Corporate Psychopathy

Katarina Fritzon · Nathan Brooks ·
Simon Croom

Corporate Psychopathy

Investigating Destructive Personalities in the Workplace

Katarina Fritzon
Bond University
Robina, QLD, Australia

Nathan Brooks
Central Queensland University
Townsville, QLD, Australia

Simon Croom
University of San Diego
San Diego, CA, USA

ISBN 978-3-030-27187-9   ISBN 978-3-030-27188-6   (eBook)
https://doi.org/10.1007/978-3-030-27188-6

This Palgrave Macmillan imprint is published by the registered company Springer Nature Switzerland AG
The registered company address is: Gewerbestrasse 11, 6330 Cham, Switzerland

Contents

Notes on Contributors

Dr. Belinda Board, Ph.D., C. Psychol. Clin. is a Chartered Clinical Psychologist with postgraduate degrees in Organisational and Forensic Psychology and a Ph.D. in leadership behaviours and workplace well-being. She is an Associate Fellow of the British Psychological Society, a Visiting Lecturer at the University of Hertfordshire, and her research investigates leadership potential, toxic leadership, women in leadership and cultural workplace well-being. She is the Founder and CEO of PeopleWise, a global business psychology consultancy that focuses on performance and potential to future-proof organisations.

Dr. Nathan Brooks, Ph.D., MPsych (Forensic), GradDip Psych, BPsychSc, MAPS is a Senior Lecturer at Central Queensland University and an experienced Forensic Psychologist with a demonstrated history of working in the criminal justice sector. He is skilled in personality testing, crime analysis, risk management, criminal profiling and psychological assessment. He commonly consults on a variety of forensic matters and completed his Ph.D. on psychopathic personality.

Simon Croom, Ph.D., MSc, MSc (Psych), PgDip., BA (Hons), FCIPS, CPSM, MBPsS is a Distinguished University Professor of Supply Chain Management at the University of San Diego, CA, USA. After experiences in management and running his own successful business, he has spent the last 30 years in academia. He is currently researching psychopathy in executives, sustainable business practices and world-class supply chain operations.

Keith Duncan is Professor of Accounting and Finance at Bond Business School, a Director of Founders Forum and has also served on the Advisory Board for the John Heine Entrepreneurial Challenge and the Gold Coast Innovation Group. His research interests span auditing, governance, finance, financial accounting and strategic management. He taught at leading institutions in Australia, USA, New Zealand, South Africa and throughout East Asia and has held visiting professor positions at University of Southern California, Los Angeles, and Northeastern University, Boston. In addition to his extensive teaching and research experience, Keith has consulted to and conducted executive development for commercial and government organisations.

Rozalija Erdelyi, GradDip Psych, BPsych is a Registered Psychologist and is also a Teaching Fellow, while concurrently completed Ph.D. research at Bond University (Gold Coast, Australia). Her research is in the area of personality as associated with risk of white-collar crime and counterproductive work behaviours, with particular interest in dark triad personalities. She has gained approximately 15 years of combined experience in both community and corporate sectors and also in private practice.

Dr. Katarina Fritzon, Ph.D., MSc, MA (Hons), MAPS is an Associate Professor at Bond University, on the Gold Coast, Australia. Her research interests include Internet sexual offending, the links between early trauma and offending behavior, the psychology of firesetting and personality characteristics in corporate settings. She has also been a Practicing Forensic Psychologist for 25 years.

Dr. Adrian Gepp, Ph.D. is an Associate Professor of Statistics in the Bond Business School at Bond University. He is also an inaugural member of Bond University's Centre for Actuarial and Financial Big Data

Analytics and Manager of the Centre's industry relationships. A recipient of the American Accounting Association Best Dissertation Award in the Forensic Accounting Section for his work on financial statement fraud detection, he uses big data and predictive modelling to reveal unique insights about problems of economic and social importance. His research spans fraud detection, business failure prediction, financial literacy, health analytics, marketing analytics and workplace design.

Dr. Lars Bang Madsen is a Clinical and Forensic Psychologist with advanced training in Schema Therapy. He has worked for the last ten years largely in the private sector in Australia and prior to that in the National Health Service (NHS) in England. He completed his Ph.D. in the use of the polygraph in the management of supervision of community based sexual offenders. He has expertise in working with offending populations, specifically individuals who present with personality disorder, sexual behaviour problems, violence and other problematic behaviours. In his current role, he works primarily with mandated violent and sexual offenders.

Russell Mills is an experienced Fraud Manager, with a demonstrated history of working in the insurance industry. Prior to working in Insurance, he spent 10 years in the New South Wales Police Force, attaining the rank of Sergeant.

He is a Certified Fraud Examiner, a Justice of the Peace (Qualified) in Queensland, and an ANZIIF Senior Associate (CIP). He has a Graduate Diploma of Fraud Investigation Management and is currently conducting research towards a Masters of Philosophy (M.Phil.) in the field of Linguistic Analysis for Fraud Detection in Insurance Claims.

Simone Ray, BPsych (Hons), MPsych (Clinical) is a Registered Psychologist from Melbourne, Australia. In 2019, she completed a Master of Psychology (Clinical) from Bond University (Gold Coast, Australia) under the supervision of Dr. Katarina Fritzon. Her research interests include malignant personality characteristics and workplace outcomes.

Caroline Turner is a Chartered Occupational Psychologist with comprehensive experience in all aspects of workforce development and talent management. Specialised in scoping, designing and providing assessment and development solutions, both psychometric and competency based. Her career history includes consulting engagements across a variety of sectors as well as talent management. She is an executive coach and an experienced writer and presenter, having additional experience in journalism and sub-editing. She is currently completing her Ph.D. at Royal Holloway University, focusing on the assessment of risk-based personality factors at work.

Dr. Bruce Watt, Ph.D., MAPS is an Associate Professor and Head of the School of Psychology at Bond University in Australia. He is also a Forensic and Clinical Psychologist, and his research interests include juvenile and adult firesetting, forensic mental health, violence, and fitness for trial. Having practiced as a forensic psychologist for 25 years, Dr. Watt provides frequent expert testimony in diverse legal proceedings.

List of Additional Contributors

We would like to acknowledge the following additional contributors:

Kathryn Anderson, Bond University
Morgan Hughes, Bond University
Sayona Rodriga, Bond University
Nicola Uechtritz, Bond University
Cindy Walsh, Bond University
Emily Wiseman, Bond University

List of Figures

List of Tables

1

Overview of Theories and Empirical Findings Relevant to Psychopathic Personality Characteristics Amongst High-Functioning Populations

Nathan Brooks, Katarina Fritzon and Bruce Watt

Definition and Characteristics of Psychopathy

The clinical construct of psychopathy is defined by a constellation of interpersonal, affective and lifestyle characteristics (Cleckley, 1941; Hare, 1999b). Traits associated with psychopathy include: insincerity, pathological lying, egocentricity, unreliability, lack of remorse and an inability to experience empathy or concern for others (Cleckley, 1941; Hare, 1999b; Hare & McPherson, 1984). Psychopathy has been described as one of the most important forensic concepts in the early stages of the twenty-first century (Monahan et al., 2006). Experts suggest that psychopathic traits

N. Brooks (✉)
Central Queensland University, Townsville, QLD, Australia
e-mail: nathan@nathanbrooks.com.au

K. Fritzon · B. Watt
Bond University, Robina, QLD, Australia
e-mail: kfrtizon@bond.edu.au

B. Watt
e-mail: bwatt@bond.edu.au

© The Author(s) 2020
K. Fritzon et al., *Corporate Psychopathy*,
https://doi.org/10.1007/978-3-030-27188-6_1

1

are best viewed based on a continuum, also allowing for research to examine the construct outside of institutional settings (Dutton, 2012; Edens, Marcus, Lilienfeld, & Poythress, 2006; Hare & Neumann, 2010).

While the violence and criminal behaviour that is commonly associated with psychopathy is of paramount concern to society, many individuals with psychopathy never commit acts of violence or serve a period of incarceration in a correctional facility (Dutton, 2012; Hare, 1999a). Indeed, Hickey (2010) suggested that psychopaths might be more likely to operate as white-collar criminals than violent murderers. However, research has overwhelmingly focused on incarcerated populations, with prevalence rates for correctional inmates ranging from 15 to 25% (Hare, 1996), while the community prevalence (i.e. the general population) is estimated to be only approximately one in 100 (Hare, 1999b). More recently, literature has turned towards examining manifestations of psychopathy in high-functioning populations, such as the corporate and political sectors, and three key strands of research have emerged as crucial in understanding this "new" form of psychopathy. These are: (1) theoretical and conceptual explanations for high-functioning psychopathy; (2) the core defining personality, cognitive and affective components of high-functioning psychopathy, including differences between the high-functioning and low-functioning criminal psychopath; and (3) the most appropriate ways of measuring or assessing psychopathy in noncriminal populations. Of practical concern, the need for appropriate assessment tools is illustrated by the vast differences reported in prevalence rates, ranging from 3% (Babiak, Neumann, & Hare, 2010) using the short form of the Psychopathy Checklist-Revised (PCL-SV; Hart, Cox, & Hare, 1995) to 12% (Croom, 2017) using the Psychopathic Personality Inventory-Revised (PPI-R; Lilienfeld & Widows, 2005).

Psychopathy has always been recognised as a paradoxical condition, with individuals being devoid of outwardly obvious signs and symptoms of mental disorder, while possessing significant emotional and cognitive deficits (Cleckley, 1988, Lilienfeld et al., 2012, Lykken, 1995). Cleckley (1941, 1976) described psychopathic individuals as charming, fearless and bold, interpersonally dominant, with intact intellectual functioning and low anxiety, yet also reckless and dishonest. Extending on this, Hare (1999b, 2003) described psychopathy as characterised by interpersonal, affective, lifestyle and antisocial features, with much of Hare's conceptualisation of psychopathy, and indeed subsequent research, developed from North American criminal offenders. The current chapter will focus on a broad overview of the psychopathic personality and will present research from various perspectives on the aetiological foundations of the construct. Subsequent chapters will highlight the empirical findings on the sequelae of psychopathy in relation to its criminal and noncriminal manifestations.

Brief History of the Psychopathy Construct

German psychiatrist Julius Ludwig August Koch in his monograph *Die Psychopathischen Minderwertigkeiten (Psychopathic Inferiorities)* published in 1891 was one of the first people to introduce the term, psychopath. Koch in his preliminary writing described the "psychopathic inferiorities" which were marked by differences in congenital and acquired forms. In similar vein to Koch, Henderson (1939) in his book, *Psychopathic States*, described psychopaths as suffering from an illness causing badness and antisocial behaviour for which there was no known explanation. The first comprehensive clinical conceptualisation of psychopathy (Blonigen, Hicks, Krueger, Patrick, & Iacono, 2006; Hicks, Markon, Patrick, Krueger, & Newman, 2004) was provided by Hervey Cleckley (1941) in his book The *Mask of Sanity*. Cleckley's work on psychopathy was based on his widespread experience working with psychiatric patients at a Georgia Hospital (Cleckley, 1941; Skeem, Polaschek, Patrick, & Lilienfeld, 2011). Cleckley identified 16 key characteristics that he believed captured the psychopathic personality. The title of Cleckley's book, the "Mask of Sanity", refers to the ability of psychopaths to present as personable, confident and well adjusted in comparison with other psychiatric patients; however, behind the mask, a character is revealed with a severe underlying pathology evident through their actions and attitudes (Cleckley, 1941, 1976; Skeem et al., 2011). Cleckley believed that psychopaths were not of unsound mind or suffering from any form of insanity of psychosis, but rather were calculated and reasoned in their actions, having limited moral regard for any consequences.

Building on the work of Cleckley (1941), Dr. Robert Hare operationalised the construct of psychopathy, identifying 22 core characteristics that he argued depicted psychopathic personality (Hare, 1980). These characteristics were developed into a criterion-based protocol, consisting of an interview and review of collateral documentation to assess the presence of psychopath. Hare (1980) called the measure the Psychopathy Checklist (PCL; Hare, 1980). After its introduction, the PCL was revised by Hare (PCL-R; Hare, 1991, 2003) and reduced to a 20-item checklist of characteristics that defined psychopathy. Table 1.1 shows a side-by-side comparison of Cleckley's 16 characteristics and Hare's final 20 characteristics, and highlights some important differences between the two—namely that Cleckley emphasised an absence of neurotic and suicidal affect, while Hare has expanded on the antisocial and behavioural manifestations of psychopathy.

Research has also identified neurobiological, cognitive, affective and developmental differences that suggest important distinctions between subgroups of individuals with psychopathic characteristics (Hall & Benning, 2006; Patrick, 2007; Patrick, & Zempolich, 1998). This distinction, based on similar, yet unique, dimensions, provides support for the notion of psychopathic personality variants marked by aetiological pathways, temperament, motivation, and social and emotional expression (Fowles & Dindo, 2009; Hall & Benning, 2006; Willemsen & Verhaeghe, 2012).

Aetiological Causes of Psychopathy

The aetiology of psychopathy has been subject to much debate (Blair, Mitchell, & Blair, 2005; Hare, 2003). Research has found evidence suggesting genetic (Blonigen, Carlson, Krueger, & Patrick, 2003; Larsson, Andershed, & Lichtenstein, 2006; Viding, Blair, Moffitt, & Plomin, 2005), neurological or environmental (Blonigen et al., 2003; Meloy & Shiva, 2007; Raine, Phil, Stoddard, Bihrle, & Buchsbaum, 1998) contributions to the personality disorder. Findings from a number of studies have provided evidence that each risk factor domain may contribute differently in individual cases (Baron-Cohen, 2011; Blair et al., 2005; Glenn & Raine, 2014; Hare, 2003; Raine et al., 1998). Commonly cited environmental

Table 1.1 Cleckley and Hare criteria for Psychopathy

Cleckley (1941, 1976)	Hare (1980, 1991)
Superficial charm and good intelligence	Glib, superficial charm
Pathological egocentricity and incapacity for love	Grandiose (exaggeratedly high) estimation of self
Fantastic and uninviting behavior, with drink and sometimes without	Need for stimulation
Untruthfulness and insincerity	Pathological lying
Unresponsiveness in general interpersonal relations	Conning and manipulative
Lack of remorse or shame	Lack of remorse or guilt
General poverty in major affective reactions	Shallow affect (superficial emotional responsiveness)
Sex life impersonal, trivial and poorly integrated	Sexual promiscuity
Failure to follow any life plan	Lack of realistic long-term goals
Specific loss of insight	Impulsivity
Unreliability	Irresponsibility
Poor judgement and failure to learn from experience	Failure to accept responsibility for own actions
	Callousness and lack of empathy
	Parasitic lifestyle
	Poor behavioural controls
	Many short term marital relationships
	Early behavioural problems
	Juvenile delinquency
	Revocation of conditional release
Inadequately motivated antisocial behaviour	Criminal versatility
Absence of 'nervousness' or psychoneurotic manifestations	
Absence of delusions and other signs of irrational thinking	
Suicide rarely carried out	

factors contributing to the development of psychopathic personality traits include childhood neglect and physical and sexual abuse (Meloy & Shiva, 2007; Raine et al., 1998).

The pioneering research of McCord and McCord (1964) demonstrated that factors including parental rejection, an antisocial parent and erratic and inconsistent discipline influenced the development of psychopathy. Similarly, Lykken (1957, 2006) also highlighted the importance of parental competence and socialisation in the distinction between sociopathy and psychopathy. Despite this, studies of adult psychopathy have largely neglected the role of family factors, whereas this has been the predominant focus of researchers who are interested in adolescent psychopathic symptoms (Farrington, Felthous, & Sass, 2000; Marshall & Cooke, 1999).

Two important prospective longitudinal studies have specifically investigated the development of psychopathic symptoms in adults: the Cambridge Study in Delinquent Development (CSDD; Farrington et al., 2000) and the Pittsburgh Youth Study (PYS; Loeber, Farrington, Stouthamer-Loeber, & White, 2008). In the CSDD, poor parental supervision at 8 years old significantly predicted high psychopathy scores aged 48 (Farrington, 2006). In the PYS, inconsistent discipline at age 13 was a predictor of the interpersonal facet of psychopathy at the age of 24 after researchers controlled for early psychopathic symptoms at age 13, along with 12 other individual and family variables (Lynam, Caspi, Moffitt, Loeber, & Stouthamer-Loeber, 2007). In a four-year longitudinal study, negative parenting, including poor supervision, discipline and low parental involvement, was a strong predictor of a wide range of psychopathic symptoms (Frick et al., 2003). Researchers have also highlighted important methodological difficulties in assessing family predictors of psychopathy, including retrospective reporting of parenting variables (e.g. Marshall & Cooke, 1999), and different findings being produced depending on whether the informants are the children themselves, or their parents (Frick et al., 2003). Research on parenting factors and psychopathy has also highlighted some inconsistent findings, including large family size (which predicted psychopathy in males but not females), low SES (socioeconomic status), and the link between young parents and antisociality and psychopathy in their children. In the CSDD, young mothers had children with higher antisocial personality scores at age 32 (Farrington et al., 2000), but not higher psychopathy scores. Research has suggested that early abuse may be differentially related to the two factors (interpersonal and affective, and lifestyle and antisocial) of psychopathy. In a sample of $n = 702$ North American prisoners, Poythress, Skeem, and Lilienfeld (2006) found that the relationship between overall abuse and total psychopathy score was largely attributable to scores on the irresponsible-antisocial factor (Factor 2) of psychopathy.

Findings from the CSDD also supported the intergenerational transmission of psychopathy (Auty, Farrington, & Coid, 2015) with high psychopathy scores in the original cohort of boys (G2) being predictive of scores in both their male and female offspring (G3). With the development of medical technology over the past two decades, research has begun to provide greater insight and understanding into the specific genetic basis of psychopathy. Science has observed what has been termed a "warrior gene", with some individuals possessing a monoamine oxidase-A polymorphism called MAOA-L (Dutton, 2012; McDermott, Tingley, Cowden, Frazzetto, & Johnson, 2009; Shih & Chen, 1999). The variation to this gene has been linked with "dangerous and psychopathic behaviour" (Dutton, 2012; Frydman, Camerer, Bossaerts, & Rangel, 2011; McDermott et al., 2009). One notable study supporting a relationship between psychopathy and MAOA involved the examination of several generations of a Dutch family. The research found that over a number of generations the family had incidences of violent and criminal behaviour in male family members who were found to have an abnormality in the MAOA gene (Brunner, Nelen, Breakefield, Ropers, & van Oost, 1993; McDermott et al., 2009).

Neurobiological research has identified notable differences in brain structures relevant to emotions, autonomic arousal and attachment in psychopathic individuals (Blair et al., 2005; Kiehl, 2014). Studies have found that psychopathic personality is associated with abnormal brain structures, observing significant variances in several areas of the brain relevant to emotional and moral processing. These areas include the amygdala, hippocampus, and the anterior and posterior cingulate (Blair et al., 2005; Dolan, Deakin, Roberts, & Anderson, 2002; Glenn & Raine, 2014; Glenn, Han, Yang, Raine, & Schug, 2017; Kiehl, 2014; Kiehl et al., 2001). Initial neuroanatomical research has provided a promising contribution to understanding psychopathic personality (Fallon, 2014; Glenn & Raine, 2014); however, consistent replication across studies is needed to identify shared aetiological causes (Glenn & Raine, 2014; Hare, 2003; Müller et al., 2003). For example, while some studies investigating activation in the amygdala have found increases in response to aversive conditioning stimuli (Schneider et al., 2000), others found reduced activation when processing affective stimuli (Kiehl et al., 2001). Similarly inconsistent findings have been observed in relation to the hippocampus with one study finding that reduced grey-matter volume within the hippocampus and orbitofrontal cortex explained 22% of the variance in psychopathy scores (Cope et al., 2012), which contrasted with an earlier finding that enlargement in the lateral borders of the hippocampus was associated with psychopathy (Boccardi et al., 2010). Finally, fMRI research has produced findings of both increased (Kiehl et al., 2001; Intrator et al., 1997) and decreased (Finger et al., 2011) responsiveness in the orbitofrontal regions. These inconsistencies are also compatible with the view that there are different forms of psychopathy, with distinct brain deficits (Yang & Raine, 2018). While the development of this area of research appears promising, further consistent empirical evidence is required to establish the validity and reliability of neuroanatomical patterns and functional deficits related to psychopathic individuals. Additionally, some researchers have cautioned that focusing on neuroanatomical research findings may have potentially unhelpful consequences in legal settings (Skeem et al., 2011), in that evidence presented about an offender possessing such deficits does not necessarily mean that the deficits caused the individual to commit the offence, over and above social and psychological causal factors. Any such implication raises the possibility that jurors may assume that the individual is absolved of criminal responsibility.

Affective and Cognitive Deficits Associated with Psychopathy

In his early writings, Cleckley described psychopathic individuals as being absent of emotion, immoral and incapable of love (Cleckley, 1941). The limited and/or reduced ability to form sustained affectional attachments to other living people or objects is considered as a cornerstone feature of psychopathic personality (Bowlby, 1944; Meloy & Shiva, 2007). According to Gray (1987), emotion, motivation, and approach and avoidance behaviour are the fundamental aspects of personality (Corr, 2008). A pattern of emotional unresponsiveness has been found in those with psychopathy and is one of the leading factors believed to contribute to their callous disregard for others, lack of moral concern and the subsequent harm that occurs as a result of their actions (Hare, 2003; Lykken, 1995). A number of studies have empirically evaluated evidence that individuals with psychopathic personality features respond differently to emotionally valenced stimuli from those who do not have such personality features (Brook & Kosson, 2013; Christianson et al., 1996; Garofalo, Neumann, Zeigler-Hill, & Meloy, 2019).

Brook and Kosson (2013) investigated the emotional and empathic capacities of psychopathic and non-psychopathic offenders using the PCL-R to assess psychopathy. The study included 103 adult male offenders from a county jail. The Interpersonal Reactivity Index (Davis, 1983) was used to measure empathy and an empathic accuracy task (see Ickes, 1997) was employed to examine accuracy at detecting emotional states. Participants were required to view video vignettes of targets describing an emotional event in their life and rank the emotions experienced by the target in the vignette, as well as their perception of their own accuracy. Psychopathic offenders were found to have lower levels of empathic accuracy in comparison with non-psychopathic offenders after controlling for intelligence, reading ability and perceived emotional intelligence (Brook & Kosson, 2013).

The relationship between psychopathy and empathy has also been investigated in a community setting by Mullins-Nelson, Salekin, and Leistico (2006) and Watt and Brooks (2012). Mullins-Nelson et al. (2006) investigated the relationship between psychopathy and emotional processing capabilities in 44 male and 130 female undergraduate students, and found no significant relationship between psychopathy, empathy and gender; however, a significant negative relationship was found between total psychopathy scores, perspective-taking and affective empathy. A similar pattern of results was found by Watt and Brooks (2012) in Australia community sample, using the Self-Report Psychopathy Scale, Third Edition (SRP-III; Paulhus, Hemphill, & Hare, 2016). The authors found that participants with higher levels of callous affect had greater deficits in empathic concern, in comparison with participants with lower levels of callous affect. The interpersonal manipulation subscale of the SRP-III was found to be associated with a deficit in empathic concern and perspective-taking. Higher scores were found, however, for the fantasy scales of the Interpersonal Reactivity Index (IRI; Davis, 1983) and total psychopathy scores. This suggested that those with higher psychopathy scores had a tendency for greater imagination and creativity, which may serve to enhance the capacity for manipulation and deceit.

Despite a number of findings suggesting that individuals with psychopathic characteristics have strong impression management skills and are manipulative, deceptive and capable of detecting and exploiting vulnerability, some researchers disagree over the ability of individuals with psychopathy to process and understand emotions (Wheeler, Book, & Costello, 2009). Johns and Quay (1962) famously coined the phrase that individuals with psychopathic traits "know the words but not the music" (p. 217). For example, in a study that investigated the relationship between psychopathy and recognition of facial affect, psychopathic traits were found to be negatively related to affect recognition, which was most notable for expressions of sadness (Hastings, Tangney, & Stuewig, 2008). A similar finding was noted by Long and Titone (2007), with participants who scored higher on a self-report measure of psychopathy less efficient at processing the negative emotional states of sadness and fear in comparison with other emotional states. However, Glass and Newman (2006) and Book, Quinsey, and Langford (2007) both found that people with psychopathic traits did not have deficits in their ability to recognise facial emotional expression, suggesting that the fault does not lie with the cognitive but rather the affective component of emotional identification. In a study conducted by Blair, Jones, Clark, and Smith (1997), participants with high levels of psychopathic traits were found to have reduced arousal responses to distress cues. However, participants with higher levels of psychopathy were not found to have a complete deficit in perceiving distress cues. The authors concluded that this finding was due to a deficient physiological response to distress cues in people with psychopathic traits rather than a deficiency in the perception of distress (Blair et al., 1997). This finding suggests that individuals with psychopathic traits know the emotional state, yet do not experience the accompanying physiological symptoms associated with distressing emotional states.

This relationship between psychopathy and observation of emotional states was investigated by Fecteau, Pascual-Leone, and Théoret (2008). The authors examined mirror neurons, which refer to neural circuits in the brain that are activated in an individual when observing the actions of another person, or when an individual copies or executes an act previously performed by another person (Chartrand & Bargh, 1999; Fecteau et al., 2008; Iacoboni, 2009). The researchers hypothesised that psychopathy would be negatively associated with mirror neuron activation and empathic concern in response to four sets of videos pertaining to needles penetrating various objects (e.g. hand, fruit). Using transactional magnetic stimulation to measure motor evoked potentials, the authors found a number of important results. Total psychopathy scores (as measured by the PPI; Lilienfeld & Andrews, 1996) were not significantly correlated with neural activation during observation of the painful video-imagery condition (Fecteau et al., 2008). Notably, a significant relationship was found between the coldheartedness (callous affect) subscale of the PPI and motor evoked potentials (mirror neuron activation). The relationship between the coldheartedness subscale and motor evoked potentials in response to painful stimuli was positive in nature (Fecteau et al., 2008). In interpreting this finding, the researchers drew attention to the fact that the aspect of empathy measured by motor cortex modulation was sensory, as opposed to emotional, and that an ability to understand another's experience at an embodied sensory level could be advantageous to individuals wishing to cause harm (Rogers, Viding, Blair, Frith, & Happe, 2006).

Decety, Chen, Harenski, and Kiehl (2013) investigated the relationship between psychopathy and perspective-taking in offenders. The findings of the study indicated that offenders with high levels of psychopathy had an atypical response to adopting an imagine-other perspective, although displayed a normal pattern of response for imagine-self perspectives. This suggested that psychopathic offenders had self-awareness, but were limited in their ability to adopt the perspective of others (Decety et al., 2013). The implications of these two studies suggest that psychopathy may be positively associated with sensory aspects of the empathy construct (ability to observe and understand the affective/emotional states). However, on the other hand, psychopathy may be negatively related to emotional, state or trait empathy (Decety et al., 2013; Fecteau et al., 2008). This suggested that those with higher levels of psychopathy may in fact have the ability to observe and take on the perspective of the victim (presence of mirror neuron functioning), yet lack emotional concern or regard (emotional empathy) for the victim (Dolan & Fullam, 2004; Fecteau et al., 2008).

Further adding to the complexity of these findings is an intriguing study by Meffert, Gazzola, den Boer, Bartels, and Keysers (2014). In this study, the researchers first exposed twenty male offenders with scores above 26 on the PCL-R and 26 control participants to a series of videos depicting hand interactions while measuring whole-brain activation using fMRI. After the videos, the men participated in interactions similar to those depicted in the video, via the researcher touching the participants' hands. Following this, participants were asked to rate the video interactions and they were instructed to empathise with the actors in the videos. During the observation phase, participants with psychopathy showed reduced activations across a wide network of brain areas compared to the controls. However, following the physical interaction and when instructed to empathise, there were no differences in brain activations observed between the two groups, suggesting that the capacity to learn empathic responses in individuals with psychopathy can be enhanced through direct experience.

Findings that highlight enhancements rather than deficits associated with psychopathy have also emerged from recent research focusing on the ability to identify micro-expressions (Demetrioff, Porter, & Baker, 2017), perceptions of emotional authenticity (Dawel, Wright, Dumbleton, & McKone, 2019) and intensified emotional experiences (Garofalo et al., 2019). The latter identified in a large ($n = 1997$) non-clinical sample that psychopathic traits as assessed by the SRP-III and the TriPM were positively associated with heightened experiencing of spitefulness and contempt, leading to the suggestion that far from being devoid of emotions, individuals with psychopathic traits may experience certain negative emotions at more intense levels than other individuals, which may explain their engagement in negative acts directed at others (Garofalo et al., 2019).

The lack of conscience, reduced fear arousal and emotional deficits, makes psychopathy a personality pattern that is interpersonally and affectively disengaged and disconnected from others and social norms (Hare, 1999b). The differences in emotional processing discussed in the aforementioned areas have important implications for psychopathy research as well as clinical implications. The impairments of emotional capacity for attachment-based emotions associated with psychopathy are evidenced in both the community and forensic setting. This indicates evidence suggesting that emotional deficits are found irrespective of the particular population of psychopathic people being examined, with lower levels of empathy observed in offenders and individuals residing in the community.

Gender Differences in Psychopathy

Although in his initial conceptualisation of psychopathy, Cleckley (1941, 1976) included several female case studies indicating that psychopathy does fully manifest in women, the vast majority of subsequent research has been developed primarily using males (Hare, 1980; Kreis, Cooke, Stanford, & Felthous, 2011; Logan & Weizmann-Henelius, 2012). Additionally, the PCL-R and its derivatives were developed to measure this definition of the construct and validated using primarily male samples (Kreis et al., 2011; Logan & Weizmann-Henelius, 2012). This raises several questions regarding the utility of current models and measures of psychopathy and their applicability to the female population and whether the expression of key traits of psychopathy is similar across genders (Forouzan & Cooke, 2005; Logan & Weizmann-Henelius, 2012; Verona & Vitale, 2018).

The prevalence of psychopathy in women in community, forensic mental health and correctional samples as assessed by the PCL-R and its derivatives is generally found to be lower than the 15–25% prevalence found in men (Hare, 1996; Logan & Weizmann-Henelius, 2012). One study of 103 females incarcerated in the USA reported that 16% of the sample scored above a cut-off score of 29 on the PCL-R (Salekin, Rogers, & Sewell, 1997), while 11% of a Finnish sample of $n = 61$ incarcerated women were found to score above the cut-off on the PCL-R (Weizmann-Henelius, Viemero, & Eronen, 2004). Research has supported utilising a lowered cut-off score of 25 for females (Weizmann-Henelius et al., 2004). Of a matched sample of 36 male and 36 female violent offenders in Sweden, 11% of the females met or exceeded a lowered cut-off score of 26 on the PCL-R, while 31% of the male participants scored above (Grann,

2000). The results of these studies suggest that the PCL-R may be less sensitive to the presentation of psychopathy in (incarcerated) females, and this suggestion is also supported by inconsistent findings in relation to the factor structure of the PCL-R in female samples, with some supporting a two-factor structure (Kennealy, Hicks, & Patrick, 2007) while others (Drislane & Patrick, 2017; Weizmann-Henelius et al., 2010) have shown a better fit for a three-factor model. Furthermore, findings at the individual item level in relation to women, specifically the cross-loading of "poor behavioural controls", "impulsivity" and "lack of realistic long-term goals" on Factors 1 and 2 (Salekin et al., 1997), reinforce the suggestion that the PCL-R functions differently in women than in men, perhaps due to its reliance on criminal history variables (Logan & Weizmann-Henelius, 2012). Since research indicates that females are more likely to employ relational forms of aggression (Logan & Weizmann-Henelius, 2012; Verona & Vitale, 2018), and to target known individuals (family members, friends, work colleagues), this type of aggression is less likely to result in criminal charges.

An exploration of differences in psychopathic traits between men and women has revealed that certain characteristics, such as emotional instability (Kreis & Cooke, 2012) and sexual risk-taking (Kreis et al., 2011), may be more prevalent in females, whereas others, such as early behavioural problems (Silverthorn & Frick, 1999) and risk of criminal recidivism (Edens et al., 2006), are more prevalent in males. Studies have also investigated differences in the meaning or function of certain psychopathic traits, where although prevalence is similar between men and women, the motivation may be different. For example, Forouzan and Cooke (2005) found that impulsivity and conduct problems in males were more likely to manifest as violent behaviours, while conduct problems in females consisted of running away, self-harming behaviours, manipulation and complicity in committing financially motivated crimes (Forouzan & Cooke, 2005). Additionally, it was reported that psychopathic females may use their sexuality in order to manipulate and exploit others, while promiscuity in male psychopaths may be a form of sensation seeking (Forouzan & Cooke, 2005).

In conclusion, although psychopathic men and women have similar underlying emotional and interpersonal deficits, these may manifest differently, and/or current assessments, particularly the PCL-R, do not adequately capture the behavioural expressions of the deficits in women (Verona & Vitale, 2018). As observed in a recent training event, "women are not just funny-shaped men" (Caroline Logan 2019 personal communication), and future research should move away from attempting to generalise findings derived from male samples and focus instead on grounded conceptualisation of the psychopathy construct in women.

Effective Aspects of Psychopathy

The charming and superficial traits associated with psychopathy may allow individuals with psychopathic characteristics to exploit these traits for self-gain. Proyer, Flisch, Tschupp, Platt, and Rush (2012) examined the witty, charismatic and superficial traits associated with psychopathy, specifically the use of humour and laughter. The authors utilised a series of self-report measures to assess humour, the fear of being laughed at and psychopathy in 90 male and 143 female university students. Participants with higher levels of psychopathic traits reported greater enjoyment in laughing at others and were less likely to experience fear of being laughed at. Psychopathy traits were significantly related to greater use of verbal humour, and traits of superficial charm and callousness were significantly related to all facets of humour except for enjoyment. Psychopathy was significantly positively correlated with enjoyment at being laughed at, while the callous and unemotional features of the personality construct were significantly negatively related to enjoyment at being laughed at. The finding that participants with psychopathy traits found enjoyment in laughing at others suggests that individuals with psychopathic characteristics may use laughter as a means of controlling and manipulating others, rather than as a shared joy with others (Proyer et al., 2012). Although the research utilised a student sample, the findings by Proyer et al. have important implications for psychopathy in the community and professional contexts. The ability to use humour to achieve a purpose and build rapport may explain why some individuals with psychopathy are considered successful and others unsuccessful, due to the ability to adapt and apply social skills to a given situation (Babiak & Hare, 2006).

It is an unusual phenomenon that a personality type found to be associated with destructive and criminal behaviour is also related to levels of success and achievement (Babiak & Hare, 2006; Boddy, 2011; Brooks, 2017). There have been many historical figures who have reflected features of psychopathy, with some achieving great success, while others have fallen victim to their own shortcomings. This has included: Winston Churchill (Carter, 1965; Lykken, 2006; Manchester, 1986, 1988), Saddam Hussein (Dutton, 2016), African explorer Sir Richard Burton (Farwell, 1963; Lykken, 2006; Rice, 1990), Adolf Hitler (Dutton, 2016), Lyndon Johnson (Caro, 1982, 2002; Lykken, 2006), Joseph Stalin (Lykken, 2006) and Donald Trump (Dutton, 2016). According to Lykken (2006, p. 12), a case of a well-documented psychopath is that of "*Oskar Schindler, the savior of hundreds of Krakow Jews whose names were on Schindler's list. Opportunist, bon vivant, lady's man, manipulator, unsuccessful in legitimate business by his own admission but widely successful in the moral chaos of wartime, Schindler's rescue of those Jews can be best understood as a 35-year-old conman's response to a kind of ultimate challenge, Schindler against the Third Reich*".

The ability to charm another person and remain confident and socially poised in a social situation may explain why some psychopathic individuals are able to reach positions of higher career and social status, and why not all people with psychopathic traits end up in jail (Dutton, 2012; Hare, 1999a, 2003). Research suggests that individuals with psychopathic characteristics are entitled, selfish, grandiose and experience difficulties working with others (Jonason, Li, & Teicher, 2010; Kajonius, Persson, & Jonason, 2015; ten Brinke, Black, Porter, and Carney, 2015). In contrast, traits of charm, humour and confidence are often desirable qualities within society, with people who display these traits deemed more likeable and popular. Most typically whether someone is liked or disliked is determined within the first few occasions of meeting a given person. Subsequently, those that are initially liked often become more likeable and those that are initially disliked remain that way (Babiak & Hare, 2006). This process of socialisation works to the advantage of psychopathic people who are able to appear charming, charismatic, socially poised and confident when needed (Babiak & Hare, 2006; Hare, 1999b). Over time, however, the true persona of psychopathic individuals emerges, typically leading to harm and destruction (Hare, 1999b, 2003).

Research has identified that an aptitude for creating positive impressions can have significant implications for the criminal justice system. Porter, ten Brinke, and Wilson (2009) conducted a study that examined crime profiles and the likelihood of being granted conditional release in psychopathic and non-psychopathic sexual offenders. Offenders with high levels of psychopathic traits were found to have a higher rate of non-sexual recidivism, but not sexual recidivism. Despite the findings suggesting that psychopathic offenders were of greater likelihood to reoffend for non-sexual crimes, they were two and a half times more likely than non-psychopathic offenders to be successful in their application for conditional release. The findings suggest that individuals with high levels of psychopathic traits are capable of presenting an impression that persuaded the parole boards that they in fact represented a reduced risk to the community. In a related study, Porter, ten Brinke, Baker, and Wallace (2011) found that psychopathic traits, particularly facet 2, were related to less unintentional emotional "leakage" when engaging in an emotional deception task. The research by Porter and colleagues highlights that the role of impression management is vital to understanding why some individuals with psychopathic traits may potentially reach positions of high status in the professional field (Babiak & Hare, 2006; Boddy, 2011; Dutton, 2012; Hare, 1999b). The ability to defraud, con, cheat and manipulate people without concern about their victim or the repercussions of their actions is a central characteristic of psychopathy (Hare, 1999b, 2003).

The charismatic nature of people with psychopathic traits assists in creating positive impressions and allows for manipulation and control of social situations (Babiak & Hare, 2006). The confidence and belief that is held by people with psychopathic characteristics regarding their own abilities to persist in the face of adversity assists individuals with psychopathy to overcome uncertainty and achieve outcomes (Sandvik, Hansen, Hystad, Johnsen, & Bartone, 2015). Individuals with psychopathic traits are resilient and not easily emotionally deterred by criticism or setbacks, resembling qualities of psychological hardiness (Dutton, 2012; Sandvik et al., 2015). Hardiness, in a similar vein to resiliency, refers to a person's capacity to protect themselves from physical and mental effects of stress (Kobasa, 1979). Due to people with psychopathic traits having low levels of anxiety and high self-esteem, they possess the ability to remain cool under pressure (Dutton, 2012; Lykken, 1957). For example, in his research Professor Kevin Dutton highlighted the adaptive psychopathic traits of former decorated SAS soldier, Andy McNab. Dutton based on his analysis of McNab contended that he exhibited a psychopathic personality, yet was able to express psychopathic tendencies in a prosocial, legal and acceptable manner (Dutton, 2012; McNab & Dutton, 2014).

In a study specifically related to business-related outcomes, the ability of individuals with psychopathic traits to negotiate with others was examined by ten Brinke et al. (2015). The researchers sought to explore the social and cognitive biases held by those with psychopathic traits. Participants completed a hypothetical negotiation task in which they were assigned the role of a buyer or seller. Four issues were required to be negotiated by the pairs and each issue was assigned an economic value represented by points. Psychopathy was assessed by the Dirty Dozen self-report questionnaire (Jonason & Webster, 2010). The results of the research did not find a significant relationship between levels of psychopathic traits and total number of points achieved in the negotiation task. Higher levels of psychopathic traits were found to be significantly associated with extracting more value than those with lower levels of psychopathic traits in the negotiation task; however, overall psychopathic traits were significantly associated with lower levels of achievement. These findings suggest that higher levels of psychopathic traits lead to selfish and competitive behaviour. ten Brinke et al. (2015) concluded that due to the competitive nature of individuals with psychopathic traits, these individuals were just as likely to excel as to fail at bargaining tasks. The desire of those with psychopathy to maximise personal achievement and self-gain at the cost of others was likely to become a liability in tasks where cooperation was required. In a more recent study aptly named "hedge fund managers with psychopathic tendencies make for worst investors", ten Brinke, Kish, and Keltner (2018) identified that 10-year financial performance was significantly worse for hedge fund managers rated as having psychopathic characteristics. Together these research findings have important implications for individuals with psychopathic traits that manage to reach positions of professional status, suggesting that these people are entitled, selfish and ineffective at working with others.

Many researchers have proposed that people with psychopathic characteristics that manage to avoid incarceration and function in the community are considered as being "successful psychopaths" (Babiak & Hare, 2006; Dutton, 2012; Hall & Benning, 2006; Mullins-Sweatt, Glover, Derefinko, Miller, & Widiger, 2010). The concept of successful psychopathy has emerged after several leading experts have identified that people with psychopathic traits have managed to survive and thrive in the community and workplace (Babiak & Hare, 2006; Dutton, 2012; Fritzon, Bailey, Croom, & Brooks, 2016). Ullrich, Farrington, and Coid (2008) investigated the relationship between psychopathic personality traits and life success. The authors aimed to examine whether features of psychopathy were related to life success in a large community sample of males all aged 48 years old. The sample was collected for a longitudinal study ($N = 411$), which commenced in 1961 by Farrington and West (1990) in England when participants were aged eight years old and was focused on delinquent development in males. The PCL:SV (Hart et al., 1995) was used to assess levels of psychopathy, while an interview was utilised to assess life success across a number of areas including: wealth and status, contribution to society, personal and professional fulfilment, family and relationships, and security.

The study by Ullrich et al. (2008) found no significant relationship between the categories of life success and psychopathy. Results demonstrated that the interpersonal facet of psychopathy was not associated with life success, while the affective facet was found to have a negative relationship with status, wealth and successful intimate relationships (Ullrich et al., 2008). The authors concluded that psychopathic traits did not lead to greater success in life and therefore raised doubts pertaining to theories regarding successful psychopathy. One limitation of the research was that of the sample of 304 men, only two participants met the cut-off score on the PCL:SV for a diagnosis of psychopathy, potentially limiting the sensitivity of the research.

Mullins-Sweatt et al. (2010) examined the relationship between psychopathy and success, sampling clinical psychology professors ($n = 58$), psychologists ($n = 118$) and attorneys ($n = 31$). Each profession was provided with a description of a psychopathic individual and asked whether they knew anyone fitting this description, and if that person had been successful in their endeavours. If participants knew an individual matching that description, they were required to describe in their own words why the person was successful. Participants were also required to rate this individual on the five-factor rating form which corresponded to the five-factor model of personality, and complete a psychopathy rating form about the individual.

The narratives provided by the participants across the three professions were significantly related, and described a successful psychopath as being exploitative, dishonest, arrogant, shallow, lacking remorse and minimising self-blame. The profile of a successful individual with psychopathic characteristics was found to have a number of significant relationships with prototypic personality disorders as measured by the five-factor rating form. This included a significant negative relationship with obsessive-compulsive personality disorder and a significant positive relationship with narcissistic and antisocial personality disorders. Indicators of success provided by participants to depict successful psychopathy included: "a top notch detective and a hero, dean from a major university, successful retail business, made a large sum of money and was mayor for three years, managerial position in government organization, full professor of two major universities, and an endowed professor with numerous federal grants" (p. 556, Mullins-Sweatt et al., 2010). The authors contended that successful psychopathy may be distinguished from unsuccessful or prototypical psychopathy based on the levels of adaptive traits, particularly conscientiousness. Typical characteristics of an unsuccessful psychopath are marked by impulsivity, irresponsibility and negligence, often reflecting poor awareness and lower levels of conscientiousness. However, a successful psychopath presents as controlled, aware and deliberate, exhibiting a higher degree of conscientiousness (Mullins-Sweatt et al., 2010).

Corporate Psychopathy

Until recently, the notion of psychopathy in the workplace was primarily the stuff of clinical lore (Smith & Lilienfeld, 2013); however, research has begun to emerge examining the psychopathic personality in the corporate setting. Board and Fritzon (2005) compared personality traits across a series of samples, with the aim of investigating personality patterns associated with the psychopathic personality. The authors utilised a sample of 317 forensic patients, 768 mentally ill patients and 39 senior business managers. The business sample was comprised of chief executives and senior business managers from British companies. The forensic and mentally ill sample was comprised of 1085 current and former clients from Broadmoor Special Hospital in England. Forensic patients were differentiated based on a legal classification of psychopathic personality disorder (Mental Health Act, 1983), while the mentally ill sample consisted of participants diagnosed with a mental illness. All participants were assessed on the Minnesota Multiphasic Personality Inventory Scales (MMPI-PD; Morey, Waugh, & Blashfield, 1985), which was developed based on DSM-III personality disorders.

Board and Fritzon (2005) found that the sample of senior business managers had significantly higher levels of histrionic personality patterns than both the mentally ill and psychopathic samples. Senior business managers had greater levels of narcissistic and obsessive-compulsive personality traits in relation to all comparison groups, although this finding was not statistically significant. The authors attributed the higher levels of histrionic, narcissist and obsessive-compulsive personality patterns to resembling the Factor 1, interpersonal and affective, features of psychopathy. The authors concluded that senior business managers displayed greater levels of grandiosity, superficial charm, egocentricity, lack of empathy, rigidness, exploitation and manipulation than the forensic sample. In addition, the senior business sample was found to have lower levels of antisocial personality disorder, suggesting a prosocial orientation and ability to function within a demanding social setting (Board & Fritzon, 2005). This finding provides support to the dual-process theory of noncriminal psychopathy proposed by Hall and Benning (2006), suggesting that individuals higher on psychopathic traits in the community may have elevated levels of interpersonal-affective traits and lower levels of antisocial tendencies. The conclusions of Board and Fritzon (2005), however, were limited by measuring psychopathic characteristics without using a specific psychopathy assessment tool (Skeem et al., 2011).

The prevalence of corporate psychopathy was more explicitly investigated by Babiak et al. (2010) in a study of 203 corporate professionals in the USA. The authors found approximately 4% of the sample met the diagnostic criteria for psychopathy (score of 30 or higher on the PCL-R: Hare, 2003). This finding suggested a higher prevalence of psychopathy in the business domain, in comparison with community rates of psychopathy, reported to be approximately 1% (Hare, 1999b, 2003). The study found that some individuals holding positions in companies, including titles of vice-president, supervisor or director, could be considered as having high levels of psychopathic traits.

Recently, Fritzon et al. (2016) examined the presence of psychopathic traits in the supply chain management industry, an area of business typically of a buying and selling nature. The sample consisted of 261 participants working in the industry with an overall mode value of a $50 million budget for pricing negotiations. The study utilised self-report measures including: the Paulhus Deception Scales (PDS; Paulhus, 1999), Psychopathic Personality Inventory-Revised (PPI-R; Lilienfeld & Widows, 2005) and the Corporate Psychopathy Inventory (Fritzon et al., 2016). Results of the study found the supply chain professions obtained higher mean scores on the PPI-R, compared to the normative offender and community samples for the PPI-R. The results suggested that the prevalence rate of psychopathy found in the sample of supply chain professions was comparative to prevalence rates found in criminal population (Fritzon et al., 2016; Hare, 1996). Although this research reports extremely high prevalence rates of psychopathic traits and has yet to be replicated in other studies of supply chain professions or varying workplace contexts, the findings provide preliminary support for psychopathic traits being prominently found in individuals managing to hold down positions of corporate status.

Lilienfeld et al. (2012) conducted a notable study that investigated fearless dominance and psychopathic traits amongst past presidents of the USA. The authors utilised historical experts on the 42 US presidents up to and including George W. Bush to rate each president's personality, leadership and presidential performance. The 121 expert raters recruited by Rubenzer and Fashingbauer (2004) completed a 596-item questionnaire comprised of a series of measures to evaluate their respective presidents' personality and behaviour. Part of the measure was comprised of the revised NEO Personality Inventory Form R (NEO-PI-R; Costa & McCrae, 1992), an observer version of the NEO-PI for rating personality. Using the five-factor model (FFM) underlying the NEO-PI, the authors mapped the 30 facets of the FFM onto the two factors of the PCL-R (Lilienfeld et al., 2012) to assess psychopathic traits. Based on the facets of the FFM indicative of fearless dominance, Theodore Roosevelt, John Kennedy, and Franklin Roosevelt were found to be the most fearless and boldest American presidents. Fearless dominance was also related to greater ratings of presidential leadership, performance, persuasiveness and crisis management. The findings suggested that while presidents of America were not considered to be psychopathic, they were found to display traits associated with psychopathy that contributed to primarily positive, although at times negative, performance during their periods as president.

Theories of Successful Psychopathy

The recent focus on noncriminal psychopathy and difficulties conceptualising psychopathy outside of the correctional setting has highlighted the importance of adequate theoretical models to capture the diversity of the psychopathy construct (Benning, Venables, & Hall, 2018; Hall & Benning, 2006; Kujacic, Medjedovic, & Knezevic, 2015). Three models have been proposed giving rise to noncriminal and criminal variants of the psychopathic construct. The first proposal is that noncriminal psychopathy is a "subclinical manifestation of the disorder" (Hall & Benning, 2006, p. 462), characterised by lower levels of the pathological tendencies underlying the full expression of psychopathy. This explanation is consistent with Gustafson and Ritzer's (1995) concept of "aberrant self-promoters", which is characterised by individuals with subclinical psychopathy who possess narcissistic traits and commit crimes sporadically.

While the subclinical model conceives of psychopathy as a unitary construct, with successful individuals being partially afflicted of the full disorder, the second proposal is that noncriminal psychopathy involves the presence of adaptive attributes which promote success, and thus, non-criminal psychopathy is a "moderated expression of the full disorder" (Hall & Benning, 2006, p. 463). Here, the suggestion is that criminal and noncriminal psychopathy is based on a common aetiology; however, the manifestation of traits is moderated by compensatory factors such as education, intelligence and socio-economic status. Therefore, intelligent and well-disciplined individuals with psychopathic characteristics may recognise the consequences of antisocial behaviour and instead use socially sanctioned outlets, including business, athletics and politics, as means to express psychopathic desires (Hall & Benning, 2006). Some support for the moderated expression theory was found in the research by Spencer and Byrne (2016) who identified that contrary to expectation, the presence of primary psychopathic characteristics amongst senior managers did not attenuate high levels of intrinsic job satisfaction as reported by mid-level managers and low-level employees. It may be that the presence of psychopathy in senior management was buffered by the ability of those same individuals to create and maintain a positive impression. However, contrary to these findings, Babiak et al. (2010) found poorer overall performance by psychopathic employees, suggesting that while capable of managing initial impressions, over time the negative impact of psychopathic tendencies may emerge. These findings collectively highlight the importance of recognising that corporate psychopathy may not necessarily convey entirely egregious effects upon a workplace environment, yet the costs and benefits to organisations over the long term should be closely examined (Smith and Lilienfeld, 2013).

The third proposed explanation for noncriminal psychopathy is a multiprocess model in which psychopathy encompasses several underlying processes which converge to form the phenotypic features of the disorder. One possibility is that the interpersonal-affective features of psychopathy are aetiologically distinct from the mechanisms that give rise to antisocial and aggressive behavioural tendencies. The authors suggest that due to this distinction, it is possible to have elevated traits for one dimension but not the other, allowing some individuals to function adaptively in the community, while others have a greater likelihood of incarceration (Hall & Benning, 2006). This theoretical model is supported by the fact that many assessments of psychopathy, for example the PCL-R and the PPI-R, have orthogonal factor structures, with each domain exhibiting varying associations with external criteria.

There is empirical support for all three of the theories of successful psychopathy. For example, studies of noncriminal community participants have found that psychopathic traits are associated with similar deficits on cognitive-executive tasks as shown for criminal psychopaths (Adams, 2019; Bagshaw, Gray, & Snowden, 2014) implying continuity of the disorder along a scale of severity. The moderated expression theory is supported by findings including that successful psychopaths have higher executive functioning than unsuccessful individuals with psychopathy (Ishikawa, Raine, Lencz, Bihrle, & Lacasse, 2001) and are also more similar to healthy controls in terms of neuroanatomy (Raine et al., 2004; Yang, Raine, Colletti, Toga, & Narr, 2010). Finally, as mentioned previously, consistent with multiprocess theory, distinct features of psychopathy have been found to be related to different external measures (Benning, Patrick, Blonigen, Hicks, & Iacono, 2005; Hicks & Patrick, 2006). These theories of successful psychopathy therefore provide an account of how different manifestations of psychopathic personality may vary based on traits, characteristic adaptations and environmental factors (Costa & McCrae, 2003; Skeem et al., 2011). The paradox of psychopathy, reflected in the various perspectives from prior research with samples from diverse population, presents a challenge when trying to develop a comprehensive conceptualisation of the psychopathy syndrome.

Conceptualisations of Psychopathy

A model which unifies the phenotypic traits underlying both criminal and noncriminal manifestations of psychopathy is the triarchic model developed by Patrick, Fowles, and Krueger (2009). The three components of the triarchic model are: Disinhibition, Boldness and Meanness. Disinhibition entails a general propensity towards impulse control problems, including a lack of planning or foresight, insistence on immediate gratification, inhibited regulation of affect or urges and deficient behavioural restraint (Patrick et al., 2009; Skeem et al., 2011). The term boldness refers to a capacity to remain calm and focused in threatening and pressured situations, the ability to rapidly recover from stressful events, a tolerance for danger and unfamiliarity, as well as a high level of self assurance and social efficacy (Patrick et al., 2009; Skeem et al., 2011). The third construct of the triarchic model, Meanness, entails a constellation of attributes including deficient empathy, disdain for and a lack of close attachments/relationships with others, excitement seeking, exploitativeness, rebelliousness and empowerment through cruelty (Patrick et al., 2009; Skeem et al., 2011). Figure 1.1 depicts the hypothesised interrelation between the components of the triarchic model.

One major advantage of the triarchic model is that it provides a framework that overlaps with the factor structure of the major assessment tools for measuring psychopathy, making it possible to compare results derived from different samples using different measures (Polaschek, 2015; Skeem et al., 2011). The model is *"a point of reference for the reader to organise and think about (a) differing conceptualizations and operationalizations of psychopathy and (b) how research findings based on well validated measures apply to policy and practice"* (Skeem et al., 2011, p. 105). This allows psychopathy to be conceptualised as a construct separate to factor structures of assessment instruments, allowing the construct to have a standalone

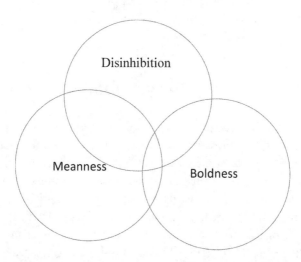

Fig. 1.1   The triarchic model of psychopathy (Patrick et al., 2009)

theoretical basis that can account for similarities and differences across contexts and psychometric tools.

The Comprehensive Assessment of Psychopathic Personality-Concept Map (CAPP-CM; Cooke, Hart, Logan, & Michie, 2012) acts as a conceptual model for understanding the dynamic personality traits of psychopathy (Sellbom, Cooke, & Hart, 2015). The CAPP concept map of psychopathy, like the triarchic model, details core overarching domains associated with the personality construct. The CAPP model consists of six broad domains (self, emotional, dominance, attachment, behavioural and cognitive), which are characterised by 33 personality traits or symptoms (Sellbom et al., 2015). A strength of the model is that it only details personality traits associated with psychopathy, rather than behaviours, as behaviour related to personality traits often varies as a function of gender, age and culture (Cooke et al., 2012). The focus on personality, rather than expressed behaviour, separates the model from the PCL-R (Cooke & Michie, 2001; Cooke et al., 2012). The self-domain reflects issues with individuality and identity, such as being self-aggrandising and self-centred. The emotional domain is characterised by problems with regulating moods, including the experience of shallow and labile emotions. The dominance domain reflects problems with interpersonal agency, typically striving for excessive status, focusing on power and being over-assertive. The attachment domain reflects issues with interpersonal affiliation, including difficulties forming close relationships and stable emotional bonds with others. The behavioural domain is characterised by issues with the organisation of goal-directed activities, typically including behavioural regulation difficulties, impulsiveness and sensation seeking. The cognitive domain reflects problems with adaptability and mental flexibility, such as being intolerant, suspicious, distractible and having poor information processing (Cooke et al., 2012; Sellbom et al., 2015). Figure 1.2 depicts the CAPP conceptual model of psychopathy, including the six domains and 33 traits/symptoms.

The CAPP and triarchic models share consistencies with several leading theories and measures of psychopathy, including the PCL-R, PPI-R, Cleckley's 16 psychopathy criteria, and Karpman's primary and secondary psychopathy (Cooke et al., 2012; Patrick et al., 2009; Sellbom et al., 2015; Skeem et al., 2011). The advantage of models that provide a phenotypical account of psychopathy is that a diverse operationalisation of

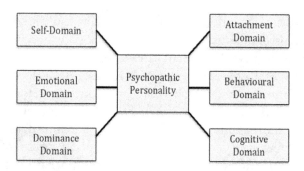

Fig. 1.2 The Comprehensive Assessment of Psychopathic Personality (CAPP) (Adapted from Cooke et al. [2012, p. 246])

the construct is possible across different samples, contexts and practical applications. Rather than a construct being defined by a sole measure, an overarching conceptualisation allows for an array of theoretical positions and assessment instruments to exist and demonstrate psychometric utility at a given point in time (Skeem et al., 2011).

Summary and Conclusions

Research supports the global construct of psychopathy, which has largely been established around Cleckley's early work (1941, 1976) and since refined by Robert Hare (1999b, 2003). There has been considerable empirical analysis of psychopathy in offender population; however, to date, little is known regarding psychopaths who have managed to avoid involvement with the criminal justice system (Ullrich et al., 2008). Noncriminal psychopathy refers to individuals with psychopathic traits who manage to reside in the community without a period of incarceration and/or minimal involvement with the criminal justice system (Mullins-Sweatt et al., 2010; Skeem et al., 2011). Such an individual may still be exploitative, commit ethical and moral violations, or even criminal acts, but, however, manages to avoid incarceration (Babiak & Hare, 2006; Cleckley, 1976; Dutton, 2012; Skeem et al., 2011). Recently, Dutton (2012) contended that psychopaths can be distinguished as "good psychopaths" and "bad psychopaths", arguing that some psychopaths are capable of using their personality disposition for good, such as serving in the military, while others use it for bad by violating the rights of others. However, whether measured by the PCL-R or other assessment measures, psychopathy is not monolithic, instead a combination of multiple traits that when present together form psychopathic personality, such as boldness, disinhibition and meanness (Skeem et al., 2011).

Preliminary research has identified significantly elevated levels of psychopathic traits in people of both high corporate status and in positions of responsibility (Babiak et al., 2010; Fritzon et al., 2016). Understanding the differences between criminal and noncriminal psychopathy, specifically successful or corporate psychopathy, is important for several reasons. First, the empirical understanding of criminal psychopathy may not be generalisable to noncriminal psychopathy (Gao, Raine, Felthous, & Sass, 2010; Hall & Benning, 2006; Mullins-Nelson et al., 2006). By relying on research conducted on offender samples, aetiological distinctions between criminal and noncriminal psychopathy may be missed. It is possible that noncriminal psychopathy may in the long term be more destructive and problematic for society (ten Brinke et al., 2018; Mathieu & Babiak, 2015; Gao et al., 2010). Second, studying noncriminal psychopathy allows researchers to focus specifically on the attributes and aetiologies of successful psychopathy (Hall & Benning, 2006; Skeem et al., 2011), rather than examining the relationship between psychopathy, criminality and antisocial behaviour (Cooke et al., 2012; Gao et al., 2010). Further, through understanding the traits and aetiology of noncriminal psychopathy, it may be possible to identify protective factors that prevent successful and noncriminal psychopathic individuals from engaging in a criminal lifestyle (Gao et al., 2010; Hall & Benning, 2006; Mullins-Nelson et al., 2006). Finally, it is important to further understand the notion of the "corporate" psychopath due to conflicting evidence about the impact of psychopathic personality traits on workplaces. For example, some research suggests that corporate psychopaths exert a toxic influence on colleagues and subordinates and may also engage in unethical and illegal business practices (Boddy, 2011; Boddy & Taplin, 2017; Clarke, 2005). Research has also reported, however, high levels of psychopathy in senior-level managers concurrent with high levels of subordinate job satisfaction (Spencer

& Byrne, 2016). These contradictory findings will be examined in later chapters within this book, along with further exploration of the contextual factors and additional personality factors that may moderate or mediate the relationship between psychopathy and workplace outcomes.

References

Adams, E. (2017). *The psychopath next door: How similar are they to those behind bars? Criminality, executive functioning, and emotion processing in 'noncriminal' psychopathy.* Submitted in fulfilment of the requirements for the degree of Doctor of Philosophy, Queensland University of Technology.

American Psychiatric Association. (2013). *Diagnostic and statistical manual of mental disorders* (5th ed.). Arlington, VA: American Psychiatric Publishing.

Auty, K., Farrington, D., & Coid, J. (2015). Intergenerational transmission of psychopathy and mediation via psychosocial risk factors. *The British Journal of Psychiatry: The Journal of Mental Science, 206*(1), 26–31. https://doi.org/10.1192/bjp.bp.114.151050.

Babiak, P., & Hare, R. D. (2006). *Snakes in suits: When psychopaths go to work.* New York, NY: HarperCollins.

Babiak, P., & Hare, R. D. (2012). *The B-Scan 360 Manual.* Manuscript in preparation.

Babiak, P., Neumann, C. S., & Hare, R. D. (2010). Corporate psychopathy: Talking the walk. *Behavioural Sciences and the Law, 28,* 174–193. https://doi.org/10.1002/bsl.925.

Bagshaw, R., Gray, N., & Snowden, R. (2014). Executive function in psychopathy: The Tower of London, Brixton Spatial Anticipation and the Hayling Sentence Completion Tests. *Psychiatry Research, 220*(1–2), 483–489. https://doi.org/10.1016/j.psychres.2014.07.031.

Baron-Cohen, S. (2011). *Zero degrees of empathy: A new theory of human cruelty* (Vol. 30). London, UK: Penguin.

Bechara, A., Damasio, A. R., Damasio, H., & Anderson, S. W. (1994). Insensitivity to future consequences following damage to human prefrontal cortex. *Cognition, 50*(1–3), 7–15. https://doi.org/10.1016/0010-0277(94)90018-3.

Benning, S. D., Patrick, C. J., Blonigen, D. M., Hicks, B. M., & Iacono, G. (2005). Estimating facets of psychopathy from normal personality traits: A step toward community epidemiological investigations. *Assessment, 12,* 3–18. https://doi.org/10.1177/1073191104271223.

Benning, S. D., Venables, N. C., & Hall, J. R. (2018). Successful psychopathy. In C. J. Patrick (ed.), *Handbook of psychopathy* (2nd ed., pp. 585–608). New York: Guilford Press.

Blair, J., Mitchell, D., & Blair, K. (2005). *The Psychopath emotion and the brain.* Oxford, UK: Blackwell Publishing.

Blair, R. J. R., Jones, L., Clark, F., & Smith, M. (1997). The psychopathic individual: A lack of responsiveness to distress cues? *Psychophysiology, 34,* 192–198. https://doi.org/10.1111/j.1469-8986.1997.tb02131.x.

Blonigen, D., Carlson, S., Krueger, R., & Patrick, C. (2003). A twin study of self-reported psychopathic personality traits. *Personality and Individual Differences, 35*(1), 179–197. https://doi.org/10.1016/S0191-8869(02)00184-8.

Blonigen, D., Hicks, B., Krueger, R., Patrick, C., & Iacono, W. (2006). Continuity and change in psychopathic traits as measured via normal-range personality: A longitudinal–biometric study. *Journal of Abnormal Psychology, 115*(1), 85–95. https://doi.org/10.1037/0021-843X.115.1.85.

Board, B. J., & Fritzon, K. (2005). Disordered personalities at work. *Psychology, Crime and Law, 11*(1), 17–32. https://doi.org/10.1080/10683160310001634304.

Boccardi, M., Ganzola, R., Rossi, R., Sabattoli, F., Laakso, M., Repo-Tiihonen, E., ... Tiihonen, J. (2010). Abnormal hippocampal shape in offenders with psychopathy. *Human Brain Mapping, 31*(3), 438–447. https://doi.org/10.1002/hbm.20877.

Boddy, C. R. (2010). Corporate psychopaths and organizational type. *Journal of Public Affairs, 10,* 300–312. https://doi.org/10.1002/pa.365.

Boddy, C. R. (2011). The corporate psychopaths theory of the global financial crisis. *Journal of Business Ethics, 102,* 255–259. https://doi.org/10.1007/s10551-011-0810-4.

Boddy, C., & Taplin, R. (2017). A note on workplace psychopathic bullying – Measuring its frequency and severity. *Aggression and Violent Behavior, 34,* 117–119. https://doi.org/10.1016/j.avb.2017.02.001.

Book, A. S., Quinsey, V. L., & Langford, D. (2007). Psychopathy and the perception of affect and vulnerability. *Criminal Justice and Behavior, 34,* 531–544. https://doi.org/10.1177/0093854806293554.

Bowlby, J. (1944). Forty-four juvenile thieves. Their character and home-life. *International Journal of Psych-Analysis, 25,* 107–128.

Brook, M., & Kosson, D. S. (2013). Impaired cognitive empathy in criminal psychopathy: Evidence from a laboratory measure of empathic accuracy. *Journal of Abnormal Psychology, 122,* 156–166. https://doi.org/10.1037/a0030261.

Brooks, N. (2017). *Understanding the manifestation of psychopathic personality traits across populations* (Doctoral thesis).

Brunner, H., Nelen, M., Breakefield, X., Ropers, H., & van Oost, B. (1993). Abnormal behavior associated with a point mutation in the structural gene for monoamine oxidase A. *Science, 262,* 578–580.

Bushman, B. J., & Baumeister, R. F. (1998). Threatened egotism, narcissism, self esteem, and direct and displaced aggression: Does self-love or self-hate lead to violence? *Journal of Personality and Social Psychology, 75,* 219–229. https://doi.org/10.1037/0022-3514.75.1.219.

Caro, R. A. (1982). *The path to power.* New York: Knopf.

Caro, R. A. (2002). *Master of the senate.* New York: Knopf.

Carter, V. B. (1965). *Winston Churchill: An intimate portrait.* New York: Konecky & Konecky.

Chartrand, T., & Bargh, J. (1999). The chameleon effect: The perception–behavior link and social interaction. *Journal of Personality and Social Psychology, 76*(6), 893–910. https://doi.org/10.1037/0022-3514.76.6.893.

Christianson, S.-Å., Forth, A. E., Hare, R. D., Strachan, C., Lidberg, L., & Thorell, L.-H. (1996). Remembering details of emotional events: A comparison between psychopathic and nonpsychopathic offenders. *Personality and Individual Differences, 20,* 437–443. https://doi.org/10.1016/0191-8869(95)00220-0.

Clarke, J. (2005). *Working with monsters: How to identify and protect yourself from the workplace psychopath.* Sydney: Random House.

Cleckley, H. (1988). *The mask of sanity.* St Louis, MO: Mosby.

Cleckley, H. M. (1941). *The mask of sanity: An attempt to reinterpret the so-called psychopathic personality.* London: The C. V. Mosby Company.

Cleckley, H. M. (1976). *The mask of sanity* (5th ed.). St Louis, MO: Mosby.

Cooke, D., Hart, S., Logan, C., & Michie, C. (2012). Explicating the construct of psychopathy: Development and validation of a conceptual model, the Comprehensive Assessment of Psychopathic Personality (CAPP). *International Journal of Forensic Mental Health, 11*(4), 242–252. https://doi.org/10.1080/14999013.2012.746759.

Cooke, D. J., & Michie, C. (2001). Refining the construct of psychopathy. *Psychological Assessment, 13,* 171e188.

Cope, L., Shane, M., Segall, J., Nyalakanti, P., Stevens, M., Pearlson, G., … Kiehl, K. (2012). Examining the effect of psychopathic traits on gray matter volume in a community substance abuse sample. *Psychiatry Research: Neuroimaging, 204*(2–3), 91–100. https://doi.org/10.1016/j.pscychresns.2012.10.004.

Corr, P. J. (2008). *The reinforcement sensitivity theory of personality*. Cambridge: Cambridge University Press.

Costa, P. T., & McCrae, R. R. (1992). *Neo PI-R professional manual*. Odessa, FL: PAR Inc.

Costa, P. T., & McCrae, R. R. (2003). *Personality in adulthood: A five-factor theory perspective* (2nd ed.). New York: Guilford Press.

Coyne, S. M., & Thomas, T. J. (2008). Psychopathy, aggression, and cheating behavior: A test of the Cheater-Hawk hypothesis. *Personality and Individual Differences, 44*, 1105–1115. https://doi.org/10.1016/j.paid.2007.11.002.

Cronbach, L. J., & Meehl, P. E. (1955). Construct validity in psychological tests. *Psychological Bulletin, 52*(4), 281–302. https://doi.org/10.1037/h0040957.

Croom, S. (2017). *An examination of the incidence of psychopathic personality disorder in supply executives compared to general business executives*. Thesis submitted for degree of MSc Psychology, University of Liverpool, Liverpool, UK.

Davis, M. H. (1983). Measuring individual differences in empathy: Evidence for a multidimensional approach. *Journal of Personality and Social Psychology, 44*, 113–126. https://doi.org/10.1037/0022-3514.44.1.113.

Dawel, A., Wright, L., Dumbleton, R., & Mckone, E. (2019). All tears are crocodile tears: Impaired perception of emotion authenticity in psychopathic traits. *Personality Disorders: Theory, Research, and Treatment, 10*(2), 185–197. https://doi.org/10.1037/per0000301.

Decety, J., Chen, C., Harenski, C., & Kiehl, K. A. (2013). An fMRI study of affective perspective taking individuals with psychopathy: Imaging another in pain does not evoke empathy. *Frontiers in Human Neuroscience, 7*, 1–12. https://doi.org/10.3389/fnhum.2013.00489.

Demetrioff, S., Porter, S., & Baker, A. (2017). I know how you feel: The influence of psychopathic traits on the ability to identify micro-expressions. *Psychology, Crime & Law, 23*(3), 274–290. https://doi.org/10.1080/1068316X.2016.1247159.

Dolan, M., Deakin, J., Roberts, N., & Anderson, I. (2002). Quantitative frontal and temporal structural MRI studies in personality-disordered offenders and control subjects. *Psychiatry Research, 116*(3), 133–149.

Dolan, M., & Fullam, R. (2004). Theory of mind and mentalizing ability in antisocial personality disorders with and without psychopathy. *Psychological Medicine, 34*, 1093–1102. https://doi.org/10.1017/S0033291704002028.

Drislane, L., & Patrick, C. (2017). Integrating alternative conceptions of psychopathic personality: A latent variable model of triarchic psychopathy constructs. *Journal of Personality Disorders, 31*(1), 110–132. https://doi.org/10.1521/pedi_2016_30_240.

Dutton, K. (2012). *The wisdom of psychopaths: What saints, spies, and serial killers can teach us about success.* New York, NY: Scientific American.

Dutton, K. (2016). Would you vote for a psychopath? *Scientific American Mind, 27,* 50–55.

Edens, J. F., Marcus, D. K., Lilienfeld, S. O., & Poythress, N. G. (2006). Psychopathic, not psychopath: Taxometric evidence for the dimensional structure of psychopathy. *Journal of Abnormal Psychology, 115,* 131–144. https://doi.org/10.1037/0021-843X.115.1.131.

Falkenbach, D. M., Howe, J. R., & Falki, M. (2013). Using self-esteem to disaggregate psychopathy, narcissism, and aggression. *Personality and Individual Differences, 54*(7), 815–820.

Fallon, J. (2014). *The psychopath inside: A neuroscientist's personal journey into the dark side of the brain.* New York: Current.

Farrington, D. (2006). Family background and psychopathy. In C. J. Patrick (Ed.), *Handbook of psychopathy* (pp. 229–250). New York: Guilford Press.

Farrington, D., Felthous, A., & Sass, H. (2000). Psychosocial predictors of adult antisocial personality and adult convictions. *Behavioral Sciences & the Law, 18*(5), 605–622. https://doi.org/10.1002/1099-0798(200010)18:5<605::AID-BSL406>3.0.CO;2-0.

Farrington, D. P., & West, D. J. (1990). The Cambridge study in delinquent development: A longterm follow-up of 411 London males. In H. J. Kerner & G. Kaiser (Eds.), *Kriminalitat: Personlichkeit, Lebensgeschichte und Verhalten* [Criminality: Personality, Behaviour and Life History] (pp. 115–138). Berlin: Springer-Verlag.

Farwell, B. (1963). *Burton: A biography of Sir Richard Francis Burton.* New York: Holt, Rinehart & Winston.

Fecteau, S., Pascual-Leone, A., & Théoret, H. (2008). Psychopathy and the mirror neuron system: Preliminary findings from a non-psychiatric sample. *Psychiatry Research, 160,* 137–144. https://doi.org/10.1016/j.psychres.2007.08.022.

Finger, E., Marsh, A., Blair, K., Reid, M., Sims, C., Ng, P., … Blair, R. (2011). Disrupted reinforcement signaling in the orbitofrontal cortex and caudate in youths with conduct disorder or oppositional defiant disorder and a high level of psychopathic traits. *The American Journal of Psychiatry, 168*(2), 152–162. https://doi.org/10.1176/appi.ajp.2010.10010129.

Forouzan, E., & Cooke, D. J. (2005). Figuring out la femme fatale: Conceptual and assessment issues concerning psychopathy in females. *Behavioral Sciences & the Law, 23*, 765–778.

Fowles, D. C., & Dindo, L. (2009). Temperament and psychology: A dual pathway model. *Current Directions in Psychological Science, 18*(3), 179–183. https://doi.org/10.1111/j.1467-8721.2009.01632.x.

Frick, P., Kimonis, E., Dandreaux, D., Farell, J., Petrila, J., & Skeem, J. (2003). The 4 year stability of psychopathic traits in non-referred youth. *Behavioral Sciences & the Law, 21*(6), 713–736. https://doi.org/10.1002/bsl.568.

Frick, P. J., Lilienfeld, S. O., Ellis, M., Loney, B., & Silverthorn, P. (1999). The association between anxiety and psychopathy dimensions in children. *Journal of Abnormal Child Psychology, 27*(5), 383–392. https://doi.org/10.1023/a:1021928018403.

Fritzon, K., Bailey, C., Croom, S., & Brooks, N. (2016). Problem personalities in the workplace: Development of the corporate personality inventory. In P.-A. Granhag, R. Bull, A. Shaboltas, & E. Dozortseva (Eds.), *Psychology and law in Europe: When west meets east.* Boca Raton: CRC Press.

Frydman, C., Camerer, C., Bossaerts, P., & Rangel, A. (2011). MAOA-L carriers are better at making optimal financial decisions under risk. *Proceedings. Biological Sciences, 278*(1714), 2053–2059. https://doi.org/10.1098/rspb.2010.2304.

Gao, Y., Raine, A., Felthous, A., & Sass, H. (2010). Successful and unsuccessful psychopaths: A neurobiological model. *Behavioral Sciences & the Law, 28*(2), 194–210. https://doi.org/10.1002/bsl.924.

Garofalo, C., Neumann, C., Zeigler-Hill, V., & Meloy, J. (2019). Spiteful and contemptuous: A new look at the emotional experiences related to psychopathy. *Personality Disorders: Theory, Research, and Treatment, 10*(2), 173–184. https://doi.org/10.1037/per0000310.

Glass, S. J., & Newman, J. P. (2006). Recognition of facial affect in psychopathic offenders. *Journal of Abnormal Psychology, 115*, 815–820. https://doi.org/10.1037/0021-843X.115.4.815.

Glenn, A., Han, H., Yang, Y., Raine, A., & Schug, R. (2017). Associations between psychopathic traits and brain activity during instructed false responding. *Psychiatry Research: Neuroimaging, 266*, 123–137. https://doi.org/10.1016/j.pscychresns.2017.06.008. https://doi.org/10.1016/j.biopsych.2009.06.018.

Glenn, A. L., & Raine, A. (2014). *Psychopathy: An introduction to biological findings and their implications.* New York, NY: University Press.

Goleman, D. (1995). *Emotional intelligence.* London: Bloomsbury.

Gray, J. A. (1975). *Elements of a two-process theory of learning.* New York, NY: Academic Press.

Gray, J. A. (1982). *The neuropsychology of anxiety: An enquiry into the functions of the septo-hippocampal system.* Oxford: Oxford University Press.

Gray, J. A. (1987). *The psychology of fear and stress.* Cambridge: Cambridge University Press.

Grieve, R., & Panebianco, L. (2013). Assessing the role of aggression, empathy, and self-serving cognitive distortions in trait emotional manipulation. *Australian Journal of Psychology, 65,* 79–88. https://doi.org/10.1111/j.1742-9536.2012.00059.x.

Gustafson, S. B., & Ritzer, D. R. (1995). The dark side of normal: A psychopathy-linked pattern called aberrant self-promotion. *European Journal of Personality, 9,* 147–183. https://doi.org/10.1002/per.2410090302.

Habel, U., Kühn, E., Salloum, J. B., Devos, H., & Schneider, F. (2002). Emotional processing in psychopathic personality. *Aggressive Behavior, 28,* 394–400. https://doi.org/10.1002/ab.80015.

Hall, J. R., & Benning, S. D. (2006). The "successful" psychopath: Adaptive and subclinical manifestations of psychopathy in the general population. In C. J. Patrick (Ed.), *Handbook of psychopathy* (pp. 459–478). New York, NY: Guilford Press.

Hare, R. D. (1980). A research scale for the assessment of psychopathy in criminal populations. *Personality and Individual Differences, 1*(2), 111–119. https://doi.org/10.1016/0191-8869(80)90028-8.

Hare, R. D. (1991). *The Hare psychopathy checklist—Revised (PCL-R).* Toronto, ON: Multi-Health Systems.

Hare, R. D. (1996). Psychopathy: A clinical construct whose time has come. *Criminal Justice and Behavior, 23*(1), 25–54. https://doi.org/10.1177/0093854896023001004.

Hare, R. D. (1999a). Psychopathy as a risk factor for violence. *Psychiatric Quarterly, 70,* 181–197. https://doi.org/10.1023/A:1022094925150.

Hare, R. D. (1999b). *Without conscience: The disturbing world of psychopaths among us.* New York, NY: Guilford Press.

Hare, R. D. (2003). *The Hare psychopathy checklist—Revised* (2nd ed.). Toronto, ON: Multi-Health Systems.

Hare, R. D., & McPherson, L. M. (1984). Violent and aggressive behavior in criminal psychopaths. *International Journal of Law and Psychiatry, 7,* 35–50. https://doi.org/10.1016/0160-2527(84)90005-0.

Hare, R. D., & Neumann, C. S. (2010). The role of antisociality in the psychopathy construct: comment on Skeem and Cooke (2010). *Psychological Assessment, 22*(2), 446–454. https://doi.org/10.1037/a0013635.

Hart, S. D., Cox, D. N., & Hare, R. D. (1995). *The Hare psychopathy checklist: Screening version.* Toronto, ON: Multi-Health Systems.

Hart, S. D., & Hare, R. D. (1997). Psychopathy: Assessment and association with criminal conduct. In D. Stoff, J. Breiling, & J. Maser (Eds.), *Handbook of antisocial behavior* (pp. 22–35). New York, NY: Wiley.

Hastings, M. E., Tangney, J. P., & Stuewig, J. (2008). Psychopathy and identification of facial expressions of emotions. *Personality and Individual Differences, 44*, 1474–1483. https://doi.org/10.1016/j.paid.2008.01.004.

Hickey, E. W. (2010). *Serial murder, the encyclopedia of victimology and crime prevention.* Thousand Oaks, CA: Sage.

Hicks, B., & Patrick, C. (2006). Psychopathy and negative emotionality: Analyses of suppressor effects reveal distinct relations with emotional distress, fearfulness, and anger-hostility. *Journal of Abnormal Psychology, 115*(2), 276–287. https://doi.org/10.1037/0021-843X.115.2.276.

Hicks, B. M., Markon, K. E., Patrick, C. J., Krueger, R. F., & Newman, J. P. (2004). Identifying psychopathy subtypes on the basis of personality structure. *Psychological Assessment, 16*(3), 276–288. https://doi.org/10.1037/1040-3590.16.3.276.

Hicks, B. M., Vaidyanathan, U., & Patrick, C. J. (2010). Validating female psychopathy subtypes: Differences in personality, antisocial and violent behavior, substance abuse, trauma, and mental health. *Personality Disorders: Theory, Research, and Treatment, 1*, 38–57. https://doi.org/10.1037/a0018135.

Iacoboni, M. (2009). Imitation, empathy, and mirror neurons. *Annual Review of Psychology, 60*, 653–670. https://doi.org/10.1146/annurev.psych.60.110707.163604.

Ickes, W. J. (1997). *Empathic accuracy.* New York, NY: Guilford Publications.

Intrator, J., Hare, R., Stritzke, P., Brichtswein, K., Dorfman, D., Harpur, T., ... Machac, J. (1997). A brain imaging (single photon emission computerized tomography) study of semantic and affective processing in psychopaths. *Biological Psychiatry, 42*(2), 96–103. https://doi.org/10.1016/S0006-3223(96)00290-9.

Ishikawa, S., Raine, A., Lencz, T., Bihrle, S., & Lacasse, L. (2001). Autonomic stress reactivity and executive functions in successful and unsuccessful criminal psychopaths from the community. *Journal of Abnormal Psychology, 110*(3), 423–432. https://doi.org/10.1037/0021-843X.110.3.423.

Johns, J. H., & Quay, H. C. (1962). The effect of social reward on verbal conditioning in psychopathic and neurotic military offenders. *Journal of Consulting Psychology, 26,* 217–220. https://doi.org/10.1037/h0048399.

Jonason, P. K., Li, N. P., & Teicher, E. A. (2010). Who is James Bond? The dark triad as an agentic social style. *Individual Differences Research, 8,* 111–120.

Jonason, P. K., & Webster, G. D. (2010). The dirty dozen: A concise measure of the dark triad. *Psychological Assessment, 22*(2), 420–432. https://doi.org/10.1037/a0019265.

Jones, D. N., & Hare, R. D. (2015). The mismeasure of psychopathy: A commentary on Boddy's PM-MRV. *Journal of Business Ethics.* https://doi.org/10.1007/s10551-015-2584-6.

Jones, D. N., & Paulhus, D. L. (2010). Different provocations trigger aggression in narcissists and psychopaths. *Social Psychological and Personality Science, 1*(1), 12–18. https://doi.org/10.1177/1948550609347591.

Kajonius, P. J., Persson, B. N., & Jonason, P. K. (2015). Hedonism, achievement, and power: Universal values that characterize the dark triad. *Personality and Individual Differences, 77,* 173–178. https://doi.org/10.1016/j.paid.2014.12.055.

Kantor, M. (2006). *The Psychopathy of everyday life: How antisocial personality disorder affects all of us.* Westport, CT: Praeger.

Karpman, B. (1941). On the need of separating psychopathy into two distinct clinical types: The symptomatic and the idiopathic. *Journal of Criminal Psychopathology, 3,* 112–137. Retrieved from http://psycnet.apa.org/psycinfo/1942-00202-001.

Karpman, B. (1948). Conscience in the psychopath: Another version. *American Journal of Orthopsychiatry, 18,* 455–491. https://doi.org/10.1111/j.1939-0025.1948.tb05109.x.

Kiehl, K. (2014). *The psychopath whisperer: The science of those without a conscience* (1st ed.). New York: Crown Publishers.

Kiehl, K., Smith, A., Hare, R., Mendrek, A., Forster, B., Brink, J., & Liddle, P. (2001). Limbic abnormalities in affective processing by criminal psychopaths as revealed by functional magnetic resonance imaging. *Biological Psychiatry, 50*(9), 677–684. https://doi.org/10.1016/S0006-3223(01)01222-7.

Kobasa, S. C. (1979). Stressful life events, personality, and health: An inquiry into hardiness. *Journal of Personality and Social Psychology, 37*(1), 1–11. https://doi.org/10.1037/0022-3514.37.1.1.

Koch, J. L. A. (1891). *Die Psychopathischen Minderwertigkeiten.* Whitefish, MT: Kessinger Publishing.

Kreis, M., & Cooke, D. (2012). The manifestation of psychopathic traits in women: An exploration using case examples. *International Journal of Forensic Mental Health, 11*(4), 267–279. https://doi.org/10.1080/14999013.2012. 746755.

Kreis, M., Cooke, D., Stanford, M., & Felthous, A. (2011). Capturing the psychopathic female: A prototypicality analysis of the Comprehensive Assessment of Psychopathic Personality (CAPP) across gender. *Behavioral Sciences & the Law, 29*(5), 634–648. https://doi.org/10.1002/bsl.1003.

Kujacic, D., Medjedovic, J., & Knezevic, G. (2015). The relations between personality traits and psychopathy as measured by ratings and self-report. *Psihologija, 48*(1), 45–59.

Larsson, H., Andershed, H., & Lichtenstein, P. (2006). A genetic factor explains most of the variation in the psychopathic personality. *Journal of Abnormal Psychology, 115*(2), 221–230. https://doi.org/10.1037/0021-843X.115.2.221.

Legislation.gov.uk. (2015). *Mental Health Act 1983* [online]. Available at: http://www.legislation.gov.uk/ukpga/1983/20/contents. Accessed 13 January 2015.

Levenson, M. R., Kiehl, K. A., & Fitzpatrick, C. M. (1995). Assessing psychopathic attributes in a non institutionalized population. *Journal of Personality and Social Psychology, 68,* 151–158. https://doi.org/10.1037/0022-3514.68. 1.151.

Lilienfeld, S. O., & Andrews, B. P. (1996). Development and preliminary validation of a self report measure of psychopathic personality traits in noncriminal populations. *Journal of Personality Assessment, 66,* 488–524. https://doi.org/10.1207/s15327752jpa6603_3.

Lilienfeld, S. O., Patrick, C. J., Benning, S. D., Berg, J., Sellbom, M., & Edens, J. F. (2012). The role of fearless dominance in psychopathy: Confusions, controversies, and clarifications. *Personality Disorders: Theory, Research, and Treatment, 3,* 327–340. https://doi.org/10.1037/a0026987.

Lilienfeld, S. O., & Widows, M. R. (2005). *Psychopathic personality inventory-revised (PPI-R) professional manual.* Odessa, FL: Psychological Assessment Resources.

Loeber, R., Farrington, D., Stouthamer-Loeber, M., & White, H. (2008). *Violence and serious theft: Development and prediction from childhood to adulthood* (pp. 1–404). https://doi.org/10.4324/9780203933237.

Logan, C., & Weizmann-Henelius, G. (2012). Psychopathy in women: Presentation, assessment and management. In H. Hakkanen-Nyholm & J. O. Nyholm (Eds.), *Psychopathy and law: A practitioner's guide* (pp. 99–125). London, England: Wiley.

Long, S. L., & Titone, D. A. (2007). Psychopathy and verbal emotion processing in non-incarcerated males. *Cognition and Emotion, 21,* 119–145. https://doi.org/10.1080/02699930600551766.

Lorenz, A. R., & Newman, J. P. (2002). Deficient response modulation and emotion processing in low-anxious Caucasian psychopathic offenders: Results from a lexical decision task. *Emotion, 2*(2), 91–104. https://doi.org/10.1037/1528-3542.2.2.91.

Lykken, D. T. (1957). A study of anxiety in the sociopathic personality. *The Journal of Abnormal and Social Psychology, 55,* 6–10. https://doi.org/10.1037/h0047232.

Lykken, D. T. (1995). *The antisocial personalities.* Mahwah, NJ: Erlbaum.

Lykken, D. T. (2006). Psychopathic personality: The scope of the problem. In C. J. Patrick (Ed.), *Handbook of psychopathy* (pp. 3–13). New York, NY: Guilford Press.

Lynam, D., Caspi, A., Moffitt, T., Loeber, R., & Stouthamer-Loeber, M. (2007). Longitudinal evidence that psychopathy scores in early adolescence predict adult psychopathy. *Journal of Abnormal Psychology, 116*(1), 155–165. https://doi.org/10.1037/0021-843X.116.1.155.

MacDonald, A. W., & Iacono, W. (2006). Toward an integrated perspective on the etiology of psychopathy. In C. J. Patrick (Ed.), *Handbook of psychopathy* (pp. 373–386). London: Guilford Press.

Manchester, W. (1986). *The last lion: Winston Spencer Churchill—Visions of glory, 1874–1932.* New York: Little, Brown.

Manchester, W. (1988). *The last lion: Winston Spencer Churchill—Visions of glory, 1932–1940.* New York: Little, Brown.

Mathieu, C., & Babiak, P. (2015). Tell me who you are, I'll tell you how to lead: Beyond the full-range leadership model, the role of corporate psychopathy on employee attitudes. *Personality and Individual Differences, 87,* 8–12. https://doi.org/10.1016/j.paid.2015.07.016.

Marshall, L., & Cooke, D. (1999). The childhood experiences of psychopaths: A retrospective study of familial and societal factors. *Journal of Personality Disorders, 13*(3), 211–225. https://doi.org/10.1521/pedi.1999.13.3.211.

McCord, W., & McCord, J. (1964). *The Psychopath: An essay on the criminal mind.* Princeton, NJ: Van Nostrand.

McDermott, R., Tingley, D., Cowden, J., Frazzetto, G., & Johnson, D. (2009). Monoamine Oxidase A Gene (MAOA) predicts behavioral aggression following provocation. *Proceedings of the National Academy of Sciences of the United States of America, 106*(7), 2118–2123. https://doi.org/10.1073/pnas.0808376106.

McNab, A., & Dutton, K. (2014). *The good psychopath's guide to success*. Random House.

Meffert, H., Gazzola, V., den Boer, J. A., Bartels, A. A., & Keysers, C. (2014). Reduced spontaneous but relatively normal deliberate vicarious representations in psychopathy. *Brain, 136*(8), 2550–2562.

Meloy, J. R., & Shiva, A. (2007). A psychoanalytic view of the psychopath. In A. Felthous & H. Sass (Eds.), *International handbook on psychopathic disorders and the law: Laws and policies* (Vol. 1, pp. 335–346). Diagnosis and Treatment. Chichester: Wiley.

Monahan, J., Steadman, H. J., Appelbaum, M. D., Grisso, T., Mulvey, E. P., Roth, L. H., … Silver, E. (2006). The classification of violence risk. *Behavioural Sciences & The Law, 24*(6), 721–730. https://doi.org/10.1002/bsl.725.

Morey, L. C., Waugh, M. H., & Blashfield, R. K. (1985). MMPI scales for DSM-III Personality disorders: Their derivation and correlates. *Journal of Personality Assessment, 49*(3), 245–251. https://doi.org/10.1207/s15327752jpa4903_5.

Morrison, D., & Gilbert, P. (2001). Social rank, shame and anger in primary and secondary psychopaths. *The Journal of Forensic Psychiatry, 12,* 330–356. https://doi.org/10.1080/09585180110056867.

Müller, J., Sommer, M., Wagner, V., Lange, K., Taschler, H., Röder, C., … Hajak, G. (2003). Abnormalities in emotion processing within cortical and subcortical regions in criminal psychopaths: Evidence from a functional magnetic resonance imaging study using pictures with emotional content. *Biological Psychiatry, 54*(2), 152–162. https://doi.org/10.1016/S0006-3223(02)01749-3.

Mullins-Nelson, J. L., Salekin, R. T., & Leistico, A. M. (2006). Psychopathy, empathy, and perspective-taking ability in a community sample: Implications for the successful psychopathy concept. *International Journal of Forensic Mental Health, 5,* 133–149. https://doi.org/10.1080/14999013.2006.10471238.

Mullins-Sweatt, S. N., Glover, N. G., Derefinko, K. J., Miller, J. D., & Widiger, T. A. (2010). The search for the successful psychopath. *Journal of Research in Personality, 44,* 554–558. https://doi.org/10.1016/j.jrp.2010.05.010.

Newman, J. P., & Kosson, D. S. (1986). Passive avoidance learning in psychopathic and nonpsychopathic offenders. *Journal of Abnormal Psychology, 95*(3), 252–256. https://doi.org/10.1037/0021-843X.95.3.252.

Newman, J. P., Curtin, J. J., Bertsch, J. D., & Baskin-Sommers, A. R. (2010). Attention moderates the fearlessness of psychopathic offenders. *Biological Psychiatry, 67*(1), 66–70. https://doi.org/10.1016/j.biopsych.2009.07.035.

Ogloff, J. R. P., Wong, S., & Greenwood, A. (1990). Treating criminal psychopaths in a therapeutic community program. *Behavioral Sciences & the Law, 8*(2), 181–190. https://doi.org/10.1002/bsl.2370080210.

Patrick, C. J. (2007). Getting to the heart of psychopathy. In H. Herve & J. C. Yuille (Eds.), *The psychopath: Theory, research, and practice* (pp. 207–252). Mahwah, NJ: Lawrence Erlbaum Associates.

Patrick, C. J., Fowles, D. C., & Krueger, R. F. (2009). Triarchic conceptualization of psychopathy: Developmental origins of disinhibition, boldness, and meanness. *Development and Psychopathology, 21,* 913–938. https://doi.org/10.1017/S0954579409000492.

Patrick, C. J., & Zempolich, K. A. (1998). Emotion and aggression in the psychopathic personality. *Aggression and Violent Behavior, 3,* 303–338. https://doi.org/10.1016/S1359-1789(97)00003-7.

Paulhus, D. L. (1999). *Paulhus deception scales (PDS): The Balanced Inventory of Desirable Responding-7.* New York, NY: Multi-Health Systems.

Paulhus, D. L., Hemphill, J. D., & Hare, R. D. (2016). *Manual for the self report psychopathy scale.* Toronto: Multi-Health Systems.

Paulhus, D. L., & Williams, K. M. (2002). The dark triad of personality: Narcissism, machiavellianism, and psychopathy. *Journal of Research in Personality, 36,* 556–563. https://doi.org/10.1016/S0092-6566(02)00505-6.

Polaschek, D. L. L. (2015). (Mis)Understanding psychopathy: Consequences for policy and practice with offenders. *Psychiatry, Psychology and Law, 22,* 500–519. https://doi.org/10.1080/13218719.2014.960033.

Porter, S., ten Brinke, L., Baker, A., & Wallace, B. (2011). Would I lie to you? "Leakage" in deceptive facial expressions relates to psychopathy and emotional intelligence. *Personality and Individual Differences, 51*(2), 133–137. https://doi.org/10.1016/j.paid.2011.03.031.

Porter, S., ten Brinke, L., & Wilson, K. (2009). Crime profiles and conditional release performance of psychopathic and non-psychopathic sexual offenders. *Legal and Criminological Psychology, 14,* 109–118. https://doi.org/10.1348/135532508X284310.

Poythress, N., Skeem, J., & Lilienfeld, S. (2006). Associations among early abuse, dissociation, and psychopathy in an offender sample. *Journal of Abnormal Psychology, 115*(2), 288–297. https://doi.org/10.1037/0021-843X.115.2.288.

Proyer, R. T., Flisch, R., Tschupp, S., Platt, T., & Ruch, W. (2012). How does psychopathy relate to humor and laughter? Dispositions toward ridicule and being laughed at, the sense of humor, and psychopathic personality traits. *International Journal of Law and Psychiatry, 35,* 263–268. https://doi.org/10.1016/j.ijlp.2012.04.007.

Raine, A., Ishikawa, S., Arce, E., Lencz, T., Knuth, K., Bihrle, S., ... Colletti, P. (2004). Hippocampal structural asymmetry in unsuccessful psychopaths. *Biological Psychiatry, 55*(2), 185–191. https://doi.org/10.1016/S0006-3223(03)00727-3.

Raine, A., Phill, D., Stoddard, J., Bihrle, S., & Buchsbaum, M. (1998). Prefrontal glucose deficits in murderers lacking psychosocial deprivation. *Neuropsychiatric, Neuropsychological, and Behavioural Neurology, 11,* 1–7.

Rice, E. (1990). *Captain Sir Richard Francis Burton.* New York: Scribner's.

Rogers, J., Viding, E., Blair, R. J., Frith, U., & Happe, F. (2006). Autism spectrum disorder and psychopathy: Shared cognitive underpinnings or double hit? *Psychological Medicine, 36,* 1789–1798.

Rubenzer, S. J., & Faschingbauer, T. R. (2004). *Personality, character and leadership in the White House.* Washington, DC: Potomac Books.

Salekin, R., Rogers, R., & Sewell, K. (1997). Construct validity of psychopathy in a female offender sample: A multitrait–multimethod evaluation. *Journal of Abnormal Psychology, 106*(4), 576–585. https://doi.org/10.1037/0021-843X.106.4.576.

Sandvik, A. M., Hansen, A. L., Hystad, S. W., Johnsen, B. H., & Bartone, P. T. (2015). Psychopathy, anxiety, and resiliency—Psychological hardiness as a mediator of the psychopathy–anxiety relationship in a prison setting. *Personality and Individual Differences, 72,* 30–34. https://doi.org/10.1016/j.paid.2014.08.009.

Schneider, F., Habel, U., Kessler, C., Posse, S., Grodd, W., & Müller-Gärtner, H. (2000). Functional imaging of conditioned aversive emotional responses in antisocial personality disorder. *Neuropsychobiology, 42*(4), 192–201. https://doi.org/10.1159/000026693.

Schoenleber, M., Sadeh, N., & Verona, E. (2011). Parallel syndromes: Two dimensions of narcissism and the facets of psychopathic personality in criminally involved individuals. *Personality Disorders: Theory, Research, and Treatment, 2*(2), 113–127. https://doi.org/10.1037/a0021870.

Sellbom, M., Cooke, D., & Hart, S. (2015). Construct validity of the Comprehensive Assessment of Psychopathic Personality (CAPP) concept map: Getting closer to the core of psychopathy. *International Journal of Forensic Mental Health, 14*(3), 172–180. https://doi.org/10.1080/14999013.2015.1085112.

Shih, J., & Chen, K. (1999). MAO-A and -B gene knock-out mice exhibit distinctly different behavior. *Neurobiology, 7,* 235–246.

Silverthorn, P., & Frick, P. (1999). Developmental pathways to antisocial behavior: The delayed-onset pathway in girls. *Development and Psychopathology, 11*(1), 101–126. https://doi.org/10.1017/S0954579499001972.

Skeem, J. L., & Cooke, D. J. (2010). Is criminal behavior a central component of psychopathy? Conceptual directions for resolving the debate. *Psychological Assessment, 22,* 433–445. https://doi.org/10.1037/a0008512.

Skeem, J. L., Polaschek, D. L. L., Patrick, C. J., & Lilienfeld, S. O. (2011). Psychopathic personality: Bridging the gap between scientific evidence and public policy. *Psychological Science in the Public Interest, 12,* 95–162. https://doi.org/10.1177/1529100611426706.

Smith, S. F., & Lilienfeld, S. O. (2013). Psychopathy in the workplace: The knowns and unknowns. *Aggression and Violent Behavior, 18*(2), 204–218. https://doi.org/10.1016/j.avb.2012.11.007.

Spector, P. E. (1997). *Job satisfaction: Application, assessment, causes, and consequences.* Thousand Oaks, CA: Sage.

Spencer, R. J., & Byrne, M. K. (2016). Relationship between the extent of psychopathic features among corporate managers and subsequent employee job satisfaction. *Personality and Individual Differences, 101,* 440–445. https://doi.org/10/1016/j.paid.2016.06.044.

ten Brinke, L., Black, P. J., Porter, S., & Carney, D. R. (2015). Psychopathic personality traits predict competitive wins and cooperative losses in negotiation. *Personality and Individual Differences, 79,* 116–122. https://doi.org/10.1016/j.paid.2015.02.001.

ten Brinke, L., Kish, A., & Keltner, D. (2018). Hedge fund managers with psychopathic tendencies make for worse investors. *Personality and Social Psychology Bulletin, 44*(2), 214–223. https://doi.org/10.1177/0146167217733080.

Ullrich, S., Farington, D. P., & Coid, J. W. (2008). Psychopathic personality traits and life-success. *Personality and Individual Differences, 44*(5), 1162–1171. https://doi.org/10.1016/j.paid.2007.11.008.

Verona, E., & Vitale, J. (2018). Psychopathy in women: Assessment, manifestations and etiology. In C. J. Patrick (Ed.), *Handbook of psychology* (2nd ed., pp. 509–528). New York: Guilford Press.

Verschuere, B., Uzieblo, K., De Schryver, M., Douma, H., Onraedt, T., & Crombez, G. (2014). The inverse relation between psychopathy and faking good: Not response bias, but true variance in psychopathic personality. *Journal of Forensic Psychiatry and Psychology, 25*(6), 705–713. https://doi.org/10.1080/14789949.2014.952767.

Viding, E., Blair, R., Moffitt, T., & Plomin, R. (2005). Evidence for substantial genetic risk for psychopathy in 7-year-olds. *Journal of Child Psychology and Psychiatry, 46*(6), 592–597. https://doi.org/10.1111/j.1469-7610.2004.00393.x.

Watt, B., & Brooks, N. (2012). Self-report psychopathy in an Australian community sample. *Psychiatry, Psychology and Law, 19,* 389–401. https://doi.org/10.1080/13218719.2011.585130.

Weizmann-Henelius, G., Putkonen, H., Grönroos, M., Lindberg, N., Eronen, M., & Häkkänen-Nyholm, H. (2010). Examination of psychopathy in female homicide offenders — Confirmatory factor analysis of the PCL-R. *International Journal of Law and Psychiatry, 33*(3), 177–183. https://doi.org/10.1016/j.ijlp.2010.03.008.

Weizmann-Henelius, G., Viemerö, V., & Eronen, M. (2004). The violent female perpetrator and her victim. *Forensic Science International, 133,* 197–203. https://doi.org/10.1016/S0379-0738(03)00068-9.

Wheeler, S., Book, A., & Costello, K. (2009). Psychopathic traits and perceptions of victim vulnerability. *Criminal Justice and Behavior, 36,* 635–648. https://doi.org/10.1177/0093854809333958.

Willemsen, J., & Verhaeghe, P. (2012). Psychopathy and internalising psychopathology. *International Journal of Law and Psychiatry, 35*(4), 269–275. https://doi.org/10.1016/j.ijlp.2012.04.004.

Yang, Y., & Raine, A. (2018). The neuroanatomical bases of psychopathy. In C. J. Patrick (Ed.). *Handbook of psychopathy* (2nd ed., pp. 380–400). New York: The Guilford Press.

Yang, Y., Raine, A., Colletti, P., Toga, A., & Narr, K. (2010). Morphological alterations in the prefrontal cortex and the amygdala in unsuccessful psychopaths. *Journal of Abnormal Psychology, 119*(3), 546–554. https://doi.org/10.1037/a0019611.

2

Conceptualising Psychopathy: Empirical, Clinical and Case Interpretations

Nathan Brooks

Common Psychopathy Instruments

There are many conceptions of psychopathy, influenced by theory, empirical research and the operationalisation of assessments (Skeem, Polaschek, Patrick, & Lilienfeld, 2011). The vast majority of psychopathy assessment instruments have been significantly influenced by the work of Hervey Cleckley and Robert Hare who have pioneered the understanding of psychopathy. The contribution from both Cleckley and Hare to understanding psychopathic personality will likely be enduring, yet, recently there has been an uprising in new theoretical models attempting to account for the considerable difference observed in cases of psychopathic personality. For many years, the two leading assessments instruments in the field were the Psychopathic Checklist-Revised (PCL-R; Hare, 2003) and Psychopathic Personality Inventory-Revised (PPI-R; Lilienfeld & Widows, 2005); however, a number of new instruments examining psychopathy

N. Brooks (✉)
Central Queensland University, Townsville, QLD, Australia
e-mail: nathan@nathanbrooks.com.au

© The Author(s) 2020
K. Fritzon et al., *Corporate Psychopathy*,
https://doi.org/10.1007/978-3-030-27188-6_2

47

have emerged recently, including the Self-Report Psychopathy Scale (SRP-III; Paulhus et al., in press), the B-Scan (Mathieu, Hare, Jones, Babiak, & Newman, 2013), CPI (Fritzon et al., 2016), the Triarchic Psychopathy measure (TRiPM; Patrick, 2009), and the various Comprehensive Assessment of Psychopathic Personality assessment protocols (CAPP; Cooke, 2018). Two of the most prominent theoretical models have been the Triarchic Model of Psychopathy (TMP; Patrick, Fowles, & Krueger, 2009) and the Compressive Assessment of Psychopathic Personality-Concept Map (CAPP-CM; Cook, Hart, Van Dogen, Marle, & Viljoen, 2013). The TMP provides an overarching conceptualisation of psychopathy, identifying boldness, meanness and disinhibition as discrete and intersecting constructs capturing psychopathic personality. The CAPP-CM consists of six broad domains (self, emotional, dominance, attachment, behavioural and cognitive), which are characterised by 33 personality traits or symptoms. A primary difference between the TMP and CAPP-CM compared to Hare's PCL-R, which has been considered as both an assessment tool and theoretical model of psychopathy (Skeem et al., 2011), is the lack of violence as a core characteristic (Brooks, 2017).

The absence of violence as a core feature of psychopathy is of importance when understanding psychopathy in contexts outside of the custodial environment, with some cases of psychopathic personality failing to display violent behaviour (Brooks, 2017; Fritzon et al., 2016; Howe, Falkenbach, Massey, 2014; Skeem et al., 2011). Understanding the underpinnings of psychopathic personality through models such as the TMP and CAPP-CM is a valuable method for comprehensively mapping the principle domains underlying the construct. However, it remains difficult to determine and interpret the various combinations of psychopathic traits whereby someone can at both a theoretical and operational level be considered psychopathic (Murphy & Vess, 2003). For example, some psychopathic individuals are callous and cruel, while others may be charming and narcissistic, both notably different presentations (Coid, Freestone, & Ullrich, 2012; Millon & Davis, 1998). Currently, the clinical categorisation of psychopathy rests on having scored highly on an assessment instrument and being assumed to be therefore essentially similar to the prototypical definition of a psychopath (Murphy & Vess, 2003). Yet this is rarely consistent with clinical observations, with personality features and behaviour often varied, reflecting both similarities and differences amongst individuals. The importance of differentiating personality and behaviour has been evidenced in the alternative model of the DSM-V diagnosis of antisocial personality disorder (ASPD), which distinguished ASPD based on characteristics of antagonism and disinhibition, including specifying the presence of psychopathic features (APA, 2013). Although this model did not replace the traditional personality diagnostic criteria, the APA have acknowledged the need for further investigation relating to personality diagnosis. Appropriately distinguishing core traits associated with personality constructs is important when making decisions related to treatment, management and safety needs, and this is arguably particularly so for psychopathy; the identification of which carries particularly acute clinical and forensic implications (Murphy & Vess, 2003). There are currently limited processes to differentiate between manifestations of psychopathic personality, with a need for reliable methods to accurately differentiate subtypes in presentations.

Assessing Psychopathy in Criminal, Forensic and Clinical Subjects

There have been attempts to classify subtypes of psychopathy throughout the years, led by both theoretical positions and empirical findings. American psychiatrist Benjamin Karpman (1941, 1948) was arguably the first person to distinguish the variations of psychopathy, coining the terms primary and secondary to capture the difference in people presenting with psychopathic personality. According to Karpman, although similarities existed between both types of psychopathy (both antisocial, hostile and irresponsible), primary psychopathy was characterised by an absence of moral conscience, while individuals with secondary psychopathy possessed a moral conscience, but their functioning was disrupted due to perceiving their environment and others as hostile (Skeem, Poythress, Edens, Lilienfeld, & Cale, 2003). Building on Karpman's findings, over a series of studies Blackburn found support for the primary and secondary subtypes of psychopathy (see Blackburn, 1971, 1975, 1986), although proposed further subtypes through a cluster analysis examining personality profiles of mentally disordered forensic patients. Based on the psychological profiles of 144 individuals who were examined on the Millon Clinical Multiaxial Inventory (MCMI; Millon, 1983) and Special Hospitals Assessment of Personality and Socialization (SHAPS; Blackburn, 1979, 1986), Blackburn (1996) identified four personality types, with two profiles reflective of under-controlled tendencies and two over-controlled. The four types included: primary psychopathy (self-confident, extraverted, hostile and impulsive), secondary psychopathy (socially anxious, moody, withdrawn, hostile and impulsive), controlled personalities (unemotional, defensive and socially conforming) and inhibited personalities (controlled, depressed, withdrawn and introverted). The research by Blackburn offered a valuable contribution to personality profiles amongst mentally disordered forensic patients and although his findings provide support for subtypes of psychopathy, the sample limited the generalisability of the research to non-mentally disordered psychopathic presentations.

Holland, Levi and Watson (1980) conducted another foundational study into the profiles of psychopathic individuals across two samples of hospitalised ($n = 80$) and incarcerated ($n = 80$) subjects. Patients and offenders were required to complete the Minnesota Multiphasic Personality Inventory (MMPI; Hathaway & McKinley, 1940), with cluster analysis results revealing five distinct profiles characterised by abnormally high levels of psychopathy. The five profiles of psychopathy included: primary or simple psychopathy (self-absorption, excessive pleasure and excitement seeking, impulsiveness, irresponsibility, and deficient foresight and judgement), hostile psychopathy (resentment, low tolerance for frustration, irritability and demandingness), paranoid schizoid psychopathy (suspicious, socially alienated and reclusive), neurotic psychopathy (withdrawal, alienation, anxious and dysphonic, and social nonconformity), and confused psychopathy (impaired intellect, underlying though disorder, wide-ranging psychopathology). The authors found that primary and hostile psychopathy was more common amongst incarcerated subjects, while paranoid, schizoid, neurotic and confused psychopathy was most common in hospitalised patients. Holland and colleagues concluded that there was considerable personality heterogeneity amongst psychopathic individuals and identified the need for further investigation of subgroups, particularly in incarcerated offenders, with psychopathy widely under-researched at the time of the publication.

Employing a similar methodology to Holland et al. (1980) and Haapasalo and Pulkkinen (1992) found support for primary and secondary subtypes of psychopathy based on cluster analysis in a sample of male offenders. The authors identified three clusters, these being primary psychopathy (glib and charming, manipulative, callous, lacking in remorse and failing to accept responsibility), secondary psychopathy (poor impulse control and antisocial) and non-psychopathy (impulsive, yet limited criminal versatility and more self-regulating than secondary psychopathy). Alterman et al. (1998) reported similar findings in a sample of 252 methadone patients, identifying six clusters, with psychopathic personality characterised by primary and secondary psychopathy. Two types of secondary psychopathy were identified in the research, with these differentiated by the onset of antisocial behaviour and the level of hostility displayed, while primary psychopathy was captured by limited emotionality, criminal diversity and moderate antisocial behaviour. The remaining clusters did not evidence significant levels of psychopathic traits. The results by Alterman and colleagues provided further support for primary and secondary psychopathy subtypes; however, the research utilised a liberal PCL-R score of 20 to determine psychopathy, having possible implications as to suitability of subjects considered to be representative of a cluster (Falkenbach, 2004). (The PCL-R typically applies a cut off at 30.)

Millon and Davis (1998) proposed a markedly different perspective to primary and secondary psychopathy, stipulating ten theoretical subtypes of psychopathy. According to the authors, the diametrically opposed conceptions of psychopathy are a result of the failure to understand that psychopathic behaviour comes from appreciably different personality patterns. According to Millon and Davis, the ten types of psychopaths are: the unprincipled, disingenuous, risk-taking, covetous, spineless, explosive, abrasive, malevolent, tyrannical and malignant. The *unprincipled psychopath* shares many similarities with the narcissist, able to avoid law enforcement and clinical attention, commonly successful, although considerably self-centred, indifferent towards others, exploitative and malicious. The *disingenuous psychopath* is characterised by histrionic features, friendly and socially adaptable, yet deceitful, unreliable, calculating, insincere and seductive. The *risk-taking psychopath* engages in risks for pleasure and excitement, with a tendency to be irresponsible, fearless, impulsive and reckless. The *covetous psychopath* is driven by envy, desire and greed, using manipulation and deceit to gain advantage over others, seeking to mask their underlying insecurities. The *spineless psychopath* is deeply insecure, often fearful, and attempts to impress others through their actions, most commonly through violence and aggression in an effort to feel powerful. The *explosive psychopath* has a tendency towards uncontrollable rage, often targeted at those close to them. This form of psychopath is quick to anger, easily threatened and harbours underlying feelings of disappointment and frustration related to their life. The *abrasive psychopath* is deliberately contentious and quarrelsome, often negativistic and paranoid, while having limited remorse and justifying their behaviour through a thin veneer of supposed principles and beliefs. The *malevolent psychopath* is vindictive and hostile, hateful and distrusting of others, defiant, ruthless and anticipating the worst in others. Many murders or serial killers commonly fit this profile, experiencing limited guilt and displaying arrogant contempt for others. The *tyrannical psychopath* is characterised by intimidation and a tendency to attack and dominate others. This form of psychopath is sadistic, unmerciful, seeks to inspire fear in others, while characteristically calm and calculated in demeanour. Lastly, the *malignant psychopath* is driven by power, envy and mistrust, however, are often defective in their attempts to achieve outcomes burdened by insecurity, paranoia and resentment (Millon & Davis, 1998).

The ten subtypes of psychopathy proposed by Millon and Davis (1998) derived through observation, experience and clinical lore, provide an inductive perspective on variations of psychopathic personality. The suggestions offer insight into how vast and varied the expression of psychopathic traits can be. A strength of the proposed subtypes is the consideration of specific types of psychopathy being associated with levels of functioning, something which many theories and empirical findings at that point had failed to explain. A limitation of many studies investigating subtypes has been the reliance on criminal or hospital samples, failing to consider noncriminal psychopathy or the differences that emerge between psychopathic traits and community contexts. While the theoretical subtypes proposed by Millon and Davis consider the context of psychopathy, there are some challenges in testing the typologies. There is considerable overlap between many of the subtypes, and components of their model are underpinned by psychodynamic constructs that are not easily operationalised and can be difficult to quantify (Murphy & Vess, 2003).

Murphy and Vess (2003) proposed an alternative clinical classification for psychopathy based on their observational and clinical experience with patients in a maximum-security forensic hospital. The authors contended that patients could be classified into one of four subtypes of psychopathy: narcissistic, borderline, sadistic and antisocial. The *narcissistic* variant of psychopathy is characterised by pathological levels of narcissism, along with features of grandiosity, entitlement and a callous disregard for others. This form of psychopathy shares similarities with Millon and Davis's (1998) unprincipled and covetous psychopath subtypes, along with Factor 1 traits on the PCL-R (Hare, 2003; Lykken, 1995; Murphy & Vess, 2003). The *borderline* variant is captured by self-destructive tendencies and affective instability, sharing some overlap with Blackburn's (1996) under-controlled subtypes, as well as characteristics of Factor 2 of the PCL-R. The *sadistic* variant of psychopathy is considered to reflect a person that derives pleasure from suffering of others. This entails that capacity to recognise the suffering of another and experience pleasure and arousal in the process, features reflective of both Factor 1 traits on the PCL-R in conjunction with sadistic tendencies (Murphy & Vess, 2003). The antisocial type is captured by repeated criminal behaviour, commonly characterised by impulsivity, poor behaviour controls, a parasitic lifestyle and need for stimulation. The authors contended that the variations of psychopathy had different clinical presentations, treatment needs, treatment responsivity and requirements relating to levels of safety precautions. Murphy and Vess (2003) recommended that further research examining patterns and clusters of psychopathy traits be undertaken to assist in distinguishing clinically meaningful subtypes. The authors acknowledged that limited inferences could be made based solely on clinical classifications of mentally ill offenders, with wider application of the four subtypes required across settings to establish reliability and validity of these forms of psychopathy.

Assessment of Noncriminal, Non-forensic Subjects

Coid et al. (2012) conducted an empirical study to differentiate psychopathic traits in a large community sample ($N = 624$). The authors utilised a series of instruments to examine British residents, with the Psychopathy Checklist-Screening Version (PCL: SV; Hart, Cox, & Hare, 1995) used to assess psychopathic personality traits amongst participants. The study employed cluster analysis to examine correlates with psychopathic traits, identifying five broad subtypes of abnormal personality pathology as determined by the PCL:SV. The five subtypes included: criminal psychopaths, non-psychopathic criminals, the impulsive and irresponsible, social failures and successful psychopaths. *Criminal psychopaths* were predominately male, with a history of criminality and drug and alcohol use. These individuals had early behavioural problems, adverse life events, elevated psychopathology and a tendency towards violence, consistent with many of the PCL-R criteria (Hare, 2003). *Non-psychopathic criminals* had severe antisocial and criminal features, were commonly impulsive, lacking goals and irresponsible. Compared to criminal psychopaths, the non-psychopathic criminals were less likely to display affective deficits and narcissistic and histrionic traits, with many similarities to antisocial personality disorder. The *impulsive and irresponsible* cluster was characterised by lower intelligence, reduced antisocial features, broad psychopathology, substance misuse and self-regulation deficits. *Social failures* had limited and less severe criminal histories, although had higher levels of social, behavioural and mental health problems. Lastly, *successful psychopaths* were characterised by higher levels of intelligence and social class, financial success and financial crisis, alcohol dependence, limited involvement with the criminal justice system and elevated narcissistic, histrionic and schizotypal traits, similar to the findings by Board and Fritzon (2005).

The findings presented above contribute to the theoretical debate about the nature of the psychopathic construct, which is essential for the evolution of knowledge, as well as clinical and operational utility of information concerning psychopathy (Lykken, 1995; Millon & Davis, 1998; Murphy & Vess, 2003). Psychopathic personality is arguably one of the most important forensic concepts of the twenty-first century (Monahan, 2006) and failing to provide appropriate specification relating to personality traits and behaviours associated with cases of psychopathy leads to decisions being made on what is considered to be a "prototypical psychopath". Consequently, there remains much confusion amongst many professionals as to what constitutes criminal or noncriminal psychopathy, or even why some psychopathic individuals become "con-artists" and others "serial murders". It remains an odd paradigm when the Chief Judge of the State of New York (see Lykken, 1995) and serial killer Theodore (Ted) Bundy (see Dielenberg, 2017; Meloy & Shiva, 2007; Ramsland, 2013) may both be considered psychopathic, a seemingly unlikely comparison. There is a proliferation of research examining psychopathic traits amongst offenders (Cornell et al., 1996; Hare, 2003; Hare & McPherson, 1984; Woodworth & Porter, 2002), while there is a growing body of empirical analysis emerging on psychopathic traits in people residing in the community and those maintaining positions of professional status (Brooks, 2017; Fix & Fix, 2015; Fritzon et al., 2016; Howe et al., 2014). The widespread examination of psychopathic personality (empirical, clinical and theoretical) has established the construct, identified many co-occurring relationships, explored trait manifestations across contexts, and investigated aetiological pathways. However, despite the progressive analysis of psychopathy, sufficient processes to differentiate variations of psychopathic personality are required. Specification criteria are important for several reasons; firstly, the current empirical understanding of psychopathy is largely generalised to the global construct and a few leading assessment instruments, with limited research on diagnostically distinguishing features (Skeem et al., 2011). Secondly, developing diagnostic specifiers serves to strengthen the clinical and operational understanding of the personality construct, is essential to risk and safety practices, law enforcement responsiveness, and management and treatment strategies (Millon & Davis, 1998; Murphy & Vess, 2003). Lastly, through determining the specifications unique to presentations, it may be possible to identify protective factors that prevent psychopathic individuals from engaging in criminal conduct or perpetrating acts of high harm (Gao & Raine, 2010; Hall & Benning, 2006; Mullins-Nelson, Salekin, & Leistico, 2006).

The Clinical Classification Criteria of Psychopathy

Determining a dominant personality type or level of pathology can be challenging and ultimately requires review of the DSM-5 criteria. According to the manual, a personality disorder is identified through behaviour that deviates from the normative expectations of a culture, characterised by inflexibility, pervasiveness, and leading to distress or impairment (APA, 2013). This may entail the individual experiencing this array of symptomology, or alternatively others being significantly impacted by the functioning of the person. Despite not being recognised as formal disorder in the DSM-5 (instead captured under ASPD; APA, 2013), psychopathy is recognised in the criminal justice system and legal frameworks (Hare, 2003; Monahan, 2006), with diagnoses based on the outcomes of assessment instruments along with clinical opinion determining the presence of psychopathic personality traits.

The Clinical Classification Criteria of Psychopathy (CCCP) is formulated to guide and assist in the decision-making related to psychopathic personality, proving structured criteria to overcome the current diagnostic and interpretative challenges concerning psychopathy as discussed by Cooke (2018) and Skeem et al. (2011). The lack of specification leads to clinical and forensic decisions being made on what is considered to be a "prototypical psychopath", a position implying that all psychopathic individuals are essentially the same. Although assessment tools such as the PCL-R and PPI-R are comprised of factors and subscales, practitioners often place limited weight to this information, instead viewing psychopathy at the global level. Without an appropriate framework to interpret assessment findings, developing an individualised profile of a patient can be problematic, dependent on the clinician's level of training and construct expertise. The CCCP seeks to overcome these current challenges by providing clinical criteria to determine the overall severity of psychopathic personality based on four core specification criteria. This information is then used to establish risk, treatment, and management and safety processes relevant to the individual. The CCCP is influenced by the recent emergence of structured professional judgement (SJP) assessment protocols (Chu, Thomas, Ogloff, & Daffern, 2013; Davis & Ogloff, 2008), consisting of structured and dynamic criteria to promote the decision-making of evaluators examining psychopathic personality. However, unlike SPJ's the CCCP is not an assessment tool, instead a clinical classification framework to implement when determining assessment outcomes for psychopathy.

The CCCP specifying criteria include: *cruelty-sadism* (mild, moderate, severe, with sadism or without sadism), *social adjustment* (poor, integrated, adept), *disinhibition* (mild, moderate, severe) and *capacity* (criminally inclined, unremarkable, accomplished, criminally inclined-accomplished). The process for implementing the CCCP is as follows: *step one* involves the administering of a standardised assessment protocol to examine psychopathy personality (e.g. PCL-R; PPI-R; CAPP-Symptom Rating Scale-Clinical Interview); *step two*, upon a significant elevation being identified on an assessment instrument, the CCCP is applied to results, determining the specific clinical features applicable to the presentation; *step three*, the assessment results and endorsement of CCCP are jointly considered to determine the severity of psychopathy; and *step four*, the culmination of clinical and assessment evidence is utilised to determine risk, treatment, management and safety strategies appropriate to the severity and clinical presentation of the person (Fig. 2.1).

Cruelty reflects intentional and unintentional attitudes or behaviour that causes physical or mental harm to another. This criterion is endorsed as *mild, moderate* or *severe, with sadism* or *without sadism*. *Severe* levels of cruelty reflect a general disregard towards others, enjoyment from the suffering of others, a desire for dominance, a proneness towards callousness and proficiency in making decisions that may result in others being harmed. This individual is clinical and detached in their decision-making and emotional reactions and may exploit weakness in others for self-gain, undeterred by any grief or suffering their behaviour may cause. *Moderate* cruelty is evidenced by some features consistent with severe cruelty; however, there may be times where the person has shown a degree of compassion, had consideration for the impact of their actions or made attempts to modify their behaviour so that it does not cause significant harm to others. For example, there may be evidence of someone showing compassion or concern at points in their life; however, this would need to be evidenced by involving both their in-group (family and friends) and their out-group (limited prior existing relationship, e.g., concern for

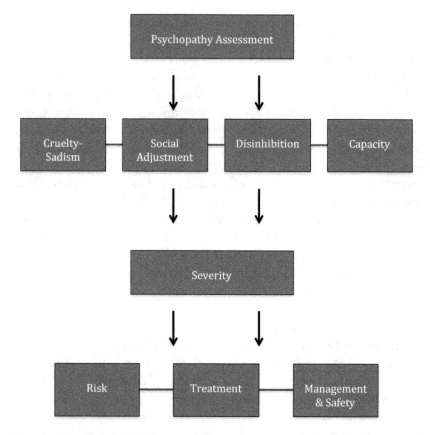

Fig. 2.1 The Clinical Classification Criteria of Psychopathy (CCCP): A Framework for the Classification of Psychopathic Personality

another prisoner). *Mild* indication of cruelty would reflect someone that does not make deliberate attempts to cause suffering to others. It may be a secondary consequence of their actions at times, yet the person does not generally derive enjoyment from the suffering or hardship of others. At a mild level, there is an absence of ruthlessness, a limited or minimal history of deliberate or calculated harm, and behavioural evidence of remorse or concern for others is evident.

Sadism concerns the tendency to derive pleasure from the suffering of others. This suffering is caused by inflicting pain and seeking to humiliate another person, resulting in the perpetrator experiencing enjoyment and gratification. It is not uncommon for the individual to find sexual pleasure and arousal through the act of causing degradation and suffering. For sadism to be endorsed, there must be clear behavioural evidence (violence) that the individual has physically harmed another person or living creature as means to gratification and pleasure. The sadistic acts have led to a person experiencing extensive or permanent physical suffering. For example, a person, who has previously kicked an animal when in state of anger, would not receive endorsement for sadism, unless an identifiable pattern of enjoyment and excitement was evident when engaging in this behaviour.

Social adjustment relates to the person's level of social integration and their ability to manage interpersonal interactions and complex social situations. The three specifiers for social adjustment are, *adept, integrated* and *poor*. *Adept* social adjustment indicates that a person has the ability to manage interpersonal conflict, can respond appropriately to setbacks, persuade others to see their side of the story, the capacity for leadership, and the capability to adjust their communication style to match the situation. A socially adjusted person is poised in social situations, able to talk on a variety of topics, is engaging and presents with a veneer of sincerity. *Integrated* social adjustment indicates that a person is able to work with others, can maintain relationships and has minimal history of relationship conflicts. However, it may also be common for those at the integrated level to experience trouble convincing others to see their side of the story, instead often resorting to lying in attempt to persuade others due to a limited ability to charm and captivate them. These individuals may be prone to ruminating on social problems and become frustrated (although rarely acting out this frustration) when failing to succeed in their pursuits. *Poor* social adjustment is likely to be characterised by conflict in relationships, difficulty with adjusting to social demands and expectations, reactive to setbacks or barriers, a disposition towards blaming others and a tendency to ruminate on grievances. This individual may be hostile or confrontational when faced with resistance, with a pattern of resorting to direct or indirect threats when feeling challenged.

Disinhibition refers to a person's capacity for self-management, self-awareness and to employ self-discipline. Disinhibition, like cruelty, is distinguished based on *mild, moderate* and *severe* levels. For a person to evidence *mild* levels of disinhibition an ability to delay gratification, utilise planning and foresight, and have behavioural restraint must be evident. A person may engage in thrill-seeking behaviour to meet their need for excitement and stimulation, such as sky-diving, car racing or flying planes. Instead of acting in a reckless manner, a person may engage in mild disinhibited behaviour such as infidelity, infrequent gambling and attending prostitutes—despite being in a relationship, or occasional excessive spending. A *moderately* disinhibited individual may have a tendency to be unreliable, often making mistakes, prone to occasional recklessness (e.g. going out for drinks and not returning home), or repeatedly fail to maintain employment or relationships. Despite a tendency towards disinhibition, a person at a moderate level will have the ability to maintain at least one form of stability in their life, this may include: employment, friendships, intimate relationships, study or hobbies. A *severely* disinhibited person is likely to have significant issues with impulse control, implementing structure and planning in their life, managing their mood states and may be prone to substance abuse. This person is likely to continually repeat the same mistakes and is unable to modify their behaviour. They will have troubled interpersonal relationships, commonly experience conflict in their life, engage in self-destructive or risk-taking behaviour, and have addictive tendencies.

Capacity refers to the person's degree of functionality within society. There are four levels of capacity, with a person rated based on which category they are deemed to be most applicable to. The four levels of capacity are, *criminally inclined, unremarkable, accomplished and criminally inclined-accomplished.* These levels may be subject to change depending on when a person is assessed. For example, a person may be assessed as being accomplished or unremarkable at a given point in time; however, if subsequently convicted of a criminal offence and sentenced to serve a period of incarceration, this person would later be determined as being criminally inclined. Although in cases where a person has previously met the criteria to be considered accomplished, yet perpetrates offences meeting the specifier for criminally inclined, and endorsement of criminally inclined-accomplished is given. This endorsement acknowledges a history of accomplishment, with a tendency towards criminality, an important consideration when determining treatment, management and risk strategies. The *criminally inclined* category becomes an absolute category once incarceration is served, considered to reflect the ongoing area of functional concern once evidence of criminal behaviour is established. To be considered criminally inclined a person must have served a period of incarceration on least one occasion or alternatively have been sentenced to a community based custodial order on more than two occasions (i.e. probation or parole orders). The category of *unremarkable* refers to someone that may have a minor criminal history (e.g. up to two community based custodial orders), yet has not met the criteria to be considered criminally inclined. This level of capacity relates to someone that has resided in the community, yet may have a history of broken relationships, failed employment or dismissals, a high school education or lower, has experienced some difficulties with self-regulation (i.e. gambling, substance use, sexual preoccupation, domestic violence, infidelity and/or financial problems) and struggles to achieve goals. The *accomplished* level of capacity refers to someone that has achieved educational standards beyond a bachelor degree, has exceeded requirement of a formal trade qualification, or alternatively has maintained a level of professional status or seniority in their career for a period of four years or more. While the person may have experienced problems in their lives, similar to the unremarkable level of capacity, the key distinguishing feature is that the accomplished person has been able to demonstrate a level of competence or achievement in one or more areas of their life over an extended time period.

Severity is determined based on the total assessment score and the classifications on the clinical criteria of psychopathy. Professional judgement is required to establish the severity of psychopathic personality, considering all the relevant information and clinical criteria to make a clinical decision as to the nature of the presentation. There are three levels of severity, *clinical, pervasive* and *pathological*. Social adjustment and capacity are consideration criteria that can influence both the severity of the presentation along with the secondary consequences that may arise with psychopathic personality. For example, an adept endorsement on social adjustment may be partially considered protective in one case, yet in another, or when coupled with other CCCP features, increase the potentiality for harm or victimisation. *Clinical severity* of psychopathy indicates that the person has significantly elevated levels of psychopathy, with the personality features and behaviours displayed by person considered to have a marked impact on their functionality and interaction with others. A person at the clinical level will likely have moderate elevations on the psychopathy assessment (e.g. PCL-R score between 25 and 30) in conjunction with moderate cruelty and/or moderate disinhibition on the CCCP. The *pervasive severity* indicates that psychopathic traits are a sustained theme in the individual's life, overt and considerably problematic. At the pervasive level, a moderate to high psychopathy assessment result (e.g. PCL-R score of 30+) is evident coupled with a severe area of deficit on the clinical classification criteria. This indicates the presence of severe cruelty or severe disinhibition. It will be challenging to engage with an individual presenting at the pervasive level, with features such as manipulation, dominance, hostility or intimidation often apparent. A person at this level will require thorough clinical recommendations to manage their risk and have resistance to treatment. Lastly, *pathological severity* indicates that the individual's severity of psychopathy is chronic, considered to be an enduring and extreme presentation. This concerns a person with a high assessment score (e.g. PCL-R score of 30+) and one or more severe (cruelty and disinhibition) classifications on the clinical criteria. If endorsement of severe cruelty with sadism is present, this indicates pathological severity, without disinhibition needing to be at the severe level. At this level, treatment will be considerably problematic and challenging, with measured judgement required relating to decisions on management, safety and risk.

Applying the CCCP to Case Studies of Psychopathic Personality

There have been many highly publicised cases of psychopathic personality throughout the years, some speculative, while others have been determined based on assessment and expert opinion. For the purpose of examining the application of the CCCP, five cases will be explored comprising of varied presentations and functionality. It is acknowledged that the author has not assessed these individuals and is instead providing a clinical opinion based on the following persons being considered to have psychopathic personalities as identified by other experts or authors publishing on the subject. Subsequently, endorsement on the CCCP is made based on the available information to the author at the time of completion. The individuals include: Theodore (Ted) Bundy, Richard Speck, Bernie Madoff, Sol Wachtler and Al Dunlap.

Ted Bundy

During the 1970s Ted Bundy was responsible for the deaths of multiple young women, across several states in the USA. In the hours prior to his execution, Bundy confessed to perpetrating 30 homicides with many of these murders involving, rape, kidnapping and necrophilia (Stone, 2009). Bundy's notoriety did not cease with his offending, escaping from custody and representing himself during his court cases. He was described by author Ann Rule (2009, p. xiv) who once worked with Bundy as a "*sadistic sociopath who took pleasure from another human's pain and the control he had over his victims, to the point of their death, and even after*". By far one of the most concerning features to Bundy's offending was his methods of targeting his victims which were considerably calculated:

> Bundy brought himself a pair of crutches and even went so far as to give the appearance of putting his leg in a cast. Thus temporarily 'disabled,' he asked for assistance from sympathetic young women who might cross the street to avoid a pass but who apparently readily stopped to lend a hand to a man with a broken leg. Bundy varied the theme-sometimes his arm was in a sling and he found his willing victim on a busy street; sometimes, with his leg problem, he targeted young women at recreational areas and gained their aid in securing his boat-"It's just down the road"-to his car. In a terrible way, the ploy was a stroke of genius. (Hare, 1999, p. 51)

In 1979, Hervey Cleckley was appointed as an expert to evaluate Bundy's competency to stand trial for the murder of two women at the Chi Omega sorority house of Florida State University (Lilienfeld, Patrick,

Watts, Smith, & Hare, 2018). Based on his assessment, Cleckley determined that Bundy was psychopathic and competent to stand trial. Several other experts in the field have commented on the extent of Bundy's psychopathic personality, including Robert Hare (1999) and J. Reid Meloy (see Meloy & Shiva, 2007).

Applying the CCCP to Bundy indicates that he would receive the following endorsement: cruelty (severe; with sadism), social adjustment (adept), disinhibition (moderate) and capacity (criminally inclined). Considering these endorsements, Bundy would be determined to evidence psychopathic personality of pathological severity. Examining Bundy across the CCCP suggests a profile of a person who has a general disregard for others, enjoys inflicting suffering and humiliation (including through serious physical violence), is callous, prone to repeatedly making the same mistakes, and is at times reckless (although capable of some stability). He has an overarching tendency towards criminality, despite being socially poised, charismatic and able to confidently manage challenging social interactions. Bundy's profile on the CCCP shares many similarities to primary psychopathy (Blackburn, 1996; Lykken, 1995) and the unprincipled and disingenuous psychopath (Millon & Davis, 1998), yet across the PCL-R scoring Bundy has elevations on both Factor 1 and Factor 2 domains, making distinguishing features of his presentation difficult to determine without an appropriate diagnostic framework. His CCCP endorsements indicate that Bundy was a cruel and sadistic psychopathic individual who was considerably socially adjusted, yet with a tendency towards failure and recklessness, ultimately evidenced through his repetitive criminal behaviour, reflective of his pathological severity of psychopathy.

Richard Speck

Unlike Bundy's serial killing, Speck is often referred to as spree killer, perpetrating a series of murders in a continuous period without a cooling-off time frame (Hickey, 2010; Stone, 2009). Before Speck committed his horrific spree killing, he had an extensive criminal history, including the murder of a waitress and the robbery and rape of a 65-year-old female

(Breo, Martin, & Kunkle, 1993). His offences that occurred on the night of 13 July and early morning hours of 14 July 1966 are described by Stone (2009, p. 48) as follows:

> Richard Speck, the alcoholic drifter who killed eight nurses in a Chicago hospital dormitory, had broken into the dorm intending to cadge money from the nurses. He then bound them and held them at gunpoint. When some of them resisted, he killed all eight that he could find, though there was another nurse who had hidden under a bed and who survived.

In killing these eight women, Speck was believed to have engaged in a frenzy of rape, strangulation, slashing and stabbing during the commission of his crimes (Breo, Martin, & Kunkle, 1993; Douglas & Olshaker, 1995). The extent of Speck's personality and presenting pathology was subject to much contention, with suggestions even proposed that Speck suffered from a chromosomal abnormality (Breo et al., 1993). In the book *Mindhunter* (1995), former FBI agent John Douglas and co-author Mark Olshaker provide the anecdotal account of Speck with a pet bird while in custody, offering an insight into his personality:

> He found an injured sparrow that had flown in through one of the broken windows and nursed it back to health. When it was healthy enough to stand, he tied a string around its leg and had it perched on his shoulder. At one point, a guard told him pets weren't allowed. "I can have it?" Speck challenged, then walked over to a spinning fan and threw the small bird in. Horrified, the guard said, "I thought you liked that bird". "I did," Speck replied. "But if I can't have it, no one can".

In 1969, Speck was admitted to trial in relation to the murder of eight student nurses. Hervey Cleckley was called upon to provide expert opinion on Speck, who at the time claimed that he experienced amnesia and could not recall his crimes. Cleckley determined that Speck did not have a memory impairment or evidence of brain damage, instead testifying that he showed "*definite signs of psychopathic personality*" (Lilienfeld et al., 2018; Ramsland, 2013). In reviewing Speck on the CCCP, his clinical endorsement indicates a severely disinhibited individual, severely cruel

and sadistic, with poor social adjustment and a capacity of being criminally inclined. His endorsements on the CCCP suggest that the severity
of his psychopathy is pathological. The profile of Speck on the CCCP
indicates: a disregard for others, callousness, violence as means to gratification, pleasure from the physical suffering of others, limited capacity for
self-awareness, substance dependence, an inability to maintain structure or
stability, self-destructive tendencies, conflictual relationships, emotional
volatility, a tendency towards blaming others, reactivity to setbacks, poor
social and communication skills, fixation on grievances and a propensity
towards criminal behaviour as an overarching life pattern.

The clinical profile of Speck shares many similarities with that of Bundy,
however, important differences are evident based on the CCCP. Although
both individuals are characterised by severe levels of cruelty and sadism,
Speck has a severe level of disinhibition, captured by being self-destructive
and unable to regulate and manage his behaviour. Bundy's endorsement
of moderate on disinhibition indicates self-destructives tendencies, yet a
capacity for stability, able to complete education and maintain employment and relationships. Bundy is also endorsed as having adept social
adjustment, having the ability to manage interpersonal interactions and
complex social situations through skilled communication and social traits.
On the other hand, Speck's life was prone to conflict and ruptures in relationships, with a poor ability to adjust to social situations or challenges
in social relationships. Speck shares many similarities with Millon and
Davis's (1998) spineless and abrasive psychopath typologies along with
secondary psychopathy (Blackburn, 1996; Lykken, 1995). The notable
exception to Speck displaying secondary psychopathy is the overt features
of cruelty and callousness captured by the CCCP framework.

Bernie Madoff

At 70 years of age, Madoff was convicted of securities fraud, investment
advisor fraud, wire and mail fraud, money laundering, making false statements, perjury, filing false documents and theft from employee benefit
funds (USA v. Madoff, 2009). Madoff was sentenced to 150 years of
incarceration for fraudulent offences exceeding $13 billion in loss, with

his offending alleged to have spanned from 1980 until his arrest in 2008 (Markopolos, 2010). He had a prominent profile in the international investment market, chairman of his own investment firm and the NAS-DAQ (American stock exchange). According to the sentencing memorandum of Acting United States Attorney Southern District of New York, Lev L. Dassin (2009), the details of Madoff's offending encompassed the following:

> A multi-billion dollar Ponzi scheme by which he defrauded thousands of inventors, including individuals, non-profit organizations and for-profit institutions, who placed money directly or indirectly with his registered broker-dealer and, later, registered investment advisory firm, Bernard L. Madoff Investment Securities ("BLMIS"). For more than two decades, Madoff solicited billions of dollars from investors under false pretences, failed to invest such funds as promised, and misappropriated and converted investors' funds for his own benefit and the benefit of others. These criminal acts caused billions of dollars of losses to investors, drove many individuals and charitable organizations to economic collapse or near collapse, and visited especially significant non-economic, emotional damage on many of Madoff's victims.

The news of Bernie Madoff's offending shocked many, with Madoff an established, prominent and powerful individual in the investment community (Markopolos, 2010). As details of his offending emerged, his years of perceived success were nothing short of calculated fraudulent behaviour, committed through a body of lies, manipulation and deceit (Dassin, 2009; Markopolos, 2010; USA v. Madoff, 2009). There has been considerable speculation concerning Madoff's motivations, personality disposition and capacity to perpetrate fraud over several decades. According to Professor Stephen Porter (2011), an expert on psychopathic personality, Madoff's personality shares many resemblances to psychopathy, reflective of what may constitute a "corporate psychopath". If Madoff were psychopathic, his personality style may explain his capacity for pathological lying, being conning and manipulative, lacking in remorse and being bold and fearless.

Applying the CCCP to Madoff reveals that he would likely be endorsed with the following ratings: cruelty (severe, without sadism), social adjustment (adept), disinhibition (mild) and capacity (criminally inclined-accomplished). His profile indicates a cruel and callous individual, undeterred by the suffering of others, skilled in interpersonal communication and managing complex social situations, a confident and engaging conversationalist, socially flexible and responsive, having the ability to delay gratification and manage desires for enjoyment, with a history of accomplishment coupled with criminal tendencies. In many aspects, Madoff's CCCP profile may support Porter's (2011) assertion of corporate psychopathy or alternatively a criminally inclined-corporate psychopath. The history of accomplishment, mild disinhibition and absence of sadism, separates Madoff from the likes of Bundy and Speck, with his presentation likely of pervasive severity and reflecting the capacity to pursue endeavours and dominate others in controlled and calculated manner without violence, notably similar to Millon and Davis's (1998) unprincipled psychopath.

Sol Wachtler

In 1968, Sol Wachtler was elected to the New York Supreme Court, before becoming the Chief Judge of the New York Court of Appeals in 1985. He was considered highly successful and wielded great power in his profession, responsible for overseeing the sentencing of many defendants facing years of incarceration (Wolfe, 1994). However, this success was brought to a sudden standstill when Wachtler was arrested in 1992 by the FBI on charges of extortion, blackmail and racketeering, eventually sentenced to 15-months imprisonment for harassment and threatening kidnapping (Levin, 2014). Lykken (1995), a former Professor of psychiatry and psychology and expert on psychopathy, provided the following commentary on the details of Sol Wachtler's offending (p. 36):

> In 1992, a wealthy divorcee named Joy Silverman began receiving letters containing blackmail demands and threatening to kidnap her 14-year old daughter (Franks, 1992). The anonymous writer knew intimate details of Mrs. Silverman's Park Avenue apartment and of her current relationship

with a New Jersey attorney, David Samson. Other letters, allegedly from a woman in New Jersey, reported that she had hired one David Purdy, a private investigator from Texas, to spy on Samson. This woman reported that Purdy had obtained photographs and tapes of Silverman and Samson and planned to use them to blackmail Mrs. Silverman. A man dressed in Texas garb left messages at both Samson's and Silverman's apartment buildings. Mrs. Silverman began receiving threatening phone calls from a man whose voice seemed disguised. She appealed to the FBI for help in dealing with this escalating and frightening harassment.

The FBI obtained a court order enabling the telephone company to "trap and trace" any calls that were made to the Silverman apartment. When the first call came through, it was traced to the car phone belonging to Sol Wachtler, the 62-year-old chief judge of the State of New York. Wachtler had been Silverman's long-time lover before she broke off the relationship a year earlier because she had come to feel that he "had increasingly tried to control her, both emotionally and financially, as trustee of the $3 million she had inherited from her stepfather." Silverman was stunned: Wachtler "had fallen into a rage when she began seeing Samson, but she could not really believe that he would do this to her".

After her marriage had failed. Silverman had turned to Wachtler although she was much younger than he and his wife was her cousin. Wachtler was the most powerful judge in the state, "said to be a very ambitious guy, who got to the top by assiduously and methodically cultivating those who could help him." I do not know that Wachtler was a primary psychopath; one would need more information about his early life to make a differential diagnosis. But, on the evidence available, this classification seems a good guess.

Lykken's (1995) opinion on Wachtler offers a valuable insight into his personality features. It is unknown if Wachtler has ever been formally assessed as psychopathic, but if Lykken's position on Wachtler was accurate, then endorsement on the CCCP would likely indicate his profile as resembling: cruelty (moderate or severe, without sadism), social adjustment (integrated or adept), disinhibition (mild) and capacity (criminally inclined-accomplished). His presentation would suggest clinical severity, although the availability of a more thorough life history may indicate a pervasive severity. From the available information on Wachtler, his CCCP profile suggests that he disregards others, is undeterred by causing others grief, is detached in decision-making, is fluid and flexible in his communication style, generally responsive to setbacks, persuasive in conversation, able to manage conflict, capable of delaying gratification and achieving goals, with controlled pursuits of excitement and enjoyment (e.g. infidelity), having a history of accomplishment and personal achievement, along with engaging in serious criminal behaviour leading to incarceration. The profile of Wachtler shares many similarities to Madoff, characterised by a significant accomplishment and the ability to manage social interactions, yet with a tendency towards being ruthless, exploitative and prepared to perpetrate criminal acts for personal gain.

Al Dunlap

In author Jon Ronson's book (2011), *The Psychopath Test*, Ronson proposed to Al Dunlap that he was in fact psychopathic. Dunlap was renowned for his pursuits as a corporate executive, most notably as Chairman of Sunbeam from 1996 to 1998, eventually dismissed due to multiple allegations of fraud and misconduct. He eventually settled these allegations without a criminal conviction for a supposed multimillion-dollar agreement (Byrne, 2003) and was ordered to never serve again as a director of a public company. It was estimated in the allegations that approximately $60 million of Sunbeams 1997 financial return was fraudulent, with the scandal eventually leading to Sunbeam filing for bankruptcy in 2002 (Byrne, 2003; Securities and Exchange Commission, 2001). Prior to these allegations, Dunlap was known in the corporate industry for his ability to "clean out" companies, firing quantities of employees to save company costs (Byrne, 2003). It was reported that when previously working at Scott, Dunlap fired nearly 20% of the company staff, equating to approximately 11,200 employees (Gallagher, 2000). According to Ronson, "*he fired people with such apparent glee that the business magazine Fast Company included him in an article about potentially psychopathic CEOs*" (p. 145).

During the course of his conversation with Dunlap, Ronson (2011) explored the items of the PCL-R, querying Dunlap on each item and discussing the behaviour that he exhibited consistent with that. For example, when questioned about displaying impulsivity, Dunlap responded, "*just another way of saying Quick Analysis. Some people spend a week weighing up the pros and cons. Me? I look at it for ten minutes. And if the pros outweigh the cons? Go!"* (Ronson, 2011, p. 157). The commentary by Ronson on Dunlap was not the first, with several other publications and books detailing his exploits in the corporate world, including Dunlap's own book which he co-authored with Bob Andelman (1996), titled, *Mean Business: How I Save Bad Companies and Make Good Companies Great.* In his own book, Dunlap refers to himself as *"Chainsaw Al"*, *"Rambo in Pinstripes"* and *"The Shredder".* He notes that *"predators are out there, circling, trying to stare you down, waiting for any sign of weakness, ready to pounce and make you their next meal".* His views share many similarities to Hare's (1999) conclusion that psychopathic individuals view the world as comprising of *"givers and takers, predators and prey, and that it would be very foolish not to exploit the weakness of others"* (p. 49).

It does not appear that Dunlap was ever formally assessed for psychopathy and Ronson's opinion of him must be taken with caution. However, if Dunlap was psychopathic, he may arguably have been one of the few documented cases of a successful corporate psychopath. Although surrounded by allegations, Dunlap managed to negotiate his way out of these and appeared to avoid sanction in several other matters where suspicion and concern were evident (Byrne, 2003). Subsequently, understanding what endorsement he would likely receive of the CCCP becomes important to investigating the idea of "successful corporate psychopathy". Based on available information and taking the position that Dunlap evidenced psychopathic personality, his endorsement would include: cruelty (severe, without sadism), social adjustment (adept), disinhibition (mild) and capacity (accomplished), with a severity rating of either clinical or pervasive. The CCCP indicates that Dunlap was considerably accomplished, having maintained several high positions of corporate status, fluent in social situations, skilled in managing conflict, with the ability to pursue goals and delay gratification, along with being ruthless, callous and capable of making decisions that caused significant grief to others. Contrary to Madoff and Wachtler, Dunlap's capacity remained as accomplished never convicted of criminal offences and required to serve time in custody. His capacity for cruelness, combined with skilled social competence, leadership and a capacity for self-awareness, suggests that Dunlap was able to cause widespread grief and destruction as a CEO, while progressing and enhancing his career at the same time.

Conclusion

The case explorations of psychopathy as discussed highlight the varied presentations of psychopathic personality. As a construct psychopathy is characterised by overarching features and domains as detailed in the TPM (see Patrick, 2010) and CAPP-CM (see Cooke et al., 2012), however, at a trait level each presenting case of psychopathic personality is unique, with similarities and differences. It is pivotal for the construct to evolve and that this heterogeneity can be understood and appropriately accounted for. In a forensic context, or even at an organisation level in the case of corporate psychopathy, being able to understand the individual presenting before a practitioner or assessor is of upmost importance. The current assessment processes to determine psychopathic personality are promising, well understood in criminal settings (see Hare, 2003) and with a body of assessment protocols emerging in noncriminal settings (see Chapters 4–6). These tools are the first step to analysing psychopathic personality; however, once elevations are identified, a systematic process is needed whereby assessment outcomes can be reviewed through a clinical classification framework to support the assessment findings, determine the specifying features of psychopathy, and to guide decision-making. The CCCP provides a set of criteria for classifying psychopathic personality, identifying distinguishing features, the capacity of the individual (which serves as a guide for future risk and management) and provides a process to determine the severity of clinical presentation. Without a clinical framework to understand psychopathic personality, there remain concerns that all psychopathic individuals are viewed the same, a fundamental issue when considering risk implications, parole hearings, court outcomes and victimology matters. Due to the multitude of risk and management concerns that arise with psychopathy, assessment should not be limited to a generalised personality analysis, instead requiring a standardised measure of psychopathic personality in conjunction with the CCCP framework, which is modelled off structured professional judgement tools. Together, psychopathy assessment with the CCCP provides a method to support interpretation, decision-making and guide recommendations pertaining to the case and individual.

References

American Psychiatric Association. (2013). *Diagnostic and statistical manual of mental disorders* (5th ed.). Washington, DC: Author.

Alterman, A. I. McDermott, P. A., Cacciola, J. S., Rutherford, M. J., Boardman, C. R., McKay, J. R., & Cook, T. G. (1998). A typology of antisociality in methadone patients. *Journal of Abnormal Psychology, 107*, 42–422.

Blackburn, R. (1971). Personality types among abnormal homicides. *British Journal of Criminology, 11*, 14–31.

Blackburn, R. (1975). An empirical classification of psychopathic personality. *British Journal of Psychiatry, 127*, 456–460.

Blackburn, R. (1979). Psychopathy and personality: The dimensionality of self-report and behaviour ratings data in abnormal offenders. *British Journal of Social and Clinical Psychology, 18*, 111–119.

Blackburn, R. (1986). Patterns of personality deviation among violent offenders: Replication and extension of an empirical taxonomy. *British Journal of Criminology, 26*, 254–269.

Blackburn, R. (1996). Replicated personality disorder clusters among mentally disordered offences and their relation to dimensions of personality. *Journal of Personality Disorders, 10*, 68–81.

Board, B. J., & Fritzon, K. (2005). Disordered personalities at work. *Psychology, Crime & Law, 11*, 17–32. https://doi.org/10.1080/10683160310001634304.

Brooks, N. (2017). *Understanding the manifestation of psychopathic characteristics across populations* (Doctoral thesis). Bond University, Robina, Australia.

Breo, D. L., Martin, W. J., & Kunkle, B. (1993). *The crime of the century: Richard Speck and the murders that shocked a nation.* New York: Bantam Books.

Byrne, J. A. (2003). *Chainsaw: The notorious career of Al Dunlap in the era of profit-at-any- price.* New York: Harper Business Publishing.

Chu, C. M., Thomas, S. D. M., Ogloff, J. R. P., & Daffern, M. (2013). The short-to-medium-term predictive accuracy of static and dynamic risk assessment measures in a secure forensic hospital. *Assessment, 20*, 230–241. https://doi.org/10.1177/1073191111418298.

Coid, J., Freestone, M., & Ullrich, S. (2012). Subtypes of psychopathy in the British household population: Findings from the national household survey of psychiatric morbidity. *Social Psychiatry and Psychiatric Epidemiology, 47,* 879–891. https://doi.org/10.1007/s00127-011-0395-3.

Cook, A. N., Hart. S. D., Van Dogen, S., Van Marle, H., & Viljoen, S. (2013, June). *Evaluation of the TriPM and PPI using the CAPP as a concept map in Canadian and Dutch samples.* Keynote Address presented at the 13th International Association of Forensic Mental Health Services, Maastricht, The Netherlands.

Cooke, D. J. (2018). Psychopathic personality disorder: Capturing elusive concept. *European Journal of Analytic Philosophy, 14,* 15–32. Retrieved from https://www.researchgate.net/publication/329630330_Psychopathic_Personality_Disorder_Capturing_an_Elusive_Concept.

Cooke, D. J., Hart, S. D., Logan, C., & Michie, C. (2012). Explicating the construct of psychopathy: Development and validation of a conceptual model, the comprehensive assessment of psychopathic personality (CAPP). *International Journal of Forensic Mental Health, 11,* 242–252. https://doi.org/10.1080/14999013.2012.746759.

Cornell, D. G., Warren, J., Hawk, G., Stafford, G., Oram, G., & Pine, D. (1996). Psychopathy in instrumental and reactive violent offenders. *Journal of Consulting and Clinical Psychology, 64,* 783–790. https://doi.org/10.1037/0022-006X.64.4.783.

Dassin, L. L. (2009). *Government sentencing memorandum: United States of America v. Bernard Madoff.* New York: United States of America District Court Southern District Court of New York.

Davis, M. R., & Ogloff, J. R. P. (2008). Key considerations and problems in assessing risk for violence. In D. V. Canter & R. Zukauskiene (Eds.), *Psychology and law: Bridging the gap.* Aldershot, UK: Ashgate.

Douglas, J., & Olshaker, M. (1995). *Mindhunter: Inside the FBI elite serial crime unit.* London: Arrow Books.

Dunlap, A. J., & Andelman, B. (1996). *Mean business: How I save bad companies and make good companies great.* New York: Fireside.

Dielenberg, R. (2017). *Ted Bundy: A visual timeline.* Retrieved from https://www.academia.edu/30617453/Ted_Bundy_A_Visual_Timeline_Hi-Res_sampler.

Falkenbach, D. M. (2004). *The subtypes of psychopathy and their relationship to hostile and instrumental aggression* (Doctoral thesis). Retrieved from https://scholarcommons.usf.edu/etd/1028/.

Fix, R. L., & Fix, S. T. (2015). Trait psychopathy, emotional intelligence, and criminal thinking: Predicting illegal behavior among college students. *International Journal of Law and Psychiatry, 42–43,* 183–188. https://doi.org/10. 1016/j.ijlp.2015.08.024.

Franks, L. (1992). To catch a judge: How the F.B.I. tracked Sol Wachtler. *The New Yorker.* Retrieved from https://www.newyorker.com/magazine/1992/12/ 21/to-catch-a-judge-how-the-f-b-i-tracked-sol-wachtler.

Fritzon, K., Bailey, C., Croom, S., & Brooks, N. (2016). Problematic personalities in the workplace: Development of the corporate personality inventory. In P. Granhag, R. Bull, A. Shaboltas, & E. Dozortseva (Eds.), *Psychology and law in Europe: When west meets east.* Boca Raton: CRC Press.

Gallagher, B. (2000). *Once a bum, always a bum.* Niagara Falls Reporter. Retrieved from http://www.niagarafallsreporter.com/gallagher50.html.

Gao, Y., & Raine, A. (2010). Successful and unsuccessful psychopaths: A neurological model. *Behavioral Sciences & the Law, 28,* 194–210. https://doi.org/ 10.1002/bsl.924.

Haapasalo, J., & Pulkkinen, L. (1992). The psychopathy checklist and non-verbal offender groups. *Criminal Behaviour & Mental Health, 2,* 315–328.

Hall, J. R., & Benning, S. D. (2006). The "successful" psychopath: Adaptive and subclinical manifestations of psychopathy in the general population. In C. J. Patrick (Ed.), *Handbook of psychopathy* (pp. 459–478): New York: Guilford Press.

Hare, R. D. (1999). *Without conscience: The disturbing world of psychopaths among us.* New York: Guilford Press.

Hare, R. D. (2003). *The Hare Psychopathy Checklist-Revised* (2nd ed.). Toronto, ON: Mutli-Health Systems.

Hare, R. D., & McPherson, L. M. (1984). Violent and aggressive behavior by criminal psychopaths. *International Journal of Law and Psychiatry, 7,* 35–50. https://doi.org/10.1016/0160-2527(84)90005-0.

Hart, S., Cox, D., & Hare, R. D. (1995). *Manual for the Psychopathy Checklist: Screening Version (PCL:SV).* Toronto, ON: Multi-Health Systems.

Hathaway, S. R., & McKinley, J. C. (1940). A multiphasic personality schedule (Minnesota): I. Construction of the schedule. *The Journal of Psychology: Interdisciplinary and Applied, 10,* 249–254. https://doi.org/10.1080/00223980. 1940.9917000.

Hickey, E. W. (2010). *Serial murderers and their victims* (5th ed.). Belmont, CA: Wadsworth Cengage Learning.

Holland, T. R., Levi, M., & Watson, C. G. (1980). Personality patterns among hospitalized vs. Incarcerated psychopaths. *Journal of Clinical Psychology, 36,* 826–832.

Howe, J., Falkenbach, D., & Massey, C. (2014). The relationship among psychopathy, emotional intelligence, and professional success in finance. *International Journal of Forensic Mental Health, 13,* 337–347. https://doi.org/10. 1080/14999013.2014.951103.

Karpman, B. (1941). On the need of separating psychopathy into two distinct clinical types: The symptomatic and the idiopathic. *Journal of Criminal Psychopathology, 3,* 112–137. Retrieved from http://psycnet.apa.org/psycinfo/ 1942-00202-001.

Karpman, B. (1948). Conscience in the psychopath: Another version. *American Journal of Orthopsychiatry, 18,* 455–491. https://doi.org/10.1111/j.1939-0025.1948.tb05109.x.

Levin, J. (2014). The judge who coined "indict a ham sandwich" was himself indicted. *Slate.* Retrieved from https://slate.com/human-interest/2014/11/ sol-wachtler-the-judge-who-coined-indict-a-ham-sandwich-was-himself-indicted.html.

Lilienfeld, S. O., Patrick, C. J., Watts, A. L., Smith, S. F., & Hare, R. D. (2018). Hervey Cleckley (1903–1984): Contributions to the study of psychopathy. *Personality Disorders: Theory, Research, and Treatment, 9,* 510–520. https://doi. org/10.1037/per0000306.

Lilienfeld, S. O., & Widows, M. R. (2005). *Psychopathic Personality Inventory-Revised (PPI-R) professional manual.* Odessa, FL: Psychological Assessment Resources.

Lykken, D. T. (1995). *The antisocial personalities.* Hillsdale, NJ: Erlbaum.

Markopolos, H. (2010). *No one would listen: A true financial thriller.* Hoboken, NJ: Wiley.

Mathieu, C., Hare, R. D., Jones, D. N., Babiak, P., & Neuman, C. S. (2013). Factor structure of the B-scan 360: A measure of corporate psychopathy. *Psychological Assessment, 25,* 288–293. https://doi.org/10.1037/a0029262.

Meloy, J. R., & Shiva, A. (2007). A psychoanalytic view of the psychopath. In A. Felthous & H. Sass (Eds.), *International handbook on psychopathic disorders and the law: Laws and policies* (Vol. 1, pp. 335–346). London: Wiley.

Millon, T. (1983). *Millon Cinical Multiaxial Inventory Manual* (3rd ed.). Minneapolis: National Computer Systems.

Millon, T., & Davis, R. D. (1998). Ten subtypes of psychopathy. In T. Millon, E. Simonsen, M. Birket-Smith, & R. Davis (Eds.), *Psychopathy: Antisocial, criminal, and violent behavior* (pp. 161–170). New York: Guilford Press.

Monahan, J. (2006). Tarasoff at thirty: How developments in science and policy shape the common law. *University of Cincinnati Law Review, 75,* 497–521. Retrieved from http://law.bepress.com/cgi/viewcontent.cgi?article=1101&context=uvalwps.

Mullins-Nelson, J. L., Salekin, R. T., & Leistico, A. M. (2006). Psychopathy, empathy, and perspective-taking ability in a community sample: Implications for the successful psychopathy concept. *International Journal of Forensic Mental Health, 5,* 133–149. https://doi.org/10.1080/14999013.2006.10471238.

Murphy, C., & Vess, J. (2003). Subtypes of psychopathy: Proposed differences between narcissistic, borderline, sadistic, and antisocial psychopaths. *Psychiatric Quarterly, 74,* 11–29. https://doi.org/10.1023/A:1021137521142.

Patrick, C. J. (2010). *Operationalizing the Triarchic conceptualization of psychopathy: Preliminary description of brief scales for assessment of boldness, meanness, and disinhibition* (Unpublished test manual).

Patrick, C. J., Fowles, D. C., & Krueger, R. F. (2009). Triarchic conceptualizations of psychopathy: Developmental origins of disinhibition, boldness, and meanness. *Development and Psychopathology, 21,* 913–938. https://doi.org/10.1017/S0954579409000492.

Porter, S. (2011, August). *Preying for parole: Psychopathy, violence and the art of manipulation.* Presentation, Australian and New Zealand Association of Psychology, Psychiatry, and Law. Gold Coast, Australia.

Ramsland, K. (2013). Crystallizing psychotherapy: Dr. Hervey Cleckley. *Forensic Examiner, 22,* 56–62.

Ronson, J. (2011). *The psychopath test: A journey through the madness industry.* New York: Penguin Books.

Rule, A. (2009). *The stranger beside me: The shocking inside story of serial killer Ted.* New York: Pocket Books.

Securities and Exchange Commission. (2001). SEC sues former top officers of Sunbeam Corporation and Arthur Andersen in connection with massive financial fraud. *Accounting and Auditing Enforcement Release.* Retrieved from https://www.sec.gov/litigation/litreleases/lr17001.htm.

Skeem, J. L., Polaschek, D. L. L., Patrick, C. J., & Lilienfeld, S. O. (2011). Psychopathic personality: Bridging the gap between scientific evidence and public policy. *Psychological Science in Public Interest, 12,* 95–162. https://doi.org/10.1177/1529100611426706.

Skeem, J. L., Poythress, N., Edens, J. F., Lilienfeld, S. O., & Cale, E. M. (2003). Psychopathic personality or personalities? Exploring potential variants of psychopathy and their implications for risk assessment. *Aggression and Violent Behaviour, 8,* 513–546. https://doi.org/10.1016/S1359-1789(02)00098-8.

Stone, M. H. (2009). *The anatomy of evil.* New York: Prometheus Books.

United States of America v. Madoff. (2009). *United State of America v. Bernard Madoff.* New York: United States of America District Court Southern District of New York.

Wolfe, L. (1994). *Double life: The shattering affair between Chief Judge Sol Watcher and socialite Joy Silverman.* New York: Integrated Media.

Woodworth, M., & Porter, S. (2002). In cold blood: Characteristics of criminal homicides as a function of psychopathy. *Journal of Abnormal Psychology, 111,* 436–445. https://doi.org/10.1037//0021-843X.111.3.436.

3

Criminal and Noncriminal Psychopathy: The Devil is in the Detail

Nathan Brooks, Katarina Fritzon, Bruce Watt, Keith Duncan and Lars Madsen

Understanding the Details

Research and case presentations have observed vast variation in psychopathic personality, from high performing executives to violent offenders (Babiak, 1995; Brooks, 2017; Cleckley, 1941, 1976; Dutton, 2012; Hare, 2003). Conceptualisations of psychopathy should consider how psychopathic personality traits may vary across contexts and settings, accounting for both the similarities and differences. Criminal psychopathy and

N. Brooks (✉)
Central Queensland University, Townsville, QLD, Australia
e-mail: nathan@nathanbrooks.com.au

K. Fritzon · B. Watt · K. Duncan
Bond University, Robina, QLD, Australia
e-mail: kfrtizon@bond.edu.au

B. Watt
e-mail: bwatt@bond.edu.au

© The Author(s) 2020
K. Fritzon et al., *Corporate Psychopathy*,
https://doi.org/10.1007/978-3-030-27188-6_3

noncriminal psychopathy are considered as similar, yet possibly etiologically distinct constructs (Hall & Benning, 2006; Polaschek, 2015; Skeem, Polaschek, Patrick, & Lilienfeld, 2011). Psychopathy, regardless of whether criminal or noncriminal manifestation, is a pervasive psychological disorder characterised by a lack of conscience (Cleckley, 1941, 1976; Hare, 1999). Successful or corporate psychopathy may describe individuals with high levels of education and personality traits that have allowed them to achieve corporate status (Boddy, 2011; Gao & Raine, 2010), while criminal psychopathy may be associated with lower socio-economic support and a tendency towards impulsivity (Hare, 2003; Skeem et al., 2011). Psychopathic criminals are typically described as cunning and manipulative, calculated, violent and reckless in nature, callous and prone to heinous and repetitive acts of crime (Hare, 1999, 2003; Stone, 2009). In contrast, individuals with psychopathic traits residing in the community are proposed to be successful and capable of functioning in society, despite being ruthless, immoral, manipulative, charming, grandiose and lacking concern for others (Babiak & Hare, 2006; Boddy, 2011; Dutton, 2012; McNab & Dutton, 2014). This chapter will examine criminal and noncriminal psychopathy, exploring research findings, similarities and discrepancies across trait presentations, and discuss implications for future investigation of psychopathic personality in specific populations.

Criminal Psychopathy

Research that has examined psychopathy in offender populations has found that psychopathy is associated with several factors related to criminality (Cornell et al., 1996; Hare, 1999, 2003; Hare & McPherson, 1984). The desire to control and dominate another has been identified as a central

K. Duncan
e-mail: kduncan@bond.edu.au

L. Madsen
Forensic Psychology Centre, Brisbane, QLD, Australia
e-mail: lars@psychclinic.com.au

trait of psychopathic personality, often engaging in threats, bullying, verbal intimidation, manipulation and physical aggression to achieve such outcomes (Hare, 1999; Hickey, 2010). Individuals with psychopathic traits in comparison with non-psychopathic offenders have been found to utilise greater levels of violence and aggression, use a weapon or commit a violent assault, engage in aggressive behaviour in the custodial setting (Hare & McPherson, 1984), perpetrate planned and instrumental acts of violence (Cornell et al., 1996; Woodworth & Porter, 2002), possess cognitions supporting violence and aggression (Watt & Brooks, 2012) and engage in behaviours that threaten and challenge those perceived to be blocking the pursuit of goals (Morrison & Gilbert, 2001). The drive to dominate others and obtain self-indulgent goals, even when at a cost to another, are the cornerstone of psychopathy (Meloy, 2005; Meloy & Shiva, 2007).

There has been body of work examining psychopathy in criminal settings, with findings indicating that psychopathic offenders are more likely to commit violent crimes for instrumental reasons and are at a greater likelihood of reoffending upon release from custody (Cornell et al., 1996; Hare, 2003; Porter, Birt, & Boer, 2001; Serin & Amos, 1995; Woodworth & Porter, 2002). Psychopathy as measured by the PCL-R and its derivate tools is commonly found to show moderate associations with most forms of crime and future violence (Douglas, Vincient, & Edens, 2018). For example, offenders with psychopathic personality were found to be five times more likely to engage in violent recidivism within five years of release from incarceration (Serin & Amos, 1995) and to consistently perpetrate more violent and non-violent crimes than their non-psychopathic counterparts (Porter et al., 2001). However, one of the major concerns regarding psychopathy is that the construct has become associated with representing recidivism, particularly for violence (Polaschek, 2015). This is troubling as the PCL-R was designed to measure a personality construct, rather than to predict crime or violence (Douglas et al., 2018). As Polaschek (2015) states, *"criminals are neither inevitably psychopathic, nor are psychopaths inevitably criminal"* (p. 2). A psychopathy assessment therefore is not representative of risk and should only be a guiding factor that is considered alongside evidence-based risk assessments. Alone, the PCL-R should never be used to make risk decisions, requiring accompanying risk assessment protocols (Douglas et al., 2018). While research has demonstrated a relationship between psychopathy and criminality, this does not suggest that crime or violence is a core characteristic of psychopathy, but rather one of many secondary consequences related to the personality construct (Lilienfeld & Widows, 2005; Polaschek, 2015).

One of the most commonly observed associations in regard to psychopathy and offending behaviour concerns violent offending (Hare, 1999; Hare & McPherson, 1984; Stone, 2001). Logan and Hare (2008) estimate that up to 90% of serial killers would meet the PCL-R criteria to be classified as psychopathic. Notably, in a study of 99 serial sexual murders, Stone (2001) found the 91% of the sample scored 30 or greater on the PCL-R; however, one of the primary criticisms of this finding was the reliance on biographical information to assess the psychopathy traits of the serial offenders (Hickey, Walters, Drislane, Palumbo, & Patrick, 2018).

It is not uncommon for serial murders to be considered as displaying psychopathy characteristics due to the brutal nature of their offending and the process by which crimes are committed, such as through torture, rape, necrophilia and cannibalism (Hickey et al., 2018). However, despite committing heinous acts violence, many serial murders only display features of psychopathic personality, rather than pervasive levels of the personality. Although there is often evidence of callousness and coldheartedness in the crimes of serial killers, it is unclear to what extent these individuals exhibit boldness-fearlessness and impulsivity-disinhibition features (Patrick, Fowles, & Krueger, 2009). For example, based on cases being rated by trained diagnosticians using the PCL-R, Hickey et al. (2018) assessed Theodore Bundy (Total = 34, Factor 1 = 16, Factor 2 = 15.5), John Wayne Gacy (Total = 27, Factor 1 = 16, Factor 2 = 9), Edmund Kemper (Total = 26, Factor 1 = 13, Factor 2 = 11), Jeffrey Dahmer (Total = 23, Factor 1 = 9, Factor 2 = 12) and Gary Ridgeway (Total = 19, Factor 1 = 11, Factor 2 = 4.5). Contrary to the view that most serial murders are clinically psychopathic, the author's found that only one of the five cases, Theodore (Ted) Bundy, was endorsed as exceeding the PCL-R diagnostic scores.

A common misconception concerning psychopathy is that an isolated event, such as a violent murder, is attributed to be representative of psychopathic personality. As Hare (2003) notes, psychopathy is characterised by life-course-persistent traits and behaviours. One of the main challenges of determining the relationship between psychopathy and repeated offending is that serial murder is a rare occurrence, with limited subjects available for examination, and some offenders apprehended for single acts of violence despite having suspected repeated victims (Hickey et al., 2018). Moreover, it is unknown whether serial murders who evade detection (such as the Zodiac Killer who operated in California in the 1960s and 1970s) for their serial offending display different personality features possibly associated with their ability to avoid detection. Whether offending is committed by a serial offender or perpetrated as a singular act, it appears that the disinhibitory characteristics (such as substance use, deviancy, paraphilias and impulsivity) may be greater predictors of violence than the totality of psychopathic personality (Hickey et al., 2018; Polaschek, 2015).

One of the features considered to be associated with psychopathy and crime is the tendency for psychopathic individuals to be impulsive and violent. Interestingly, despite impulsivity being considered a core feature of psychopathy, research has consistently found that in psychopathic offenders, instrumental offending is evident, commonly characterised by premeditation and the desire to achieve an external goal. Woodworth and Porter (2002) investigated the association between psychopathy and instrumental violence in a sample of homicide perpetrators. The authors found that 93.3% of the homicides committed by psychopathic offenders were instrumentally motivated, compared to non-psychopathic individuals who were less likely to perpetrate homicide for instrumental reasons (48.4%). The findings were in contrast to the notion that psychopathic individuals are highly spontaneous and impulsive, something which the authors attributed to "selective impulsivity". According to Woodworth and Porter, psychopathic people may behave in a more instrumental manner based on the gravity or seriousness of an event or situation, planning their actions in a calculating manner when the stakes are high (e.g. perpetrating an act of homicide, which has the consequences of lifetime incarceration). The findings by Woodworth and Porter (2002) highlight that psychopathic offending can be instrumental in nature; however, the tendency to towards "selective impulsivity" may also vary as a function of disinhibition (Polaschek, 2015). It is possible that general impulsivity is related to higher levels of disinhibition, but in cases where fewer traits of disinhibition are apparent and coupled with affective deficits, instrumental offending may emerge.

The empathy and emotional deficits associated with psychopathy may also serve to explain the relationship between psychopathic personality and offending behaviour (Blair, Mitchell, & Blair, 2005; Hare & Quinn, 1971; Williamson, Harpur, & Hare, 1991). Early literature on psychopathy focused on the study of criminal samples and identified that offenders with high levels of psychopathy demonstrated a profound lack of empathic concern for others, as well as difficulties recognising and responding to emotions (Blair, Jones, Clark, & Smith, 1997; Cleckley, 1941, 1976; Hare & Quinn, 1971; Johns & Quays, 1962; Lykken, 1957; Williamson et al., 1991). This early research often concluded that criminal and antisocial behaviour was partially due to the empathy deficits associated with psychopathy. Research on the construct has seen a wide range of studies examining psychopathy, empathy and criminality. For example, Brook and Kosson (2013) observed that psychopathic offenders had lower levels of empathic accuracy in comparison with non-psychopathic offenders after controlling for intelligence, reading ability and perceived emotional intelligence. While the relationship between the PCL-R factors and the subscales of the IRI was not reported in the research (other than perspective-taking), the research suggested that cognitive empathy deficits were most notable for the antisocial/behavioural and lifestyle features of psychopathy.

Despite an established relationship between low empathy and psychopathy, interesting research has been noted when reviewing the construct of empathy, shedding light on the potential functionality of psychopathic personality. Using the PCL-R and MRI evaluations to examine psychopathy, Decety, Chen, Harenski, and Kiehl (2013) examined the neurological responses of 121 offenders. Subjects were required to view stimuli of body injuries and requested to adopt imagine-self and imagine-other perspectives (Decety et al., 2013). When presented with stimuli and adopting an imagine-self perspective, the high psychopathy group demonstrated typical neurological patterns of response for the brain regions involved in empathy for pain; however, an atypical pattern of brain activation was observed for the psychopathic group when adopting the imagine-other perspective (Decety et al., 2013). The atypical pattern of neural activation for the imagine-other perspective was significantly different for offenders with elevated scores on Factor 1 of the PCL-R, indicating a reduced arousal to others' pain or concerns (Hare, 2003; Hare & Quinn, 1971). Elevated scores on Factor 1 were found to be associated with an increase in activity in the ventral striatum, suggesting pleasure in observing the distress of others. This pattern of activation in the ventral striatum, which is typically activated during reward anticipation (Diekhof, Kaps, Falkai, & Gruber, 2012), was only found for elevations on Factor 1 and not Factor 2. The findings of the research suggested that offenders with high levels of psychopathy were capable of imagine-self perspective-taking abilities, however, were characterised by marked deficits in imagine-other perspective-taking (Decety et al., 2013). The research provided an important understanding of the perspective-taking element of empathy in offenders and raised the questions as to whether perspective-taking plays a central role in noncriminal or successful psychopathy.

The finding by Decety et al. (2013) suggested that Factor 1 of the PCL-R was associated with perspective-taking deficits; however, high scores on Factor 2 may not lead to lower levels of perspective-taking. Mullins-Nelson, Salekin, and Leistico (2006) contend that the relationship between psychopathy and empathy depends largely on the type of psychopathy evaluated (e.g. factor or total score), gender of the individual, as well at the population being examined. For example, general levels of empathy may be lower in custodial settings rather than in the community. While higher overall scores on the PCL-R for some offenders may be largely due to a greater propensity of lifestyle and antisocial traits, rather than interpersonal and affective features, therefore, resulting in an elevated PCL-R score. Consequently, the interpersonal and affective traits, often identified as the core personality characteristics of psychopathy (Brook & Kosson, 2013), may not be solely representative of criminal samples, instead an important feature in noncriminal samples where lifestyle and antisocial traits may be less common (Hall & Benning, 2006; Mullins-Nelson et al., 2006).

Like empathy, the relationship between psychopathy and manipulation has important implications for understanding psychopathy across populations. For example, Porter, ten Brinke, and Wilson (2009) found that psychopathic offenders, while having a greater history of criminal offending, were two and half times more likely to be granted conditional release than non-psychopathic offenders. Similar findings were reported by Häkkänen-Nyholm and Hare (2009) in a study of 546 Finnish homicide offenders. The authors examined psychopathy and post offence behaviour for homicide cases. The researchers conducted a case file review and assessed psychopathy retrospectively on the PCL-R. Eighteen per cent of the sample was identified as having a score of 30 or more on the PCL-R. Notably, one-third of offenders sampled achieved the maximum score on the PCL-R item pathological lying (Häkkänen-Nyholm & Hare, 2009). Due to the seriousness of their offence, individuals with higher levels of psychopathy were referred to higher levels of court, however, were paradoxically more likely to be convicted of a lesser offence. High levels of psychopathic traits were also related to reduced levels of remorse, placing blame on external factors for the offence, and denial of responsibility for actions. When the stakes are high, psychopathic people demonstrate a sound ability to manipulate and deceive others. Despite high-level processes in place to mitigate deception and manipulation in the criminal justice system, psychopathic individuals are successfully able to overcome obstacles, raising questions regarding what could be achieved in the community where both awareness and barriers are considerably lower. Moreover, in cases where psychopathic individuals have lower levels of disinhibition, greater social adjustment, generally positive upbringings and receive higher levels of education, notably different life trajectories may emerge. According to Benning, Venables, and Hall (2018), there are multiple pathways to the development of psychopathy, with personality features moderated by life events, exposing some individuals to factors associated with criminality, while for others positive socialisation may lead to integration within the community.

Noncriminal and Successful Psychopathy

It is an unusual phenomenon that a personality type found to be associated with destructive and criminal behaviour is also related to levels of success and achievement (Babiak & Hare, 2006; Boddy, 2011; Brooks, 2017; Fritzon, Bailey, Croom, & Brooks, 2016). The corporate and business sector is a vast contrast to the custodial environment, requiring levels of social and interpersonal skills, responsibility, education and performance standards (Benning et al., 2018; Boddy, 2011, 2015; Perri, 2013). Yet, despite skill and educational demands, research has identified several successful individuals that have elevated levels of psychopathic traits (Babiak, Neumann, & Hare, 2010; Brooks, 2017; Fritzon et al., 2016). These include, US presidents (Lilienfeld et al., 2012), high court justices, city mayors, academic deans (Mullins-Sweatt, Glover, Derefinko, Miller, & Widiger, 2010; Stevens, Deuling, & Armenakis, 2012), corporate executives and directors (Babiak et al., 2010), a leading neuroscientist (Fallon, 2014), and a decorated special forces officer (Dutton, 2012; McNab & Dutton, 2014).

Ishikawa, Raine, Lencz, Bihrle, and LaCasse (2001) examined the concept of successful and unsuccessful psychopathy. The authors examined psychopathy in the community and determined success based on whether participants had ever been convicted of a crime. Psychopathy was assessed on the PCL-R and participants completed the Wisconsin Card Sorting Test (WCST) and the Wechsler Memory Scale-Revised (WMS-R). The successful psychopathy group comprised of 13 participants (never convicted of a crime), unsuccessful psychopathy group of 16 participants (convicted of a crime) and the control comparison group of 26 non-psychopathic (low scoring psychopathy and never convicted of a crime) participants. Results revealed that successful psychopathy was associated with greater executive functioning on the WCST and an elevated heart rate for stress reactivity in comparison with unsuccessful psychopathy and control groups (Ishikawa et al., 2001). The unsuccessful psychopathy group were found to have a lower heart rate and reduced executive functioning compared to the successful psychopathy and non-psychopathy groups. No difference was found between the two psychopathy groups for intelligence. The authors concluded that the elevated autonomic responding and greater executive functioning displayed by the successful psychopathy group served to protect from detection and arrest in the community, responsive to cues and consequences (Ishikawa et al., 2001). The research provided an important comparison of criminal and noncriminal psychopathy for stress reactivity and executive functioning, however, the study did not include a comparison group of unsuccessful non-psychopathy participants, or account for social and emotional skills which may further serve to protect from detection and arrest.

A similar study investigating intelligence, executive functioning, empathy and psychopathy was conducted by Mahmut, Homewood, and Stevenson (2008). The study comprised of 27 males and 74 females recruited from a university sample. The measures used in the research included the SRP-III (Paulhus, Hemphill, & Hare, in press), Iowa Gambling Task (IGT; Bechara, Damásio, Damásio, & Anderson, 1994), the Emotional Empathy Questionnaire (EEQ; Mehrabian & Epstein, 1972), National Adult Reading Test (NART; Nelson, 1991), and Trail-Making Test-Part B (TMT-B; Reitan, 1992). The authors dichotomised the data into high and low psychopathy groups based on the highest 30% and lowest 30% of scores on the SRP-III. The SPR-III subscale of criminal tendencies was excluded from the analyses to avoid conflating psychopathy with antisocial behaviour (Mahmut et al., 2008). Results found that the high psychopathy group performed significantly poorer on the IGT in comparison with the low psychopathy group, making riskier choices and concluding the game with less money. A significant deficit in emotional empathy was found for the high psychopathy group, although the deficit in emotional empathy was not observed for the low psychopathy group. No significant difference was found between the psychopathy groups for IQ or executive functioning based on the NART and TMT-B.

Mahmut et al. (2008) compared the results to a previous study (Mitchell, Colledge, Leonard, & Blair, 2002) that had employed the IGT with a criminal sample, concluding that findings from the two studies were similar and that criminal and noncriminal psychopathy are qualitatively similar, sharing psychophysiological and neurophysiological characteristics. The researchers contended that the manifestation of interpersonal and affective traits, as well as the extent to which individuals engaged in antisocial behaviours, may be the only differentiating features between criminal and noncriminal psychopathy (Mahmut et al., 2008). Due to the challenges of contrasting psychopathy across populations, the authors recommended that future research employ the same measurement protocols across populations to control for measurement variance and to allow for consistent comparison. The notable limitations of the research were that the study comprised predominately of females and that the authors

dichotomised psychopathy rather than examined the construct on a continuum, excluding a large percentage of the sample from the analyses.

Another study examining noncriminal psychopathy, emotional intelligence and criminal thinking was conducted by Fix and Fix (2015) utilising a sample of 111 university students. The authors employed the PPI-R
(Lilienfeld & Widows, 2005) to examine psychopathy, Bar-On EQ-i (EQ-
i; Bar-On, 2008) to measure emotional intelligence, Inventory of Callous-
Unemotional Traits-Youth Version (ICU; Frick, 2006) to assess callousness, Texas Christian University Criminal Thinking Scales (TCU; Knight,
Garner, Simpson, Morey, & Flynn, 2006) and Illegal Behaviours Checklist
(IBC; McCoy et al., 2006). Despite the sample being community-based,
psychopathy was found to be a significant predictor of violent offending, property offending and illegal behaviour. Regression analyses showed
that psychopathy was predicted by lower interpersonal and mood scores,
and higher scores on stress management and interpersonal relationships.
Higher scores on the uncaring subscale of the ICU also significantly predicted psychopathy. Fix and Fix (2015) contended that the results provided
a portrait of successful psychopathy, characterised by interpersonal skills,
but lacking in empathy and social responsibility, displaying little concern
for others, troubled by understanding emotions and holding a pessimistic
emotional outlook, although fluid in managing levels of stress (Fix &
Fix, 2015). The findings by the authors demonstrated that psychopathy
was characterised by positive adaptive features such as stress management,
yet also significantly predicted criminal behaviour, supporting research on
psychopathy and stress immunity (Fowles & Dindo, 2009; Lilienfeld &
Widows, 2005; Lykken, 1995; Patrick et al., 2009) and suggesting that
successful psychopathy may be associated with avoiding detection.

Howe, Falkenbach, and Massey (2014) investigated the relationship
between psychopathic personality traits, emotional intelligence and success in 55 participants working in the financial industry in New York.
The authors used the PPI-R, the Mayer-Salovey-Caruso Emotional Intelligence Test (MSCEIT; Mayer, Salovey, & Caruso, 2002) and a series of
demographic questions to assess income and position within the company.
The results of the study revealed that 7.3% of the sample were found to
score two standard deviations above the normative mean score for the PPI-
R. Significant elevations above the clinical cut-off T score were observed

for fearless dominance (12.7%) and coldheartedness (9.1%); however, no notable elevated levels of self-centred impulsivity were found in the sample. Total PPI-R scores were negatively related to overall emotional intelligence as well as subscales of the MSCEIT. A significant negative relationship was found for self-centred impulsivity and total MSCEIT scores, although no significant associations were found between fearless dominance and total or subscale MSCEIT scores. Statistical analysis of income groups revealed that significant differences were only identified for fearless dominance, with no differences found for total PPI-R scores or remaining subscales. Fearless dominance was found to significantly predict the income bracket of $100,000–$200,000, with higher scores found for this level of income compared to the less than 100,000 and over $200,000 groups (Howe et al., 2014). No significant differences were observed for total psychopathy or subscales for corporate rank. The authors postulated that the interpersonal-affective features of psychopathy may help an individual to obtain a moderate level of success; however, they suggested that an optimal level of psychopathic traits may exist and that exceeding this level could have a detrimental effect on career success.

What Does It All Mean?

It is evident that psychopathic traits exist in criminal, noncriminal and business populations. Hare (1999, 2003) contends that regardless of the setting, psychopathic personality is comprised of interpersonal, affective, lifestyle and antisocial features. However, emerging research suggests that psychopathic traits may cluster to form specific typologies, including criminal, noncriminal and successful psychopathy, each characterised by a specific constellation of psychopathic characteristics, with a dominant phenotypic pattern often evident (Dutton, 2012; Hall & Benning, 2006; Skeem et al., 2011). These differences in psychopathy typologies are marked through etiological pathways, temperament, motivation and social and emotional expression (Costa & McCrae, 2003; Fowles & Dindo, 2009; Hall & Benning, 2006; Millon & Davis, 1998; Willemsen & Verhaeghe,

2012). For example, research suggests that the interpersonal and affective features of psychopathy are negatively associated with fear and anxiety, while the behavioural traits are positively related to fear and anxiety (Willemsen & Verhaeghe, 2012). Considering the three distinct but intersecting constructs of the triarchic model (Patrick et al., 2009), a greater unique contribution of boldness, and reduced features of disinhibition may explain noncriminal and successful psychopathy.

The unique role of fearless dominance/boldness/interpersonal-affective features and the self-centred impulsivity/ disinhibition/lifestyle-antisocial characteristics in distinguishing subtypes of psychopathy has been the centrepiece of much debate amongst leading experts (Hall et al., 2014; Lilienfeld et al., 2012; Poythress et al., 2010; Skeem et al., 2011). Notably, psychopathy is a paradoxical disorder, with individuals appearing high functioning and interpersonally skilled, yet marked by emotional and cognitive processing deficits (Cleckley, 1988, Lilienfeld et al., 2012; Lykken, 1995). In his pioneering work, Cleckley (1941, 1976) described psychopathic people as charming, fearless and bold, interpersonally dominant, with intact intelligence and low anxiety, yet reckless and dishonest. The Cleckley depiction of psychopathy was characterised by a prominent pattern of interpersonal and affective features, with traits of disinhibition that were not necessarily marked by violence. In contrast, Hare (1999, 2003) describes psychopathy as characterised by shared interpersonal, affective, lifestyle and antisocial features. Hare's conceptualisation of the psychopathic individual is of a callous, impulsive, egocentric, hostile and ruthless person, characterised by self-centred behaviour, poor interpersonal relationships, destructive actions and criminality. Sharing somewhat similar views to both Cleckley and Hare, Lykken (1957, 1995) and Karpman (1941, 1948) detailed primary and secondary psychopathy, which were characterised by differences in emotionality and psychopathy trait patterns. The emergence of recent research investigating noncriminal psychopathy has proposed that psychopathy is characterised by positive adaptive features, suggesting that the right constellation of psychopathic traits could lead to success in the community (Broad & Fritzon, 2005; Dutton, 2012; Howe et al., 2014).

Cleckley (1941, 1976) and Hare's (2003) conceptualisations of psychopathy are markedly different; yet, these differences may be a result of how their formulations of psychopathy were determined, with both experts conducting research on vastly different populations. Cleckley's assessment of psychopathy was largely determined based on his work with patients in a Georgia psychiatric facility, as well as community-based patients. Hare's work has been predominately based on North American offenders, with the origins of his PCL-R based on criminals. Recent work on psychopathy in the corporate and business sectors has examined the notion that psychopathy can be related to success and has adaptive features. For example, psychologist Kevin Dutton (2012) determined former decorated SAS soldier Andy McNabb to be psychopathic based on neuropsychological testing. Dutton contends that certain trait qualities associated with psychopathy can lead to success and functioning in the community. Consequently, the debate regarding psychopathy traits appears to depend on who is being assessed, where the assessment is occurring, and what assessment protocol is used to measure psychopathy.

Due to variations in assessment methodologies and samples, consensus is yet to be reached in establishing baseline prevalence rates of psychopathy in business settings. For example, the occurrence of psychopathic personality in corporate settings has been suggested to range between 4% and 20% (Babiak et al., 2010; Fritzon et al., 2016; Howe et al., 2014). These figures, while higher than the approximate one per cent found in the general community (Hare, 1999), fall in between the community base rate and the level of psychopathy identified in offender populations (15–25%; Hart & Hare, 1996). Understanding the prevalence of psychopathy across populations is an important starting point when attempting to contrast and draw conclusions about the construct in business settings. One of the main challenges to comparing findings on psychopathic personality across studies is that research often reports overall scores and fails to provide a descriptive overview of subscales and score dispersions, making it difficult to determine the overall distribution of psychopathic traits in a study, along with identifying the prominent personality factors associated with the sample (Benning et al., 2018). Interestingly, a recent study has provided some insight into the comparison of psychopathic traits across populations by employing the same methodology across samples. Using the PPI-R to assess psychopathy, Brooks (2017) contrasted psychopathic personality traits in noncriminal (community), business and criminal samples. Based on a T score of 65, consistent with one and a half standard deviations above the mean score, all samples were identified to have individuals with clinically significant levels of psychopathy.

The noncriminal sample had 21 (18.3%) participants with clinically elevated levels of psychopathy, while 94 (81.7%) were without elevations. In the business sample, seven (11.67%) participants were found to have clinical levels of psychopathy, while 53 participants did not. For the criminal sample, four participants (9.1%) were found to have clinically elevated levels of psychopathy, while 40 participants did not have clinically elevated levels. The distribution of the percentage of clinically elevated psychopathy traits for the business, criminal and noncriminal samples can be seen in Fig. 3.1.

Further investigation of results in the study, which were examined through regression analysis, revealed that higher levels of fearless dominance were found in the business sample compared to the noncriminal and criminal samples. Brooks (2017) concluded that this finding provided support for the dual pathways model of psychopathy (Benning et al., 2018;

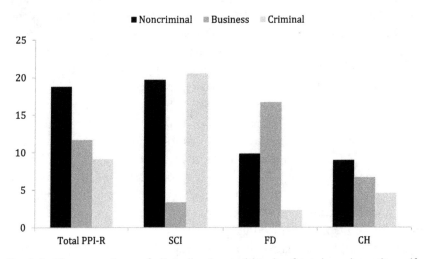

Fig. 3.1 The percentage of clinically elevated levels of total psychopathy, self-centred impulsivity, fearless dominance and coldheartedness in the noncriminal, business and criminal samples

Hall & Benning, 2006), as well as the depiction of primary psychopathy as described by Lykken (1995) and Cleckley (1941, 1976). Although consideration must be given to the finding that fearless dominance differentiated the business sample from the criminal and noncriminal samples, elevation on this facet alone does not indicate psychopathy (Lilienfeld et al., 2012). The elevation of fearless dominance suggested that the business sample had a significant pattern of psychopathy traits and when coupled with higher levels of disinhibition and/or meanness would suggest a psychopathic individual (Board & Fritzon, 2005; Hall & Benning, 2006; Hall et al., 2014; Lilienfeld et al., 2012; Skeem et al., 2011). Benning et al. (2018) suggest that fearlessness without deficits in cognitive or executive functioning may lead to social assertiveness, confidence, persuasiveness and limited sensitivity to the feelings of others due to reduced personal responsivity to fear or anxiety. Hence, successful psychopathy may be characterised by high levels of fearless dominance/ boldness, with moderate levels of self-centred impulsivity/disinhibition and coldheartedness/ meanness.

The results relating to the criminal sample from the findings by Brooks (2017) provided support for Hare's (2003) research on psychopathy in offenders, as well as secondary psychopathy (Lykken, 1957; 1995). The results indicated a significant elevation in self-centred impulsivity in the criminal sample, although this elevation alone does not suggest a psychopathic individual. This appeared to reflect greater similarities with Factor 2 of the PCL-R, suggesting features of disinhibition, impulsivity and recklessness. The elevation of self-centred impulsivity/ disinhibition in the criminal sample suggested that criminal psychopathy may form a different profile, characterised by higher levels of disinhibition and moderate levels of boldness and/or meanness (Hall & Benning, 2006; Hare, 2003; Lilienfeld et al., 2012). One limitation of the results relating to the criminal sample is in determining whether the elevation in self-centred impulsivity captures a unique profile of psychopathy, associated with greater lifestyle and antisocial features, or alternatively is reflective of overarching features of antisocial personality disorder.

The findings also suggested that psychopathy traits in the community, shared a different profile compared to both the business and the criminal samples. Terming this noncriminal psychopathy, Brooks (2017) contended that elevated levels of both fearless dominance/ boldness and self-centred impulsivity/ disinhibition captured this sample. The findings suggested that noncriminal psychopathy may be distinct from criminal and successful psychopathy, reflecting a pattern of boldness and disinhibition. Based on the CAPP model of psychopathy (Cooke, Hart, Logan, & Michie, 2012), it is theorised that noncriminal and criminal psychopathy share similarities in the behavioural, cognitive and emotional domains, yet noncriminal psychopathy is marked by traits from the self and dominance domains. In relation to the triarchic model (Patrick et al., 2009), the results suggested that noncriminal psychopathy may be characterised by moderate to high levels of both boldness and disinhibition and low to moderate levels of meanness. This finding was further supported by the pattern in clinical levels of psychopathy based on T scores of 65 and above on the PPI-R (Lilienfeld & Widows, 2005).

The PPI-R manual describes fearless dominance as the perception of oneself as a risk-taker, unafraid of physical danger, free of nervous habits and social anxiety, remaining cool under pressure, socially confident, charming and engaging, and verbally fluent and able to influence others (Lilienfeld & Widows, 2005). In contrast self-centred impulsivity is depicted as seeing oneself as superior, being manipulative and exploitive, reckless and defiant of social norms, blaming, poor at problem-solving, failing to consider consequences and failing to learn from mistakes (Lilienfeld & Widows, 2005). Interestingly, the Cleckley (1941, 1976) depiction of psychopathy appears to reflect a greater resemblance of fearless dominance characteristics, while Hare's psychopathy description, particularly Factor 2 of the PCL-R, suggests an individual with greater self-centred impulsivity features. The results of the research indicated that both Cleckley and Hare's (2003) theories captured psychopathy; however, each theory described psychopathy in a specific population. Hare's psychopathy reflected criminal psychopathy, with some overlap with noncriminal psychopathy, while Cleckley's conceptualisation of psychopathy typified successful and noncriminal psychopathy. However, the results also provided support for the CAPP concept map and triarchic model, which appear to account for the differences across samples, serving as overarching theoretical models for conceptualising psychopathic personality. As the results failed to find a difference between the samples for coldheartedness, the researcher believed that it was likely that this trait shared overlap of varying degrees with both fearless dominance and self-centred impulsivity across all populations (Patrick et al., 2009; Polaschek, 2015).

The results by Brooks (2017) are consistent with Lilienfeld et al. (2012) who found elevated levels of fearless dominance traits in US presidents. The authors concluded that boldness/fearless dominance, but not disinhibition or meanness, was significantly positively associated with greater presidential leadership and performance ranking. It remained unclear in the findings by Lilienfeld et al. as to whether a cut-off point existed in which traits of boldness/ fearless dominance became problematic and impeded performance. The observed results for the noncriminal and business samples also shared similarities with Board and Fritzon (2005) who observed elevated levels of histrionic, narcissistic and obsessive-compulsive personality traits in a sample of senior business managers. The findings by Brooks suggested that the business sample had greater levels of interpersonal-affective psychopathy features compared to the criminal and noncriminal samples, similar to Factor 1 traits of the PCL-R (Hare, 2003) and resembling Cleckley's (1976) depiction of psychopathy. The marked elevation for this facet is of relevance to understanding successful psychopathy.

In the research by Brooks (2017), 17% of the business sample was identified as having clinically elevated levels of fearless dominance. Clinically elevated levels are indicative of prototypical psychopathic traits, suggesting clinical significance (Lilienfeld & Widows, 2005). The findings for the business sample are consistent with Howe et al. (2014) who found that 7 of 55 (12.7%) financial investors had elevated levels of fearless dominance based on two standard deviations above the standardised mean score. Howe et al. suggested that boldness may serve as a positive adaptive psychopathy trait in moderate levels, leading to greater achievement (Dutton, 2012; Lilienfeld et al., 2012); yet in clinical levels was likely to be problematic and impair success. The number of participants with elevated traits of fearless dominance in both Brooks' and Howe et al.'s research has implications for the business sector. Psychopathic traits can lead to illegal and unethical business practices and have a toxic influence on colleagues and relationships (Babiak & Hare, 2006; Boddy, 2011; Mathieu & Babiak, 2016; Spector, 1997); however, it is unclear as to the extent to which fearless dominance/ boldness may contribute to immoral and problematic behaviour. Brooks recommended that future research investigates differences in levels of psychopathy and success, determining whether subclinical levels may serve as a protective factor, while clinical levels may be deemed problematic (Gao & Raine, 2010; Hall & Benning, 2006; Mullins-Nelson et al., 2006).

Determining the presence of a pervasive personality pattern or disorder requires that the behaviour associated with a person's personality deviates from the normative expectations and is characterised by inflexibility, persistence and results in distress or impairment (APA, 2013). Psychopathic personality is examined across a continuum; however, at moderate levels problems with integration, following rules and expectations, and reacting to concern are likely to be evident. At high levels, psychopathy will be pervasive and pathological, commonly causing significant distress to those associated with the person. There are many pathways to the development of psychopathy, including the dual and moderated pathways as discussed by Benning et al. (2018) and Hall and Benning (2006). These pathways provide an understanding as to why one individual may exhibit criminal psychopathy, yet another presents with psychopathy and reaches corporate success. According to Benning et al. (2018), fearlessness is pertinent feature of psychopathy and may differentiate forms of psychopathy when accompanied by either deficits or functionality in areas of cognitive and executive functioning. Successful psychopathy may be characterised by fearlessness and proficient cognitive and executive functioning, consistent with Ishikawa et al. (2001). Unsuccessful psychopathy, while being associated with fearlessness, is also related to deficits in cognitive and executive functioning. This form of psychopathy may also be further perpetuated by the experience of adverse events promoting social detachment, hostility and distrust towards others (Benning et al., 2018).

It is evident that the manifestation of psychopathic traits has been found to vary across contexts and samples examining psychopathy, with differences observed between criminal and business samples (Board & Fritzon, 2005; Brooks, 2017; Howe et al., 2014). While the difference between types of psychopathy can be identified at the trait level, there is a lack of research exploring behavioural and physiological differences between criminal and noncriminal psychopathy. There is need for studies examining the relationship between psychopathy traits, success and physiological reactions in response to stress. This form of research may employ stress design paradigms measuring galvanic skin response to stimuli similar to that employed by Hare (1966) and Ogloff and Wong (1990) with offender samples. Research on psychopathic traits and response to stress in a successful sample would provide a greater understanding as to whether fearlessness and boldness serve as adaptive traits in the community, or if successful psychopathy is associated with the same physiological markers or deficits that have been observed in studies on criminal psychopathy (Hare, 1966; Ishikawa et al., 2001). There has recently been a preliminary body of research emerging on behavioural outcomes of psychopathic personality in the workplace, such as work cohesion, leadership, bullying and performance (Babiak et al., 2010; Boddy, 2011; Lilienfeld et al., 2012; Mathieu & Babiak, 2016); however, there remain several areas for further investigation. Additional outcomes to examine in relation to psychopathy, particularly noncriminal or successful psychopathy, include: annual income, accumulation of income, ability to maintain intimate relationships, engagement in risk-taking behaviours, and preservation of friendships and family relationships (Benning et al., 2018; Jonason & Kavanagh, 2010; Martens, 2014). Lastly, there is still contention regarding what constitutes successful or noncriminal psychopathy. For some time, the point of differences was the absence of a criminal record, yet, this appears to be only a component of determining noncriminal psychopathy. The Clinical Classification Criteria of Psychopathy (CCCP), as discussed in Chapter 2, specifies a range of criteria that can be applied to differentiating presentations of psychopathic personality. The CCCP classifies the capacity of a psychopathic person, attributing a classification of accomplished, unremarkable, criminally inclined or criminally inclined-accomplished. Implementing specification criteria assists in assigning a level of capacity to a psychopathic individual, allowing for clear clinical determination of the relationship between a psychopathic person, competency and individual contextual factors. Although the CCCP is a proposed clinical framework and in need of further empirical analysis, without a process to operationalise or define noncriminal and criminal psychopathy, there will remain contention and confusion in relation to the "threshold limit", the point whereby psychopathy can be considered criminally, noncriminally or even successfully inclined.

References

American Psychiatric Association. (2013). *Diagnostic and statistical manual of mental disorders* (5th ed.). Washington, DC: Author.

Babiak, P. (1995). When psychopaths go to work: A case study of an industrial psychopath. *Applied Psychology: An International Review, 44,* 171–188.

Babiak, P., & Hare, R. D. (2006). *Snakes in suits: When psychopaths go to work.* New York: HarperCollins.

Babiak, P., Neumann, C. S., & Hare, R. D. (2010). Corporate psychopathy: Talking the walk. *Behavioural Sciences and the Law, 28,* 174–193. https://doi.org/10.1002/bsl.925.

Bar-On, R. (2008). *Emotional quotient inventory: Higher education (EQ-i:HEd).* North Tonawanda, NY: Multi-Health Systems.

Bechara, A., Damásio, A. R., Damásio, H., & Anderson, S. W. (1994). Insensitivity to future consequences following damage to human prefrontal cortex. *Cognition, 50,* 7–15. https://doi.org/10.1016/0010-0277(94)90018-3.

Benning, S. D., Venables, N. C., & Hall, J. R. (2018). Successful psychopathy. In C. J. Patrick (Ed.), *Handbook of psychopathy* (2nd ed., pp. 585–608). New York: Guilford Press.

Blair, J., Mitchell, D., & Blair, K. (2005). *The psychopath emotion and the brain.* Oxford, UK: Blackwell.

Blair, R. J. R., Jones, L., Clark, F., & Smith, M. (1997). The psychopathic individual: A lack of responsiveness to distress cues? *Psychophysiology, 34,* 192–198. https://doi.org/10.1111/j.1469-8986.1997.tb02131.x.

Board, B. J., & Fritzon, K. (2005). Disordered personalities at work. *Psychology, Crime & Law, 11,* 17–32. https://doi.org/10.1080/10683160310001634304.

Boddy, C. R. (2011). *Corporate psychopaths: Organisational destroyers.* London: Palgrave Macmillan.

Boddy, C. R. (2015). Organisational psychopaths: A ten year update. *Management Decisions, 53,* 2407–2432. https://doi.org/10.1108/MD-04-2015-0114.

Brook, M., & Kosson, D. S. (2013). Impaired cognitive empathy in criminal psychopathy: Evidence from a laboratory measure of empathic accuracy. *Journal of Abnormal Psychology, 122,* 156–166. https://doi.org/10.1037/a0030261.

Brooks, N. (2017). *Understanding the manifestation of psychopathic characteristics across populations* (Doctoral thesis). Bond University.

Cleckley, H. M. (1941). *The mask of sanity: An attempt to reinterpret the so-called psychopathic personality.* London: The C. V. Mosby Company.

Cleckley, H. M. (1976). *The mask of sanity* (5th ed.). St. Louis: Mosby.

Cleckley, H. (1988). *The mask of sanity: An attempt to clarify some issues about the so-called psychopathic personality* (5th ed.). Augusta: E. S. Cleckley.

Cooke, D. J., Hart, S. D., Logan, C., & Michie, C. (2012). Explicating the construct of psychopathy: Development and validation of a conceptual model, the comprehensive assessment of psychopathic personality (CAPP). *International Journal of Forensic Mental Health, 11,* 242–252. https://doi.org/10.1080/14999013.2012.746759.

Cornell, D. G., Warren, J., Hawk, G., Stafford, G., Oram, G., & Pine, D. (1996). Psychopathy in instrumental and reactive violent offenders. *Journal of Consulting and Clinical Psychology, 64,* 783–790. https://doi.org/10.1037/0022-006X.64.4.783.

Costa, P. T., & McCrae, R. R. (2003). *Personality in adulthood: A five-factor theory perspective* (2nd ed.). New York: Guilford Press.

Decety, J., Chen, C., Harenski, C., & Kiehl, K. A. (2013). An fMRI study of affective perspective taking individuals with psychopathy: Imaging another in pain does not evoke empathy. *Frontiers in Human Neuroscience, 7,* 1–12. https://doi.org/10.3389/fnhum.2013.00489.

Diekhof, E., Kaps, L., Falkai, P., & Gruber, O. (2012). The role of the human ventral triatum and the medial orbitofrontal cortex in the representation of reward magnitude: An activation likelihood estimation meta-analysis of neuroimaging studies of passive reward expectancy and outcome processing. *Neuropsychologia, 50,* 1252–1256. https://doi.org/10.1016/j.neuropsychologia.2012.02.007.

Douglas, K. S., Vincent, G. M., & Edens, J. F. (2018). Risk for criminal recidivism: The role of psychopathy. In C. J. Patrick (Ed.), *Handbook of psychopathy* (2nd ed., pp. 682–709). New York: Guilford Press.

Dutton, K. (2012). *The wisdom of psychopaths: What saints, spies, and serial killers can teach us about success.* New York: Scientific American.

Fallon, J. (2014). *The psychopath inside.* New York: Penguin Group.

Fix, R. L., & Fix, S. T. (2015). Trait psychopathy, emotional intelligence, and criminal thinking: Predicting illegal behavior among college students. *International Journal of Law and Psychiatry, 42–43,* 183–188. https://doi.org/10. 1016/j.ijlp.2015.08.024.

Fowles, D. C., & Dindo, L. (2009). Temperament and psychopathy: A dual-pathway model. *Current Directions in Psychological Science, 18*(3), 179–183. https://doi.org/10.1111/j.1467-8721.2009.01632.x.

Frick, P. J. (2006). Developmental pathways to conduct disorder. *Child and Adolescent Psychiatric Clinics of North America, 15,* 311–331. https://doi.org/ 10.1016/j.chc.2005.11.003.

Fritzon, K., Bailey, C., Croom, S., & Brooks, N. (2016). Problematic personalities in the workplace: Development of the corporate personality inventory. In P. Granhag, R. Bull, A. Shaboltas, & E. Dozortseva (Eds.), *Psychology and law in Europe: When West meets East.* Boca Raton: CRC Press.

Gao, Y., & Raine, A. (2010). Successful and unsuccessful psychopaths: A neurological model. *Behavioral Sciences & the Law, 28,* 194–210. https://doi.org/ 10.1002/bsl.924.

Häkkänen-Nyholm, H., & Hare, R. D. (2009). Psychopathy, homicide, and the courts: Working the system. *Criminal Justice and Behavior, 36,* 761–777. https://doi.org/10.1177/0093854809336946.

Hall, J. R., & Benning, S. D. (2006). The "successful" psychopath: Adaptive and subclinical manifestations of psychopathy in the general population. In C. J. Patrick (Ed.), *Handbook of psychopathy* (pp. 459–478). New York: Guilford Press.

Hall, J. R., Drislane, l. E., Patrick, C. J., Morano, M., Lilienfeld, S. O., & Poythress, N. G. (2014). Development and validation of triarchic construct scales from the psychopathic personality inventory. *Psychological Assessment, 26*(2), 447–461. https://doi.org/10.1037/a0035665.

Hare, R. D. (1966). Psychopathy and choice of immediate and delayed punishment. *Journal of Abnormal Psychology, 71,* 25–29. https://doi.org/10.1037/ h0022909.

Hare, R. D. (1999). *Without conscience: The disturbing world of psychopaths among us.* New York: Guilford Press.

Hare, R. D. (2003). *The Hare Psychopathy Checklist—Revised* (2nd ed.). Toronto: Mutli-Health Systems.

Hare, R. D., & McPherson, L. M. (1984). Violent and aggressive behavior by criminal psychopaths. *International Journal of Law and Psychiatry, 7*(1), 35–50. https://doi.org/10.1016/0160-2527(84)90005-0.

Hare, R. D., & Quinn, M. J. (1971). Psychopathy and autonomic conditioning. *Journal of Abnormal Psychology, 77,* 223–235.

Hart, S. D., & Hare, R. D. (1996). Psychopathy and antisocial personality disorder. *Current Opinion in Psychiatry, 9,* 129–132.

Hickey, E. W. (2010). *Serial murderers and their victims* (5th ed.). Belmont, CA: Wadsworth Cengage Learning.

Hickey, E. W., Walters, B. K., Drislane, L. E., Palumbo, I. M. & Patrick, C. J. (2018). Deviance at its darkest: Serial murder and psychopathy. In C. J. Patrick (Ed.), *Handbook of psychopathy* (2nd ed., pp. 570–584). New York: Guilford Press.

Howe, J., Falkenbach, D., & Massey, C. (2014). The relationship among psychopathy, emotional intelligence, and professional success in finance. *International Journal of Forensic Mental Health, 13,* 337–347. https://doi.org/10.1080/14999013.2014.951103.

Ishikawa, S. S., Raine, A., Lencz, T., Bihrle, S., & Lacasse, L. (2001). Autonomic stress reactivity and executive functioning in successful and unsuccessful psychopaths from the community. *Journal of Abnormal Psychology, 110,* 423–432. https://doi.org/10.1037/0021-843X.110.3.423.

Johns, J. H., & Quay, H. C. (1962). The effect of social reward on verbal conditioning in psychopathic and neurotic military offenders. *Journal of Consulting Psychology, 26,* 217–220.

Jonason, P. K., & Kavanagh, P. (2010). The dark side of love: Love styles and the dark triad. *Personality and Individual Differences, 49,* 606–610.

Karpman, B. (1941). On the need of separating psychopathy into two distinct clinical types: The symptomatic and the idiopathic. *Journal of Criminal Psychopathology, 3,* 112–137. Retrieved from http://psycnet.apa.org/psycinfo/1942-00202-001.

Karpman, B. (1948). Conscience in the psychopath: Another version. *American Journal of Orthopsychiatry, 18,* 455–491. https://doi.org/10.1111/j.1939-0025.1948.tb05109.x.

Knight, K., Garner, B. R., Simpson, D. D., Morey, J. T., & Flynn, P. M. (2006). An assessment for criminal thinking. *Crime & Delinquency, 52,* 159–177. https://doi.org/10.1177/0011128705281749.

Lilienfeld, S. O., Waldman, I. D., Landfield, K., Watts, A. L., Rubenzer, S., & Faschingbauer, T. R. (2012). Fearless dominance and the U.S. presidency: Implications of psychopathic personality traits for successful and unsuccessful political leadership. *Journal of Personality and Social Psychology, 103*(3), 489–505. https://doi.org/10.1037/a0029392.

Lilienfeld, S. O., & Widows, M. R. (2005). *Psychopathic Personality Inventory-Revised (PPI-R) professional manual.* Odessa, FL: Psychological Assessment Resources.

Logan, M. H., & Hare, R. D. (2008). Criminal psychopathy: An introduction for police. In M. St-Yves & M. Tanguay (Eds.), *Psychology of criminal investigation: The search for the truth* (pp. 359–405). Cowansville, QC: Editions Yvon Blais.

Lykken, D. T. (1957). A study of anxiety in the sociopathic personality. *Journal of Abnormal and Clinical Psychology, 55,* 6–10. https://doi.org/10.1037/h0047232.

Lykken, D. T. (1995). *The antisocial personalities.* Hillsdale, NJ: Erlbaum.

Mahmut, M. K., Homewood, J., & Stevenson, R. J. (2008). The characteristics of non-criminals with high psychopathy traits: Are they similar to criminal psychopaths? *Journal of Research in Personality, 42,* 679–692. https://doi.org/10.1016/j.jrp.207.09.002.

Martnes, W. J. H. (2014, October 7). The hidden suffering of the psychopath. *Psychiatric Times.* Retrieved from https://www.psychiatrictimes.com/psychotic-affective-disorders/hidden-suffering-psychopath.

Mathieu, C., & Babiak, P. (2016). Corporate psychopathy and abusive supervision: Their influence on employees' job satisfaction and turnover intentions. *Personality and Individual Differences, 91,* 102–106. https://doi.org/10.1016/j.paid.2015.12.002.

Mayer, J. D., Salovey, P., & Caruso, D. R. (2002). *Mayer-Salovey-Caruso Emotional Intelligence Test (MSCEIT) user's manual.* Toronto: Multi-Health Systems.

McCoy, K., Fremouw, W., Tyner, E., Clegg, C., Johansson-Love, J., & Strunk, J. (2006). Criminal-thinking styles and illegal behaviour among college students: Validation of the PICTS. *Journal of Forensic Science, 51,* 1174–1177. https://doi.org/10.1111/j.1556-4029.2006.00216.x.

McNab, A., & Dutton, K. (2014). *The good psychopath's guide to success.* London: Bantam Press.

Mehrabian, A., & Epstein, N. (1972). A measure of emotional empathy. *Journal of Personality, 40,* 525–543. https://doi.org/10.1111/j.1467-6494.1972.tb00078.x.

Meloy, J. R. (2005). *Violent attachments.* Oxford: Roman & Littlefield.

Meloy, J. R., & Shiva, A. (2007). A psychoanalytic view of the psychopath. In A. Felthous & H. Sass. (Eds.), *International handbook on psychopathic disorders and the law: Laws and policies* (Vol. 1, pp. 335–346). Chichester, UK: Wiley & Sons.

Millon, T., & Davis, R. D. (1998). Ten subtypes of psychopathy. In T. Millon, E. Simonsen, M. Birket-Smith, & R. Davis (Eds.), *Psychopathy: Antisocial, criminal, and violent behaviour* (pp. 161–170). New York: Guilford Press.

Mitchell, D. G. V., Colledge, E., Leonard, A., & Blair, R. J. R. (2002). Risky decisions and response reversal: Is there evidence of orbitofrontal cortex dysfunction in psychopathic individuals? *Neuropsychologist, 40,* 2013–2022. Retrieved from http://citeseerx.ist.psu.edu/viewdoc/download?doi=10.1.1.455.3494& rep=rep1&type=pdf.

Morrison, D., & Gilbert, P. (2001). Social rank, shame and anger in primary and secondary psychopaths. *The Journal of Forensic Psychiatry, 12,* 330–356. https://doi.org/10.1080/09585180110056867.

Mullins-Nelson, J. L., Salekin, R. T., & Leistico, A. M. (2006). Psychopathy, empathy, and perspective-taking ability in a community sample: Implications for the successful psychopathy concept. *International Journal of Forensic Mental Health, 5,* 133–149. https://doi.org/10.1080/14999013.2006.10471238.

Mullins-Sweatt, S. N., Glover, N. G., Derefinko, K. J., Miller, J. D., & Widiger, T. A. (2010). The search for the successful psychopath. *Journal of Research in Personality, 44*(4), 554–558. https://doi.org/10.1016/j.jrp.2010.05.010.

Nelson, H. E. (1991). *National Adult Reading Test (NART): Test manual.* Windsor: NFER-Nelson.

Ogloff, J. R., & Wong, S. (1990). Electrodermal and cardiovascular evidence of a coping response in psychopaths. *Criminal Justice and Behavior, 17,* 231–245. https://doi.org/10.1177/0093854890017002006.

Patrick, C. J., Fowles, D. C., & Krueger, R. F. (2009). Triarchic conceptualizations of psychopathy: Developmental origins of disinhibition, boldness, and meanness. *Development and Psychopathology, 21,* 913–938. https://doi.org/10.1017/S0954579409000492.

Paulhus, D. L., Hemphill, J. F., & Hare, R. D. (in press). Manual for the *self-report psychopathy scale.* Toronto: Multi-Health Systems.

Perri, F. S. (2013). Visionaries or false prophets. *Journal of Contemporary Criminal Justice, 29,* 331–350. https://doi.org/10.1177/1043986213496008.

Polaschek, D. L. L., (2015). (Mis)understanding psychopathy: Consequences for policy and practice with offenders. *Psychiatry, Psychology and Law.* Advanced online publication. https://doi.org/10.1080/13218719.2014.960033.

Porter, S., Birt, A. R., & Boer, D. P. (2001). Investigations of the criminal and conditional release profiles of Canadian federal offenders as a function psychopathy and age. *Law and Human Behavior, 25,* 647–661.

Porter, S., ten Brinke, L., & Wilson, K. (2009). Crime profiles and conditional release performance of psychopathic and non-psychopathic sexual offenders.

Legal and Criminological Psychology, 14, 109–118. https://doi.org/10.1348/135532508X284310.

Poythress, N. G., Lilienfeld, S. O., Skeem, J. L., Douglas, K. S., Edens, J. F., Epstein, M., & Patrick, C. J. (2010). Using the PCL-R to help estimate the validity of two self-report measures of psychopathy with offenders. *Assessment, 17,* 206–219. https://doi.org/10.1177/1073191109351715.

Reitan, R. M. (1992). *Trail making test: Manual for administration and scoring.* Tucson: Reitan Neuropsychology Laboratory.

Serin, R. C., & Amos, N. L. (1995). The role of psychopathy in the assessment of dangerousness. *International Journal of Law and Psychiatry, 18,* 231–238.

Skeem, J. L., Polaschek, D. L. L., Patrick, C. J., & Lilienfeld, S. O. (2011). Psychopathic personality: Bridging the gap between scientific evidence and public policy. *Psychological Science in Public Interest, 12,* 95–162. https://doi.org/10.1177/1529100611426706.

Spector, P. E. (1997). *Job satisfaction: Application, assessment, causes and consequences.* Thousand Oaks, CA: Sage.

Stevens, G. W., Deuling, J. K., & Armenakis, A. (2012). Successful psychopaths: Are they unethical decision-makers and why? *Journal of Business Ethics, 105,* 139–149. https://doi.org/10.1007/s10551-011-0963-1.

Stone, M. H. (2001). Serial sexual homicide: Biological, psychological, and sociological aspects. *Journal of Personality Disorders, 15,* 1–18.

Stone, M. H. (2009). *The anatomy of evil.* New York: Prometheus Books.

Watt, B., & Brooks, N. (2012). Self-report psychopathy in an Australian community sample. *Psychiatry, Psychology and Law, 19,* 389–401. https://doi.org/10.1080/13218719.2011.585130.

Willemsen, J., & Verhaeghe, P. (2012). Psychopathy and internalising psychopathology. *International Journal of Law and Psychiatry, 35,* 269–275. https://doi.org/10.1016/j.ijlp.2012.04.004.

Williamson, S. E., Harpur, T. J., & Hare, R. D. (1991). Abnormal processing of affective words by psychopaths. *Psychophysiology, 28,* 260–273. https://doi.org/10.1111/j.1469-8986.1991.tb02192.

Woodworth, M., & Porter, S. (2002). In cold blood: Characteristics of criminal homicides as a function of psychopathy. *Journal of Abnormal Psychology, 111,* 436–445. https://doi.org/10.1037//0021-843X.111.3.436.

4

The Assessment of Psychopathic Personality Across Settings

Nathan Brooks and Katarina Fritzon

Early Theoretical Conceptualisations and Measurement of Psychopathy

The understanding of psychopathic personality has evolved from work based on psychiatric patients, criminal offenders, and a criterion checklist, through to present assessment methods that involve self-report measures in the community. In his book *The Mask of Sanity*, Cleckley (1941, 1976) operationalised the construct of psychopathy based on 16 key characteristics which he believed classified the features associated with the personality. The characteristics proposed by Cleckley to account for the psychopathic persona included: superficial charm and intelligence, poor judgment, and a failure to learn, lack of remorse and shame, unreliability, untruthfulness

N. Brooks (✉)
Central Queensland University, Townsville, QLD, Australia
e-mail: nathan@nathanbrooks.com.au

K. Fritzon
Bond University, Robina, QLD, Australia
e-mail: kfritzon@bond.edu.au

© The Author(s) 2020
K. Fritzon et al., *Corporate Psychopathy*,
https://doi.org/10.1007/978-3-030-27188-6_4

and insincerity, absence of delusions or nervousness, impersonal sex life, absence of suicidal acts, antisocial behaviour, loss of insight, poverty in affective reactions, pathological egocentricity and an incapacity to love (Cleckley, 1941, 1976). Notably, Cleckley did not depict psychopathic people as predatory, violent, cruel, or dangerous, despite recent research suggesting the contrary (see Hare, 1999b, 2003; Hare & McPherson, 1984). Instead, Cleckley believed that the harm caused by these individuals was a secondary consequence of the shallow and feckless nature (Cleckley, 1941; Skeem, Polaschek, Patrick, & Lilienfeld, 2011). In his book, Cleckley cited not only criminals as being psychopathic, but also provided case examples of businessmen, scientists, doctors, and psychiatrists who had psychopathic personalities.

The work of Cleckley was expanded upon by Hare (1980) who reviewed and refined the characteristics associated with psychopathic personality, developing the Psychopathy Checklist (PCL; Hare, 1980). After its introduction, the PCL was revised by Hare (PCL-R; Hare, 1991, 2003) and reduced to a 20-item checklist of characteristics. Much of Hare's conceptualisation of psychopathy was developed from his research on North American criminal offenders, with Hare proposing that impulsivity and aggression were a core trait of the personality construct, rather than a secondary symptom (Hare, 2003; Skeem et al., 2011). In reviewing the work of Checkley and Hare, it is evident that much of Hare's early work on psychopathy was influenced by offender characteristics, while Cleckley's understanding of psychopathy was largely based on community/hospital patients.

Since the work of these two pioneering experts, several psychometric measures and conceptual theories have recently emerged to counterbalance the large body of literature that exists on psychopathy based on the PCL-R criteria (Butcher et al., 2001; Cooke, Hart, Logan, & Michie, 2012; Levenson, Kiehl, & Patrick, 1995; Lilienfeld & Widows, 2005; Patrick, Fowles, & Krueger, 2009). The different assessment measures and theoretical conceptualisations of psychopathy each provide important contributions to the empirical knowledge of the construct. Self-report measures allow for a broader understanding of different populations of people (such as community and business) with psychopathic personality characteristics, other than the forensic population that the PCL-R instrument was designed to measure (Lilienfeld & Widows, 2005).

Several measures have in recent times been proposed, adding to the large body of literature that exists on psychopathy based on the PCL-R criteria. These measures mainly are self-report in nature and commonly used for research purposes, although some support for clinical utility has been observed. There has also been an emergence of instruments focused on psychopathic personality in the workplace. Some of the prominent self-report measures have included: Self-Report Psychopathy Scale-III (SRP-III; Paulhus, Neumann, & Hare, 2016), Levenson Self-Report Psychopathy Scale (LSPR; Levenson et al., 1995); Minnesota Multiphasic Personality Inventory Psychopathic Deviate Scale (Butcher et al., 2001); and Psychopathic Personality Inventory-Revised (PPI-R; Lilienfeld & Widows, 2005). Measures developed to examine psychopathy in the workplace include: Business-Scan 360 (B-Scan 360; Mathieu, Hare, Jones, Babiak, & Neumann, 2013), Corporate Personality Inventory (Fritzon, Croom, Brooks, & Bailey, 2013), and Psychopathy Measure-Management Research Version (PM-MRV (Boddy, Ladyshewsky, & Galvin, 2010).

The refinement of empirical knowledge on psychopathy, alongside the multiple assessment instruments, has raised questions as to whether psychopathic personality is of a dimensional or discrete nature. A dimensional trait is one in which there is a continuation of a trait or variable along a continuum, while a discrete category suggests that a distinct class or end point exists, qualitatively different from others or things (Edens, Marcus, Lilienfeld, & Poythress, 2006). The PCL-R score is often used to determine whether someone is a psychopath, with a cut-off score of 30 on the PCL-R routinely used to indicate whether an individual is or is not a psychopath in North America, while a score of 25 is employed in the UK (Hare, 2003; Skeem et al., 2011).

Research suggests that psychopathy is a dimensional trait rather than a discrete category or taxon. This suggests that individuals are not psychopathic per se, but instead vary from other people based on the degree rather than on kind (Dutton, 2012; Edens et al., 2006; Skeem et al., 2011). Therefore, the degree of psychopathy is founded in the relativity of psychopathic traits (Edens et al., 2006). This distinction has important implications for research, assessment, treatment, decisions based on the risk, and policy/court decision making (Hare, 2003; Skeem et al., 2011). An advantage of using a dimensional definition of psychopathy is that it overcomes arguments put forward by proponents of the taxonomic perspective that psychopathic individuals do not benefit from treatment, due to psychopaths being qualitatively distinct and different from the rest of the population (Harris & Rice, 2006). However, although the dimensional view of psychopathic personality offers a promising approach to conceptualising and understanding the construct, there also appears to be a threshold whereby psychopathic traits, or the combination of overlapping traits become pervasive and problematic. According to Boddy (2011), this threshold may be determined based on someone scoring at 75% of a total score on an assessment of psychopathy, indicating significantly elevated levels of psychopathic traits. There is clinical and operational utility in being able to propose a "tipping point" where traits are considered pervasive, yet such a position is also dependent on measures being standardised and results reflective of an elevation in comparison with a normative group.

Since the development of the PCL (Hare, 1980) and the PCL-R (Hare, 1991, 2003), psychopathy has largely been assessed based on Hare's instrument. The body or research and application of the PCL-R has contributed immensely to the understanding of psychopathy. However, some researchers suggest that the PCL-R has effectively usurped the construct (Skeem & Cooke, 2010) and become heralded as the only sole representation of psychopathy (Skeem et al., 2011). According to Cronbach and Meehl (1955), all measures of constructs are fallible, with Skeem et al. (2011) suggesting that inferences made about psychopathy based solely on one measure may prove misleading or problematic. Subsequently, a large body of knowledge exists about "the psychopathic offender as defined by the PCL-R" (MacDonald & Iacono, 2006, p. 383), but not necessarily about the nature, structure, and boundaries of the psychopathy construct as a whole (Skeem et al., 2011). The current chapter will review the array of assessment instruments developed to examine psychopathic personality, discussing the suitability of measures, dimensional or taxonomic nature, and exploring the clinical or operational utility of tools.

The Psychopathy Checklist-Revised (PCL-R)

Building on the work of Cleckley (1941), Dr. Robert Hare identified 22 core characteristics that he argued depicted psychopathic personality (Hare, 1980). These characteristics were developed into a criterion-based protocol, consisting of an interview and review of collateral documentation to assess the presence of psychopathy. Hare (1980) called the measure the Psychopathy Checklist (PCL; Hare, 1980). After its introduction, the PCL was revised by Hare (PCL-R; Hare, 1991, 2003) and reduced to a 20-item checklist of characteristics.

According to Hare (2003), the construct of psychopathy is characterised by two overarching factors, these being, an interpersonal-affective factor comprising of an interpersonal facet and an affective facet, and an antisocial factor which consisted of a lifestyle facet and an antisocial facet. Interpersonal features included: glibness and superficial charm, manipulation, pathological lying, and a grandiose sense of self-worth. Affective characteristics included: lack of remorse or guilt, callousness/lack of empathy, failure to accept responsibility for actions, and shallow affect. The lifestyle facet of psychopathy included: impulsivity, irresponsibility, lack of realistic long-term goals, need for stimulation/proneness to boredom, and parasitic lifestyle. The fourth dimension, antisocial features included: early behavioural problems, poor behavioural control, juvenile delinquency, criminal versatility, and revocation of conditional release (Hare, 1999a, 2003).

Alternative factor structures have been found for the PCL-R, including three- (Cooke & Michie, 2001; Johansson, Andershed, Kerr, & Levander, 2002) and five-factor models (Hare, 1980; Međedović, Petrović, Kujačić, Želeskov Đorić, & Savić, 2015), which challenge the theoretical underpinnings of the PCL-R.

The difference in trait constellation has led researchers to suggest that the interpersonal-affective features and the antisocial-lifestyle characteristics of psychopathy are etiologically distinct from one another (Hall & Benning, 2006; Patrick, 2007). It remains possible that an individual could meet a diagnosis of psychopathy based on the PCL-R due to elevated scores on one factor, yet low to moderate scores on factor two (Hall & Benning, 2006). The two-psychopathy factors therefore, although similar, are unique dimensions. This position provides support for the notion of psychopathic personality variants (Hall & Benning, 2006). For example, (Balsis, Busch, Wilfong, Newman, & Edens, 2017) contend that not all psychopathic traits are weighted equally, with some features of more significance to the global construct. The authors argued that at raw score of 21 on the PCL-R may have higher construct severity in terms of presentation than a less severe combination of traits that result in a raw score of 30. Although the score of 30 on the PCL-R is determined to be the diagnostic threshold, psychopathic traits may be of a lesser or severer concern depending on what traits are endorsed and the specific context or population being examined (Balsis et al., 2017).

Despite recent debate and commentary about the use of the PCL-R and the tools operationalisation of psychopathy, the assessment tool remains as the "gold standard" measure for examining psychopathic personality. The PCL-R is widely validated for use with offenders, and when scored by trained and experienced raters is demonstrated to be highly reliable (Hare, 2003; Bolt, Hare, & Neumann, 2007). Researchers may argue that the instrument is uniquely tailored to forensic settings, considering the association between psychopathy and criminal behaviour; and that the overlap between psychopathy, criminality, and risk is an artefact of the test, rather than the underlying personality features (Cooke & Michie, 2001). Due to violence or criminality being considered as a core aspect of psychopathy, the use of the PCL-R in noncriminal populations is cautioned. There have also been administration issues when using the instrument in noncriminal settings, based on the in-depth collateral information needed and the formalised interview process (Skeem et al., 2011).

Psychopathy Checklist-Screening Version (PCL:SV)

The PCL:SV (Hart, Cox, & Hare, 1995) is a 12-item criterion-based assessment protocol initially developed for use in the MacArthur Risk Assessment study (see Steadman et al., 2000). The measure is designed as a screening tool for psychopathy and recommends that if elevated scores are identified that a follow-up-formalised assessment is conducted with the PCL-R. The authors of the PCL:SV stipulate that a score of 18 or above is reflective of psychopathy and requires further investigation. The PCL:SV is similar to the PCL-R, based on a two-factor scale structure and correlates highly with the PCL-R (Hare & Neumann, 2005; Hart et al., 1995). Due to the instrument being a screening tool and not requiring the same level of collateral information as needed in the PCL-R, the PCL:SV has been able to be used in noncriminal settings and in the corporate sector (see Babiak, 1995). Evidence has been found to support the psychometric properties of the PCL:SV, including research indicating the ability of the instrument to predict violence and aggression in both forensic and civil contexts (Hare & Neumann, 2005). The use of PCL:SV in noncriminal settings has utility and provides a promising approach to screening for psychopathic traits, however, as antisocial behaviour is considered a core component of the operationalisation of psychopathy in the measure, along with the close association that the tool has with the PCL-R, caution should be taken when using the assessment. As noncriminal subjects may have a limited history of antisocial actions, there remains the potential that the PCL:SV will fail to capture features associated with psychopathy in the community or workplace.

The Psychopathic Personality Inventory-Revised (PPI-R)

The PPI-R was originally developed by Lilienfeld and Andrews (1996) and revised by Lilienfeld and Widows (2005). The tool is comprised of 154 self-report items designed to measure the construct of psychopathy. The PPI-R consists of eight content scales and three validity scales. In addition to the total score, the eight content scales form three separate factors: self-centred impulsivity, fearless dominance and coldheartedness. The measure consists of two higher order factors (fearless dominance and self-centred impulsivity), and one subscale (coldheartedness) that remains primarily independent of the other two factors (Lilienfeld, & Widows, 2005; Skeem et al., 2011). Higher scores on the PPI-R are indicative of a greater level of psychopathic traits. Scores can be interpreted as either raw scores or standardised scores, with normative sample data available to compare scoring. Standardised scores and base rates for the PPI-R are based on the T scores, consisting of a mean score of 50 and a standard deviation of 10. The measure provides clinical cut-off levels for the PPI-R for total, factor, and content scores, indicating that a T score of 65 or above is considered to represent clinically significant levels of psychopathic traits (Lilienfeld & Andrews, 1996; Lilienfeld & Widows, 2005). This allows scores to be examined either as dimensional or based on a discrete threshold.

The PPI-R (Lilienfeld & Widows, 2005) has been established as a sound psychometric self-report measure of psychopathy. In comparison with other assessment instruments, the PPI-R has had widespread use in community and criminal samples (Lilienfeld & Widows, 2005), as well as being heavily utilised for research (Lilienfeld & Andrews, 1996; Lilienfeld & Widows, 2005). The measure is established based on Cleckley's (1941) conceptualisation of psychopathy, considers antisocial behaviour including violence to be separate or secondary to the core features of psychopathy, and yet is relatively concordant with the PCL-R (Patrick & Zempolich, 1998; Skeem, Poythress, Edens, Lilienfeld, & Cale, 2003). The PPI has been found to moderately correlate with the PCL-R (.54), while moderate correlations have also been found between the PPI total score and factor one (.54) and factor two (40) of the PCL-R (Poythress, Edens, & Lilienfeld, 1998). A full analysis and discussion of the PPI-R will be provided in Chapter 5.

Comprehensive Assessment of Psychopathic Personality (CAPP)

The Comprehensive Assessment of Psychopathic Personality model (CAPP; Cooke et al., 2012) was initially developed as a concept map for understanding the dynamic personality traits of psychopathy (Sellbom, Cooke, & Hart, 2015). The CAPP concept map details six overarching domains associated with the personality construct, these being: self, emotional, dominance, attachment, behavioural and cognitive domains. Each domain is captured by several accompanying personality traits and symptoms, with 33 personality characteristics specified in the concept map

(Sellbom et al., 2015). Since the development of the concept map, several assessment measures have been produced to examine psychopathy, with this range of tools including: CAPP-Symptom Rating Scale (CAPP SRS-CI; Cooke & Logan, 2018); CAPP SRS-Informant Report (CAPP SRS-IR); CAPP Lexical Ratings Scale (CAPP-LRS; Sellbom et al., 2015); and, CAPP Self Report Scale (CAPP-SR; Cooke & Logan, 2015).

The CAPP SRS-CI is suggested to provide the most detailed analysis of psychopathic personality, evaluating overall symptom severity, functional impairment, and trait extremity (Cooke & Logan, 2018). The interview examines all 33 symptoms within the CAPP concept map and requires a trained interviewer to complete a semi-structured interview with the subject (Cooke, 2018). The CAPP SRS-IR is used to support the CAPP SRS-CI, although in cases where a client refuses a clinical interview, may serve as a substitute assessment tool. The measure requires a third party or supervising informant (in the case of prison or a secure hospital) to evaluate the client and provide an alternative perspective on the person's psychopathic symptomatology (Cooke, 2018). The CAPP-LRS provides lexical markers, used to rate trait extremity in contexts or situations where it is not possible to examine functional impairment. This version of the tool has greater utility for research rather than clinical purposes, with participants required to rate the adjective or personality descriptions as applicable to them, rather than determining the clinical severity of symptoms (Cooke, 2018). Lastly, the CAPP-SR is a self-report measure comprising of 99 items tested with samples in the USA and New Zealand, reported to show a promising pattern of convergent and discriminant validity based on preliminary research findings (Cooke, 2018; Sellbom, Cooke, & Shou, 2018).

According to Cooke (2018), the development of different measures by which the concept map is instantiated allows for the progression of psychological science through refining existing models and in turn devising new measures. Preliminary research on the CAPP has found support for the factor structure and validity of the model (Cooke et al., 2012; Kreis & Cooke, 2011; Pedersen, Kunz, Elass, & Rasmussen, 2010). Early findings of the research on the CAPP suggest evidence of an overall global psychopathy factor, characterised by residual sub-facets reflecting boldness/emotional stability, emotional detachment, and disinhibition (Sellbom et al., 2015).

This factor structure suggests that psychopathy shares a core set of characteristics, yet can be distinguished by variations in domains such as boldness and impulsivity (Drislane et al., 2014; Sellbom et al., 2015). Research has indicated that traits in the attachment, cognitive, and behavioural domains are marginally more prototypical of males, while traits of manipulative, unstable self-concept, and lacking emotional stability are more prototypical of females (Kreis & Cooke, 2011). Early results examining the CAPP SRS-CI have found support for the measure, with total scores more related to personality pathology, finding associations with paranoid, narcissistic, and antisocial personality disorders, than with drug use or criminal behaviour (Flórez et al., 2018). The findings also suggest that the CAPP model shares similarities with the triarchic model (Cook, Hart, Van Dogen, Van Marle, & Viljoen, 2013; Sellbom et al., 2015), with the CAPP model providing a detailed domain and trait analysis of psychopathy.

Triarchic Psychopathy Measure (TriPM)

The triarchic model provides a conceptual overview of psychopathic personality and a theoretical basis to contrast varied findings across studies that have investigated psychopathy (Hall et al., 2014; Patrick & Drislane, 2014; Polaschek, 2015; Skeem et al., 2011). Similar to the CAPP, the triarchic model was initially developed as a conceptual framework for psychopathic personality, however, the overarching factors (boldness, meanness, and disinhibition) have formed the Triarchic Psychopathy Measure (TriPM; Patrick, 2010). The TriPM is a 58-item self-report measure designed predominantly for research and study relating to psychopathy. The measure comprises of three separate subscales based on the triarchic factors, with overall scores summed to derive a total score on the instrument (Somma, Borroni, Drislane, Patrick, & Fossati, 2019).

The factor structure of the TriPM has received support through empirical analysis (Somma et al., 2019), while convergent and discriminant validity has been found to support the three scales. The TriPM has shown a promising relationship with both the PPI-R and PCL-R. Boldness has been found to have positive associations with fearless dominance (PPI-R), the interpersonal facet (PCL-R), and Extraversion. A negative relationship has been observed for boldness with Neuroticism and behavioural inhibition (Hall et al., 2014). Disinhibition has been shown to relate positively with the lifestyle face of the PCL-R, self-centred impulsivity factor of the PPI-R, and negatively with contentiousness (Hall et al., 2014). Meanness has been identified to positively relate to the affective facet (PCL-R), coldhearted-ness (PPI-R), narcissism, machiavellianism, and negatively associate with Conscientiousness, Agreeableness and Openness (Hall et al., 2014). Total TriPM scores have also been shown to predict the overall PCL-R score, suggesting that the three factors of the TriPM and triarchic model ade-quately account for the construct of psychopathy (Patrick, 2010; Skeem et al., 2011).

The preliminary findings on the TriPM provide support for the measure and indicate positive associations with established psychopathy tools such as the PPI-R and PCL-R. As a research instrument, the TriPM has sufficient empirical evidence to validate the assessment as a measure of psychopathic personality (Hall et al., 2014; Patrick & Drislane, 2014; Skeem et al., 2011; Somma et al., 2019). Although the instrument is limited in clinical utility at present, there appear to be several strengths to the TriPM based on its association with other assessment tools, underlying theoretical structure, and suitability for research purposes. The advantage of the triarchic model and the TriPM is that it provides a phenotypical account of psychopathy and allows for diverse operationalisation of the construct across different samples, contexts, and practical applications (Skeem et al., 2011).

The Self-Report Psychopathy Scale (SRP-4)

The Self-Report Psychopathy Scale (SRP-4; Paulhus et al., 2016). The SRP-4 is the fourth version of the original SRP which was developed by Robert Hare and colleagues from an original item pool of 75 variables derived from the PCL (Sellbom, Lilienfeld, Fowler, & McCrary, 2018). Despite this, the original version of the SRP had only modest correla-tion with the PCL, and so was further revised to increase coverage of the core personality traits of psychopathy (Hare, Harpur, & Hemphill, 1989). The SRP-II contained two factors identical to the PCL-R, and the SRP-III was further developed to reduce the number of (negatively loading) anxiety-related items, improve coverage of the antisocial facet, and increase reliability of factor scores (Williams, Paulhus, & Hare, 2007). The SRP-4 now contains 64 items and has a reliable four-factor structure of Interpersonal Manipulation ($\alpha = 082$), Callous Affect ($\alpha = .78$), Erratic Lifestyle ($\alpha = .79$), and Criminal Tendencies ($\alpha = .75$) (Debowska, Boduszek, Kola, & Hyland, 2014; Neal & Sellbom, 2012; Williams et al., 2007).

In terms of validity, Paulhus and Williams (2002) reported that SRP-II scores correlated modestly with Narcissism and Machiavellianism, as well as with the FFM; specifically in the expected (negative) directions with Agreeableness, Neuroticism, and Conscientiousness, and positively with Extraversion and Openness to Experience. The SRP-III was also shown to be a strong predictor of various forms of "misbehaviour" (O'Boyle, Forsyth, Banks, & Mcdaniel, 2012), including: bullying, drug use, dangerous driving, criminal behaviour, and anti-authority attitudes. Although this pattern of correlations supports the use of the SRP-4 as a valid and reliable overall measure of psychopathy, research has also suggested that certain features of psychopathy are not captured by the measure, namely the interpersonal-affective traits, and Boldness (Sandvik et al., 2012, Sellbom et al., 2018). Crego and Widiger (2014) found a strong pattern of correlations among the PPI-R Fearless Dominance, TriPM Boldness, and EPA Emotional Stability; but the SRP-III did not correlate with any of these measures. The SRP-III therefore arguably does not tap into the potentially adaptive aspects of psychopathy, as captured by the fearlessness/boldness constructs of the PPI/ triarchic model, respectively. This may in turn explain the relatively weak predictive relationships found between psychopathy and job performance and CWB in meta-analytic studies (O'Boyle et al., 2012; O'Boyle, Forsyth, Banks, Story, & White, 2015), given that many of the samples included in the meta-analyses employed the SRP-III as a measure of psychopathy. It may be that the aspects of psychopathy that have the strongest relationships with job performance outcomes are those that are not well represented in currently validated self-report measures of psychopathy.

The Levenson Self-Report Psychopathy Scale

Levenson Self-Report Psychopathy Scale (LSRP; Levenson et al., 1995) contains 26 items and a two-factor structure was originally found representing primary and secondary psychopathy. More recent studies have reported a three-factor structure using a modified 19-item version of the LSRP (Sellbom, 2011). The convergent and discriminant validity of the three-factor model has not, however, held as well as the original two-factor model (Salekin et al., 2014). The LSRP Factor 1 (Primary psychopathy) correlates poorly with the PPI Factor 1 (fearless dominance; Ross, Benning, Patrick, Thompson, & Thurston, 2009); however, the LSRP Factor 2 correlates strongly with the PPI Factor 2 (self-centred impulsivity). Similarly to the SRP-III, the LRSP has been found to assess maladaptive traits and outcomes only, without considering any form of adaptive behaviours, and consequently correlates poorly with items reported in the literature as potentially reflecting positive traits associated with psychopathy (Durand, 2019). A recent item-response theory analysis (Tsang, Salekin, Coffey, & Cox, 2017) indicated that items in the LSRP PP factor were relatively good at discriminating among individuals with varying levels of primary psychopathy, while items in the LSRP SP were not sensitive enough to distinguish individuals with secondary psychopathy, in an undergraduate student sample with presumably low levels of psychopathy overall, but who may nevertheless endorse some impulsive and antisocial behaviour.

Finally, a comment that has been made in relation to self-report measures of psychopathy generally is that many of them contain negatively worded items, the endorsement of which is assumed to reflect psychopathic traits. As has been noted in psychometric personality assessment generally (Crego, & Widiger, 2014; Ray, Frick, Thornton, Steinberg, & Cauffman, 2016), and in relation to psychopathy specifically (Sellbom et al., 2018; Tsang et al., 2017) there may be a problem with inferring that the absence of a trait such as anxiety or empathy, is equivalent to endorsement of its opposite, i.e. fearlessness, callousness.

The Short Dark Triad

The SD3 is a 27-item self-report measure designed to examine the dark triad personality traits, most specifically, psychopathy, narcissism, and Machiavellianism. The measure was originally developed through a review of seminal sources on each of the constructs associated with the dart triad (Jones & Paulhus, 2011), with the aim of operationalising each construct. The scales were of the measure were developed from theory and empirical associations with the construct (Jones & Paulhus, 2014). According to Jones and Paulhus (2011), narcissism is associated with ego-identity goals, Machiavellianism, and psychopathy with instrumental-based behaviour, while Machiavellianism is distinct from psychopathy based upon temporal focus. All three constructs are related to Interpersonal Manipulation and comprised by a callous core (Jones & Paulhus, 2011, 2014).

The original version of the SD4 comprised of 41 items and was later reduced to 27 items through item refinement and structural analysis. Preliminary studies on the SD3 have found support for the validity and reliability, observing convergent validity with the SRP-III, Mach-IV, NPI and Dirty Dozen measure of Dark Triad traits (Ashton-James & Levordashka, 2013; Jones & Paulhus, 2014). The SD3 appears to have usefulness in research settings and, as the authors note, requires further investigation in relation to behavioural outcomes to demonstrate the operational utility of the measure for use in clinical practice. Researchers using the SD3 have questioned the distinctiveness among the DT constructs (Miller, Hyatt, Maples-Keller, Carter, & Lynam, 2017; Persson, 2019). In particular, very high correlations between Machiavellianism and psychopathy have been found, which may partly be due to inadequate construct coverage of the SD3 (Malesza, Ostaszewski, Büchner, & Kaczmarek, 2017).

Elemental Psychopathy Assessment (EPA)

The EPA is a self-report measure of psychopathy designed based on the relationship between psychopathic personality traits and the five-factor model (Lynam et al., 2011). According to Lynam and Widiger (2007), there are a number of traits from the five-factor model of personality

(FFM) that are consistently found to be associated with the conceptualisation of psychopathy. Wilson, Miller, Zeichner, Lynam, and Widiger contend that much of the speculation and dispute around the factor structure of psychopathy is misattributed, with factor structure only representative of the specific instrument measuring psychopathy, rather than defining the basic structure of psychopathic personality. Based on this theoretical view of personality traits representing the building blocks of a personality construct, Lynam et al. (2011) developed the EPA, comprising of extreme and maladaptive variants of corresponding FFM traits. The authors identified 299 items across 18 scales considered to be associated with psychopathic personality. The scales included: antagonism (distrust, manipulation, self-centeredness, opposition, arrogance, and callousness), Conscientiousness (disobliged, impersistence, and rashness), Extraversion (coldness, dominance, and thrill seeking), and Neuroticism (unconcern, anger, self-contentment, self-assurance, urgency, and invulnerability).

Initial empirical analysis of the EPA has found strong convergent validity between the measure and the PPI-R, LSRP, and SRP-III (mean $r =$ .72; Wilson, Miller, Zeichner, Lynam, & Widiger, 2011). Support for the EPA in relation to externalising behaviours was also identified, with total EPA scores significantly related to reactive and proactive aggression, along with a history of antisocial behaviour, alcohol use, and substance use. Wilson and colleagues suggested that one of the primary strengths of the instrument was the focus on lower levels of Neuroticism or negative emotionality, a feature that often receives limited content in assessment instruments such as the PCL-R, SRP-III and LSRP. The findings related to the EPA suggest support for the validity of the tool and the instrument provides a unique conceptualisation of psychopathy based upon the building blocks of personality traits. The authors noted some challenges in relation to operationalising features such as arrogance due to discrepancies between perception and ability (Lynam et al., 2011), although this may be more reflective of some of the methodological limitations of self-report instruments (Lilienfeld & Fowler, 2006). The EPA would benefit from further study to support the initial findings on the assessment, with the effectiveness of the tool in the corporate setting unknown at this stage in time, an area for possible further psychometric development and application.

Corporate Psychopathy Measures

In addition to these general self-report measures for psychopathy, a number of specific assessments have been developed for use with a corporate population. These are the Business-Scan 360 (B-Scan 360; Babiak & Hare, 2012), the Psychopathy Measure-Management Research Version (PM-MRV; Boddy et al., 2010), and the Corporate Personality Inventory (CPI; Fritzon, Croom, Brooks, & Bailey, 2013).

Business-Scan 360

The Business-Scan is based on Hare's four-factor model of psychopathy (see Hare, 2003; Hare & Neumann, 2005) and comprises of a 360 degree assessment tool (B-Scan 360; Mathieu et al., 2013) and a self-report version (B-Scan Self; Mathieu & Babiak, 2015). The B-Scan 360 measure is designed as a third-party rater tool, requiring respondents to rate subjects (i.e., managers, supervisors or peers) on psychopathy-relevant statements (e.g. "comes across as smooth, polished and charming"). Initially 113 items were developed, although this was later refined to 20 items. Exploratory factor analysis delineated a four-factor model for the B-Scan 360, similar to that found in the PCL-R. The author's also found an appropriate fit for items according to this factor structure based on confirmatory factor analysis, supporting four factors comprised of five items each (Mathieu et al., 2013). The derived factors and items of the B-Scan 360 include: manipulative and unethical (ingratiates, glib, uses charm, claims expertise, and rationalises), callous and insensitive (insensitive, rarely shows emotions, cold inside, remorseless, and no empathy), unreliable and unfocused (not loyal, no planning, unfocused, not patient, and unreliable), and intimidating and aggressive (intimidating, angry, asks harsh questions, threatens co-worker, and dramatic). The application of the B-Scan 360 to examine psychopathy in the business setting appears promising, with the third-party rating process allowing for objective oversight, rather than solely a subjects self-report. It is not clear whether multiple B-Scan 360 assessments would be carried out in cases where a concern is identified, or if one rating is considered sufficient to identify concern. The authors acknowledged that a limit of the research to date has been the challenges with gaining access to suitable participants, instead using online survey methods to gather data. While appearing to be a progressive tool for examining psychopathy in business settings, there remains limited information on the psychometric properties of the B-Scan 360, beyond its construct validity in terms of factor structure. Subsequently, its usefulness is unclear in terms of external criterion validity as well as discriminant validity.

The B-Scan Self was developed from theory and modelled of the PCL-R items and factors. The measure is comprised of 15 out of the 20 PCL-R facet items, slightly modified to the corporate setting. The assessment maintains the four-factor structure as reported in the PCL-R, with an acceptable four-factor model identified through confirmatory factor analysis (Mathieu & Babiak, 2015). The four factors and facet items include the following: interpersonal (insincere, arrogant, untrustworthy, and manipulative/unethical), affective (remorseless, shallow, insensitive, and blaming), lifestyle (impatient, selfish, unfocused, erratic, and unreliable), and antisocial (dramatic and bullying). Support was also found for the convergent and discriminant validity of the B-Scan Self based on the correlations with the SRP-III, Five-Factor Model and Dark Triad traits—narcissism and machiavellianism. The B-Scan Self shared the same correlational patterns with the FFM as the SRP-II, with a negative relationship with both Conscientiousness and Agreeableness. Positive relationships were observed between the B-Scan Self and narcissism, machiavellianism and the SRP-III, although factors three and four (lifestyle and antisocial) of the B-Scan Self were more highly correlated with factor one from the SRP-III than factors three and four (Erratic Lifestyle and Criminal Tendencies) of the SRP-III (Mathieu & Babiak, 2015). The author's suggested that these correlational results were due to the modification in facet items within the B-Scan Self, with criminal behaviour removed from the tool. Early research on the B-Scan Self appears positive; however, this measure is still in the preliminary stages of development and requires further validation and exploration to determine the operational utility of the instrument in corporate settings.

Psychopathy Measure-Management Research Version

The PM-MRV (Boddy et al., 2010) is a third-party report measure requiring respondents to rate their managers on a series of behavioural traits considered to reflect psychopathic personality. The instrument is comprised of eight items scored on a three-point scale, comprising of not present (0), somewhat present (1), and present (2). The eight items include: glib and superficially charming, accomplished liars, manipulative and conning, grandiose sense of self-worth, lack of remorse about actions, emotionally shallow, calculating and cold, lack of empathy and no capacity to experience the feelings of others, and refuse to take responsibility (Boddy et al., 2010). According to Boddy (2011), psychopathy is indicated by a score of 75% of the total score, this being represented as 13 out of 16. Scores between 9 and 12 were considered to reflect dysfunctional managers, while a score of 8 or below was reflective of a normal manager. Boddy (2011) suggests an alternative view of these scoring categories can be interpreted as, non-psychopaths, intermediate psychopaths and psychopaths.

The PM-MVR has been found to have strong internal consistency, while the measure has been compared with outcome-based criteria, indicating a significant positive relationship between psychopathy scores and withdrawal, workload, bullying, organisational constraints, and conflict. Significant negative relationships were observed between psychopathy scores, job satisfaction, and social responsibility. However, despite the relationship between psychopathy and these work-related outcomes, the PM-MVR has been criticised for its limited scope and lack of ability to discriminate between broader personality traits, such as psychopathy, machiavellianism, and narcissism. A primary critique is that the tool does not account for lifestyle or antisocial features of psychopathy, which are considered to be necessary for the characterisation of psychopathic personality (Cooke & Michie, 2001; Jones & Hare, 2016). Before the PM-MVR can be applied to organisational settings, further research is required to establish the empirical validity of the measure, particularly its ability to exclusively measure psychopathy, differentiating the construct from other similar, yet separate personality dimensions.

The Corporate Personality Inventory

The Corporate Personality Inventory (Fritzon et al., 2013) consists of both a self-report and third-party report version (CPI-3R; Fritzon et al., 2013). The self-report version consists of 61 items, while the third-party version has 57 items. Both measures were based on an exploratory approach to test construction with items being generated by an expert panel comprising of academics with research and professional experience in forensic psychology and business management.

For the self-report version, an initial item pool of 120 items was drawn from the core personality descriptors of psychopathy as translated into statements that would reflect the business environment, and a number of these items ($n = 47$) also reflected potentially positive constructions or manifestations of psychopathic personality traits in a business context (e.g. "*I am not afraid to make bold business decisions*"; "*I am a talented communicator*"), some of which also reflected the concepts of fearlessness and social influence as central features of the psychopathic personality. Exploratory factor analysis revealed a number of items with cross-loading or nil loadings on factors, and the final solution consisted of 61 items with a three-factor structure accounting for 23.14% of the variance. The three factors reflect similarities with the triarchic model of psychopathy (Patrick et al., 2009).

For the third-party version (CPI-3R), exploratory factor analysis also yielded a three-factor structure with subscale alphas of .91 for adaptive façade, .92 for ruthless determination, and .75 for impulsive egocentricity (Fritzon, Wiseman, & Gabriel, 2015). Preliminary validity evidence supporting the internal structure of the CPI-3R was also found during development, with the three-factor solution accounting for 35.95% of the variance. In terms of discriminant and concurrent validity, the CPI correlates significantly with the Paulhus Deception Scale ($r = .361$, $p < .001$; Fritzon et al., 2016) and the Psychopathy Personality Inventory-Revised ($r = .231$, $p < .001$). The finding that the PDS correlated positively with the CPI, while negatively with the PPI-R supports research by Verschuere et al. (2014) finding an inverse relationship between psychopathy and impression management based on the assumption that psychopaths have a disregard for social convention. However, the disparate pattern of correlations between the CPI and PPI-R suggests that impression management may be a central part of the defining criteria for corporate psychopathy and differentiates the successful psychopath from the non-successful variant. This finding also supports the moderated expression theory of corporate psychopathy (Hall & Benning, 2006) in that the ability to successfully create and maintain a positive impression acts as a protective factor that buffers against the negative aspects of psychopathy, and allows individuals to succeed in a business environment.

The research on the CPI-3R (Fritzon et al., 2015) also found an interesting pattern of correlations using the NEO-PI-R to examine criterion validity. Individuals obtaining high scores on the CPI-3R were rated as low on Agreeableness on the NEO-PI-R, in line with previous research (DeShong, Grant, & Mullins-Sweatt, 2015). Gender differences were also noted, in that female participants with high ratings on the CPI-3R also had high ratings on Openness and Conscientiousness. These findings were in contrast to prior research linking high ratings on psychopathy measures to low ratings on Openness and Conscientiousness. However, this also potentially aligns with the moderated expression of successful psychopathy, suggesting that gender may be a second variable that buffers against the negative effects of psychopathic personality. This latter possibility extends to other variables linked with gender that were not included in the Fritzon et al. (2016) study such as empathy.

Finally, recent research by Spencer and Byrne (2016) identified that contrary to expectation, the presence of primary psychopathic characteristics amongst senior managers did not attenuate high levels of intrinsic job satisfaction as reported by mid-level managers and low-level employees. It may be that the presence of psychopathy in senior management was buffered by the ability of those same individuals to create and maintain a positive impression such that individuals working alongside these psychopathic managers overall did not perceive a negative impact. These findings collectively highlight the importance of recognising that corporate psychopathy may not necessarily convey entirely egregious effects upon a workplace environment and calls for a more balanced approach to examining both the costs and benefits to organisations (Smith & Lilienfeld, 2013). Table 4.1 provides an overview of psychopathy measures and some considerations for their use in business settings.

Table 4.1 Summary of psychopathic personality assessment tools and findings relevant to workplace assessments

Name of assessment	Factors/scales	Correlations with other measures (of psychopathy)	Criterion validity	Workplace findings	Possible limitations
PCL-R (Hare, 1991)	Interpersonal-affective; Antisocial	Not reported since this is the original psychopathy measure	Numerous outcomes relating to antisocial and dishonest behaviour	Babiak, Neumann, and Hare (2010) using the short form found that high scores were positively related to ratings of creativity, strategic thinking, and communication skills, and negatively associated with ratings of being a team player, management skills, and overall accomplishments	Variable factor structure, The required collateral information difficult to obtain in non-institutionalized samples Relevance of antisocial factor to non-forensic samples, and indeed to psychopathy construct as a whole has been questioned (Cooke, Michie, Hart, & Clarke, 2004)

(continued)

Table 4.1 (continued)

Name of assessment	Factors/scales	Correlations with other measures (of psychopathy)	Criterion validity	Workplace findings	Possible limitations
SRP-4 (Paulhus et al., 2016) (derived from PCL-R)	Interpersonal manipulation; Callous affect; Erratic lifestyle; Criminal tendencies	Narcissism and Machiavellianism (Paulhus & Williams, 2002); correlations in the expected directions with the FFM	Bullying, drug use, dangerous driving, criminal behavior, anti-authoritarian attitudes (Williams & Paulhus, 2004)	Is frequently used as a measure of psychopathy in studies predicting CWB (e.g. studies included in meta-analyses by O'Boyle et al., 2012, 2015)	Interpersonal-affective traits and Boldness (see Triarchic model described in Chapter 1) not well captured (Sellbom et al., 2018) Did not correlate with PPI-R Fearless Dominance, TriPM Boldness, EPA Emotional Stability (Crego & Widiger, 2014)

Name of assessment	Factors/scales	Correlations with other measures (of psychopathy)	Criterion validity	Workplace findings	Possible limitations
LSRP (Levenson et al., 1995) (derived from PCL-R)	Primary (Factor 1); secondary (Factor 2) Alternative factor structure Egocentric, Callous, and Antisocial (Brinkley, Diamond, Magaletta, & Heigel, 2008)	Factor 2 correlates strongly with PPI Self Centred impulsivity (Ross et al., 2009) Factor 1 associated with PPI Coldheartedness	Buss-Perry Aggression Questionnaire, PAI (Morey, 2007) Antisocial personality scale (Brinkley et al., 2008); Machiavellianism and Narcissism Impulsivity, anger, antisociality, and addiction (Sellbom, 2011)	Rardin, Nadler, Bartels, & Ro (2017) found that individuals higher in (LSRP) psychopathic traits are attracted to organisations with a less formal hierarchical structure Scores on LSRP related to ethical business decision making (Watson, Teaque, & Papamarcos, 2017)	Construct validity of Primary scale has been questioned due to its relationship with antisocial behaviours rather than affective/interpersonal features of psychopathy (Sellbom et al., 2018) Does not appear to capture traits of fearlessness, stress immunity, or social influence associated with Boldness (Lilienfeld et al., 2012)

(continued)

Table 4.1 (continued)

Name of assessment	Factors/scales	Correlations with other measures (of psychopathy)	Criterion validity	Workplace findings	Possible limitations
PPI-R (Lilienfeld & Widows, 2005)	Self-centred impulsivity, Fearless Dominance and Coldheartedness	Total score correlates with PCL-R; also several other self-report measures of psychopathy and measures of personality (e.g. MMPI, MPQ, and CPI)	Alcohol and drug problems, child and adult antisocial symptoms (Benning, Patrick, Salekin, & Leistico, 2005). Aggression, Institutional misbehavior (Edens, Poythress, & Watkins, 2001), Drug abuse Treatment Program failure (McCoy & Edelstein, 2010)	Coldheartedness and SCI were predictive of economic self-ishness (Berg, Lilienfeld, Waldman, 2013) Higher levels of Stress Immunity amongst professionals compared to general community (Pegrum & Pearce, 2015)	Fearless dominance (as aligned to Boldness) has been found to correlate with adaptive outcomes. There is debate about whether Boldness is a core trait of psychopathy; irrelevant (Lynam & Miller, 2012), or can be considered an "impact trait" which determines the interpersonal manifestation of psychopathy (Lilienfeld, Watts, Smith, & Latzman, 2018)

Name of assessment	Factors/scales	Correlations with other measures (of psychopathy)	Criterion validity	Workplace findings	Possible limitations
CAPP (Cooke et al., 2012)	Boldness/emotional stability; Emotional detachment; disinhibition (Sellbom et al., 2015)	Significant associations with IPDE diagnoses of paranoid, antisocial, and narcissistic (Flórez et al., 2018)	Associated with criminal versatility, violent crime, and entitlement; aggression (total, physical, hostility, anger, verbal); and interpersonal conflict (Hanniball, Gatner, Douglas, Viljoen, & Aknin, 2019)		Limited research at this stage has examined the predictive validity of the CAPP, but one study on a forensic psychiatric population found that the CAPP may not perform as well as the PCL-R at predicting recidivism risk (De Page, Mercenier, & Titeca, 2018)

(continued)

Table 4.1 (continued)

Name of assessment	Factors/scales	Correlations with other measures (of psychopathy)	Criterion validity	Workplace findings	Possible limitations
TriPM (Patrick, 2010)	Boldness; Meanness; Disinhibition	Moderate to strong correlations with PCL-R (Patrick, 2010); between TriPM meanness and PPI total; Self-centred impulsivity subscale of PPI and disinhibition of TriPM (Sellbom & Phillips, 2013)	Sensation seeking (Sellbom & Phillips, 2013). Meanness and Disinhibition related to violent crime and criminal versatility, as well as less direct (e.g., nonviolent) crime, and fraud (Hanniball et al., 2019)		Research examining predictive validity is limited at this stage, and it has not been used with clinical or occupational samples

Name of assessment	Factors/scales	Correlations with other measures (of psychopathy)	Criterion validity	Workplace findings	Possible limitations
EPA (Lynam et al., 2011)	Antagonism, Emotional Stability, Disinhibition, and Narcissism	Significant correlations between total scores of EPA with PPI-R, LRSP, and SRP-4	Substance use, Reactive and Proactive aggression, Anti-social behaviour, Alcohol and substance use (Wilson et al., 2011)	Antagonism and Disinhibition significantly related to Computer Crime, Identity fraud and website defacing (Seigfried-Spellar, Villacís-Vukadinović, & Lynam, 2017)	Research examining predictive validity is limited at this stage

(continued)

Table 4.1 (continued)

Name of assessment	Factors/scales	Correlations with other measures (of psychopathy)	Criterion validity	Workplace findings	Possible limitations
B-Scan 360 (Mathieu et al., 2013)	Manipulative and unethical; Callous and insensitive; Unreliable and unfocused; and Intimidating and aggressive	Correlations with SRP-III, Five Factor Model and Narcissism and Machiavellianism			Research examining predictive validity is limited at this stage
CPI (Fritzon et al., 2013)	Boldness, Ruthlessness and Interpersonal Dominance	Correlations with the PPI-R for the self-report version, and between the third party (CPI-3R) and the CAPP SRS-Informant Report. Boldness correlates with Narcissism (NPI), and Ruthlessness correlates with Machiavellianism (Mach-IV) (see Chapter 8 for further details)	Proactive and reactive aggression, academic dishonesty, and self-report criminal behaviour	Counter-productive work behaviour, bullying, complaints, career success and leadership style (see Chapter 8)	Research is limited to mainly unpublished studies using University students, and requires replication across larger and more diverse samples

Personality Assessment Instruments

There are a range of personality assessment tools designed to examine a broad range of personality traits and other associated mental health symptomology. These measures are commonly quite extensive, of a self-report nature, and encompass validity indexes to control for response distortions. Some of the leading personality assessments include: Minnesota Multiphasic Personality Inventory (MMPI; Hathaway & McKinley, 1940), Millon Clinical Multiaxial Inventory (MCMI-IV; Millon, Grossman, & Millon, 2015); Eysenck Personality Questionnaire (EPQ; Eysenck & Eysenck, 1975); Personality Assessment Inventory (PAI; Morey, 2007); California Personality Inventory (CPI; Gough & Bradley, 1996), and Personality Inventory for DSM-5 (PID-5; Krueger, Derringer, Markon, Watson, & Skodol, 2012). Personality assessments are generally considered to compressively examine personality features; however, these instruments are also nonspecific measures of behavioural deviance, globally measuring traits, rather than specific core features (Lilienfeld & Fowler, 2006). Many instruments have scales developed to measure features of antisocial or criminal behaviour, such as the Psychopathic Deviant (Pd) and Hypomania scales (Ma) of the MMPI, Socialisation (So) scale of the CPI, Antisocial Scale (ANT) from the PAI, and the Antisocial and Aggressive/Sadist Scales of the MCMI.

Several studies have evaluated the relationship between personality assessment measure scales and psychopathy instruments. Harpur, Hare, and Halstian (1989) found negligible or low correlations ($r = .05-.15$) for factor one and moderate correlations ($r = .3-.5$) for factor two of the PCL with the MMPI Pd and Ma scales, the CPI So scale, and EPQ Psychoticism scale. Similar findings were observed by Edens, Hart, Johnson, Johnson, and Olver (2000) based on the association between the PCL:SV and PAI-ANT scale. A moderate correlation was observed between factor one ($r = .44$) slightly higher correlation ($r = .56$) between factor two and the PAI-ANT in a sample of psychiatric patients. However, in a sample of sexual offenders, a non-significant relationship was found between the PCL-R factor one and PAI-ANT ($r = .07$), while a moderate correlation was found for factor two and PAI-ANT ($r = .53$).

One of the most recently developed personality assessments is the PID-5, a 220-item self-report inventory developed to assess personality traits corresponding to the five traits of personality disorder described in Section III of the DSM-5 (Krueger et al., 2012). This is the first edition of the DSM to include a psychopathy specifier for ASPD, which emphasises traits previously neglected under the DSM definition of ASPD, including low anxiousness, and attention seeking. These traits are similar to the concepts of fearless dominance or boldness captured in other psychopathy measures such as the PPI-R or TriPM (Anderson, Sellbom, Wygant, Salekin, & Krueger, 2014). The five domains of the PID-5 are: Disinhibition, Antagonism, Negative Affect, Detachment, and Psychoticism. Early research on the PID-5 in relation to psychopathy observed varied results based on correlational analysis between the instrument and TRiPM and the PPI-R (Anderson et al., 2014). Although the DSM-5 Section III facet profile demonstrated greater associations with the psychopathy measures than the DSM-IV ASPD, they did not provide coverage of disinhibitory psychopathy traits. Additionally, some features of antisocial personality disorder (ASPD) such as hostility, were found to be negatively associated with psychopathy, with hostility more related to negative affectivity, rather than the affective and interpersonal traits of psychopathy (Anderson et al., 2014). Finally, the PID-5 psychopathy specifier was negatively associated with the PPI-R self-centred impulsivity scale, and the TriPM Disinhibition scale.

The research findings suggest that personality assessment tools tend to measure antisocial and criminal behaviour, yet do not encompass all of the core characteristics of psychopathy, such as the interpersonal and affective traits. This has commonly been one of the central debates regarding ASPD and psychopathy (see Hare, 2003), with ASPD traits often failing to sufficiently capture psychopathic personality, an issue apparent in many personality measures, conflating ASPD with psychopathy (Anderson et al., 2014; Lilienfeld & Fowler, 2006). As many personality instruments are modelled off the DSM-IV or DSM-5, comprising of clinical scales designed to measure the personality disorders specified in the manuals, concerns exist regarding the measurement of psychopathy, as psychopathic personality is not part of the nomenclature of personality disorders (Mathieu & Babiak, 2015). Subsequently, personality assessments capture features of psychopathy, although fail to exclusively and comprehensively measure the construct. Although a combination of features based on the results from a personality measure may suggest psychopathy, there is considerable clinical interpretation and expertise required to determine that such profile elevations are suggestive of psychopathic personality (Hare, 2003; Lilienfeld & Fowler, 2006).

Conclusion

The assessment of psychopathy has largely been based upon Hare's (1980, 2003) PCL (later revised as PCL-R) since the 1980s, with the measure shaping much of what is known about modern-day psychopathy. The PCL-R has for many years been the gold standard psychopathy assessment and arguably remains the leading assessment tool of psychopathy in offender populations (Hare, 2003; Hare & Neumann, 2005; Skeem et al., 2011). Although there has been concern raised that the construct of psychopathy has become equated and solely represented by the theoretical underpinnings and criteria of the PCL-R(Skeem & Cooke, 2010), the body of empirical research on Hare's measure has been important for construct development. The PCL-R has paved the way for refining the empirical knowledge related to psychopathic personality and provided a platform for further refinement and progression. Subsequently, several psychometric measures and conceptual theories have recently emerged to both expand upon and counterbalance the large body of literature that exists on psychopathy based on the PCL-R criteria (Butcher et al., 2001; Cooke et al., 2012; Levenson et al., 1995; Lilienfeld & Widows, 2005; Patrick et al., 2009).

The different assessment measures and theoretical conceptualisations of psychopathy each provide important contributions to the empirical knowledge of the construct. The PPI-R (Lilienfeld & Widows, 2005) was one of the earlier assessment tools to propose an alternative conceptualisation and method of psychopathy assessment, suggesting that three factors captured psychopathy, with criminal behaviour not considered to be a defining feature. The self-report measure has had wide use as both a clinical instrument and a research tool (Polaschek, 2015; Skeem et al.,

2011). The body of empirical literature on the PPI-R has supported the instrument as valid measure of psychopathy and has demonstrated application in both criminal and noncriminal settings (Brooks, 2016; Patrick & Zempolich, 1998; Skeem et al., 2003, 2011). Other promising assessment tools include the CAPP SRS-IR (Cooke & Logan, 2018,) EPA (Lynam et al., 2011), B-Scan 360 (Mathieu et al., 2013) and CPI-R (Fritzon et al., 2016). These measures have encouraging findings in relation to examining psychopathic personality and the overlapping personality features associated with the construct. The CAPP SRS-IR and EPA appear to have utility in multiple settings; however, further investigation of these tools in the corporate setting is required before this can be conclusive. The B-Scan 360 and CPI-R have been specifically developed for use in the corporate domain, designed to examine personality features applicable to the workplace. The B-Scan 360 is solely a measure of psychopathy, while the CPI-R examines various problematic personality traits, including psychopathic characteristics. These two tools have had preliminary validation with business samples and the findings have supported the use of the measures in determining problematic traits and behaviours in the workplace setting. There are also a number of assessment instruments that have been developed to measure psychopathy in the research setting. The TRiPM (Patrick, 2010) has demonstrated promising findings based on early studies (Hall et al., 2014), while tools such as the LSRP (Levenson et al., 1995) and SRP-III (Paulhus et al., 2016) are alternative measures of psychopathy that have greater research, rather than clinical utility, particularly in populations that are expected to possess accompanying adaptive traits.

References

Anderson, J., Sellbom, M., Wygant, D., Salekin, R., & Krueger, R. (2014). Examining the associations between DSM-5 section III antisocial personality disorder traits and psychopathy in community and university samples. *Journal of Personality Disorders, 28*(5), 675–697. https://doi.org/10.1521/pedi_2014_28_134.

Ashton-James, C. E., & Levordashka, A. (2013). When the wolf wears sheep's clothing: Individual differences in the desire to be liked influence nonconscious behavioural mimicry. *Social Psychological and Personality Science, 4,* 643–648.

Babiak, P. (1995). When psychopaths go to work: A case study of an industrial psychopath. *Applied Psychology: An International review, 44*(2), 171–188.

Babiak, P., & Hare, R. D. (2012). *The B-Scan 360 manual.* Manuscript in preparation.

Babiak, P., Neumann, C. S., & Hare, R. D. (2010). Corporate psychopathy: Talking the walk. *Behavioral Sciences & the Law, 28*(2), 174–193. https://doi.org/10.1002/bsl.925.

Balsis, S., Busch, A. J., Wilfong, K. M., Newman, J. W., & Edens, J. F. (2017). A statistical consideration regarding the threshold of the Psychopathy Checklist-Revised. *Journal of Personality Assessment, 99,* 494–502. https://doi.org/10.1080/00223891.2017.1281819.

Benning, S., Patrick, C., Salekin, R., & Leistico, A. (2005). Convergent and discriminant validity of psychopathy factors assessed via self-report: A comparison of three instruments. *Assessment, 12*(3), 270–289. https://doi.org/10.1177/1073191105277110.

Berg, J., Lilienfeld, S., & Waldman, I. (2013). Bargaining with the devil: Using economic decision-making tasks to examine the heterogeneity of psychopathic traits. *Journal of Research in Personality, 47*(5), 472–482. https://doi.org/10.1016/j.jrp.2013.04.003.

Boddy, C. R. (2011). *Corporate psychopaths: Organisational destroyers.* London: Palgrave Macmillian.

Boddy, C. R., Ladyshewsky, R. K., & Galvin, P. (2010). The influence of corporate psychopaths on corporate social responsibility and organizational commitment to employees. *Journal of Business Ethics, 97,* 1–19. https://doi.org/10.1007/s10551-010-0492-3.

Bolt, D. M., Hare, R. D., & Neumann, C. S. (2007). Score metric equivalence of the Psychopathy Checklist-Revised (PCL-R) across criminal offenders in North America and the United Kingdom: A critique of Cooke, Michie, Hart, and Clark (2005) and new analyses. *Assessment, 14,* 44–56. https://doi.org/10.1177/1073191106293505.

Brinkley, C., Diamond, P., Magaletta, P., & Heigel, C. (2008). Cross-validation of Levenson's psychopathy scale in a sample of federal female inmates. *Assessment, 15*(4), 464–482. https://doi.org/10.1177/1073191108319043.

Brooks, N. (2016). *Understanding the manifestation of psychopathic personality characteristics across populations.* Gold Coast, QLD: Bond University.

Butcher, J. N., Graham, J. R., Ben-Porath, Y. S., Tellegen, A., Dahlstrom, W. G., & Kaemmer, B. (2001). *The Minnesota Multiphasic Personality Inventory-2 (MMPI-2): Manual for administration and scoring.* Minneapolis: University of Minnesota Press.

Cleckley, H. M. (1941). *The mask of sanity: An attempt to reinterpret the so-called psychopathic personality.* London: C. V. Mosby.

Cleckley, H. M. (1976). *The mask of sanity* (5th ed.). St. Louis: Mosby.

Cook, A. N., Hart. S. D., Van Dogen, S., Van Marle, H., & Viljoen, S. (2013, June). *Evaluation of the TriPM and PPI using the CAPP as a concept map in Canadian and Dutch samples.* Keynote Address presented at the 13th International Association of Forensic Mental Health Services, Maastricht, The Netherlands.

Cooke, D. (2018). Psychopathic personality disorder: Capturing an elusive concept. *European Journal of Analytic Philosophy, 14*(1), 15–32. https://doi.org/10.31820/ejap.14.1.1.

Cooke, D. J., Hart, S. D., Logan, C., & Michie, C. (2012). Explicating the construct of psychopathy: Development and validation of a conceptual model, the Comprehensive Assessment of Psychopathic Personality (CAPP). *International Journal of Forensic Mental Health, 11*, 242–252. https://doi.org/10.1080/14999013.2012.746759.

Cooke, D. J., & Logan, C. (2015). Capturing clinical complexity: Towards a personality-oriented measure of psychopathy. *Journal of Criminal Justice, 43*, 262–273. Retrieved from https://daneshyari.com/article/preview/882729.pdf.

Cooke, D. J., & Logan, C. (2018). Capturing psychopathic personality: Penetrating the mask of sanity through clinical interview. In C. J. Patrick (Ed.), *Handbook of psychopathy* (2nd ed.). New York: Guilford Press.

Cooke, D. J., & Michie, C. (2001). Refining the construct of psychopathy: Towards a hierarchical model. *Psychological Assessment, 13*, 171–188. https://doi.org/10.1037/1040-3590.13.2.171.

Cooke, D., Michie, C., Hart, S., & Clark, D. (2004). Reconstructing psychopathy: Clarifying the significance of antisocial and socially deviant behavior in the diagnosis of psychopathic personality disorder. *Journal of Personality Disorders, 18*(4), 337–357. https://doi.org/10.1521/pedi.2004.18.4.337.

Crego, C., & Widiger, T. (2014). Psychopathy, DSM-5, and a caution. *Personality disorders: Theory, research, and treatment, 5*(4), 335–347. https://doi.org/10.1037/per0000078.

Cronbach, L. J., & Meehl, P. E. (1955). Construct validity in psychological tests. *Psychological Bulletin, 52*, 281–302. https://doi.org/10.1037/h0040957.

De Page, L., Mercenier, S., & Titeca, P. (2018). Assessing psychopathy in forensic schizophrenia spectrum disorders: Validating the comprehensive assessment of the psychopathic personality-institutional rating scale (CAPP-IRS). *Psychiatry Research, 265,* 303–308. https://doi.org/10.1016/j.psychres.2018.05.019.

Debowska, A., Boduszek, D., Kola, S., & Hyland, P. (2014). A bifactor model of the Polish version of the Hare Self-Report Psychopathy Scale. *Personality and Individual Differences, 69*(C), 231–237. https://doi.org/10.1016/j.paid.2014.06.001.

DeShong, H., Grant, D., & Mullins-Sweatt, S. (2015). Comparing models of counterproductive workplace behaviors: The Five-Factor Model and the Dark Triad. *Personality and Individual Differences, 74*(C), 55–60. https://doi.org/10.1016/j.paid.2014.10.001.

Drislane, L. E., Patrick, C. J., Sourander, A., Sillanmäki, L., Aggen, S. H., Elonheimo, H., … Kendler, K. S. (2014). Distinct variants of extreme psychopathic individuals in society at large: Evidence from a population based sample. *Personality Disorders, 5,* 154–163. https://doi.org/10.1037/per0000060.

Dutton, K. (2012). *The wisdom of psychopaths: What saints, spies, and serial killers can teach us about success.* New York: Scientific American.

Edens, J., Hart, S., Johnson, D., Johnson, J., & Olver, M. (2000). Use of the personality assessment inventory to assess psychopathy in offender populations. *Psychological Assessment, 12*(2), 132–139. https://doi.org/10.1037/1040-3590.12.2.132.

Edens, J., Poythress, N., & Watkins, M. (2001). Further validation of the psychopathic personality inventory among offenders: Personality and behavioral correlates. *Journal of Personality Disorders, 15*(5), 403–415. https://doi.org/10.1521/pedi.15.5.403.19202.

Edens, J. F., Marcus, D. K., Lilienfeld, S. O., & Poythress, N. G. (2006). Psychopathic, not psychopath: Taxometric evidence for the dimensional structure of psychopathy. *Journal of Abnormal Psychology, 115,* 131–144. https://doi.org/10.1037/0021-843x.115.1.131.

Eysenck, H. J., & Eysenck, S. B. (1975). *Manual of the Eysenck Personality Questionnaire.* London: Hodder and Stoughton.

Flórez, G., Ferrer, V., García, L. S., Crespo, M. R., Pérez, M., Saíz, P. A., & Cooke, D. J. (2018). Clinician ratings of the Comprehensive Assessment of Psychopathic Personality (CAPP) in a representative sample of Spanish prison inmates: New validity evidence. *PloS ONE, 13*(4), e0195483. https://doi.org/10.1371/journal.pone.0195483.

Fritzon, K., Bailey, C., Croom, S., & Brooks, N. (2016). Problematic personalities in the workplace: Development of the Corporate Personality Inventory. In P.

Granhag, R. Bull, A. Shaboltas, & E. Dozortseva (Eds.), *Psychology and law in Europe: When west meets east.* Boca Raton: CRC Press.

Fritzon, K., Croom, S., Brooks, N., & Bailey, C. (2013). *The Corporate Personality Inventory—Third Party Report* (Unpublished).

Fritzon, K., Wiseman, E., & Gabriel, J. (2015). *Factor structure of the third party version of the Corporate Personality Inventory (CPI-3R).* Unpublished manuscript.

Gough, H. G., & Bradley, P. (1996). *"CPI Manual." Ed.3.* Palo Alto, CA: Consulting Psychologists Press.

Hall, J. R., & Benning, S. D. (2006). The "successful" psychopath: Adaptive and subclinical manifestations of psychopathy in the general population. In C. J. Patrick (Ed.), *Handbook of psychopathy* (pp. 459–478): New York: Guilford Press.

Hall, J., Drislane, L., Patrick, C., Morano, M., Lilienfeld, S., & Poythress, N. (2014). Development and validation of triarchic construct scales from the psychopathic personality inventory. *Psychological Assessment, 26*(2), 447–461. https://doi.org/10.1037/a0035665.

Hanniball, K. B., Gatner, D. T., Douglas, K. S., Viljoen, J. L., & Aknin, L. B. (2019). Examining the triarchic psychopathy measure and comprehensive assessment of psychopathic personality in self-identified offender populations. *Personality Disorders: Theory, Research, and Treatment, 10*(4), 340–353. https://doi.org/10.1037/per0000333.

Hare, R. D. (1980). A research scale for the assessment of psychopathy in criminal populations. *Personality and Individual Differences, 1,* 111–119. https://doi.org/10.1016/0191-8869(80)90028-8.

Hare, R. D. (1991). *The Hare Psychopathy Checklist-Revised.* Toronto, ON: Multi-Health Systems.

Hare, R. D. (1999a). *Without conscience: The disturbing world of psychopaths among us.* New York: Guilford Press.

Hare, R. D. (1999b). Psychopathy as a risk factor for violence. *Psychiatric Quarterly, 70,* 181–197. https://doi.org/10.1023/a:1022094925150.

Hare, R. D. (2003). *The Hare Psychopathy Checklist-Revised* (2nd ed.). Toronto, ON: Mutli-Health Systems.

Hare, R. D., Harpur, T. J., & Hemphill, J. D. (1989). *Scoring pamphlet for the self-report psychopathy scale: SRP-II* (Unpublished manuscript). Vancouver, BC, Canada: Simon Fraser University.

Hare, R. D., & McPherson, L. M. (1984). Violent and aggressive behavior by criminal psychopaths. *International Journal of Law and Psychiatry, 7,* 35–50. https://doi.org/10.1016/0160-2527(84)90005-0.

Hare, R. D., & Neumann, C. S. (2005). Structural models of psychopathy. *Current Psychiatry Reports, 7*(1), 57–64. https://doi.org/10.1007/s11920-005-0026-3.

Harris, G. T., & Rice, M. E. (2006). Treatment of psychopathy: A review of empirical findings. In C. Patrick (Ed.), *Handbook of psychopathy* (pp. 555–572). New York: Guilford.

Hart, S., Cox, D., & Hare, R. D. (1995). *Manual for the psychopathy checklist: Screening version (PCL:SV).* Toronto, ON: Multi-Health Systems.

Hathaway, S. R., & McKinley, J. C. (1940). *The MMPI Manual.* New York: Psychological Corporation.

Johansson, P., Andershed, H., Kerr, M., & Levander, S. (2002). On the operationalization of psychopathy: Further support for a three-faceted personality oriented model. *Acta Psychiatrica Scandanavica, 106*, 81–83. https://doi.org/10.1034/j.1600-0447.106.s412.18.x.

Jones, D., & Hare, R. (2016). The mismeasure of psychopathy: A commentary on Boddy's PM-MRV. *Journal of Business Ethics, 138*(3), 579–588. https://doi.org/10.1007/s10551-015-2584-6.

Jones, D. N., & Paulhus, D. L. (2011). Differentiating the dark triad within the interpersonal circumplex. In L. M. Horowitz & S. Strack (Eds.), *Handbook of interpersonal psychology: Theory, research, assessment, and therapeutic interventions* (pp. 249–268). New York: Wiley.

Jones, D. N., & Paulhus, D. L. (2014). Introducing the short dark triad (SD3): A brief measure of dark personality traits. *Assessment, 21*, 28–41. https://doi.org/10.1177/1073191111351405.

Kreis, M. K., & Cooke, D. (2011). Capturing the psychopathic female: A prototypicality analysis of the Comprehensive Assessment of Psychopathic Personality (CAPP) across gender. *Behavioural Sciences & the Law, 29*, 638–648. https://doi.org/10.1002/bsl.1003.

Krueger, R. F., Derringer, J., Markon, K. E., Watson, D., & Skodol, A. E. (2012). Initial construction of a maladaptive personality trait model and inventory for DSM–5. *Psychological Medicine, 42*, 1879–1890. https://doi.org/10.1017/S0033291711002674.

Levenson, M. R., Kiehl, K. A., & Fitzpatrick, C. M. (1995). Assessing psychopathic attributes in a non institutionalized population. *Journal of Personality and Social Psychology, 68*, 151–158. https://doi.org/10.1037/0022-3514.68.1.151.

Lilienfeld, S. O., & Andrews, B. P. (1996). Development and preliminary validation of a self report measure of psychopathic personality traits in noncriminal populations. *Journal of Personality Assessment, 66,* 488–524. https://doi.org/10.1207/s15327752jpa6603_3.

Lilienfeld, S. O., & Fowler, K. (2006). The self-report assessment of psychopathy: problems, pitfalls, and promises. In C. J. Patrick (Ed.), *Handbook of psychopathy* (pp. 107–132). New York: Guilford Press.

Lilienfeld, S., Patrick, C., Benning, S., Berg, J., Sellbom, M., & Edens, J. (2012). The role of fearless dominance in psychopathy: Confusions, controversies, and clarifications. *Personality Disorders, 3*(3), 327–340. https://doi.org/10.1037/a0026987.

Lilienfeld, S. O., Watts, A. L., Smith, S. F., & Latzman, R. D. (2018). Boldness: Conceptual and methodological issues. In C. J. Patrick (Ed.), *Handbook of psychopathy* (2nd ed., pp. 165–186). New York, NY: Guilford Press.

Lilienfeld, S. O., & Widows, M. R. (2005). *Psychopathic Personality Inventory-Revised (PPI-R) professional manual.* Odessa, FL: Psychological Assessment Resources.

Lynam, D., Gaughan, E., Miller, J., Miller, D., Mullins-Sweatt, S., & Widiger, T. (2011). Assessing the basic traits associated with psychopathy: Development and validation of the elemental psychopathy assessment. *Psychological Assessment, 23*(1), 108–124. https://doi.org/10.1037/a0021146.

Lynam, D., & Miller, J. (2012). Fearless dominance and psychopathy: A response to Lilienfeld et al. *Personality Disorders, 3*(3), 341–353. https://doi.org/10.1037/a0028296.

Lynam, D. R., & Widiger, T. A. (2007). Using a general model of personality to identify the basic elements of psychopathy. *Journal of Personality Disorders, 21,* 160–178. https://doi.org/10.1521/pedi.2007.21.2.160.

MacDonald, A. W., & Iacono, W. G. (2006). Towards an integrated perspective on the etiology on psychopathy. In C. J. Patrick (Ed.), *Handbook of psychopathy* (pp. 375–385). New York: Guilford Press.

Malesza, M., Ostaszewski, P., Büchner, S., & Kaczmarek, M. C. (2017). The adaptation of the Short Dark Triad personality measure—Psychometric properties of a German sample. *Current Issues in Psychology.* https://doi.org/10.1007/s12144-017-9662-0.

Mathieu, C., & Babiak, P. (2015). Tell me who you are, I'll tell you how you lead: Beyond the Full-Range Leadership Model, the role of corporate psychopathy on employee attitudes. *Personality and Individual Differences, 87,* 8–12. https://doi.org/10.1016/j.paid.2015.07.016.

Mathieu, C., Hare, R., Jones, D., Babiak, P., & Neumann, C. (2013). Factor structure of the B-Scan 360: A measure of corporate psychopathy. *Psychological Assessment, 25*(1), 288–293. https://doi.org/10.1037/a0029262.

McCoy, K., & Edelstein, B. (2010). *Incremental validity of the psychopathic personality inventory—Revised in predicting program failure* (ProQuest Dissertations Publishing). Retrieved from http://search.proquest.com/docview/910874868/.

Millon, T. D., Grossman, S., & Millon, C. (2015). *The Millon Clinical Multiaxial Inventory (MCMI-IV) manual.* Bloomington, MN: Pearson Inc.

Međedović, J., Petrović, B., Kujačić, D., Željeskov Đorić, J., & Savić, M. (2015). What is the optimal number of traits to describe psychopathy. *Primenjena Psihologija, 8,* 109–130.

Miller, J. D., Hyatt, C. S., Maples-Keller, J. L., Carter, N. T., & Lynam, D. R. (2017). Psychopathy and Machiavellianism: A distinction without a difference? *Journal of Personality, 85,* 439–453. https://doi.org/10.1111/jopy.12251.

Morey, L. C. (2007). *The Personality Assessment Inventory professional manual.* Lutz, FL: Psychological Assessment Resources.

Neal, T. M., & Sellbom, M. (2012). Examining the factor structure of the Hare self-report psychopathy scale. *Journal of Personality Assessment, 94,* 244–253. https://doi.org/10.1080/00223891.2011.648294.

O'Boyle, E., Forsyth, D., Banks, G., & Mcdaniel, M. (2012). A meta-analysis of the Dark Triad and work behavior: A social exchange perspective. *Journal of Applied Psychology, 97*(3), 557–579. https://doi.org/10.1037/a0025679.

O'Boyle, E., Forsyth, D., Banks, G., Story, P., & White, C. (2015). A meta-analytic test of redundancy and relative importance of the Dark Triad and Five-Factor Model of personality. *Journal of Personality, 83*(6), 644–664. https://doi.org/10.1111/jopy.12126.

Patrick, C. J. (2007). Getting to the heart of psychopathy. In H. Herve & J. C. Yuille (Eds.), *Psychopathy: Theory, research, and social implications* (pp. 207–252). Mahwah, NJ: Erlbaum.

Patrick, C. J. (2010). *Operationalizing the triarchic conceptualization of psychopathy: Preliminary description of brief scales for assessment of boldness, meanness, and disinhibition* (Unpublished manual). Tallahassee, FL: Department of Psychology, Florida State University. Retrieved from http://www.phenxtoolkit.org.

Patrick, C. J., & Drislane, L. E. (2014). Triarchic model of psychopathy: Origins, operationalizations, and observed linkages with personality and general psychopathology. *Journal of Personality, 83,* 627–643. https://doi.org/10.1111/jopy.12119.

Patrick, C. J., & Zempolich, K. A. (1998). Emotion and aggression in the psychopathic personality. *Aggression and Violent Behaviour, 3*, 303–338. https://doi.org/10.1016/s1359-1789(97)00003-7.

Patrick, C. J., Fowles, D. C., & Krueger, R. F. (2009). Triarchic conceptualizations of psychopathy: Developmental origins of disinhibition, boldness, and meanness. *Development and Psychopathology, 21*, 913–938. https://doi.org/10.1017/s0954579409000492.

Paulhus, D. L., Neumann, C. S., & Hare, R. D. (2016). *Manual for the Hare Self-Report Psychopathy scale.* Toronto, ON, Canada: Multi-Health Systems.

Paulhus, D. L., & Williams, K. M. (2002). The Dark Triad of personality: Narcissism, Machiavellianism, and psychopathy. *Journal of Research in Personality, 36*, 556–563. https://doi.org/10.1016/S0092-6566(02)00505-6.

Pedersen, L., Kunz, C., Elass, P., & Rasmussen, K. (2010). Psychopathy as a risk factor for violent recidivism: Investigating the Psychopathy Checklist Screening Version (PCL:SV) and the Comprehensive Assessment of Psychopathic Personality (CAPP) in a forensic psychiatric setting. *International Journal of Forensic Mental Health, 9*, 308–315. https://doi.org/10.1080/1499013.2010.526681.

Pegrum, J., & Pearce, O. (2015). A stressful job: Are surgeons psychopaths? *The Bulletin of the Royal College of Surgeons of England, 97*(8), 331–334. https://doi.org/10.1308/rcsbull.2015.331.

Persson, B. N. (2019). Searching for Machiavelli but finding psychopathy and narcissism. *Personality Disorders: Theory, Research, and Treatment*, 1–11. http://dx.doi.org/10.1037/per0000323.

Polaschek, D. (2015). (Mis)understanding psychopathy: Consequences for policy and practice with offenders. *Psychiatry, Psychology and Law, 22*(4), 500–519. https://doi.org/10.1080/13218719.2014.960033.

Poythress, N. G., Edens, J. F., & Lilienfeld, S. O. (1998). Criterion related validity of the in a prison sample. *Psychological Assessment, 10*, 426–430. Retrieved from https://www.researchgate.net/profile/John_Edens/publication/232440323_Criterionbased_validity_of_the_Psychopathic_Personality_Inventory_in_a_prison_sample/links/0deec537cd138c0d03000000.pdf.

Rardin, E., Nadler, J., Bartels, L., & Ro, E. (2017). *Corporate psychopaths and their proclivity for Infiltrating Organizations* (ProQuest Dissertations Publishing). Retrieved from http://search.proquest.com/docview/1925592797/.

Ray, J., Frick, P., Thornton, L., Steinberg, L., & Cauffman, E. (2016). Positive and negative item wording and its influence on the assessment of callous-unemotional traits. *Psychological Assessment, 28*(4), 394–404. https://doi.org/10.1037/pas0000183.

Ross, S., Benning, S., Patrick, C., Thompson, A., & Thurston, A. (2009). Factors of the psychopathic personality inventory: Criterion-related validity and relationship to the BIS/BAS and five-factor models of personality. *Assessment, 16*(1), 71–87. https://doi.org/10.1177/1073191108322207.

Salekin, R. T., Chen, D. R., Sellbom, M., Lester, W. S., & MacDougall, E. (2014). Examining the factor structure and convergent and discriminant validity of the Levenson self-report psychopathy scale: Is the two-factor model the best fitting model? *Personality Disorders: Theory, Research, and Treatment, 5,* 289–304. https://doi.org/10.1037/per0000073.

Sandvik, A., Hansen, A., Kristensen, M., Johnsen, B., Logan, C., & Thornton, D. (2012). Assessment of psychopathy: Inter-correlations between psychopathy checklist revised, comprehensive assessment of psychopathic personality—Institutional rating scale, and self-report of psychopathy scale-III. *International Journal of Forensic Mental Health, 11*(4), 280–288. https://doi.org/10.1080/14999013.2012.746756.

Seigfried-Spellar, K. C., Villacís-Vukadinović, N., & Lynam, D. R. (2017). Computer criminal behavior is related to psychopathy and other antisocial behavior. *Journal of Criminal Justice, 51,* 67–73.

Sellbom, M. (2011). Elaborating on the construct validity of the Levenson self-report psychopathy scale in incarcerated and non-incarcerated samples. *Law and Human Behavior, 35,* 440–451.

Sellbom, M., Cooke, D. J., & Hart, S. H. (2015). Construct validity of the Comprehensive Assessment of Psychopathic Personality (CAPP) concept map: Getting closer to the core of psychopathy. *International Journal of Forensic Mental Health, 14,* 172–180. https://doi.org/10.1080/14999013.2015.1085112.

Sellbom, M., Cooke, D. J., & Shou, Y. (2018). *Development and initial validation of the Comprehensive Assessment of Psychopathic Personality-Self Report (CAPP-SR).* Paper under review.

Sellbom, M., Lilienfeld, S. O., Fowler, K. A., & McCrary, K. L. (2018). The self-report assessment of psychopathy: Challenges, pitfalls, and promises. In C. J. Patrick (Ed.), *Handbook of psychopathy* (pp. 211–258). New York: Guilford Press.

Sellbom, M., & Phillips, T. R. (2013). An examination of the triarchic conceptualization of psychopathy in incarcerated and nonincarcerated samples. *Journal of Abnormal Psychology, 122,* 208–214. https://doi.org/10.1037/a0029306.

Skeem, J. L., & Cooke, D. J. (2010). Is criminal behavior a central component of psychopathy? Conceptual directions for resolving the debate. *Psychological Assessment, 22,* 433–445. https://doi.org/10.1037/a0008512.

Skeem, J. L., Polaschek, D. L. L., Patrick, C. J., & Lilienfeld, S. O. (2011). Psychopathic personality: Bridging the gap between scientific evidence and public policy. *Psychological Science in Public Interest, 12,* 95–162. https://doi.org/10.1177/1529100611426706.

Skeem, J. L., Poythress, N., Edens, J. F., Lilienfeld, S. O., & Cale, E. M. (2003). Psychopathic personality or personalities? Exploring potential variants of psychopathy and their implications for risk assessment. *Aggression and Violent Behaviour, 8,* 513–546. https://doi.org/10.1016/s1359-1789(02)00098-8.

Smith, S., & Lilienfeld, S. (2013). Psychopathy in the workplace: The knowns and unknowns. *Aggression and Violent Behavior, 18*(2), 204–218. https://doi.org/10.1016/j.avb.2012.11.007.

Somma, A., Borroni, S., Drislane, L., Patrick, C., & Fossati, A. (2019). Modeling the structure of the triarchic psychopathy measure: Conceptual, empirical, and analytic considerations. *Journal of Personality Disorders, 33*(4), 470–496. https://doi.org/10.1521/pedi_2018_32_354.

Spencer, R., & Byrne, M. (2016). Relationship between the extent of psychopathic features among corporate managers and subsequent employee job satisfaction. *Personality and Individual Differences, 101,* 440–445. https://doi.org/10.1016/j.paid.2016.06.044.

Steadman, H., Silver, E., Monahan, J., Appelbaum, P., Robbins, P., Mulvey, E., … Banks, S. (2000). A classification tree approach to the development of actuarial violence risk assessment tools. *Law and Human Behavior, 24*(1), 83–100. https://doi.org/10.1023/A:1005478820425.

Tsang, S., Salekin, R. T., Coffey, C. A., & Cox, J. (2017). A comparison of self-report measures of psychopathy among non-forensic samples using item response theory analyses. *Psychological Assessment, 30*(3), 311–327. https://doi.org/10.1037/pas000481.

Verschuere, B., Uzieblo, K., De Schryver, M., Douma, H., Onraedt, T., & Crombez, G. (2014). The inverse relation between psychopathy and faking good: Not response bias, but true variance in psychopathic personality. *The Journal of Forensic Psychiatry & Psychology, 25*(6), 705–713. https://doi.org/10.1080/14789949.2014.952767.

Watson, G., Teaque, B., & Papamarcos, S. (2017). Functional psychopathy in morally relevant business decisions. *Ethics & Behavior, 27*(6), 458–485. https://doi.org/10.1080/10508422.2016.1224188.

Williams, K. M., & Paulhus, D. L. (2004). Factor structure of the Self Report Psychopathy Scale (SRP-II) in non-forensic samples. *Personality and Individual Differences, 37,* 765–778.

Williams, K. M., Paulhus, D. L., & Hare, R. D. (2007). Capturing the four-factor structure of psychopathy in college students via self-report. *Journal of Personality Assessment, 88*, 205–219. https://doi.org/10.1080/00223890701268074.

Wilson, L., Miller, J. D., Zeichner, A., Lynam, D. R., & Widiger, T. A. (2011). An examination of the validity of the Elemental Psychopathy Assessment: Relations with other psychopathy measures, aggression, and externalizing behaviors. *Journal of Psychological Behavioural Assessment, 33*, 315–322. https://doi.org/10.1007/s10862-010-9213-6.

5

Empirical Findings Relating to Psychopathy

Simon Croom

The Complexity of the Psychopathy Construct

A central issue with psychopathy is the degree to which there is a coherent, consistent and universally agreed definition of psychopathic personality disorder, and consequently a uniform and universal means of measurement and diagnosis. As Skeem, Polaschek, Patrick, and Lilienfeld (2011) note, the psychopathy construct has, to a large extent, become synonymous with Hare's Psychopathy Checklist Revised (PCL-R) assessment, yet examination of prior research indicates a range of other instruments and constructs have been employed to provide insights into the construct of psychopathy, examine its prevalence and discern its characteristics across diverse populations, as we saw in Chapter 3. While the omission of psychopathy as a disorder in the DSM-V has provided opportunities for researchers to undertake more explorative studies aimed at delineating the construct(s) related to psychopathy, it has conversely posed a challenge for diagnosis. For instance, a reliance on forensic samples for the

S. Croom (✉)
University of San Diego, San Diego, CA, USA

© The Author(s) 2020
K. Fritzon et al., *Corporate Psychopathy*,
https://doi.org/10.1007/978-3-030-27188-6_5

development of psychopathy instruments will emphasise the antisocial and illegal behaviours associated with criminal psychopathy, while the use of non-forensic samples diminishes the role of such traits and behaviours in the conceptualisation of psychopathy so that noncriminal psychopathy is characterised very differently (Marcus, Fulton, & Edens, 2012). Thus, the scales and constructs employed in a measurement instrument play a critical role in the definition of psychopathic personality disorder.

The Psychopathic Personality Inventory-Revised (PPI-R) (Lilienfeld & Widows, 2005) has been established as a sound psychometric self-report measure of psychopathy. It has been used in both community and criminal samples (Lilienfeld & Widows, 2005) and for research (Lilienfeld & Andrews, 1996; Lilienfeld & Widows, 2005). From the initial publications of Cleckley (1941) and those of Robert Hare (inc. Hare & Neumann, 2008), psychopathy has often been regarded as a disorder associated with criminal and antisocial behaviours, and thus Lilienfeld and Widows argued that the prevailing assessments were more focused on criminality than on wider manifestations of psychopathic behaviour (such as narcissism, social influence and lack of compassion). Consequently, their development, as we will discuss, aimed to embrace a much wider range of behaviours and traits.

Analysis of the PPI-R Factors/Subscales

The PPI-R is a self-report tool developed for use with general populations rather than institutional or incarcerated ones and is founded principally on the conceptualisation of psychopathy arising from the work of Cleckley (1941) rather than Hare's PCL-R conceptualisation. Lilienfeld and Andrews (1996) argue that their exploratory approach and its inclusion of both behavioural items and personality traits provide a valid assessment of psychopathy in the general population. Significantly, the assumption underpinning the PPI-R is that personality traits are dimensional (i.e. are present in differing combinations and degrees across the population), rather than taxonic (i.e. can describe an identifiable class of individuals possessing distinctive traits) and they contend that psychopathy is a syndrome marked by varying patterns of psychopathic features. Thus, individuals can "score" highly on psychopathic instruments, but demonstrate markedly differing characteristics and traits between each other (Babiak, Neumann, & Hare, 2010; Edens, Marcus, Lilienfeld, & Poythress, 2006; Skeem et al., 2011).

The structure of the PPI-R is consistent with the triarchic model of psychopathy (Patrick, Fowles, & Krueger, 2009) and has been found to possess moderate concurrent validity with the PCL-R. However, it is not a psychopathy diagnostic instrument per se (Skeem et al., 2011), rather it examines three latent factors of psychopathy incorporating two higher-order factors—*fearless dominance* and *self-centered impulsivity*—and one subscale—*cold-heartedness,* which remains primarily independent of the other two factors (Lilienfeld & Widows, 2005; Skeem et al., 2011). Since the PPI-R was essentially developed using pre-existing subscales it has been found to have strong validity (Skeem et al., 2011), noted by Nikolova (2010) for "high internal consistency, test-retest reliability, as well as convergent validity with other measures of psychopathy and antisocial behaviour, or theoretically related concepts such as empathy, sensation seeking or driving anger" (p. 19). However, the body of literature that has examined the factor structure of the PPI-R and its relationship to other personality assessments has identified somewhat inconsistent results, and these will be discussed in the following section.

The Structure of the PPI-R

The initial samples employed in the development of the PPI were drawn from undergraduate psychology students in Minnesota, an arguably homogenous population on the basis of age (mean age range for their initial three rounds was between 20.4 years and 22.1 years), social and demographic characteristics, and with low levels of criminality. The initial conceptualisation of psychopathy as a personality disorder led Lilienfeld and Andrews (1996) to originally target 24 constructs, including guiltlessness, lack of anxiety and neurotic symptoms, and low frustration tolerance, which were subsequently reduced using principal components analysis to retain eight significant measurement scales. Methodologically, this was a robust approach because it initially expands the boundary of psychopathy to embrace associated constructs derived from existing instruments and the literature, which then allowed the extraction of significant constructs accounting for the key variance in the development of the instrument. Following factor analysis, Lilienfeld and Andrews extracted eight primary subscales, which they group into two key factors, Fearless Dominance (3 subscales) and Self-Centred Impulsivity (4 subscales) with an individual subscale, Cold-heartedness, constituting a separate, third, factor. Their model is shown in Fig. 5.1.

It was initially intended that the PPI would provide a fundamental measure of psychopathy consisting of 8 subfactors, and thus psychopathy was viewed as a homogenous or taxonic condition. Subsequent studies by Lilienfeld and colleagues have moved away from the view that psychopathy is taxonic to a view that psychopathy is more appropriately considered by use of a dimensional model. In the attempt to verify the nature of psychopathy as either taxonic or dimensional, factor analytical studies

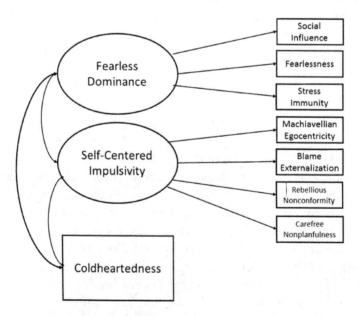

Fig. 5.1 Structure of the PPI-R three-factor model (Lilienfeld & Widows, 2005)

have been conducted by a number of authors to explore the fit of one-factor (thus taxonic), two- or three-factor models to the conceptualisation of psychopathy as envisaged by the PPI. Marcus et al. (2012) published the results of a meta-analytical study of 45 studies using variants of the PPI-R (which includes the original PPI and the short form version—PPI-SF) in which they examined the factor structure of the PPI-R. Their findings were interesting in several aspects. Firstly, the Fearless Dominance and Self-Centred Impulsivity factors are weakly correlated with each other (overall the average r was .12) and thus describe separate and potentially unrelated factors that do not necessarily co-occur. Secondly, they found that this relationship was influenced by the population being sampled. For forensic (prison or psychiatric institutional) populations, there was no correlation between the two factors ($r = .03$), but in community (general population) studies, there was in fact a significant, but small, correlation ($r = .15$). Thirdly, the Cold-heartedness factor was found not to be strongly associated with either of the PPI factors. In concluding their meta-analysis, Marcus et al. (2012) repeated the fundamental challenge in delineating psychopathic personality disorder, questioning whether psychopathy is indeed a coherent and unitary construct, specifically when the PPI-R is employed.

A more recent meta-analysis by Ruchensky et al., (2018) of 60 studies employing the PPI or PPI-R also found differences in the higher-order structure of both the PPI and PPI-R between forensic (offender) samples and community samples. They found that community sample studies gen-erated two dominant factors, similar to the findings of Benning, Patrick, Hicks, Blonigen, and Krueger (2003). Further, for this population the Fearlessness scale loaded onto the Fearless Dominance scale and cross loaded onto the other dominant factor, which was similar to the Self-Centred Impulsivity factor. However, their analysis of offender or forensic samples studies found that fearlessness did not load onto the Fearless Dominance factor, being more strongly associated with the Self-Centred Impulsivity factor. Furthermore, their analysis found that offender sam-ples also generated a third factor from the PPI and PPI-R, consisting of the Cold-heartedness and Carefree Nonplanfulness.

In a comparison of psychopathy measures, Tsang, Salekin, Coffey, and Cox (2017) used item response theory analysis to evaluate the PPI (in short form [PPI-SF] format) and concluded that subscales were moderately correlated with each, supporting the validity of each subscales as distinct item measurements. A consequence of the factor structure analyses of the PPI-R is to reinforce the view that the instrument provides a dimensional, not taxonic, approach to psychopathy, and thus examination of the facets of psychopathy that characterise subjects is a critically important contribution of the instrument (Patrick, Edens, Poythress, Lilienfeld, & Benning, 2006).

Incarcerated and Forensic Sample Studies

Neumann, Malterer, and Newman (2008) attempted to replicate Benning et al. (2003) with a sample of 1224 incarcerated males but found support for a different subscale grouping. Specifically, their PPI-1 consisted of rebellious nonconformity, blame externalisation, Machiavellian Egocentricity and fearlessness; PPI-2 subscales of stress immunity and social influence and PPI-3 consisted of cold-heartedness and carefree non-planfulness. They also note significant overlap between the PPI subscales and proposed that their interpretation of not only their study, but prior research by Lilienfeld in his doctoral thesis (1990) and the two studies by Benning et al. (2003) and Benning, Patrick, Salekin, and Leistico (2005) supports the contention that incarcerated samples do not significantly differ from community samples and thus a common PPI-R model is supportable. In concluding, Neumann et al. (2008) propose a three-factor PPI-R structure represented by factor 1 approximating *fearless, impulsive antisociality*, factor 2 approximating *high extroversion/low neuroticism* and a third *callous-indifferent* factor. The association between PPI factors and criminality tend to highlight the connection between distinctive components of psychopathy, supporting an orthogonal relationship between Fearless Dominance and Self-Centred Impulsivity (e.g., see also, Ross, Benning, Patrick, Thompson, & Thurston, 2009).

In a study of incarcerated females using the original version of the PPI, Berardino, Meloy, Sherman, and Jacobs (2005) found support for the three-factor model mirroring the model structure seen in Fig. 5.1, although the PPI's terminology is slightly different to that of the revised version (PPI-R). Similarly, Patrick et al.'s (2006) reassessment of prior data from offender samples supported Benning et al.'s (2003) two-factor structure.

In a report of two studies of hospitalised male (forensic) patients using firstly the PPI and then PPI-R, Gonsalves, McLawsen, Huss, and Scalora (2013), while not specifically delineating their factor analyses, did not support Benning et al. (2003) two-factor model but they do emphasise that their findings stress that the method of assessment of psychopathy is inseparable from clear definition of the disorder. A forensic sample study of incarcerated females by Phillips, Sellbom, Ben-Porath, and Patrick (2014) employed the PPI and Minnesota Multiphasic Personality Inventory-2-Restructured Form (MMPI-2-PF) and used data from a prior study by Sellbom et al. (2012) to conclude that both (forensic) female and male psychopathy are consistent with the original PPI two-factor model. Further, both studies compared two instruments (PPI and MMPI-2-PF) rather than necessarily "testing" the structure of psychopathy. Since the scales of the PPI were originally derived from pre-existing instruments, including MMPI, correlations between the two instruments may be more connected to measurement error than underlying psychopathy. Similarly, Poythress et al. (2010) used a large offender sample to contrast the PPI with Levenson's Primary and Secondary Psychopathy (LPSP) scales using the PCL-R as reference due to its recognition as the "most extensively validated measure of psychopathy for offenders" (ibid., p. 214), concluding that PPI offers a more valid measure of psychopathy than the LPSP when compared to PCL-R results. However, it is significant to note that their correlations for PPI Factor 1 of $r = .25$ and for PPI Factor 2 of $r = .39$ recognises that the PPI factors operationalise psychopathy in a distinctly different fashion than PCL-R factors. They thus argue that PPI factor 1 is more akin to the "boldness" phenotype of the triarchic model while PCL-R factor 1 is more closely aligned to "meanness".

An interesting study intended to examine the characteristics that discriminate between various manifestations of psychopathy undertaken by Ray, Poythress, Weir, and Rickelm (2009) specifically explored how scores on impulsivity-related traits can distinguish between primary (as measured by PPI factor1) and secondary (PPI factor 2) psychopathy. They found that urgency and lack of perseverance in particular were associated with Self-Centred Impulsivity but not Fearless Dominance.

Community Sample Studies

One of the earliest studies (Benning et al. 2003) conducted with 353 male participants from the Minnesota Twin Registry supported the two dominant factors of Lilienfeld and Andrews (1996), namely PPI-1 or Fearless Dominance and PPI-2 or Self-Centred Impulsivity, with a third factor (PPI-3) consisting solely of the Cold-heartedness subscale. Uzieblo, Verschuere, Van den Bussche, and Crombez (2010) examined the factor structure using a Belgian community sample of 675 participants and found little support for a two-factor model of the PPI-R, notably that the *blame externalization* subscale had a low factor loading to PPI-R 2 and the *stress immunity* subscale had a low factor loading on PPI-R 1. They also argue for the inclusion of *coldheartedness* as a third (PPI-R 3) factor on the basis of its focus on lack of empathy and guilt, and relation to associated (external) factors such as low enjoyment of friendships, low affective and cognitive empathy, and high scores in callousness, low sentimentality.

Anestis, Caron, and Carbonell (2011) conducted a study with 360 undergraduates of the impact of gender on the factor structure of the PPI-R using confirmatory factor analysis, initially finding inadequate fit from all 3 previous proposed factor structure models (one-, two- and three-factor models) of the PPI. However, when group analyses were conducted, there was support for fit of both one- and two-factor models. The PPI-R was found to have utility when gender differences are separated. In a study of 501 business executives (Croom, 2017), not only was significant difference found in total level of PPI scores between males and females (males scoring statistically higher than females in the PPI-R Total scale), but the nature of the dominant construct also was significant. Males scoring high in psychopathy (i.e. PPI-R T scores greater than 1.5 SD above mean or $T > 65$) were characterised by a high prevalence of the Fearlessness, Stress Immunity and Cold-heartedness subscales, while females scoring above 65 in PPI-R T scores were characterised by high scores in the Rebellious Nonconformity subscale.

In further analysis of model fit, results revealed that it was difficult to generate an acceptable model fit using the short form PPI-R (Croom & Svetina, 2019 [in review]). The results suggested that the construct of psychopathy, as measured by the PPI-R and its various subscales, was difficult to capture in the sample of business executives. However, amongst the factor analyses conducted, the most convincing evidence to support valid interpretation of psychopathy was observed with regards to Fearless Dominance and Self-Centred Impulsivity, separately. Specifically, Fearless Dominance was supported in the study as a second-factor model with Social Influence (SoI), Fearlessness (FE) and Stress Immunity (SI) as first-order factors, suggesting that items on the subscales related to SoI, FE and SI relate to a larger construct of Fearless Dominance. Similarly, Self-Centred Impulsivity was supported as a second-order factor with Machiavellian Egocentricity, Blame Externalisation, Rebellious Nonconformance, and Carefree Nonplanfulness as first-order factors, again suggesting that items related to ME, BE, RN and CN are related to Self-Centred Impulsivity. Moreover, it was difficult to find support as to how these subconstructs (alongside Cold-heartedness) relate to each other.

Summarising the PPI-R in Community and Forensic Studies

In their meta-analysis of studies employing the PPI and PPI-R, Ruchensky et al. (2018) found that the higher-order structure of both PPI and PPI-R between forensic and community sample studies differed in "meaningful ways" (p. 713), with the Stress Immunity scale being a significant difference—forensic samples demonstrated a strong negative correlation between stress immunity and both narcissistic and callous unemotional attributes in offenders. For such samples, the fearlessness scale was associated not with Fearless Dominance factor, but with Self-Centred Impulsivity. Ruchensky et al. (2018) thus appears to highlight the distinctive taxonic qualities of psychopathy and its manifestations between offenders, general population and "successful" psychopaths. Neumann, Uzieblo, Crombez, and Hare (2013) note the differences between community and offender sample correlations between Fearless Dominance and Self-Centred Impulsivity, arguing that the former scale items lack the sensitivity to discern between offenders, non-offenders, psychopaths and non-psychopaths.

Intriguingly, Chapman, Gremore, and Farmer (2003) conducted a study of females, both community and forensic (correctional) samples, but found no difference in PPI sample means and further concluded that because the subscales of Cold-heartedness, Social Potency and Stress Immunity had non-significant or negative correlations with other PPI subscales, low or negative component loadings from their principal components analysis (PCA) and relatively small or insignificant correlations with other psychopathy measure, they may "largely assess something other than the psychopathy construct among female inmates" (p. 171).

Relating PPI-R to Other Personality and Psychological Instruments

Five-Factor Model

Studies to link the five-factor model (FFM) of personality (Ross et al., 2009) used a mixed forensic/community sample to examine the PPI with the FFM (using NEO-PI-R and NEO-FFI). Fearless Dominance was found to be closely associated with low Neuroticism, high Extraversion and low Agreeableness, while Impulsive Antisociality (the PPI's original term for Self-Centred Impulsivity) was significantly associated with high Neuroticism and low Agreeableness and Conscientiousness. Cold-heartedness was significantly predicted by low Neuroticism, Extraversion, Openness and Agreeableness.

Lynam has been associated with a series of studies using the FFM to classify psychopathy (Lynam & Miller, 2015; Lynam & Widiger, 2007; Miller, Lynam, Widiger, & Leukefeld, 2001) in which the association between psychopathy and low levels of agreeableness, low levels of self-consciousness and vulnerability (from the Neuroticism scale) and high assertiveness (from the Extraversion scale) has been tested. Lynam and Miller (2015) used an interesting approach to review prior studies by

Table 5.1 Association between psychopathy and traits in the five-factor model of personality

Psychopathy is most positively associated with FFM traits of	Psychopathy is most negatively associated with traits of
Angry hostility	Extroversion (specifically, warmth)
Impulsivity	Agreeableness
Gregariousness	Conscientiousness
Assertiveness	Openness
Activity	Anxiety
Excitement seeking	Depression
Anger	Self-consciousness
Anxiety	Vulnerability

firstly consulting fifteen experts in the field of psychopathy to characterise the "prototypical" psychopath (which they describe as the "classic Cleckley" psychopath) and then they reviewed a number of studies (see Lynam & Widiger, 2007; Mullins-Sweatt, Glover, Derefinko, Miller, & Widiger, 2010; Smith & Lilienfeld, 2013) to compare prototypical psychopaths with so-called successful psychopaths. Their review of existing studies concluded that a significant difference exists between prototypical psychopaths, who score highly on impulsiveness and excitement seeking, and low in anxiety, depression, self-consciousness, vulnerability, warmth, openness to feelings, low in all aspect of Agreeableness, as well as low in dutifulness, self-discipline and deliberation. The prototypical psychopath is also high in impulsiveness, assertiveness and excitement seeking, openness to actions and competence. Successful psychopaths tend to score average on all of these same traits and were thus associated with antagonism and low Neuroticism and high Extraversion. Heroes, however, were characterised as "an emotionally stable extravert" (ibid., p. 621). Table 5.1 highlights the relationship between psychopathy and the FFM across studies (Lynam, Whiteside, & Jones, 1999; Miller et al., 2001; Ross, Lutz, & Bailley, 2004).

Psychopathy Checklist Revised (PCL-R)

Often described as the "gold standard" of psychopathy assessments, the PCL-R is "the most extensively validated measure of psychopathy for offenders" (Poythress et al., 2010, p. 214) and as such arguably provides a different assessment of psychopathy to that focused on community, non-offender and "successful" psychopathy. Its structure and assessment method differs from the PPI-R in a number of important ways. Firstly, the PCL-R consists of 4 factors (shown in Fig. 5.2), including antisocial behaviour as a factor which reflects the focus of the PCL-R as an assessment employed with criminal, incarcerated populations.

Second, the method of assessment includes review of medical and criminal records, health and psychological history and face-to-face interviews, which is markedly different to the sole use of self-reporting by respondents in PPI-R assessment.

A number of studies have set out to evaluate the PPI-R with reference to the PCL-R. Poythress et al. (2010), for example, used the PCL-R as a benchmark to compare and contrast Levenson's Primary and Secondary Psychopathy scales (LPSP) with the PPI-R, finding the latter

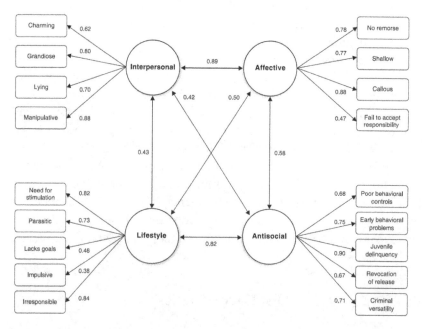

Fig. 5.2 The PCL-R structure of psychopathy

to be more statistically correlated to the PCL-R factor structure. However, they emphasise that their findings do not imply that the PPI-R and PCL-R factors are isomorphic. Using external correlates, Benning et al. (2003) found parallels between the PPI-R and PCL-R in the assessment of both the emotional-interpersonal and the antisocial deviance features of psychopathy, and regression analysis also found associations between the PPI-R Fearless Dominance factor (PPI-I) and PCL-R factor 1 (emotional-interpersonal factors). In terms of PPI-R Self-Centred Impulsivity factor (PPI-II), they found a strong association with antisocial behaviour, impulsiveness and thus "suggest a link between PPI-II and the externalising factor of psychopathology" (Benning et al., 2003, p. 346), which was also supported by the study of Berardino et al. (2005) who found a connection between PPI-II and deviant antisocial behaviour. Tonnaer, Maaike, Sijtsma, Uzieblo, and Lilienfeld (2013) found correlations of between .39 and .42 of total PCL-R to PPI-R scores. It is worth noting, however, that the correspondence in *factor structures* of the PPI-R and PCL-R has been found lacking in a number of studies. While Malterer, Lilienfeld, Neumann, and Newman (2010) found identical moderate correlations to those of Tonnaer et al. (2013) between the total scores of the PCL-R and PPI-R (at .39–.42), they did not find any direct relationship between the factor structures of the two instruments, which was also the conclusion of Copestake, Gray, and Snowden (2011), who conclude that it is inappropriate to consider the factor structure of the two instruments as being synonymous. Miller and Lynam (2012) conducted a meta-analysis of PPI studies and found that the PPI-R's Fearless Dominance factor and PCL-R Factor 1 shared only 4% of their variance and thus, contrary to the assertion by Benning et al. (2003), the construct of the two factors are not similar.

The fact that the PCL-R was developed primarily for use with offender populations has been seen to have a significant impact on how its measurement results compare to the PPI-R, developed for non-forensic/offender samples. Furthermore, there are likely differences between the two measures due to their data collection method, the PPI-R being a self-report tool. Issues of validity and bias are largely addressed in the PPI-R instrument, using items to help evaluate validity. One of the challenges with self-report survey methods using long questionnaires is careless response

(Meade & Craig, 2012) which includes *content responsive faking* (including social desirability bias) and *content nonresponsivity* (such as random response). In designing psychometric surveys, there has long been concern for issues of bias in participant response (Tourangeau, Rips, & Rasinski, 2000). However, in using the PPI-R, three major validity scales are incorporated into the survey itself (Lilienfeld & Widows, 2005)—Virtuous Responding (VR), Deviant Responding (DR) and Inconsistent Responding (IR). These scales provide the ability for screening responses to discount invalid or biased/faked responses.

Other Psychopathy Measures and the PPI-R

Berardino et al. (2005) used MMPI-2 and ASP scales to test discriminant validity (the distinctiveness or lack of overlap between individual items and scales) of the PPI and concluded that the PPI-R also offers incremental validity (or predictive ability) beyond these measures. In a network analysis comparing the PPI-SF with three other psychopathy measures—the LSRP, Personality Assessment Inventory-Antisocial Features subscale (PAI-ANT) and the Self-Report Psychopathy Scale-II (SRP-II), Tsang and Salekin (2018) set out to discern the core traits of psychopathy common to these measures. Manipulativeness/low agreeableness were found to be core traits associated with psychopathy and central to the PPI-SF (as well as the LSRP and PAI-ANT) and Impulsive Nonconformity was also central to the PPI-SF.

The meta-analysis by Miller and Lynam (2012) provided a well-structured summary of the relationship between PPI-R factors and items and scales across a number of instruments, presented in Fig. 5.3.

The comparison of PPI-R factor scales with the FFM, Multidimensional Personality Questionnaire Behavioral Activation Scale and the Diagnostics and Statistical Manual of Mental Disorders (DSM-V) criteria related to a range of personality disorders all help to provide a robust overview of association between the PPI-R and traits and scales most commonly associated with psychopathy.

Mean ES	PPI F1 (Fearless Dominance)	PPI F2 (Self-centered Impulsivity)
>.50	Behavioral inhibition scale (-) FFM Neuroticism FFM Extraversion (+)	Factor 2 psychopathy (+) MPQ constraint (-) Impulsivity (+) Antisocial PD (+) Psychopathy total (+) FFM conscientiousness (-)
.40-.49	Sensation seeking (+) MPQ Positive emotionality (+) BAS: Fun seeking (+)	FFM Agreeableness (-) Borderline PD (+) Externalizing (+) Sensation seeking (+) Aggression (+)
.30-.39	Narcissism/narcissistic PD (+) BAS total (+) Anxiety (-) Internalizing (-) MPQ negative emotionality (-)	Factor 1 psychopathy (+) Antisocial behaviour (+) MPQ Negative emotionality (+) BAS: fun seeking (+) FFM Neuroticism (+)
.20-.29	BAS: Drive (+) FFM openness (+) Factor 1 psychopathy (+) Mood (-)	Internalizing (+) Substance use (+) Anxiety (+) Empathy (-) Narcissism/narcissistic PD (+) Mood (+)
.10-.19	MPQ constraint (-) Borderline PD (-) Psychopathy total (+) Antisocial behaviour (+) FFM agreeableness (-)	BAS Total (+) MPQ positive emotionality (-) Behavioural inhibition scale (-) FFM extraversion (-)
<.10	Empathy (-) BAS: reward responsiveness (+) Factor 2 psychopathy (+) Antisocial PD (+) Substance use (+) Externalizing (+) Aggression (-) Impulsivity (-) FFM conscientiousness (-)	BAS: Drive (+) FFM openness (+) BAS: reward responsiveness (+)

Fig. 5.3 Summary of meta-analytically derived effect sizes for PPI factors 1&2 (*Note* ES = effect size; FFM = Five Factor Model; MPQ = Multidimensional Personality Questionnaire; BAS = Behavioural Activation Scale; PD = Personality Disorder. Reported by Miller and Lynam [2012, p. 317])

Link Between PPI-R and Profession

Noncriminal psychopathy had relatively little attention until the last decade or so. The association between profession and psychopathy emerged as an area of interest to include a stream of studies related to "successful" psychopaths—those professions or professionals for whom psychopathic traits are a valuable, if not necessary, prerequisite for effectiveness. In his book, *The Wisdom of Psychopaths*, Dutton (2012) cites ten careers with the highest incidence of psychopathy (in order): CEOs, lawyers, broadcast media performers, salespeople, surgeons, journalists, police officers, clergy, chefs and civil servants. He also notes the association between high-risk environments (such as bomb disposal technicians and special forces troops) and psychopathy.

As discussed in Chapter 3, there have been a number of empirical studies of workplace psychopathy, and a notable early contribution here was the study by Board and Fritzon (2005) which compared business managers with psychiatric patients and hospitalised criminals, identified some significantly elevated personality traits in the managers, specifically histrionic, narcissistic and obsessive personality disorders. Although the authors did not use a specific measure of psychopathy, the findings were significant in terms of drawing attention to the existence of dysfunctional personality constructs within a high-functioning sample.

Direct assessment of the association between psychopathy and profession using the PPI-R has been employed in a study of hospital doctors (Pegrum & Pearce, 2015) in which they found very high frequency (78%) of their study sample scoring highly for stress immunity, followed by 26% for carefree nonplanfulness, 24% for cold-heartedness and 22% for fearlessness. They also found a higher mean PPI score amongst pediatricians and surgeons, while teaching hospital doctors has significantly higher mean PPI score than district hospitals.

In studies of undergraduate students, Clow and Scott (2007) compared two majors (criminal justice and nursing) and found a significantly higher score for criminal justice majors than nursing indicated by elevated scores in the Machiavellian Egocentricity dimension, while Wilson and McCarthy's (2011) study of arts, science, commerce and law students found a higher score for commerce students than the remaining 3 subject majors. Neither of these studies is a systematic study of the relationship between psychopathy and career choice (using the proxy of university major), according to Lilienfeld, Latzman, Watts, Smith, and Dutton (2014), rather they present a limited focus using convenience samples of undergraduate students, with the attendant problems arising from such samples in terms of narrow demographic profile (Henrich, Heine, & Norenzayan, 2010).

Conclusion

The PPI-R is perhaps one of the most frequently employed instruments in the field of psychopathy, after the PCL-R, and its focus on non-forensic population studies provides significant utility for examining psychopathic characteristics in a wide range of settings. It is perhaps indicative of the evolution of the study of psychopathy that the PPI-R characterises the disorder in a distinctly different way to forensic instruments, particularly the PCL-R. Its dimensional nature provides for distinctly different manifestations of psychopathy, and thus provides informed insights into dark triad, corporate, noncriminal and other areas of interest to researchers of psychopathic personality disorder. Factor analyses of the PPI-R have often reflected the innate characteristics of the sample studied—from undergraduate students through to corporate executives. Clearly, there will be difference between such groups, and the PPI-R has been found to recognise these differences. Notwithstanding the differences shown in the factor analyses discussed, the PPI-R serves to inform the ongoing study of psychopathy and underscore the wide potential array of consequences that can arise from psychopathic individuals in any social and organisational setting.

References

Anestis, J. C., Caron, K. M., & Carbonell, J. L. (2011). Examining the impact of gender on the factor structure of the Psychopathic Personality Inventory-Revised. *Assessment.* https://doi.org/10.1177/1073191111403243.

Babiak, P., Neumann, C. S., & Hare, R. D. (2010). Corporate psychopathy: Talking the walk. *Behavioral Sciences & the Law, 28*(2), 174–193. https://doi.org/10.1002/bsl.925.

Benning, S. D., Patrick, C. J., Hicks, B. M., Blonigen, D. M., & Krueger, R. F. (2003). Factor structure of the Psychopathic Personality Inventory: Validity and implications for clinical assessment. *Psychological Assessment, 15*(3), 340.

Benning, S. D., Patrick, C. J., Salekin, R. T., & Leistico, A.-M. R. (2005). Convergent and discriminant validity of psychopathy factors assessed via self-report a comparison of three instruments. *Assessment, 12*(3), 270–289.

Berardino, S. D., Meloy, J. R., Sherman, M., & Jacobs, D. (2005). Validation of the Psychopathic Personality Inventory on a female inmate sample. *Behavioral Sciences & the Law, 23*(6), 819–836.

Board, B., & Fritzon, K. (2005). Disordered personalities at work. *Psychology, Crime & Law, 11*(1), 17–32.

Chapman, A. L., Gremore, T. M., & Farmer, R. F. (2003). Psychometric analysis of the Psychopathic Personality Inventory (PPI) with female inmates. *Journal of Personality Assessment, 80*(2), 164–172.

Cleckley, H. (1941). *The mask of sanity.* Augusta: C.V. Mosby Co.

Clow, K. A., & Scott, H. S. (2007). Psychopathic traits in nursing and criminal justice majors: A pilot study. *Psychological Reports, 100*(2), 495–498.

Copestake, S., Gray, N. S., & Snowden, R. J. (2011). A comparison of a self-report measure of psychopathy with the Psychopathy Checklist-Revised in a UK sample of offenders. *Journal of Forensic Psychiatry & Psychology, 22*(2), 169–182.

Croom, S. (2017). *An examination of the incidence of psychopathic personality disorder in supply executives compared to general business executives* (MSc Psychology). University of Liverpool, Liverpool, UK.

Croom, S., & Svetina, M. (2019, in review). *Psychometric properties of the psychopathic personality inventory: Application to high-functioning business population.*

Dutton, K. (2012). *The wisdom of psychopaths: What saints, spies and serial killers.* Scientific American / Farrar, Straus and Giroux.

Edens, J. F., Marcus, D. K., Lilienfeld, S., & Poythress, N. G., Jr. (2006). Psychopathic, not psychopath: Taxometric evidence for the dimensional structure of psychopathy. *Journal of Abnormal Psychology, 115*(1), 131.

Gonsalves, V. M., McLawsen, J. E., Huss, M. T., & Scalora, M. J. (2013). Factor structure and construct validity of the Psychopathic Personality Inventory in a forensic sample. *International Journal of Law and Psychiatry, 36*(2), 176–184.

Hare, R. D., & Neumann, C. S. (2008). Psychopathy as a clinical and empirical construct. *Annual Review of Clinical Psychology, 4,* 217–246.

Henrich, J., Heine, S. J., & Norenzayan, A. (2010). The weirdest people in the world? *Behavioral and Brain Sciences, 33*(2–3), 61–83.

Lilienfeld, S., & Andrews, B. P. (1996). Development and preliminary validation of a self-report measure of psychopathic personality traits in noncriminal population. *Journal of Personality Assessment, 66*(3), 488.

Lilienfeld, S., & Widows, M. R. (2005). *Psychopathic Personality Inventory-Revised (PPI-R) professional manual.* Odessa, FL: Psychological Assessment Resources.

Lilienfeld, S., Latzman, R. D., Watts, A. L., Smith, S. F., & Dutton, K. (2014). Correlates of psychopathic personality traits in everyday life: Results from a large community survey. *Frontiers in Psychology, 5*, 740.

Lynam, D., & Miller, J. (2015). Psychopathy from a basic trait perspective: The utility of a five-factor model approach. *Journal of Personality, 83*(6), 611–626.

Lynam, D., Whiteside, S., & Jones, S. (1999). Self-reported psychopathy: A validation study. *Journal of Personality Assessment, 73*(1), 110.

Lynam, D., & Widiger, T. (2007). Using a general model of personality to identify the basic elements of psychopathy. *Journal of Personality Disorders, 21*(2), 160–178.

Malterer, M. B., Lilienfeld, S. O., Neumann, C. S., & Newman, J. P. (2010). Concurrent validity of the Psychopathic Personality Inventory with offender and community samples. *Assessment, 17*(1), 3–15.

Marcus, D. K., Fulton, J. J., & Edens, J. F. (2012). The two-factor model of psychopathic personality: Evidence from the Psychopathic Personality Inventory. *Personality Disorders: Theory, Research, and Treatment, 3*(2), 140–154.

Meade, A. W., & Craig, S. B. (2012). Identifying careless responses in survey data. *Psychological Methods, 17*(3), 437.

Miller, J., & Lynam, D. (2012). An examination of the Psychopathic Personality Inventory's nomological network: A meta-analytic review. *Personality Disorders: Theory, Research, and Treatment, 3*(3), 305–326. https://doi.org/10.1037/a0024567.

Miller, J., Lynam, D., Widiger, T., & Leukefeld, C. (2001). Personality disorders as extreme variants of common personality dimensions: Can the five factor model adequately represent psychopathy? *Journal of Personality, 69*(2), 253–276.

Mullins-Sweatt, S. N., Glover, N. G., Derefinko, K. J., Miller, J. D., & Widiger, T. A. (2010). The search for the successful psychopath. *Journal of Research in Personality, 44*(4), 554–558.

Neumann, C. S., Malterer, M. B., & Newman, J. P. (2008). Factor structure of the Psychopathic Personality Inventory (PPI): Findings from a large incarcerated sample. *Psychological Assessment, 20*(2), 169–174. https://doi.org/10.1037/1040-3590.20.2.169.

Neumann, C. S., Uzieblo, K., Crombez, G., & Hare, R. D. (2013). Understanding the Psychopathic Personality Inventory (PPI) in terms of the unidimensionality, orthogonality, and construct validity of PPI-I and -II. *Personality Disorders: Theory, Research, and Treatment, 4*(1), 77–79.

Nikolova, N. (2010). *The Psychopathic Personality Inventory-Revised: Evaluation of its psychometric properties, incremental validity and moderating effects of gender in a correctional sample* (PhD thesis). Simon Fraser University.

Patrick, C. J., Edens, J. F., Poythress, N. G., Lilienfeld, S., & Benning, S. D. (2006). Construct validity of the Psychopathic Personality Inventory two-factor model with offenders. *Psychological Assessment, 18*(2), 204–208. https://doi.org/10.1037/1040-3590.18.2.204.

Patrick, C. J., Fowles, D. C., & Krueger, R. F. (2009). Triarchic conceptualization of psychopathy: Developmental origins of disinhibition, boldness, and meanness. *Development and Psychopathology, 21*(Special Issue 03), 913–938. https://doi.org/10.1017/s0954579409000492.

Pegrum, J., & Pearce, O. (2015). A stressful job: Are surgeons psychopaths? *The Bulletin of the Royal College of Surgeons of England, 97*(8), 331–334.

Phillips, T. R., Sellbom, M., Ben-Porath, Y. S., & Patrick, C. J. (2014). Further development and construct validation of MMPI-2-RF indices of global psychopathy, fearless-dominance, and impulsive-antisociality in a sample of incarcerated women. *Law and Human Behavior, 38*(1), 34.

Poythress, N. G., Lilienfeld, S. O., Skeem, J. L., Douglas, K. S., Edens, J. F., Epstein, M., & Patrick, C. J. (2010). Using the PCL-R to help estimate the validity of two self-report measures of psychopathy with offenders. *Assessment, 17*(2), 206–219.

Ray, J. V., Poythress, N. G., Weir, J. M., & Rickelm, A. (2009). Relationships between psychopathy and impulsivity in the domain of self-reported personality features. *Personality and Individual Differences, 46*(2), 83–87.

Ross, S. R., Benning, S. D., Patrick, C. J., Thompson, A., & Thurston, A. (2009). Factors of the Psychopathic Personality Inventory: Criterion-related validity and relationship to the BIS/BAS and five-factor models of personality. *Assessment, 16*(1), 71–87.

Ross, S. R., Lutz, C., & Bailley, S. (2004). Psychopathy and the five factor model in a noninstitutionalized sample: A domain and facet level analysis. *Journal of Psychopathology and Behavioral Assessment, 26*(4), 213–223. https://doi.org/10.1023/B:JOBA.0000045337.48535.a5.

Ruchensky, J. R., Edens, J. F., Corker, K. S., Donnellan, M. B., Witt, E. A., & Blonigen, D. M. (2018). Evaluating the structure of psychopathic personality traits: A meta-analysis of the Psychopathic Personality Inventory. *Psychological Assessment, 30*(6), 707.

Sellbom, M., Ben-Porath, Y. S., Patrick, C. J., Wygant, D. B., Gartland, D. M., & Stafford, K. P. (2012). Development and construct validation of MMPI-2-RF indices of global psychopathy, fearless-dominance, and impulsive-antisociality. *Personality Disorders: Theory, Research, and Treatment, 3*(1), 17.

Skeem, J. L., Polaschek, D. L. L., Patrick, C. J., & Lilienfeld, S. O. (2011). Psychopathic personality: Bridging the gap between scientific evidence and public policy. *Psychological Science in Public Interest, 12*, 95–162.

Smith, S. F., & Lilienfeld, S. O. (2013). Psychopathy in the workplace: The knowns and unknowns. *Aggression and Violent Behavior, 18*(2), 204–218.

Tonnaer, F., Maaike, C., Sijtsma, K., Uzieblo, K., & Lilienfeld, S. (2013). Screening for psychopaths: A validation with norm scores of the Dutch Psychopathic Personality Inventory-screening device. *Journal of Psychopathology and Behavioral Assessment, 35*(2), 153–161.

Tourangeau, R., Rips, L., & Rasinski, K. (2000). *The psychology of survey response.* Cambridge: Cambridge University Press.

Tsang, S., & Salekin, R. (2018). *The network of psychopathic personality traits: A network analysis of four self-report measures of psychopathy.* Personality Disorders: Theory, Research, and Treatment.

Tsang, S., Salekin, R., Coffey, C., & Cox, J. (2017). A comparison of self-report measures of psychopathy among nonforensic samples using item response theory analyses. *Psychological Assessment, 30*(3), 311–327.

Uzieblo, K., Verschuere, B., Van den Bussche, E., & Crombez, G. (2010). The validity of the Psychopathic Personality Inventory-Revised in a community sample. *Assessment, 17*(3), 334–346.

Wilson, M. S., & McCarthy, K. (2011). Greed is good? Student disciplinary choice and self-reported psychopathy. *Personality and Individual Differences, 51*(7), 873–876.

6

A Critical Review of the Measurement of Potential Risk-Posing Personality Traits and Their Application in the Workplace

Caroline Turner and Belinda Board

Introduction

For organisations, the cost of making poor talent decisions is high. The cost of a poor hiring decision in general managerial roles, for example, is reportedly between four to 15 times the incumbent's annual salary (Smart, 2012). This does not account for the associated covert costs such as potential litigation or labour disputes, poor team morale, culture, opportunity loss and potential reputational risk for the business, all of which increase exponentially as the seniority of the appointment increases. It's unsurprising then that organisations rely heavily on occupational assessment to minimise risk around people decisions and to provide a level of comfort

C. Turner
Royal Holloway University, Egham, UK
e-mail: caroline@cjt.london

B. Board (✉)
University of Hertfordshire, Hertfordshire, UK
e-mail: Belinda.board@peoplewise.co.uk

© The Author(s) 2020
K. Fritzon et al., *Corporate Psychopathy*,
https://doi.org/10.1007/978-3-030-27188-6_6

that their employees will demonstrate desirable and positive workplace behaviours (Furnham, 2008).

Assessment of personality, while at times contested, is generally accepted (where valid instruments are used) as a more robust and reliable method of understanding an employee's (or potential employee's) likely behaviours in the workplace than the still popular unstructured interviews and reference checks (Furnham, 2008). Typically, the approach in deploying personality measures in occupational selection is to clarify the traits that are likely to be linked to desirable workplace or role outcomes (e.g. conscientiousness or assertiveness) and to seek candidates who demonstrate higher levels of these traits. In other words, the approach is to focus on positive attributes, on the assumption that lower scores on these dimensions will result in less desirable behaviours.

An exception is the use of specific measures of counterproductive work behaviours (CWBs) that seek to ascertain the extent to which an individual is likely to engage in deliberate actions that harm the organisation or its members (Cohen, 2016). These assessments appeal to businesses seeking to understand whether employees or prospective employees are likely to engage in undesirable behaviours such as theft, dishonesty, bullying, violence, sabotage or unwarranted absenteeism. These assessments typically require respondents to indicate the extent to which they have to (or would) demonstrate these behaviours. In this instance, however, it is specific *behaviours* that are targeted. Some measures of integrity seek to uncover the underlying traits driving these behaviours, such as honesty or regard for others (Furnham, 2008). Integrity measures are a subset of personality assessment and as such usually embody a similar assumption that high levels of positive attributes (e.g. altruism) will result in an increase in desirable behaviours and decrease in CWBs.

Recently, however, there has been increasing interest in the so-called dark side of personality, with researchers claiming that workplace failure may be more related to "having undesirable qualities than lacking desirable ones" (Hogan & Hogan, 2001, p. 41). These undesirable qualities make up the "dark side" of personality and are more difficult to detect because they often coincide with well-demonstrated social skills that tend to result in favourable impressions (in the short term at least). However, the longer-term repercussions of these "dark" attributes may be significant for both individual and organisational well-being. As a result, measures of "dark" or risky personality attributes are gaining popularity in occupational assessment (Smith & Lilienfeld, 2013). These focus on identifying risk factors and potential "derailers" for the individual, their co-workers and the organisation.

This chapter considers the so-called dark-side or risk-posing personality traits in the workplace and their implications, beginning with an attempt to define and understand how these are conceptualised. Furthermore, a growing body of researchers are beginning to challenge the seemingly intuitive conclusion that these traits are by definition and without exception negative or maladaptive (Babiak & Hare, 2006; Smith & Lilienfeld, 2013) arguing that certain "dark-side" personality traits may in fact be adaptive or enabling in certain contexts. This notion is considered and explored. Thereafter, attention is diverted to assessments available for the identification of potentially risk-posing personality traits in occupational settings. A review and critique of these assessments and their applications are offered. It is necessary to note here that criteria for inclusion in this review are that the instruments selected must have been developed for occupational (rather than clinical) use and that they were specifically designed to identify and mitigate risk in predicting workplace behaviour. The focus then moves to next steps and suggestions for future research.

Defining "Dark-Side" or Risk-Posing Personality Traits and Their Impact in the Workplace

Personality in the context of occupational assessment is generally understood to represent pervasive, enduring behavioural patterns or preferences (Hogan & Hogan, 2009). Distinguishing between the so-called bright side and dark side of personality is a relatively recent endeavour in applying personality to organisational behaviour (Kaiser, Le Breton, & Hogan, 2015). While the "bright side" can be understood to apply to those traits generally considered to be adaptive, positive and enabling (e.g. Agreeableness and Conscientious in the well-known five-factor model) (Kaiser et al., 2015), the "dark side" refers to those traits typically considered maladaptive, derailing or detrimental.

In occupational settings, the notion of "dark-side" personality traits usually refers to personality disorders (PDs) that, while subclinical, are sufficiently prevalent to impact interactions or performance at work (Furnham & Crump, 2014). This view follows the dimensional (rather than categorical) representation of PDs, which holds that the characteristics of PDs are exaggerated or extreme forms of normal behaviour rather than qualitatively distinct from normal behaviour (Board & Fritzon, 2005). From this position, it is likely that so-called normal individuals may in fact also demonstrate less desirable personality traits in the workplace, which could in turn result in CWBs and/or impact interactions with colleagues.

Certain authors focus on particular PDs, such as psychopathy, and their impact on the workplace (Smith & Lilienfeld, 2013), while others focus on the broader "dark triad" of Psychopathy, Narcissism and Machiavellianism (Cohen, 2016). Other researchers, such as Moscoso and Salgado (2004, in Kaiser et al., 2015), identify 14 "dysfunctional personality styles" (Kaiser et al., 2015, p. 58). Hogan and Hogan (2001) propose a framework of 11 dimensions based on the Axis II dimensions outlined in the Diagnostic and Statistical Manual of Mental Disorders IV (DSM IV) (Kaiser et al., 2015).

The "dark side" has also been defined as the "impression people make when they let down their guard – when they are stressed, tired, or otherwise less vigilant about how they are perceived...rest[ing] on flawed assumptions about how one expects to be treated or how best to serve one's personal interests" (Kaiser et al., 2015, p. 58). This contrasts with "bright side" behaviours in evidence when people are doing their best to get along and get ahead (Hogan & Hogan, 2009).

As of yet, therefore, there does not appear to be a universally accepted taxonomy of "dark-side" traits in organisations (Kaiser et al., 2015). This is compounded by a lack of agreement around the impact and outcomes of these traits in the workplace.

The majority of the research that does exist in this area focuses, perhaps naturally, on the "toxicity" that is likely to result from the demonstration of "dark-side" traits in organisations (Smith & Lilienfeld, 2013). Hogan and Hogan (2009), for example, found that what they term "dysfunctional" personality traits linked to poor performance and impeded individuals' ability to capitalise on strengths identified in "bright side" measures. They confidently claim, therefore, that "dark-side" personality traits are "robust predictors of unsuccessful performance" (4). Furthermore, given that some PDs—in particular, psychopathy—have been identified as significant correlates and predictors of violence in other settings (Hare, 2003) conceptually, it seems logical to infer that these would result in similarly negative outcomes at work. Particularly, the link between counterproductive workplace behaviours (deliberate actions that result in harm to the organisation or to its members) and psychopathy has received considerable interest (Cohen, 2016), as has the link between psychopathic traits and white-collar crime and workplace bullying (Smith & Lilienfeld, 2013). Furthermore, researchers have shown interest in the impact of leaders with PD traits on subordinates' well-being (Kaiser et al., 2015) and, more broadly, on organisational culture as well as public perception of the organisation (Fennimore & Sementelli, 2016).

Findings have, however, not been as conclusive as one may expect in linking PD traits with negative workplace behaviours. In fact, only weak relationships have been found between CWBs and, for example, psychopathic traits (Cohen, 2016; Schutte et al., 2015). There are a number of possible explanations for these inconclusive results. These range from methodological flaws (Smith & Lilienfeld, 2013) (including choices around statistical modelling methods—for example, Landay, Harms, and Crede (2019) found that curvilinear relationships could obscure results if regression models were used that consider only high and low quantities of the traits under review) to a failure to consider the mediating effect of certain organisational variables such as perceptions of organisational politics and perceived accountability (Cohen, 2016).

Other explanations for these weaker correlations relate to the conceptualisation of the construct or PD. Some studies suggest (e.g. Benning, Patrick, Blonigen, Hicks, & Iacono, 2003; Harpur et al., 1989 in Smith & Lilienfeld, 2013) that, unlike those with certain diagnosed PDs, individuals with subclinical PD traits may tend to show higher levels of the affective and interpersonal aspects of PDs such as psychopathy (e.g. grandiosity, manipulativeness and lack of empathy) than the behavioural aspects (e.g. aggression and irresponsibility). They also assert that this is the reason that there may in fact be positive, or at least adaptive, outcomes linked to PD traits such as psychopathic traits at work.

This somewhat controversial claim (by definition psychological disorders are maladaptive) (Smith & Lilienfeld, 2013) is not new. One of the first major authors to explore psychopathy, Hervey Cleckley (1941) wrote of a psychopath who was in fact a successful businessman. Despite demonstrating pronounced psychopathic traits, this individual, apart from the "periodic spree" of irresponsible behaviour, tended to work industriously and contributed significantly to the business (in Smith & Lilienfeld, 2013, p. 206). Prominent authors in this field, Paul Babiak and Robert Hare (2006) also note that the organisational context, often characterised by flux, rapid change and transition, affording excitement and stimulation as well as opportunities to influence and demonstrate charisma, may in fact predispose psychopaths and other PDs to achieve at least a degree of success. This notion has received some empirical support. For instance, one study (Board & Fritzon, 2005) found that a senior business manager sample displayed significant elements of personality disorders, particularly those that pertain to the "emotional components" (17) of psychopathy. This finding not only provides support for the continuous distribution of personality disordered traits model (Board & Fritzon, 2005), but also suggests that PD traits may not always lead to wholly negative outcomes in the workplace (at least not for the individuals displaying them).

Successful PDs can be understood in terms of three competing models: subclinical manifestation, moderated expression and a dual-process perspective. The subclinical model proposes that the PD traits exist in a milder form in certain individuals who therefore exhibit fewer social transgressions than in clinical manifestations (although the core personality features are the same). The moderated expression model proposes that moderating factors (such as education, intelligence or environmental factors) influence the manifestation of the disorder. The dual-process model purports that in PDs such as psychopathy, the interpersonal and affective elements are distinct from the behavioural outcomes. In this model, psychopathy is considered a hybrid condition consisting of certain traits that may dispose the sufferer to either maladaptive or adaptive behaviours, dependant on personality and/or situational moderating variables (Smith & Lilienfeld, 2013).

The reality, however, is that, at present, relatively little is known about how "dark-side" traits are associated with corporate status, outcomes and performance (Babiak, Neumann, & Hare, 2010). However, whether the effects are likely to be positive or negative, individuals displaying "dark-side" tendencies are likely to have an impact on those around them and the businesses in which they operate. This has two major implications. Firstly, this is an area worthy of further research to fully understand the potential outcomes of potentially risk-posing personality traits in the workplace, and secondly, being able to reliably assess to predict whether individuals do in fact possess these traits would be incredibly valuable to businesses who may inadvertently or otherwise onboard these individuals.

The authors of this chapter acknowledge that certain so-called dark-side traits may in fact result in successful outcomes in certain contexts. For this reason, henceforth reference is made to potentially risk-based personality traits rather than "dark-side" traits. These potentially risk-based personality traits are defined as attributes that do not necessarily represent clinical personality disorders as they do not impair significant life functioning as required for a clinical diagnosis. Rather, they are elements of "normal" personality, which can nonetheless affect interpersonal functioning and judgement (Kaiser et al., 2015). Certainly, identifying these traits would have practical advantages for selecting and managing individuals, mitigating risk and creating productive and enabling work environments.

The Assessment of Potential Risk-Posing Personality Traits in the Workplace

Personality Measures—"Normal Range" or "Bright Side" Measures and the Case for the Assessment of Risk-Based Traits

Research has shown that well-chosen personality dimensions are moderately effective predictors of task performance, as well as reasonable predictors of how workers go about their jobs, or contextual performance (Hough, 1992; Salgado, 2003). Thus, where selected and applied appropriately, personality measures can "add significant incremental validity" to selection processes, "over and above cognitive ability testing" (Arnold et al., 2005 in Furnham, 2008, p. 39). It is unsurprising then that personality assessment remains popular in occupational settings.

Numerous assessments exist to measure personality. Type-based measures such as the Myers-Briggs Typology Indicator (MBTI) remain incredibly popular in occupational settings although the predictive validity for workplace outcomes is dubious at best (Furnham, 2008). This is largely because preferences do not equate with behaviours (a point strongly made by the test publishers themselves), along with the somewhat arbitrary point of differentiation for classification into one category versus another (at what point does an introvert become an extravert?). One critic, Hicks (1984 in Furnham, 2008, p. 86) points out that "even the [MBTI] manual provides less evidence for type than continuous trait-like measurement". Given, then, that it is difficult to predict even positive workplace outcomes on the back of type-based measures, predicting potential risk factors with these assessments is even more unlikely, although the framework does posit that certain types may be less comfortable with certain types of tasks or situations.

The trait model of personality is, therefore, more useful for predicting workplace outcomes. Over the last century, researchers have largely agreed on the basic underlying structure of personality distilling it into five core dimensions or traits, the Big Five: Openness, Conscientiousness, Extraversion, Agreeableness and Neuroticism (Furnham, 2008). To this, the HEXACO model added a sixth factor, Honesty-Humility. This dimension concerns an individual's approach to morality, social values, fairness, sincerity, greed avoidance and modesty (Muris, Merckelbach, Otgaar, & Meijer, 2017). Recent studies suggest that the two traits most relevant to all jobs are Neuroticism and Conscientiousness, with Furnham (2008, p. 39) highlighting a clear profile for successful managers: "low on Neuroticism (i.e. very stable), low on Agreeableness, average on Openness, high on Extraversion and very high on Conscientiousness". He asserts that while different jobs require different profiles, none benefit from high Neuroticism or low Conscientiousness (2008), which begin to point to potentially undesirable behaviours. Viewing these in conjunction with the additional

Honesty-Humility factor, to assess for the likelihood of acceptable inter-personal and values-based behaviours, should, therefore, give an indication of the likelihood of desirable traits and behaviours at work. Furthermore, "expanded versions" of trait measures such as the SHL OPQ32i assess traits such as Caring, Rule Following and Controlling, that may, at the extremes, point to potentially risky behaviours, albeit perhaps obliquely (SHL Occupational Personality Questionnaire, 2019 www.SHL.com).

What then, is the need for a specific focus on risk-based or potentially derailing personality factors in occupational assessment? Occupational psychologists have in fact been reticent to target these traits, perhaps for reasons beyond the (until recent) prevailing view that Big Five person-ality measures were sufficient in predicting workplace behaviours. These include concern around the infringement of candidates' legal rights or the inadvertent and unnecessary exclusion of those with mental health problems (Limits Technical Manual & User Guide). There is also perhaps concern around how to meaningfully assess these attributes, given the problem of "faking" and social desirability in occupational assessment.

However, there is a strong case to be made for the assessment of these traits, beyond the potential ramifications for organisations and individuals of failing to do so. Research in this area has shown that there are some correlations between Big Five measures and PD symptoms with, perhaps predictably, Neuroticism and Agreeableness being noteworthy correlations (positively and negatively, respectively) (De Clercq & De Fruyt, 2003). As expected, a study by Muris et al. (2017) examining the relationship between the Big Five and Dark Triad traits (Psychopathy, Narcissism and Machiavellianism) found negative correlations between the HEXACO trait of Honesty-Humility and all the dark-triad traits. However, certain dimensions, such as Extraversion, were found to correlate positively with PDs such as Narcissism (this makes sense as these individuals are typically outgoing, sociable and charming). These researchers also found a small but statistically significant correlation between Narcissism and Openness, which they explained via the feature of creativity (Muris et al., 2017). Therefore, it is possible to "miss" potential risk-based personality factors through the exclusive use of traditional or "bright side" measures that tend to take the view that the more of these traits in evidence, the better for workplace outcomes. Even an approach that notes risks of extreme scores on each dimension may miss the full picture as it is possible for an individual to score in the normal range for a trait such as conscientiousness, but also to score highly on a different measure of compulsivity and disinhibition (the extremes of conscientiousness) relative to others. This is because "traits are distributions, and people have probabilities of behaving in ways that correspond to every region of the distribution" (Limits Technical Manual & User Guide). Put simply, "bright side" and "dark-side" measures address different constructs, represented by different content domains. Therefore, preliminary research suggests that the inclusion of assessment of potential risk traits significantly enhances the predictive validity of occupational assessment and selection processes (Furnham, Hyde & Trickey, 2013; Rolland & De Fruyt, 2003).

While targetted measurement of potentially derailing personality factors may be a fairly new area of focus in the arena of occupational assessment, the notion of assessing for behavioural risk is not. In fact, integrity measures have long been used to predict the likelihood of negative or destructive CWBs. These assessments typically seek to ascertain either the degree to which individuals have engaged in these behaviours in the past (on the premise that past behaviour predicts future behaviour) or the existence of the underlying traits that could predict the likelihood of these behaviours (Furnham, 2008). It is the latter category that is of current interest in this discussion.

Assessments of Integrity

"Dark-side" behaviours or CWBs are those that pose harm to either the organisation or the individuals within them and include aggression, bullying, vandalism, absenteeism and theft (Furnham, 2008). The costs of such behaviours can be severe. For example, it is estimated that US businesses lose approximately 5% of their annual revenues to white-collar crime (O'Brien, 2017) with survey evidence suggesting that at least one-third of employees have stolen from their employer (Fine, 2013). And this does not take into account reputational damage or harm to individuals. Recent studies suggest that approximately 1.7 million Americans and 11% of British employees experience some kind of bullying including physical or verbal abuse, intimidation or sabotage (Appelbaum et al. in Baharom, Sharrfuddin, & Iqbal, 2017). While the real costs of these are difficult to quantify, it has been suggested that in the USA, workplace violence incurs costs of $4.2 billion annually (Bensimon in Baharom et al., 2017). It is little wonder then that organisations seek to identify individuals' propensity to engage in these behaviours via integrity testing. Broadly, integrity can be defined as "the adherence to a code of moral values" (Fine, 2013, p. 266).

Integrity assessments are measures designed to predict the likelihood of an individual's engaging in CWBs at work. They are either overt (i.e. upfront that it is integrity or the propensity to engage in CWBs being measured) or covert (basically, disguised as a personality assessment) (Furnham, 2008). In either case, they aim to investigate workplace attitudes and traits linked to moral, values-based or desirable (from the point of view of the organisation) behaviours. These tend to be traits such as dependability, prudence, honesty and conformity to rules (Fine 2013). These have been shown to correlate with the Big Five trait of conscientiousness (Murphy & Lee, 1994) as well as agreeableness and emotional stability (Marcus, Lee, & Ashton, 2007).

A large body of research exists to support the predictive validity of integrity assessments in relation to CWBs. Perhaps the largest of these was conducted by Ones, Viswesvaran, and Schmidt (1993) who conducted a large-scale meta-analytic study in which they analysed the results from 665 validity studies of over 25 instruments (Furnham, 2008). They reported validity of up to .47 for the prediction of CWBs (Fine, 2013). The type of CWB was found to be less relevant, as it was found that individuals likely to engage in one type of CWB were more likely to engage in others (Berry, Sackett, & Wiemann, 2007). This lends credence to the notion that there exists an underlying predilection (or "risk" trait or traits) that leads to the display of CWBs.

Ones et al. (1993) also reported that both overt and covert integrity tests are roughly equal in terms of predictive validity, and thus, there appears to be no basis to choose one type of test over another. For theft in particular, both overt and personality-oriented tests showed validity coefficients of .33 (Fine, 2013). On the whole, then, integrity tests show some validity with regard to the prediction of CWBs.

The biggest concern with integrity assessments, particularly overt ones, is the problem of fakeability—is it possible for people to "beat the test" and come out "looking virtuous when they are not?" (Furnham, 2008, p. 314). This is of concern in all self-report measures, but clearly particularly so when honesty is the construct being measured. Indeed, if responding in a socially desirable manner is considered synonymous with lying, then paradoxically, many integrity tests could have a "negative correlation with honesty" (Rust, 1999, p. 766). While the validity coefficients discussed above would suggest that this may not be as big a concern as one may think, it is still prudent to remember that most studies measured *self-reported* incidents of CWBs against integrity assessment results, rather than *actual incidents*. Furthermore, as it is likely that the majority of CWBs go undetected (Fine, 2013), a fairly rigorous approach to the application and selection of these assessments would seem warranted.

Integrity Assessments: The Giotto

The Giotto is based on the classical theory of Prudentius, who lived between 348 and 405 AD and compiled his theory of personality as composed of a series of conflicting vices (passions) and virtues (sentiments). In his framework, the Psychomachia, which depicts personality as a "battle of the mind", Prudentius posited that humankind is categorised by conflict between these vices on the one hand, and their corresponding virtues on the other. These were depicted by the artist Giotto di Bondone (1267–1377) as "justice/injustice, hope/despair, charity/envy, faith/idolatry, temperance/anger, fortitude/inconstancy and prudence/folly". The Giotto integrity test makes use of this structure as a framework for measuring integrity (Rust, 1999, p. 757). The Giotto, therefore, measures the following:

Prudence—work proficiency and cautiousness
Fortitude—work orientation and job commitment
Temperance—self-control and temperament
Justice—judgement ability
Faith—loyalty and dependability

Charity—honesty and trustworthiness
Hope—future orientation and ability to cope with change

The Giotto consists of 101 items that measure these seven scales. It comprises two parts, the first of which (Part A) being ipsative in nature, consisting of paired adjectives where respondents select the one that applies more closely to them. This forced-choice format is designed to address the problem of social desirability or faking, as each virtue is intrinsically desirable (the respondent in effect makes a decision as to which of these positive descriptors applies to them). Conversely, Part B represents the vices and consists of single items, each with a multiple-choice response format (Rust, 1999).

According to the test publishers, high scores provide a degree of protection against undesirable behaviours such as carelessness and the likelihood of causing /being involved in an accident, work absenteeism and lateness, disciplinary problems and hostility towards management and colleagues. They also state that high scores mitigate against the risk of likelihood of stealing company property, wasting resources, inability to cope with change, low self-confidence and/or anxiety along with the likelihood of being prone to dark sides of personality such as violence, hostility or intimidation. It is worth noting here that all scales are positively oriented and therefore high scores are considered to be favourable. Thus, the Giotto, while mitigating against risk, can be considered a "bright side" measure.

According to Rust (1999), a number of studies support the construct, concurrent and most importantly, predictive validity of the Giotto. He cites evidence of correlations between the fortitude, faith, charity and hope scales with supervisor ratings, with weaker support the justice scale. He notes less encouraging results for the prudence and temperance scales, but attributes this to the acknowledged unreliability of supervisor ratings and calls for further research into this instrument. The highest accolades he provides for the instrument relate to the overcoming of the "fakeability" aspect due to the ipsative format. However, other researchers (Meade, 2004; Tenopyr, 1988) note forced-choice response formats can cause psychometric issues, including difficulties in reliability estimation and challenges to construct validity.

Integrity Assessments: IP200

Consisting of 200 test items in a questionnaire format, the IP200 is marketed as the "flagship of the dedicated Integrity tests" (Integrity International, 2019). It is designed to measure individual integrity at work as well as "corporate integrity" as an organisational survey providing input as to the integrity of the entire organisation or departments, divisions or work groups.

The IP200 defines and measures eight factors pertaining to individual integrity (socialisation, trustworthiness, credibility, work ethic, integrity constraining attitudes to integrity, functional vs dysfunctional behaviour, manipulative abuse of power and values). Each of these is broken into further five subfactors (e.g. the trustworthiness factor explores reliability/dependability, honesty in practice, discretion, loyalty and moral conscientiousness). The focus shifts to corporate integrity in the ninth factor, transformation commitment and management, which expresses the respondent's perception of "how well his/her present or previous employer lives up to providing an acceptable corporate and managerial environment" as regards aspects such as empowerment and transparency (Integrity International).

As items were purposefully selected to increase face validity (Integrity International) and given the nature of the response format, which asks respondents to indicate the degree to which they agree that they would demonstrate particular behaviours (desirable and undesirable), the issue of transparency and social desirability is critical. To this end, the test developers have included the Monitor, Lie, Consistency and Exaggeration scale to assess the degree to which the respondent answered honestly and consistently. For the results of the profile to be considered valid, a minimum sten score of 6 should be achieved for this factor, to indicate that the respondent answered at least as openly and honestly as most.

However, given the transparency of the items, both for the integrity scales (e.g. "I have often before (for good reason) left a shop with goods not paid for") and for the Lie scale (e.g. "I have never lost my temper"), the issue of faking may not be adequately addressed. Additionally, a certain amount of education is required to complete this assessment (Grade 8), and so it could be argued that the majority of test-takers would be able to ascertain a way to beat the Lie scale while attaining favourable scores on the integrity factors.

Nonetheless, the test publishers report reliability coefficients ranging from .84 to .92 and validity results ranging from .42 to .66 (Integrity International) and remain confident that the IP200 is a "comprehensive, diagnostic and developmental instrument" that can be used to "make predictions about future behaviour".

Integrity Assessments: Moral Disengagement Measure

The Moral Disengagement Measure is based on the premise that the way in which people process, frame or understand information when making decisions of ethical importance plays an important role in their propensity to engage in unethical behaviour (Moore, Detert, Trevino, Baker, & Mayer, 2012). Specifically, the degree to which they are inclined to morally disengage is thought to affect the likelihood of their behaving in ways that are unethical or counterproductive to organisations.

Drawn from Bandura's work in the field of social psychology, moral disengagement denotes the breakdown of self-regulation that would ordinarily prevent an individual from engaging in these types of behaviours (Moore et al., 2012). It is, in essence, a process whereby the individual distances him/herself from ethical standards by reasoning that those standards do not apply to him/her in particular circumstances or contexts. This enables the person to engage in such behaviours without experiencing the distress that would usually accompany deviation from acceptable moral standards. Moore et al. (2012) note a body of research that suggests that greater attention should be paid to the role of cognitive processes in explaining unethical behaviour. Thus, they focused their attention on the development of an instrument to measure the extent to which an individual is likely to morally disengage, citing this as a "uniquely important predictor of a broad range of unethical behaviours" (Moore et al., 2012, p. 3).

According to the test developers, the Moral Disengagement Measure is an instrument developed primarily for use with any adult sample, across a range of contexts; however, considerable attention has been focused on workplace settings, to provide organisations with a reliable predictor of "unethical organisational behaviour". As there are reportedly eight specific mechanisms of moral disengagement (Moore et al., 2012), the Moral Disengagement Measure measures the following factors:

- Moral justification—the cognitive reframing of unethical acts as being in the service of a "greater good".
- Euphemistic labelling—the use of more positive language to reframe counterproductive behaviours to make them seem benign.
- Advantageous comparison—exploiting the contrast between the behaviour being (or about to be) exhibited and an even more unacceptable or reprehensible one.
- Displacement of responsibility—the attribution of responsibility for one's actions to an authority figure.
- Diffusion of responsibility—diffusing of responsibility for behaviour across members of a group.
- Distorting consequences—minimisation of the consequences of the behaviour.
- Attribution of blame—assigning responsibility to those who will feel the consequences of the behaviour (the victim), under the rationale that they deserve the fate that befalls them.
- Dehumanisation—the framing of those affected by unethical behaviour as sub-human or unworthy of humane consideration.

A key consideration when developing the instrument appears to have been "parsimony" (Moore et al., 2012). Therefore, the authors ultimately settled on a final eight-item (one per factor) instrument, concluding from their statistical analysis that using longer forms had no substantial benefit. They reported reliability of .80 for this version (Moore et al., 2012).

Rather than including a social desirability scale in the instrument itself, Moore and her colleagues tested the correlation between the Moral Disengagement Measure and a social desirability scale, a reduced version of the Marlowe-Crowne instrument. They reported no significant correlation with this measure and drew the conclusion therefrom that the Moral Disengagement Measure is not prone to contamination by social desirability bias (Moore et al., 2012).

Considering the relationships between the Moral Disengagement factors and constructs such as Machiavellianism, moral identity and two facets of empathy, the authors concluded that the relationships were significant to establish construct validity, but not so strong as to make the moral disengagement construct redundant. They assert that the inclusion of the instrument offers significant increased predictive validity to assessment processes seeking to uncover the likelihood of unethical or CWBs (Moore et al., 2012).

In critique of this instrument, however, it is important to note that firstly, the lack of an included social desirability scale may, in spite of the test developer's efforts to overcome this, still have implications for this instrument's use in occupational settings, where respondents may have far more of an incentive to present positively than they might in research settings. Furthermore, at a more theoretical level, one could raise the question as to whether Moral Disengagement is a by-product or a cause of unethical behaviour. In the case of the former, it may be more expedient to identify the traits or predilections that could themselves lead to CWBs.

Assessments of "Dark-Side" or Potentially Risk-Posing Traits

The past 20 years has produced a growing interest in the personality factors that could potentially derail performance and interpersonal functioning at work (Hogan & Hogan, 2009). In spite of this emerging interest, however, the number of derailing or risk-based occupational assessments is still relatively few, vastly overshadowed by clinical measures in this space. Two have been identified as having been specifically developed for use in occupational settings, the Hogan HDS and Limits (released by Podium Systems Ltd., 2019a, 2019b).

Risk-Based Assessments: Hogan Development Survey (HDS)

The Hogan HDS is probably the first and most well-known occupational assessment specifically designed to measure a number of "common dysfunctional dispositions" or "dark-side" traits that can lead to "problematic behaviours" in occupational settings (Hogan & Hogan, 2009, p. 1). However, the focus here is not on the prediction of CWBs, such as workplace violence or theft. Rather, this instrument was designed to uncover "more pervasive and often more subtle patterns of behaviour" (2), which can result in ongoing difficulties for individuals and their co-workers.

The dysfunctional dispositions are purported to reflect people's distorted beliefs regarding themselves, how they will be treated by others and the best way to achieve their personal goals. The point is clearly made that these dispositions are in fact dysfunctional and as such will "negatively influence people's careers and life satisfaction" (Hogan & Hogan, 2009). They are said to emerge in times of increased strain and to disrupt relationships, damage reputations and derail people's chances of success.

The instrument measures 11 "dysfunctional personality syndromes", with the test developers asserting that the HDS is appropriate for use both in selection procedures and to provide data to assist employees in developing their performance and/or interpersonal relationships at work (Hogan & Hogan, 2009). They also posit that dysfunctional dispositions, while being aligned with personality disorders as outlined in the DSM IV, are part of everyone's personality. Therefore, the instrument is not intended to diagnose PDs, but is intended for use in subclinical populations to measure the following "self-defeating expressions" (6) of normal personality:

- Excitable—aligned with borderline PD, high scorers on this scale are prone to be moody, difficult to please and sensitive to criticism.
- Sceptical—associated with paranoid PD, high scorers are typically cynical and distrustful. They may be easily offended and quick to perceive mistreatment.
- Cautious—with the corresponding PD being avoidant, high scorers on this factor are seen as reluctant to take risks or show initiative.

- Reserved—high scorers are seen as aloof or detached, the schizoid PD being the corresponding PD for this factor.
- Leisurely—associated with passive-aggressive PD, implications for high scorers are that they are likely to be independent and resistant to feedback. They may tend to procrastinate and be seen as stubborn.
- Bold—most closely aligned with narcissistic PD, high-scoring individuals tend to be self-confident and reluctant to admit shortcomings. They can be unwilling to share credit and can be seen as demanding.
- Mischievous—high scores tend to denote charming yet impulsive individuals who can be non-conforming and exploitative. They may take unnecessary risks and be unwilling to accept responsibility for mistakes. This scale corresponds to the antisocial PD.
- Colourful—aligned with histrionic PD, highly colourful individuals are typically expressive and attention seeking. They may be disorganised.
- Imaginative—associated with schizotypal PD, high scorers may be creative yet impractical, easily bored and likely to lack awareness of their impact on others.
- Diligent—high scores suggest individuals who are meticulous perfectionists and may find it difficult to delegate and set meaningful priorities. Aligned with obsessive-compulsive PD.
- Dutiful—corresponding with dependent PD, high scorers may be overly eager to please and reliant on others (Hogan & Hogan, 2009).

The HDS consists of 168 items that take the form of statements to which the respondent either agrees or disagrees. Each scale is composed of 14 items and higher scores indicate greater dysfunctional tendencies. The instrument also includes a 14-item social desirability scale.

The test developers began work on this instrument in 1992 and have, over the years, conducted extensive research into its reliability and validity. As a result, they have collected impressive sample sizes of working adults and applicants for jobs (reported in the technical manual as 109, 103). Most recent work appears to have focused on the development of parallel forms of the HDS (Hogan & Hogan, 2009). The tool has also been translated into 32 languages.

Extensive research on this instrument has provided support for the traits measured by the Hogan HDS as being predictive of negative workplace outcomes such as extreme, ineffective leader behaviours (Kaiser et al., 2015; Khoo & Burch, 2008). However, a study of nearly 5000 British adults conducted by Furnham, Tricky, and Hyde (2012) challenged the notion that the "dysfunctional dispositions" are always negative. While certain scales (i.e. Excitable and Sceptical) seemed consistently associated with low work outcome and potential ratings, others, such as the Bold and Diligent factors were either neutral or positively correlated (Furnham et al., 2012). Additionally, some of the other scales were reported as being highly variable in terms of positive associations with workplace outcomes. For example, high scores on the imaginative scale correlated negatively with reliability, but positively with sales potential (Furnham et al., 2012). This lends credence to the argument that "dark-side" traits may indeed have bright outcomes.

Risk-Based Assessments: Limits

Designed for use in occupational settings and a target population of healthy working-age adults, Limits is a psychometric measure of work-related derailing personality traits. Although based on personality disorders described in the DSM V, it is not intended to diagnose PDs, but rather to identify "traits that predispose individuals to personality disorder amongst normal working populations" (Limits Technical Manual & User Guide: 5). The test developers label these traits as "derailing" and are careful to note that they are both work-related and non-clinical.

The test developers posit that the use of the term derailing differentiates their model from "dark-side" research and the Hogan instrument. This is because the Hogan is based on the dimensionalised DSM IV axis II categories, whereas Limits reconceptualises derailing personality under the more recent DSM V trait framework (Limits Technical Manual & User Guide). They also drew on research around the dark triad, a cluster of derailing traits encompassing Narcissism, Machiavellianism and Psychopathy. These three traits are pulled together in the Antagonism factor of Limits.

Limits is recommended for development rather than selection, and as such, according to the test developers, the issue of faking is of less concern. However, measures have been taken to address potential social desirability effects in the Limits instrument. Two forms of the instrument exist, the first of which is a forced-choice format that prevents systematic bias (Guenole, Brown, & Cooper, 2018). However, again, ipsative formats can pose psychometric issues (Meade, 2004; Tenopyr, 1988) and render the instrument inappropriate for comparisons between individuals (Guenole et al., 2018).

The alternative form of Limits relies on the traditional single item and Likert scale response type. It includes a social desirability/unlikely virtues scale to control for faking. Alternatively, according to the test developer, they at times include a normed score of the proportion of extreme non-endorsements, which is based on a clinical faking detection technique (Guenole, 2018).

Overall, Limits is designed to measure the following six dimensions:

Antagonism—exhibits diverse manifestations of antipathy towards others, and a correspondingly exaggerated sense of self-importance.

Detachment—withdrawal from other people, ranging from intimate relationships to the world at large; restricted affective experience and expression; limited hedonic capacity.

Negative Affect—experiences a wide range of negative emotions (e.g. anxiety, depression, guilt/shame, worry, etc.), and the behavioural and interpersonal manifestations of those experiences.

Disinhibition—characterised by a high degree of impulsivity, recklessness and ease of distraction.

Compulsivity—the tendency to think and act according to narrowly defined and unchanging ideals, and the expectation that these ideals should be adhered to by everyone.

Eccentricity—exhibits a range of odd or unusual behaviours and cognitions, including both process (e.g. perception) and content (e.g. beliefs).

The authors assert, via research presented in the technical manual, that the reliability and validity results suggest that Limits is a reliable and valid measure of derailing personality at work (Limits Technical Manual & User Guide). A fairly new instrument, however, there does not yet appear to be much by way of peer-reviewed research or additional studies (beyond the test developers own research) pertaining to this instrument.

Conclusion

A review of the instruments available to measure potentially risk-based personality traits in the workplace (outside of the realm of integrity, which is largely considered a separate construct) reveals that there are few in existence. Of the two that were identified, one (Limits) appears to be a fairly new entrant into this domain and as such would benefit from ongoing research as to its applications in the workplace.

Both the Hogan HDS and Limits base their framework on subclinical manifestations of PDs outlined in the DSM (albeit from different versions) on the assertion that all "normal" personalities will display certain PD traits, which have implications for themselves and others at work. Both of these measures are self-report and as such, are both subject to all of the concerns brought to bear by these types of measures. These concerns are magnified when attempting to measure edge behaviours and risk-based traits, which, social desirability concerns aside, may not even be within the realm of the individual's awareness.

The other concern is around the use of results and how they inform decision-making. Given that "risk-based" traits can have positive as well as negative outcomes, understanding how to interpret an individual's profile could be exceedingly tricky. This necessitates that people using the results to make decisions must understand thoroughly both the inherent requirements of the job (as in all responsible assessment) and the organisational culture, climate, values and ways of engaging that could either enable or derail the individual.

Ethical assessment is always critical but perhaps never more so when assessing risk-based traits. While none of the instruments discussed purport to be diagnostic of PDs, it would be irresponsible at best to begin labelling high scorers as "Antagonistic" or "Compulsive". With its somewhat softer factor names, the Hogan has mitigated this risk somewhat; however, responsible use of results is still paramount. A perhaps unexplored area of research is how to offer meaningful development for those demonstrating risk-based traits, helping them to understand their edge behaviours and how to shift, as well as how organisations can establish environments and cultures that mitigate the risk.

This review highlighted the need for ongoing research in this area to understand more fully those traits or attributes that may pose risk to organisations and/or individuals. It would be useful to build a deeper understanding of the positive and negative impact these traits could have, and the moderating variables that may determine this.

There also appears to be a strong need for the development of a robust, objective assessment (ideally non-self-report) that could enable the identification of these traits in occupational contexts. The Corporate Personality Inventory (CPI) has been developed to address some of these issues, containing both a self-report and an observed-behaviours form that enables a review of demonstrated behaviours and how they are perceived by others. This instrument is discussed in Chapter 8.

Finally, the issue of organisational climate and context is one worth raising. No behaviour takes place in a vacuum, and organisations will never mitigate the risk of CWBs entirely by focusing on identification at the individual level only. While forewarned may be (better) forearmed, there may be times when ethical, legislative or practical reasons preclude simply excluding or removing individuals from certain positions or organisations. It behoves organisations, therefore, to build their understanding of the behaviours that are desirable, those which are non-negotiable, and build environments to sustain positive behaviours and mitigate risk.

References

Babiak, P., & Hare, R. D. (2006). *Snakes in suits: When psychopaths go to work.* New York: HarperCollins.

Babiak, P., Neumann, C. S., & Hare, R. D. (2010). Corporate psychopathy: Talking the walk. *Behavioural Science and the Law, 28,* 174–193.

Baharom, M. N., Sharrfuddin, M. D. K. B., & Iqbal, J. (2017). A systematic review on the deviant workplace behaviour. *Review Public Administration Management, 5*(3), 231.

Benning, S. D., Patrick, C. J., Blonigen, D. M., Hicks, B. M., & Iacono, W. G. (2003). Estimating facets of psychopathy from normal personality traits: A step toward community-epidemiological investigations. *Psychological Assessment, 15,* 340–350.

Berry, C. M., Sackett, P. R., & Wiemann, S. (2007). A review of recent developments in integrity test research. *Personnel Psychology, 60*(2), 271–301.

Board, B. J., & Fritzon, K. (2005). Disordered personalities at work. *Psychology, Crime and Law, 11*(1), 17–32.

Cleckley, H. (1941). *The mask of sanity* (1st ed.). St. Louis, MO: C.V. Mosby.

Cohen, A. (2016). Are they among us? A conceptual framework of the relationship between the dark triad personality and counterproductive work behaviours (CWBs). *Human Resource Management Review, 26*(1), 69–85.

De Clercq, B., & De Fruyt, F. (2003). Personality disorder symptoms in adolescence: A five factor model perspective. *Journal of Personality Disorders, 17,* 269–292.

Fennimore, A., & Sementelli, A. J. (2016). Public entrepreneurship and subclinical psychopaths: A conceptual frame and implication. *International Journal of Public Sector Management, 29*(6), 612–634.

Fine, S. (2013). A look at cross-cultural integrity testing in three banks. *Personnel Review, 42*(3), 266–280.

Furnham, A. (2008). *Personality and intelligence at work: Exploring and explaining individual differences at work.* Hove and New York: Psychology Press.

Furnham, A. F., & Crump, J. D. (2014). A bright side facet analysis of borderline personality disorder. *Borderline Personality Disorder and Emotion Dysregulation, 1*(1), 7.

Furnham, A., Hyde, G., & Trickey, G. (2013). Do your dark side traits fit? Dysfunctional personalities in different work sectors. *Applied Psychology, 63*(4), 589–606.

Furnham, A., Trickey, G., & Hyde, G. (2012). Bright aspects to dark side traits: Dark side traits associated with work success. *Personality and Individual Differences, 52,* 908–913.

Guenole, N., Brown, A., & Cooper, A. (2018). Forced choice assessment of work-related maladaptive personality traits: Preliminary evidence from an application of Thurstonian item response modelling. *Assessment, 25*(4), 513–526.

Hare, R. D. (2003). *Manual for the Revised Psychopathy Checklist* (2nd ed.). Toronto, ON: Multi-Health Systems.

Hogan, R., & Hogan, J. (2001). Assessing leadership: A view from the dark side. *International Journal of Selection and Assessment, 9,* 40–51.

Hogan, R., & Hogan, J. (2009). *Hogan Development Survey manual.* Tulsa, OK: Hogan Press.

Hough, L. M. (1992). The "big five" personality variables—construct confusion: Description versus prediction. *Human Performance, 5*(1–2), 139–155.

Integrity International. (2019). Available at https://www.integtests.com. Accessed 12 December 2018.

Kaiser, R. B., Le Breton, J. M., & Hogan, J. (2015). The dark side of personality and extreme leader behaviour. *Applied Psychology: An International Review, 64*(1), 55–92.

Khoo, H. S., & Burch, G. S. J. (2008). The 'dark side' of leadership personality and transformational leadership: An exploratory study. *Personality and Individual Differences, 44*(1), 86–89.

Landay, K., Harms, P. D., & Crede, M. (2019). Shall we serve the dark lords? A meta-analytic review of psychopathy and leadership. *Journal of Applied Psychology, 104*(1), 183–196.

Marcus, B., Lee, K., & Ashton, M. C. (2007). Personality dimensions explaining relationships between integrity tests and counterproductive behaviour: Big five, or one in addition? *Personnel Psychology, 60*(1), 1–34.

Meade, A. W. (2004). Psychometric problems and issues involved with creating and using ipsative measures for selection. *Journal of Occupational and Organizational Psychology, 77*(4), 531–552.

Moore, C., Detert, J. R., Trevino, L. K., Baker, V. L., & Mayer, D. M. (2012). Why employees do bad things: Moral disengagement and unethical organizational behavior. *Personnel Psychology, 65*, 1–48.

Moscoso, S., & Salgado, J. F. (2004). "Dark side" personality styles as predictors of task, contextual, and job performance. *International Journal of Selection and Assessment, 12*(4), 356–362.

Muris, P., Merckelbach, H., Otgaar, H., & Meijer, E. (2017). The malevolent side of human nature: A meta-analysis and critical review of the literature on the dark triad (narcissism, machiavellianism, and psychopathy). *Perspectives on Psychological Science, 12*(2), 183–204.

Murphy, K. R., & Lee, S. L. (1994). Does conscientiousness explain the relationship between integrity and job performance? *International Journal of Selection and Assessment, 2*, 226–233.

O'Brien, Connie. (2017). Can pre-employment tests identify white collar criminals and reduce fraud risk in your organization? *Journal of Forensic and Investigative Accounting, 9*(1), 621–636.

Ones, D. S., Viswesvaran, C., & Schmidt, F. L. (1993). Comprehensive meta-analysis of integrity test validities: Findings and implications for personnel selection and theories of job performance. *Journal of Applied Psychology, 78*(4), 679–703.

Podium Systems Pvt Ltd. (2019a). *Podium Systems Limited—Dark side assessment—Limits—Podium Systems Limited.* Podium365.com. Available at https://www.podium365.com/assessments/dark_side_limits. Accessed 31 January 2019.

Podium Systems Pvt Ltd. (2019b). *Limits technical manual and user guide.*

Rolland, J. P., & de Fruyt, F. (2003). The validity of FFM personality dimensions and maladaptive traits to predict negative affects at work: A six month prospective study in a military sample. *European Journal of Personality, 17*(1), 101–121.

Rust, J. (1999). The validity of the giotto integrity test. *Personality and Individual Differences, 27*(4), 755–768.

Salgado, J. F. (2003). Predicting job performance using FFM and non-FFM personality measures. *Journal of Occupational and Organizational Psychology, 76,* 323–346.

Schutte, N., Blickle, G., Frieder, R., Wihler, A., Schnitzler, F., Heupel, J., & Zettler, I. (2015). The role of interpersonal influence in counterbalancing psychopathic personality trait facets at work. *Journal of Management, 44*(4), 1338–1368.

SHL Occupational Personality Questionnaire. (2019). Available at https://www.shl.com/en/assessments/personality/shl-occupational-personality-questionnaire-opq. Accessed 28 February 2019.

Smart, B. (2012). *Topgrading 201: How to avoid costly mishires.* New York: Penguin.

Smith, S. F., & Lilienfeld, S. O. (2013). Psychopathy in the workplace: The knowns and unknowns. *Aggression and Violent Behavior, 18,* 204–218.

Tenopyr, M. L. (1988). Artefactual reliability of forced-choice scales. *Journal of Applied Psychology, 73*(4), 749–751.

7

Overview of the Impact of Psychopathy and Other Problematic Personality Constructs in the Workplace

Simone Ray and Katarina Fritzon

Counterproductive Work Behaviour

Personality has been found to be a useful predictor of work performance and other work-related outcomes, thus forming a relationship between personality psychology and organisational behaviour (Roberts, 2006). A number of longitudinal studies have demonstrated the predictive power of personality on organisational experience and work outcomes later in life (Caspi, Elder, & Bem, 1988; Judge, Higgins, Thoresen, & Barrick, 1999; Roberts, Caspi, & Moffit, 2003). Many of these studies have investigated relationships between the Big Five personality characteristics: extroversion, agreeableness, conscientiousness, neuroticism and openness to experience, and outcomes including charismatic leadership, higher income

S. Ray (✉)
Melbourne, VIC, Australia
e-mail: simone.ray@student.bond.edu.au

K. Fritzon
Bond University, Robina, QLD, Australia
e-mail: kfritzon@bond.edu.au

© The Author(s) 2020
K. Fritzon et al., *Corporate Psychopathy*,
https://doi.org/10.1007/978-3-030-27188-6_7

levels, more subordinates and a higher managerial position (Vergauwe, Wille, Hofmans, & De Fruyt, 2017). Of the Big Five, high extraversion and low neuroticism are consistently related to charisma and consequently charismatic leadership. On the other hand, charismatic leadership has been related to narcissism which is in itself negatively associated with Agreeableness (e.g. Furnham & Crump, 2014).

Over the last decade, in particular research within organisational psychology has seen a shift from focusing on topics such as transformational leadership and employee engagement (Schyns, 2015), towards an increasing emphasis on the workplace impact of so-called dark leadership (Harms & Spain, 2015). According to research, up to a third of US workers report that their leaders exhibit "high dysfunction" (intentionally lying, explosive outbursts, destructive criticism) and "low dysfunction" (withholding information, taking undue credit for work, unrealistically high expectations) (Rose, Shuck, Twyford, & Bergman, 2015).

Indeed, interest in the dark triad in general has grown rapidly over this time with two thirds of the publications on the dark triad appearing in 2014 and 2015 alone (Muris, Merckelbach, Otgaar, & Meijer, 2017), undoubtedly due to awareness of the role of unethical and fraudulent financial decision-making in major corporate accounting scandals (McKay, Stevens, & Fratzl, 2010). While *direct* fraud is estimated to cost businesses $680 billion annually (Wells, 2007), much of white-collar crime goes undetected and without an awareness or impact on staff other than the individual perpetrator (Whigham, 2014). Fraud schemes are not solely for direct personal gain, often being designed to improve the appearance of an organisation's performance, one notorious exponent of fraud being Al "Chainsaw" Dunlap (see Chapter 2) who oversaw the fraudulent manipulation of accounts to show an excessive loss in one year in order to present a picture of far greater turnaround than actually attained. Similarly, Tyco executives made $430 million by raising the share price through publishing fraudulent financial results for the company (Dorminey, Fleming, Kranacher, & Riley, 2012). Including such forms of fraud under the banner of *occupational* fraud is estimated to raise the cost to the global economy to between $US 3 and 4 trillion each year according to both the Association of Certified Fraud Examiners (2018) and the Financial Cost of Fraud 2018 report (Gee & Button, 2018) (Text Box 7.1).

Text Box 7.1 Fraud and corporate psychopathy Simon Croom, Rozalija Erdelyi, Adrian Gepp and Russell Mills

Perpetrators of fraud are commonly senior executives (Beasley, Carcello, Hermanson, & Neal, 2010; PwC, 2018) and such cases are substantially more costly (ACFE, 2018). Further, tip-offs from employees are the most common way occupational fraud is detected (ACFE, 2018).

Studies have variously attempted to evaluate the dynamics relating to the context, scale and human characteristics that result in fraud, the most frequently used being the *Fraud Triangle* (Fig. 7.1).

Fig. 7.1   The Fraud Triangle

The Fraud Triangle posits that fraud has three ingredients: (i) Motivation—a pressure or incentive to commit fraud, (ii) Opportunity to commit a fraud and (iii) Rationalisation that makes someone (or a group of people) willing to commit the fraud. Augmenting the Fraud Triangle, the MICE model (Kranacher, Riley, & Wells, 2011) incorporates coercion from others while the Fraud Diamond adds individual capability to commit fraud to the 3 existing dimensions. This is supported by Beasley et al. (2010) who revealed that the CEO, CFO or both were associated with 89% of fraud cases publicly disclosed by the US Securities Exchange Commission from 1998 to 2007.

Troy, Smith, and Domino (2011) also discovered that in addition to being direct perpetrators, CEOs have been found to instigate fraud by directing or enabling others to commit it (Troy et al., 2011), which was also recognized by the ACFE (2018) who reported that senior management often pressure other employees such as clerks to perform the data entry to implement the fraud.

Employees in positions of power such as CEOs and other staff with managerial oversight can detrimentally affect the workplace environment and have a greater opportunity to commit fraud. This is a result of the inherent powers associated with their roles, and the trust and accompanying security clearance vested in them by the organisations for which they work (Troy et al., 2011). Senior executives may also have greater financial incentives to commit fraud, such as bonuses linked to the share price that can be artificially boosted by financial statement fraud, as in the afore-mentioned Tyco case. Senior executives can also increase their chances of successfully completing a fraud if they can use their influence to distract others in the organisation (Ramamoorti, Morrison, & Koletar, 2009).

There have been a number of direct links between the likelihood and incidence of fraud and the presence of corporate psychopaths. Klarskov Jeppesen, and Leder (2016) surveyed Danish state-authorized auditors and found that 69% had experience of corporate psychopaths, (many had more than one experience) and 43% of these auditors had found that psychopathic executives had committed fraud. In a chilling discussion, Perri and Brody (2011) cite the case of the murdered insurance auditor, Sally Rohrbach, whose investigation into fraud at the Dilworth Insurance Agency led directly to her murder. The authors note other examples of workplace violence linked to fraud and psychopathy, highlighting that although corporate psychopaths generally employ non-violent means to achieve their goals, they are potentially just as capable of instrumental violence as criminal psychopaths if it is deemed necessary.

An experimental study with 101 auditors by Johnson, Kuhn, Apostolou, and Hassell (2012) found a significant, positive relationship between narcissistic client behaviour and fraud motivation, while Lingnau, Fuchs, and Dehne-Niemann (2017) conducted a first person survey to identify the connection between psychopathic traits and acceptance of fraud, finding a significant and positive relationship.

Of the negative work outcomes, counterproductive work behaviour (CWB) is one of the costliest damages incurred by an organisation (Cohen, 2016). CWB comprises a broad array of volitional behaviours that function to harm an organisation or an organisation's members (Spector & Fox, 2005). Specific forms of CWB include physical or verbal aggression, theft, withdrawal (absence, turnover, being late), sabotage or purposefully completing work incorrectly (Spector et al., 2006). CWB can be divided into two categories: CWB towards other people (CWB–I) and CWB towards the organisation (CWB–O). CWB–I refers to voluntary behaviours that harm or negatively impact an organisation's stakeholders (Bennett & Robinson, 2000). CWB–O is characteristic of behaviours that harm or negatively impact an organisation's structure, physical property or its policies (Bowling & Michel, 2011). CWB is a regular occurrence in the workplace and is linked to a number of negative outcomes. For instance, CWB is positively associated with employee emotional exhaustion (Raman, Sambasivan, & Kumar, 2016) and interpersonal conflict (Kessler, Bruursema, Rodopman, & Spector, 2013), while also negatively associated with employee satisfaction (Bowling, 2010), task performance (Shoss, Eisenberger, Restubog, & Zagenczyk, 2013), psychological health (Bowling & Michel, 2011) and organisational loyalty (Bowling, 2010).

The impact of CWB has sparked interest in the organisational community regarding its origins in individual differences and personality (Douglas, Martinko, & Murphy, 2001; Hershcovis & Barling, 2010; Penney & Spector, 2002). In terms of the five-factor model (FFM), meta-analytic studies have identified agreeableness and conscientiousness as negative predictors of CWB (Mount, Ilies, & Johnson, 2006; Salgado, 2002). Similarly, research has presented some evidence that neuroticism is a positive predictor of CWB (Scherer, Baysinger, Zolynsky, & LeBreton, 2013). Unaccounted for variance in FFM regression models as predictors of CWB has led researchers to turn to alternative models of personality, particularly the so-called dark triad of psychopathy, Machiavellianism and Narcissism (Jonason, Slomki, & Partyka, 2012; Paulhus & Williams, 2002; Wu & Lebreton, 2011). According to theory and empirical research, all three personality constructs are highly interrelated (Jakobwitz & Egan, 2006) and have a behavioural tendency towards self-promotion, dishonest and manipulative behaviours in the corporate environment (Jones & Paulhus,

2011; Jonason & Webster, 2010; Paulhus & Williams, 2002); however, the motives underlying their exploitative behaviour may differ (Rauthmann & Will, 2011). Machiavellianism is characterised by cynical, immoral beliefs, emotional detachedness, self-beneficial motives, strategic long-term planning, manipulation, exploitation and deception (Rauthmann & Will, 2011). Individuals high on psychopathy may present themselves as charismatic, but are emotionally shallow and lack remorse or concern for others (Jones & Paulhus, 2011). Individuals high in narcissism tend to have an inflated self-view, fantasy in relation to control, success and admiration, as well as the desire to have their self-love reinforced by others (Morf & Rhodewalt, 2001; Turner & Webster, 2018). It may be difficult to comprehend why such socially aversive individuals would be recruited in the workplace; however, it is likely due to their expertise in impression management and self-monitoring (Paunonen, Lönnqvist, Verkasalo, Leikas, & Nissinen, 2006). That is, DT personalities are able to veil their dark side with deceit and charm, by impersonating those attributes held by ideal leaders (Boddy, Galvin, & Ladyshewsky, 2011; Boddy, Miles, Sanyal, & Hartog, 2015; Schyns & Schilling, 2013). DT personalities also hold an insatiable desire for monetary rewards, status and power, which acts as a driving force for these individuals to ascend the corporate hierarchy (Muris et al., 2017). While this suggests that DT personalities can be successful in the workplace, it also implies that these individuals may be operating in positions that exceed their qualifications or abilities (Boddy, 2015).

In the corporate environment, Machiavellian employees can undertake unethical decision-making (Kish-Gephart, Harrison, & Trevino, 2010) and increase their co-worker's workplace cynicism and emotional exhaustion (Gkorezis, Petridou, & Krouklidou, 2015). Comparatively, narcissist employees have been shown to belittle co-workers and exploit their insecurities (Howell & Avolio, 2013), while psychopathic employees are often found to act unethically (Stevens, Dueling, & Armenakis, 2012) and aggressively towards stakeholders (Caponecchia, Sun, & Wyatt, 2012). Employees with DT personalities may increase the occurrence of CWB; however, the link between DT personalities and increased CWB may depend, in part, on the individual's level of authority within the corporate hierarchy (O'Boyle, Forsyth, Banks, & McDaniel, 2012).

The Dark Triad and Counterproductive Work Behaviour

Psychopathy

Taxometric data suggests that psychopathic traits exist on a dimensional continuum, suggesting that these traits manifest through varying degrees of trait expression (Edens, Marcus, Lilienfeld, & Poythress, 2006; Walters, Duncan, & Mitchell-Perez, 2007). Some authors argue that successful psychopathy is merely a variation along the psychopathic continuum, as these individuals possess a subclinical form of psychopathy (Westerlaken & Woods, 2013). Successful psychopaths can function reasonably in the community, as they display lower levels of antisocial behaviour and evade interaction with the criminal justice system (Neumann, Hare, & Pardini, 2015). Psychopathy comprises a constellation of deviant interpersonal, affective and behavioural traits (Hare, 2003; LeBreton, Binning, Adorno, & Melcher, 2004; Hare & Neumann, 2009), subclinical psychopaths may be harder to detect, as these individuals integrate into society by pursuing successful careers (Cohen, 2016, 2018; Fritzon & Board, 2005).

Corporate Psychopathy

As noted previously, the conjecture that psychopaths can attain career success has shifted a focus from forensic populations to the corporate environment. This led to modifiers being attached to the term "psychopath", including the corporate, successful, and organisational psychopath (Boddy, 2011). These terms represent those who are extremely career-oriented, yet remain ruthless, unethical and exploitive (Boddy, 2017). Relative to a criminogenic lifestyle, corporate psychopaths possess strong desires for success, monetary rewards and status, such that these individuals are willing to lie, cheat and manipulate to climb the corporate ladder (Babiak, Neumann, & Hare, 2010; Wu & Lebreton, 2011).

It is clear that psychopaths are able to function just as destructively in the workplace as their criminal counterparts, particularly at the senior level (Boddy, 2011). For instance, Babiak et al. (2010) revealed that 3.5% of individuals working at a senior level met characteristics of corporate psychopathy, while Boddy (2010) postulated that 3–4% of individuals in the business environment are psychopaths and exist more prevalently at the senior level. Similarly, Fritzon, and Board (2005) compared the personality profiles of 36 senior business managers with 768 mental health patients, and 317 incarcerated individuals previously identified as psychopathic. Results revealed that the senior business manager group held substantial elements of personality disorders that are most commonly associated with the emotional component of psychopathy. Indeed, to the outsider, corporate psychopaths can appear as "ideal leaders" by concealing their dark side with charm and manipulation (Boddy et al., 2015; Furnham, Richards, & Paulhus, 2013). The psychopathic manager has also been described by Smith and Lilienfeld (2013) as a double-edged sword. There is evidence that those with psychopathic traits can be beneficial in professions that require risk-taking, strategic thinking, creativity and superb communication skills (Crush, 2014; Lilienfeld et al., 2012; Smith & Lilienfeld, 2013). Conversely, psychopathic traits are reported to be a positive predictor of abusive supervision (Kiazad, Restubog, Zagenczyk, Kiewitz, & Tang, 2010) and destructive managerial behaviour (Boddy, 2017), while also a negative predictor of job performance (Mathieu, Neumann, Hare, & Babiak, 2014).

Corporate Psychopathy and CWB

Characteristics including lack of guilt, remorse or conscience suggest that individuals high in psychopathy may be undeterred by the consequences of CWB (Wu & Lebreton, 2011). Thus, it is not surprising that researchers have deemed psychopathy as the most significant and problematic of the DT personality trait with regard to CWB (O'Boyle et al., 2012). Özsoy (2018) provides support for this conjecture, reporting that of the DT traits, only psychopathy was positively related to CWB–O. While an association between CWB and psychopathy is intuitive, it is critical to highlight that some empirical studies have documented no association between employee psychopathy and CWB (Kantan, Yyesiltas, & Arslan, 2015). As such, the extant literature has offered mixed findings regarding the CWB of psychopathic employees.

While O'Boyle et al. (2012) meta-analytically revealed that of the DT personality traits, psychopaths in authority positions negatively predicted CWB, the samples evaluating psychopathy in this meta-analysis ($k = 27$) largely comprised police officers ($k = 24$) followed by police cadets ($k = 1$), military agents ($k = 1$) and corrections officers ($k = 1$). The negative associations between psychopathic personalities may presumably reflect the samples' profession (i.e. law enforcement), such that these individuals may possess more control over antisocial workplace behaviours.

The suggestion that contextual factors may operate to either suppress or activate psychopathic traits in individuals in leadership positions is also supported by a recent study by Blickle, Schütte, and Genau (2018). In this study, $n = 154$ German managers were requested to provide the email addresses of two co-workers, who were instructed to provide ratings of the individual's job performance and leadership behaviour. Psychopathy was assessed with 74 items from the German version of the Psychopathic Personality Inventory-Revised (PPI-R; Alpers & Eisenbarth, 2008; Lilienfeld & Widows, 2005). Outcome variables included considerate leadership behaviour which was assessed by subordinates using the Leader Behavior Description Questionnaire (LBDQ; Stogdill, 1963) and job performance which was assessed using a measure previously developed by the lead author (Blickle et al., 2011). The researchers also examined the moderating effects of prospects for ascendency and income increases. These were both measured by items from Seifert and Bergmann's work values inventory (1983), with questions including "In my job I can get ahead", and "In my job I have good career opportunities" (for ascendency), and "In my job I have the opportunity to make a lot of money", and "In my job I can get extra bonuses" (for income rise prospects). Results revealed that high prospects of ascendency or income have the effect of behaviourally activating the meanness dimension of psychopathy (Patrick, 2018), which has a negative impact on leadership consideration behaviour, and subsequent job performance ratings. The authors did not find the same effect for the boldness or disinhibition dimensions of psychopathy.

The notion that corporate psychopathy may be associated with increases in both CWB–O and CWB–P has been supported by DeShong, Grant, and Mullins-Sweatt (2015), who compared statistical models comprising the FFM and DT as predictors of CWB amongst 191 working undergraduate psychology students. All students completed the Elemental Psychopathy Assessment (Lynam et al., 2011), the Five-Factor Narcissism Inventory (Glover, Miller, Lynam, Crego, & Widiger, 2012), the Machiavellianism Personality Scale (Dahling, Whitaker, & Levy, 2009), the Revised NEO Personality Inventory (Costa & McCrae, 1992) and the Workplace Deviance Scale (Bennett and Robinson, 2000). Of the FFM, agreeableness and conscientiousness were negatively correlated with both CWB–O and CWB–P, while neuroticism was positively correlated to CWB–O. For all three of the DT measures, results revealed positive correlations with both CWB–O and CWB–P, although the overall path analysis indicated that the FFM was a better fit for the data, particularly low agreeableness. This study utilised a student population; therefore, results may not generalise to senior managers, as the level of investment in their workplace is likely lower for the students who were only working part-time. Additionally, within this study two of the dark triad measures were derived from the FFM; therefore, results may have been due to a mono-operation bias.

A study conducted by Boddy (2014) recruited 304 senior white-collar employees to complete an online survey. Respondents were instructed to rate more than one manager that they had worked with. Employee affective well-being was evaluated using a modified subset of the job-related affective well-being scale (Katwyk, Fox, Spector, Kelloway, & Barling, 2000), interpersonal conflict was evaluated using a modified version of the Interpersonal Conflict at Work Scale (Spector & Jex, 1998), while CWB was evaluated using specific items related to sabotage and production deviance from the Counterproductive Work Behaviour–Checklist (Spector et al., 2006). Finally, the presence of psychopathic traits was assessed using the Psychopathy Measure-Management Research Version (Boddy, Ladyshewsky, & Galvin, 2010). The researchers identified a significant correlation between interpersonal conflict and CWB ($r = .42$) and interpersonal conflict and corporate psychopaths ($r = .50$). The researchers also revealed that alarmingly, the average number of incidents per year of witnessing unfavourable treatment of others (bullying) at work was 13.2% compared to 84.4% in the presence of higher levels of psychopathy. The researchers also found that seven of the ten CWB items relating to sabotage and production deviance were significantly elevated in the presence of psychopathy. As such, the presence of a corporate psychopath in a senior position may heighten the occurrence of overall CWB.

Machiavellianism

The writings of Niccolo Machiavelli during 1469–1527 promoted the use of manipulation, amorality and deceptive behaviours to ascertain power (Kessler et al., 2010). The construct was first operationalised by Christie and Geis (1970) who created the Mach-IV using a selection of statements from Machiavelli's book *The Prince* (1532). The term Machiavellianism is now synonymous with manipulation, callousness, cynicism, deception and increased self-interest (Jakobwitz & Egan, 2006). The Machiavellian's cynical and untrusting worldview is accompanied by a lack of affective empathy and a preference for emotionally detached relationships (Brewer, Abell, Glăveanu, & Wentink Martin, 2017; Wai & Tiliopoulos, 2012). Emotional disconnection allows Machiavellians to deploy deviant and coercive tactics as the "end justifies the means" (Peeters, Cillessen, & Scholte, 2010). Machiavellians demonstrate some behavioural patterns that are alike to psychopaths, in that both personality types employ manipulation, superficial charm and a detached emotionally affective style (Belschak, Den Hartog, & Kalshoven, 2015). However, those high in Machiavellianism have a higher threshold for impulse control relative to psychopaths, allowing these individuals to employ long-term strategic planning to subtly achieve self-serving goals (Visser & Campbell, 2018). Machiavellians are also more flexible in their tactics, as they are quite adaptive to situations and are skilled at impression management and forging alliances if this proves instrumental to them (Belschak et al., 2015).

Due to a lack of emotional connection with others, Machiavellians frequently partake in unethical behaviour, including dishonesty or cheating (Kish-Gephart et al., 2010), and demonstrate increased proactive aggression (Peeters et al., 2010). However, research also demonstrates that Machiavellians can demonstrate excellent impression management and are frequently recruited for high power positions due to their capacity to appear as strong, assertive leaders (Jonason et al., 2012).

Dahling et al. (2009) argue that the construct of Machiavellianism comprises four complex characteristics. First, *distrust in others* is marked by an active cynicism about the ill intentions of others, such that Machiavellians perceive those around them as unpredictable, unreliable and threatening (Inancsi, Lang, & Bereczkei, 2015). This distrust is reported to stems from the Machiavellian's own desires to manipulate situations yet perceive that others desire the same (Dahling et al., 2009). Second, Machiavellians have a *desire for control,* such that they must exert dominance over interpersonal situations and diminish the extent to which others are threatening or hold power (Brewer & Abell, 2017). Third, Machiavellians' *desire for status* is reflected by their tendency to be extrinsically motivated, thus seeking external indicators of success, such as monetary rewards and status, instead of those that are internally fulfilling (Sakalaki, Kanellaki, & Richardson, 2009). Finally, Machiavellians' *amoral manipulation* describes their tendency to disregard the standards of morality and value self-fulfilling behaviours at the expense of others (Abell, Brewer, Qualter, & Austin, 2016).

Etiologically, Machiavellian traits are believed to be acquired over time in response to environmental experiences (Rauthmann & Will, 2011). Stewart and Stewart (2006) found that anxious attachment stemming from low levels of perceived family support drove the development of a competitive need to excel to the detriment of others. Early childhood experiences have also been linked to reward sensitivity and use of Machiavellian tactics in response to perceived opportunities for reward (Birkás, Csathó, Gács, & Bereczkei, 2015).

Machiavellianism and CWB

Employees with high Machiavellianism report dissatisfaction with their occupational status in the corporate hierarchy (Dahling et al., 2009). This dissatisfaction is ascribed to the notion that Machiavellians may desire greater rewards and control over their co-workers (Dahling et al., 2009). In turn, this suggests that Machiavellians may be more driven to reach senior positions of management. Despite this, the existing literature has focused largely on Machiavellians at the employee level (Belschak et al., 2015; Dahling et al., 2009) and to a lesser extent on Machiavellians in positions of power. While both employees and those in positions of power with Machiavellian traits have been linked to CWB (Dahling, 2009), the latter has been described as incredibly manipulative, economically opportunistic and inconsiderate of others (Kiazad et al., 2010). As such, Machiavellians employed at the senior level may be particularly detrimental to both the organisation and its stakeholders.

The cynical views of Machiavellians and their actions at the expense of morality suggest they are more likely to violate basic principles regulating social behaviour (Christie & Geis, 1970; Jones & Paulhus, 2009). CWBs derived from Machiavellians are argued to be directed at others and may include behaviours such as insulting others, engaging in aggression or "ranting" at their co-workers (Kiazad et al., 2010), resource abuse (Tang, Chen, & Sutarso, 2008), theft (Harrison, Summers, & Mennecke, 2018), bullying (Linton & Power, 2013), lying, gossiping and sabotage (Dahling, Kuyumcu, & Librizzi, 2012), causing employee emotional exhaustion and workplace cynicism (Stradovnik & Stare, 2018). These findings suggest that Machiavellianism may increase *both* CWB–O and CWB–P (Bennett & Robinson, 2000); however, there are mixed findings in the empirical literature suggesting that the association is unclear. Scholars have documented the following: positive correlations between Machiavellianism and both CWB–O and CWB–I (Cohen, Panter, Turan, Morse, & Kim, 2014; Kantan et al., 2015; Ying & Cohen, 2018); positive correlations between Machiavellianism and CWB–I, but not CWB–O (Zheng, Wu, Chen, & Lin, 2017); and negative correlations between Machiavellianism and CWB (Kessler et al., 2010; Özsoy, 2018). Very few studies have employed manager samples in examining Machiavellianism and CWB (Amir & Malik, 2016; Rehman & Shahnawaz, 2018).

Rehman and Shahnawaz (2018) conducted a survey using middle level managers ($N = 174$) from different IT ($n = 78$), marketing ($n = 42$) and sales ($n = 22$) firms in India. The Machiavellian Personality Scale (MPS; Dahling et al., 2009) was utilised to assess Machiavellianism, the Job Autonomy Scale (Breaugh, 1998) was used to assess job autonomy, and CWB was assessed using a 10-item CWB–C (Spector, Bauer, & Fox,

2010). Results identified a significant and positive correlation between Machiavellianism and CWB ($r = .25$); however, job autonomy did not act as a moderator in this relationship. This suggests that the attainment of autonomy in their roles diminished the management samples' tendency to commit CWB. The authors argue that Machiavellians must be pro-organisational in their role to create a credible and prestigious reputation. While these findings suggest that Machiavellian managers may refrain from CWB, this study is constrained by two limitations: first, the authors examined CWB as a unitary construct, which can mask patterns of CWB–I or CWB–O (Marcus, Taylor, Hastings, Sturm, & Weigelt, 2016). Second, the sample is from a collectivist culture (India), and collectivism may attenuate the association between CWB and Machiavellianism (O'Boyle et al., 2012). The results of Rehman and Shahnawaz (2018) may not generalise to Western individualistic cultures.

The second study, conducted by Amir and Malik (2016), administered a survey to 176 general managers, supervisors and employees from Pakistan. Machiavellianism was assessed using the Mach-IV (Christie & Geis, 1970), and CWB was evaluated with the 32-item CWB–C (Spector & Fox, 2002). There was a positive correlation between the total CWB–C score and Machiavellianism ($r = .66$, $p = .01$), as well as between the Abuse CWB–C subscale and Machiavellianism ($r = .64$, $p = .01$), while weaker correlations were noted between the remaining CWB–C subscales and Machiavellianism (i.e. theft, sabotage, production deviance and withdrawal from work; r range $= .26$–$.45$). Thus, the correlation between the Abuse CWB–C subscale and Machiavellianism appears to be driving the total CWB–C score and Machiavellianism correlation. The authors assert that Machiavellians are less likely to engage in "intense" CWB (i.e. theft or production deviance) and are drawn to less intense CWB, such as CWB–I. However, two constraints are salient in this study: (i) the sample comprised managers, supervisors and employees; however, supervisory responsibility was not controlled for. Thus, it is difficult to ascertain if the observed preference for CWB–I reflects the CWB patterns of Machiavellian managers; (ii) similarly to the previously reported study by Rehman and Shahnawaz (2018), participants in this study were from Iran, a collectivist culture.

The studies examining the CWB of Machiavellian managers have offered mixed results. While it is suggested that Machiavellian managers can be destructive towards others in the workplace (i.e. CWB–I, Amir & Malik, 2016), there is some data alluding to the moderating role of authority in the Machiavellianism–CWB relationship (O'Boyle et al., 2012). Indeed, the latter suggests that attaining a position of power may dampen the Machiavellian's destructive behaviour, perhaps either due to the fact that they have reached their goal, or they are aware that they must act in pro-organisational ways to maintain it (Jones & Paulhus, 2009). However, a study by Kiazad et al. (2010) found that supervisors, who had self-reported high levels of Machiavellianism, were more often perceived as abusive leaders by their subordinates. These findings suggest that Machiavellians in positions of power may be harmful to their subordinates (Zheng et al., 2017).

Contrary to the preceding research findings, some scholars have argued that the qualities of Machiavellians may align with necessary characteristics of senior positions, such as skills in handling others, detachment, capacity to make objective decisions on standards, as well as political and organisational savviness (Dorfman, Hanges, & Brodbeck, 2004; Offermann, Kennedy, & Wirtz, 1994). Therefore, provided that these individuals can mask their socially aversive interpersonal qualities, their behavioural tendencies may enhance organisational effectiveness and preclude their need to undertake CWBs (Ray & Ray, 1982). Jones and Paulhus (2009) posit that it may not be authority that dampens socially aversive characteristics linked to Machiavellianism, but rather, the *attainment* of authority. Some evidence has been identified to support this postulation. For instance, Gable and Dangello (1994) reported a moderate link between Machiavellianism and internal work locus of control (i.e. an expectancy that rewards or outcomes in life are controlled by one's actions [internal] or by factors [external]). Namely, individuals with higher internal LOC tend to report higher satisfaction, autonomy, control and less stress with their jobs as compared to individuals with external LOC (Spector, 1982).

Stănescu and Mohorea (2015) recruited 122 participants to complete Work Locus of Control Scale (Spector, 1988), Mach-IV (Christie & Geis, 1970), Narcissistic Personality Inventory (Raskin & Hall, 1979), Self-Report Psychopathy scale–version III and Counterproductive Work Behaviour–Checklist (Spector et al., 2006). The results demonstrated a positive relationship between psychopathy and CWB ($r = .44$), but no relationship was found for CWB and Machiavellianism ($r = .01$) or narcissism ($r = .06$). However, the researchers found that an internal work-related locus of control had a positive significant correlation with Machiavellianism $(r = .20)$. This suggests that the more it is perceived that reinforcements are being controlled by one's own actions, the more likely that Machiavellian tactics will be employed.

Narcissism

The term narcissism derives from the tale of Narcissus, who, according to Greek mythology, falls in love with his own reflection upon gazing into a pond and perishes away due to refusing to separate himself from his own reflection (Holtzman & Donnellan, 2015). Inspired by this tale, Sigmund Freud (1914/1991) operationalised the term "narcissism" to describe those with excessive self-admiration due to an unhealthy relationship between their ego and libido (Roberts, Woodman, & Sedikides, 2018). Since Freud's use of "narcissism", there has been debate about the core features and organisation of this construct (Brummelman, Thomaes, & Sedikides, 2016). Krizan and Herlache (2018) contend that this debate has created blurred conceptual boundaries and multi-usage of the term, such as: (i) a non-pathological trait that forms part of a normal persona contributing to one's self-esteem (Resick, Whitman, Weingarden, & Hiller, 2009), (ii) a configuration of personality traits and (iii) those pathologically impaired by grandiosity and self-infatuation (Krizan & Herlache, 2018; Wu & Lebreton, 2011).

Narcissism is recognised as a personality disorder in the Diagnostic Statistical Manual of Mental Disorders–Fifth Edition (DSM–5; American Psychiatric Association [APA], 2013). A diagnosis of Narcissistic Personality Disorder may be given if at least five of the nine DSM–5 diagnostic criteria are met and that the criteria are inflexible, maladaptive or cause persistent and significant functional impairment or distress (APA, 2013). However, if the individual denies distress and functions reasonably in their relationships and occupation, then this does not constitute a diagnosis (DuBrin, 2012). This milder display of narcissism is more characteristic of a personality type, which is denoted as subclinical narcissism (Treadway, Yang, Bentley, Williams, & Reeves, 2017).

Narcissists may initially present as confident, charming and likeable (Miller & Campbell, 2010). However, this socially desirable presentation tends to alter with time, often being substituted with arrogance, self-centeredness and competitiveness (Smith, 2015). For those with narcissism, interpersonal relationships are merely a source for bolstering their fragile self-esteem and attaining confirmation of their inflated self-view (Miller, Widiger, & Campbell, 2010). The narcissist often achieves this by boasting about or exaggerating their successes or employing guile tactics including strategic kindness or forging alliances to gain status by association (Bowling & Michel, 2011). Those with elevated narcissism hold unrealistic expectations about their acceptance by others (Okada, 2010). Thus, when these individuals perceive ego threat or rejection, they readily deploy aggressive responses such as overt aggression, rage or violence (Falkenbach, Howe, & Falki, 2013). Narcissists are evidently preoccupied with achieving status in society, and thus, these individuals often place greater importance on "getting ahead" rather than "getting along" (Jonason, Wee, & Li, 2015).

Narcissism and CWB

The empirical literature argues that there is a tendency for narcissists to assume an authoritative role in the workplace (Campbell, Hoffman, Campbell, & Marchisio, 2011). Narcissistic leaders reportedly hold strong social skills and charisma that they employ to influence and impose their will on others (Khoo & Burch, 2008). These individuals also reportedly undertake big risks in pursuit of their goals (Campbell et al., 2011). For instance, a study by Blair, Hoffman, and Hell (2008) sought to evaluate the relationship between narcissism and leadership to determine the extent to which narcissism is relevant to managerial effectiveness and integrity. The researchers found that these individuals tend to hold higher confidence with regard to their decision-making process, but were no more efficient than leaders without narcissism. The integrity of the narcissistic leader was also deemed to be well below the level of integrity of the leader without narcissistic traits.

Wonneberg and Chapman (2007) has suggested that narcissistic behaviour may lead to high levels of organisational leadership incompetency, as levels of narcissism will increase alongside rises in power. A resurgence of literature indicates that narcissists who hold positions of power often engage in unethical behaviours (Amernic & Craig, 2010; Chatterjee & Hambrick, 2011; Williams, Nathanson, & Paulhus, 2010) and ultimately produce negative outcomes related to organisational strategies (Zhu & Chen, 2015) and performance (Patel & Cooper, 2014). Studies have found that CEOs high on narcissism tend to provide less individual consideration for employees (Resick et al., 2009) and leader narcissism negatively impacts follower outcomes in terms of emotional burnout, counterproductivity and organisational citizenship (Braun, 2017).

The narcissist's toxic interpersonal style, self-centeredness, as well as grandiosity and entitlement may lead them to deploy deviant workplace behaviours to attain self-serving goals (Wu & Lebreton, 2011). This conjecture is supported by the empirical research which has reported links between narcissism and the following workplace outcomes: unjustified credit-taking (Graham & Cooper, 2013), contributions to corporate scandals (Zona, Minoja, & Coda, 2013), power abuse and stealing (Watts et al., 2013). These findings suggest that narcissists are likely to commit CWB–O and CWB–I for their own egoistic purposes. In an early examination of narcissism and CWB, Penney and Spector (2002) sought to examine the implications and ramifications present when a third party challenges a narcissist's view. The researchers revealed that narcissists will experience anger more frequently and are likely to express this through engaging in CWB. A corporate environment perceived as less threatening, however, may be viewed by the narcissist as an opportunity to climb up in the corporate hierarchy or fulfil their grandiose self-enhancement. The fulfilment of the narcissistic needs by attaining power suggests that a position of authority may attenuate the relationship between narcissism and CWB.

Aghaz, Sharifi Atashgah, and Zoghipour (2014) sought to clarify whether the link between managerial position and CWB is mediated by overt narcissism (i.e. arrogance, excessive self-esteem, grandiosity) or covert narcissism (i.e. low self-esteem, hypersensitivity). Participants comprised a senior manager group ($N = 196$) and an employee group ($N = 221$) that were recruited from ten Iranian firms. Participants self-reported their perceived level of narcissism and CWB across a battery of tests. The results of the study suggest that covert narcissism is a stronger predictor of CWB–I and CWB–O compared to overt narcissism. No direct effect of managerial position on CWB–I or CWB–O was identified; however, there was an indirect effect between these constructs that was mediated through covert narcissism. While these findings suggest that hypersensitive narcissists with low self-esteem (i.e. covert narcissists) are more likely to commit CWB, it is important to note that meta-analytical findings report that the narcissism–CWB relationship is weaker for cultures with higher levels of in-group collectivism (Grijalva & Newman, 2015; O'Boyle et al., 2012). Previous authors have reported that covert narcissism is higher in collectivist cultures (Zondag, van Halen, & Wojtkowiak, 2009). Thus, due to the collectivist culture employed in this sample (i.e. Iran), there is difficulty generalising these results to individualistic cultures.

Grijalva and Newman (2015) conducted an online survey using a sample of 433 workers. Narcissism was assessed using the Narcissistic Personality Inventory (NPI; Raskin & Hall, 1979) and Psychological Entitlement Scale (PES; Campbell, Bonacci, Shelton, Exline, & Bushman, 2004), while CWB was assessed using the Workplace Deviance Scale (WDS; Bennett & Robinson, 2000). Of the many results, narcissism positively predicted CWB ($r = .28$, $p < .05$), while the Leadership and Authoritative (L/A) subscale of the NPI negatively predicted CWB ($r = -.11$, $p < .05$). That is, it seemed that narcissistic leaders were less likely to engage in CWB once their desires for success and status were fulfilled. Note that the L/A facet of the NPI has been identified as the most adaptive dimension of narcissism (Ackerman et al., 2011), such that those with high L/A express ideal leadership behaviour including assertiveness and charisma, and being more likely to take responsibility for decisions (Raskin & Terry, 1988). Thus, it makes conceptual sense that L/A would negatively predict CWB. It is important to highlight that the researchers did not control for level of supervisory responsibility. Thus, it is difficult to ascertain if the "workers" in this study are employees or those in managerial roles. Additionally, the researchers examined CWB as a unified construct, so that specific patterns within CWB may have been masked (i.e. CWB–O versus CWB–I).

There is difficulty ascertaining whether narcissists in managerial positions are likely to commit CWB–I or CWB–O. This is due to the lack of empirical studies and mixed results offered by extant studies. While various studies reported the L/A facet of the NPI as a negative predictor to CWB, these studies often use student and employee samples (Fox, Kessler, & Spector, 2013). This subsequently creates difficulty determining whether the CWB patterns in the above-mentioned studies reflect the CWB of narcissistic managers. Thus, alike to Machiavellianism and psychopathy literature, the narcissistic literature suggests that further examination of the association between those operating in managerial roles and their engagement in CWB–I or CWB–O is crucial (Text Box 7.2).

Text Box 7.2: A Case of CWB
Nathan Brooks

One the most highly publicised examples of widespread CWB is the case of the company, Enron. The downfall of Enron was documented in the astutely titled book, *The Smartest Guys in the Room: The Amazing Rise and Scandalous Fall of Enron* (McLean & Elkind, 2003). Enron was established as a company in 1986, following the merging of two businesses that specialised in gas production and transport (Chabrak & Daidj, 2007). The company declared its intention of being a leader in energy trading, initially producing and transporting gas, and later progressing to being a market-maker in energy, a pioneer of commodities, and trader of derivatives (Chabrak & Daidj, 2007). Towards the end of the 1990s, Enron's share price saw enormous growth with the business considered an economic company for the future (Deakin & Konzelmann, 2004; McLean & Elkind, 2003). Enron became the number one trader of electricity in the world within the space of 15 years and was recognised in 2000 as the seventh largest company in the United States based on sales (Chadrak & Daidj, 2007). The rise of Enron coincided with deregulation of energy markets allowing Enron to take advantage of these regulatory changes and prosper economically (McLean & Elkind, 2003).

Until the companies decline in 2001, *"Enron was highly regarded by media, academic professors and the stock market analysts because it had broken the capital-intensive business model of the gas and electrical provider"* (Chadrak & Daidj, 2007, pp. 543–546). The widespread regard for Enron led to Chairman Kenneth Lay being described as *"revolutionary"* (Tourish & Vatcha, 2005, p. 462), Chief Financial Officer Jeffrey Skilling pronounced as *"the No. 1 CEO in the entire country"* (Knapp, 2009, p. 7) and Chief Financial Officer Andrew Fastow labelled as CFO of the year in 1999 (Goldstein, 2011; Perri, 2013).

Enron presented an image that was in complete contradiction to its internal reality (Perri, 2013). Despite appearing to produce significant profits, Enron was masking significant debt, with members of senior management having created over 700 companies and existing deals to mask the true extent of the organisation's debt (Boddy, 2015; Cuplan & Trussel, 2005; Tonge, Greer, & Lawton, 2003). These actions created confusion over Enron's profitability, concealing market losses, misleading analysts, and making an evaluation of the company nearly impossible (Boddy, 2015). According to Deakin and Konzelmann (2004), *"Enron's fall was brought about by conflicts of interest on the part of its senior managers and by a lack of oversight on the part of its board of directors"* (p. 134). In 2001, to the shock of many, Enron filed for bankruptcy, with evidence emerging of several fraudulent schemes (CNN Library, 2019). The decline of company led to the loss of approximately 4000 jobs and an estimated $65 billon dollars of debt owed to creditors and investors (Leung, 2005).

A former Enron vice president described Enron's approach to business as, *"[You can] break rules, you can cheat, you can lie, but as long as it makes money, it's alright"* (Sims & Brinkmann, 2003, p. 250). Despite a cultural of ruthlessness, some senior staff were concerned, with executive James Alexander identifying accounting irregularities and reporting these to Lay, only to be replaced by Andrew Fastow as CFO (Jennings, 2006; Perri, 2013). Further trepidations were raised by board member, Brent Scowcroft, questioning the accuracy of Enron's financial statements, however, again this was challenged by Lay. Through manipulation and placing social pressure on Scowcroft, Lay stated *"How could you be right and men of this caliber [referring to Fastow and Skilling] be wrong"* (Jennings, 2006, p. 65). Unfortunately for Alexander and Scowcroft, Lay and his senior managers did not respond well to being queried, with Alexander eventually dismissed and Scowcroft reminded of the company's expectations and his compliance with these (Perri, 2013). Boddy (2015) believed that the systemic culture of manipulation and deceit at Enron reflected a psychopathic corporation, using power and influence to benefit executives with shares and share options, despite the detriment to employees, investors and pension funds. For example, prior to the early decline of Enron, four days before the organisation announced a $618 million-dollar loss for the third quarter, many key figures within the organisation sold their shares in the company (Kadlec, 2002).

As the details of Enron's decline emerged, Lay was alleged to have mislead investors about the "*true value, sustainability and financial viability of Enron*" and in addition "*withdrew large personal amounts of money immediately prior to the corporation's collapse, while simultaneously reassuring investors as to Enron's longer term viability*" (Boddy, 2015, p. 2417). Interestingly, despite the fraudulent activity occurring at Enron, Lay conveyed his concern for humanity through philanthropic causes which modelled social responsibility and piety towards others, however, according to Perri (2013), this form of behaviour, like Bernie Maddoff's or Al Capone's attempts at humanitarianism, served as a smokescreen to mask fraudulent and unethical behaviour. According to Maccoby (2000) the leadership style of Lay and Skilling resembled that of narcissism, characterised by taking excessive risks for gains. However, Boddy (2015) and Fersch (2006) had different opinions of Lay and Skilling. Boddy (2015) speculated whether Lay's behaviour was more reflective of a psychopath, engaging in self-gratification, self-promotion, and self-enrichment at the expense of stakeholders and corporate investors. While Fersch (2006) stated "*Skilling possessed the traits of corporate psychopathy. He was manipulative, glib, superficial, egocentric, shallow, and impulsive, and he lacked guilt, remorse and empathy. Skilling ruined thousands of people's lives by committing insider trading and fraud*" (p.107).

The behaviour of Lay and Skilling was no doubt influential to the decline of Enron, however, multiple people within the organisation were also found to be involved in CWB, comprising of a prolific number of illegal and unethical acts. The fallout from the conduct by many of the senior members resulted in the following: Lay was charged and convicted of conspiracy and fraud; Skilling convicted of conspiracy, fraud, insider trading and making false statements; Fastow convicted of wire and securities fraud, Lea Fastow (wife of Andrew) the assistance treasurer of Enron convicted of tax fraud; executive Michael Koper found guilty of fraud; accountant Arthur Anderson indicted on obstruction of justice; and, vice chairman Clifford Baxter committing suicide (CNN Library, 2019).

Contextual Contributions to CWB

It is more adaptive for individuals to display their personality traits in certain organisational contexts compared to others (Jonason et al., 2015). Although narcissism, Machiavellianism and psychopathy are positively related to CWB, a call for research examining the role of contextual factors that either strengthen or weaken this relationship has been made (O'Boyle et al. 2012). Trait activation theory suggests that personality traits become activated by contextual factors (Blickle et al., 2018; Tett & Burnett, 2003); therefore, applying this theory to the behaviours of individuals with DT personality characteristics and workplace outcomes, it is possible that the contradictory findings identified in research may be due to scenarios where certain contextual cues activated these personality traits resulting in negative outcomes, whereas other contexts or "setting conditions" may have indeed activated the more adaptive aspects of dark triad personality traits resulting in positive work outcomes. In yet a third condition, there was simply no activation and therefore no effects found. While numerous suggestions have been made about variables that theoretically might moderate the relationship between dark triad personality traits and occupational outcomes, very few have been empirically tested in the business context. In relation to criminal psychopathy, variables that have been found to moderate the relationship between psychopathy and rates of offending include age (Olver & Wong, 2015), intelligence (Heilbrun, 1979), executive function (Ishikawa, Raine, Lencz, Bihrle, & Lacasse, 2001) and parenting competence (Edens, Skopp, & Cahill, 2008). Additional variables proposed by Benning, Venables, and Hall (2018) that may differentiate successful from unsuccessful psychopathy include communication skills (Babiak et al., 2010) and relatively intact neuroanatomy (Raine et al., 2004). Finally, some creative proposals have even included testing whether unethical behaviour was more likely to be carried out by individuals with dark triad traits at night-time rather than during daylight (it wasn't) (Roeser et al., 2016). In the following section, we review the major moderating variables that have been proposed specifically within the organisational context.

Occupational Stress and Support

CWBs have been presented in the literature as a form of coping with occupational stressors (Fox, Spector, & Miles, 2001). Specifically, research has confirmed the negative association between CWB and occupational stressors, including workload, role ambiguity, organisational injustice and interpersonal conflict (Spector, Fox, & Domagalski, 2005). Occupational stressors appear to be associated with both CWB–P and CWB–O, as employees feel that control is gained on the stressful situation, by harming an individual target or the organisation (Budean & Pitariu, 2015).

Intuitively, when negative perceptions of organisational support exist, deviant behaviours amongst individuals perceived as disagreeable increase (Colbert, Mount, Harter, Witt, & Barrick, 2004). Perceived organisational support delineates an individual's perception that their contribution and well-being are valued by their organisation (Cohen, 2018). This notion is supported by studies; where higher levels of occupational support are perceived, there is a decrease in CWB–O including employee absenteeism (Rhoades & Eisenberger, 2002) and withdrawal behaviours at work (Eder & Eisenberger, 2008).

The tendency for narcissistic or psychopathic individuals to engage in CWB–O may be reduced when occupational stress is decreased by a perception of organisational support. For instance, Palmer, Komarraju, Carter and Karau (2017) recruited 208 employees who were required to complete the Short Dark Triad Scale (Jones & Paulhus, 2014), Counterproductive Work Behaviour–Checklist (CWB–C; Spector et al., 2006) and the Survey of Perceived Organizational Support (Eisenberger, Huntington, Hutchison, & Sowa, 1986). The researchers found that when higher levels of support were perceived, employees with high narcissism engaged in fewer production deviance, while those high in psychopathy reported engaging in fewer sabotage, production deviance and theft. These findings suggest that increased occupational well-being as fostered by organisational support may act as a buffer against the frequency with which DT individuals engage in CWB.

Increased occupational support may enhance the narcissist's sense of self-importance and reduce ego threat. Comparatively, increased occupational support may reduce elements of provocation that prime psychopathic employees hold, which, in turn, may subsequently reduce unprovoked CWB. Machiavellian employees are consistently dissatisfied with the "status quo" and are consistently searching for ways to gain more influence over their co-workers (Fehr, Samsom, & Paulhus, 1992), leading to higher stress associated with pressure (Dahling et al., 2009). Machiavellians with increased occupational support may view their organisation as less threatening and opt to manipulate behind the scenes instead of risky overt tactics like CWB. However, Machiavellians are less likely to benefit from social support, as they view the world through a pessimistic lens, are highly cynical of others and distrust others' motives (Dahling et al., 2009). Therefore, perceiving the organisation in a more positive way may inhibit natural tendencies of employees who hold DT traits to engage in CWB.

Interpersonal Conflict and CWB

The DT personality traits share an exploitive interpersonal style, such that the goals of these individuals are self-oriented and carried out at the expense of others (Jones & Paulhus, 2010). In the case of psychopathy, managers have been cited as significant sources of conflict and bullying (Boddy, 2014), with the risk of aggression increasing in the presence of confrontational situations (i.e. conflict, physical attacks). Narcissists appear more aggressive when ego threat or rejection is perceived (Paulhus

& Williams, 2002), often triggering defensive behaviours deemed offensive to others (Kaiser & Kaplan, 2006). Machiavellians can be "subtler" in their behaviours; however, they exhibit a tendency to abuse their co-workers (Pilch & Turska, 2015). Evidently, the interpersonal style of those with DT personality traits suggests that they are prone to interpersonal conflict at work.

Interpersonal conflict is denoted as the quality of interactions between individuals in the workplace, including the frequency with which individuals yell at or argue with others (Spector & Jex, 1998). Interpersonal conflict at work is an important occupation stressor linked to adverse organisational consequences, including CWB since conflict is associated with decreased team work efficiency and lower organisational productivity (Dunlop & Lee, 2004) as well as employee helpfulness (Porath & Erez, 2007). This link between interpersonal conflict amongst employees and CWB is well established (Kessler, Bruursema, Rodopman, & Spector, 2013; Spector & Fox, 2002). According to Spector and Fox (2002) when employees experience stressors in the workplace, they will experience a range of state-based emotions and subsequently engage in CWB. While early researchers have focused on the mediating role of interpersonal conflict, others have identified a direct link between interpersonal conflict and CWB (Berry, Carpenter, & Barratt, 2012; Hershcovis et al., 2007).

Interestingly, Hershcovis and Barling (2010) meta-analytically found that sources of the aggression (i.e. supervisor or colleague) affected whether an individual engaged in CWB–O or CWB–I. These findings suggest that the perceived source of stressor is imperative for understanding when and why certain individuals in the workplace engage in CWB. Researchers have thus attempted to distinguish between sources of interpersonal conflict (Jonason et al., 2012; Meurs, Fox, Kessler, & Spector, 2013; Southard, Noser, Pollock, Mercer, & Zeigler-Hill, 2015) often citing individual traits and ineffective communication as the culprit (Hasanati, Winarsuni, & Karina, 2017). Unsurprisingly, all DT personality traits have been reported as significant and negative predictors of interpersonal communication (Southard et al., 2015). There is, however, seldom research pertinent to the CWB of those with DT personality traits in managerial positions. As sources of stress can vary the type of CWB engaged (i.e. CWB–I or

CWB–O), the aftermath of those senior managers with DT personality traits who are faced with conflict appears to be worth further examining.

The research suggests that interpersonal conflict may increase alongside higher levels of perceived autonomy. An early study by Spector and Fox (2005) found that interpersonal conflict associated with CWB–P is higher when individual autonomy is also high. These findings suggest that participants, who perceived that they were in an autonomous occupational role, increased their latitude to engage in CWB–P (specifically involving interpersonal conflict) without fear of retribution. This aligns with prior literature by Fox and Spector (1999), which found that the belief that one has the ability to harm an organisation without being punished was one of the strongest predictors of CWB. The likelihood of punishment has also been found to have differential effects for each of the dark triad personality traits, with those highest in psychopathy being more likely to persist in a gambling task even when there was a risk of retribution (Jones, 2014), whereas individuals high in Machiavellianism would not take unnecessary risks, and Narcissists will only do so if their ego is invested (Jones & Paulhus, 2011). The implications are that individuals in higher positions of authority, who possess increased autonomy, may be more likely to engage in CWB and that autonomy may moderate the relationship between DT traits and CWB.

Negative Affect and CWB

The experience of negative affect appears to be a significant precursor to CWB (Samnani, Salamon, & Singh, 2014). Negative affect delineates a dispositional tendency towards experiencing negative emotions such as anxiety, fear, sadness or anger (Watson, Clark, & Tellegen, 1988). Scholars have identified that employees with high levels of negative affect are more inclined to engage in CWB compared to those with lower levels (Spector et al., 2005). Larsen and Ketelaar (1991) assert that this is because employees with increased negative affect tend to experience increased sensitivity and emotional reactivity. Subsequently, as emotional reactivity entails a stronger translation of affect into actual behaviour, this may encourage a translation of affect into CWB.

Several explanations have been put forth to explain how negative affect leads to CWB. For instance, Penney and Spector (2005) propose that employees with high negative affect will perceive the world as more negatively and thus may have a greater propensity to engage in behaviours to help them reduce or cope with their negative emotions. Early research supports this postulation (Blau, 1964), which identified that employees who perceived their organisation as a source of negative emotions had a tendency to reciprocate by engaging in negative behaviours towards the organisation to gain a sense of retribution. Alternatively, employees may engage in CWB withdrawal to diffuse their affective state, by avoiding the problem (Dalal, Lam, Weiss, Welch, & Hulin, 2009).

Avenues that may offer insight into the relationship between negative affect and CWB relate to morals and ethics. A study by Samnani, Salamon, and Singh (2014) found that individuals with a greater tendency to experience negative emotions were more likely to engage in CWB when they had a higher propensity to morally disengage. Moral disengagement refers to an individual's ability to deactivate moral self-regulation and self-censure, allowing these individuals to engage in behaviour consistent with moral standards, without associated self-sanctions and guilt (Bandura, Barbaranelli, Caprara, & Pastorelli, 1996; Detert, Trevino, & Sweitzer, 2008). The results also found that employees with high levels of negative affect, who were not prone to morally disengage, were less likely to engage in CWB than those prone to morally disengage. These results suggest that experiencing negative emotions by itself may not be sufficient to explain why employees engage in CWB. However, the results also suggest that the tendency to morally disengage, a characteristic of the DT personality traits, may mean that individuals with DT personalities will be more inclined to participate in CWB in the context of negative affect.

A study by Garcia, Adrianson, Archer, and Rosenberg (2015) investigated the "affective profiles" of individuals with DT personality traits. The affective profiles comprised the combination of an individual's experience of high/low positive affect and high/low negative affect in individuals with DT personality traits. Participants ($n = 1000$) completed the Positive Affect Negative Affect Schedule (PANAS) and the Dark Triad Dirty Dozen. Individuals with higher affective profiles were more likely to report higher levels of all three of the dark triad traits than those with a low affective or self-fulfilling profile. This finding indicates that DT personality traits are associated with experiencing intense emotion—both positive and negative—and therefore, situations in which these emotions are activated may evoke the potential to engage in CWB. The mediating role of emotion may operate both directly on the individual with DT traits and their likelihood of engaging in CWB and also indirectly via the role of DT leadership on employee CWB. This was investigated in a study by Michel, Newness, and Duniewicz (2016), which found that work-related negative affect mediated the relationship between "abusive supervision" and workplace deviance. This also relates to research by Palmer et al. (2017), who found that perceived organisational support (POS) moderated the relationship between the DT traits and CWB. Specifically, narcissistic employees who perceived their organisation as supportive reported being less likely to purposely work slowly (Palmer et al., 2017), and POS also moderated the relationships between psychopathy and sabotage, production deviance and theft (Palmer et al., 2017).

Person-Organisation Fit

According to vocational theory (Blickle et al., 2018; Holland, 1997), work behaviour and performance outcomes are predicted by an interaction between job characteristics and personal factors. Schneider (1987) proposed that employees are attracted to organisations that are a good match for their individual personalities, and Holland (1997) proposed that there are six basic occupational types, each of which is sought after by individuals with particular characteristics. Enterprising work environments, such as sales, marketing and management, emphasise power, status and financial reward and encourage the use of manipulation and politicking to maximise self-interest, often at the expense of others (Blickle et al., 2018; Cohen, 2016). In the research conducted by Blickle et al. (2018), described earlier in this chapter, it was found that prospects of pay rises and promotions moderated the relationship between dark triad traits and supervisor considerate behaviour towards their subordinates. The researchers concluded that working in an enterprising environment, in which ascendency prospects were emphasised, activated the psycho-pathic traits of managers.

Political skill is defined as the ability to understand and influence oth-ers (Ferris et al., 2005), and research has shown that individuals lacking in this skill feel depleted as a result of having to engage in supervisor ingratiation and self-promotion (Klotz et al., 2018) and are more likely to engage in workplace deviance when thus depleted. Research also sup-ports that some dark triad traits are more likely to be skilful politically than others. For example, Narcissists can come across as self-aggrandising and insincere and are more focused on inflating their own ego rather than the interpersonal needs of others (Cohen, 2016; Wu & Lebreton, 2011), whereas Psychopathy and Machiavellianism may both possess sufficient superficial charm to be successful at a certain degree of positive impression management (Cohen, 2016; Wu & Lebreton, 2011). According to Boddy (2011), a political environment is ideal for individuals with psychopathic traits since, for example performance appraisals are less likely to be linked to objective performance criteria and more likely to be subjectively based on the perceived quality of the relationship between the appraiser and the appraisee. Dark triad personalities are arguably more likely to be attuned to the social nuances of the organisation, and the perception of a highly political environment is thus potentially rewarding in two aspects: firstly, it signals that self-interest, self-promotion and exploitation of others are tolerated or even expected, and secondly, it provides the fodder for such exploitation in the form of employees who lack the relevant political skill and are stressed (Klotz et al., 2018). Focusing on career building rather than competency development is likely to impact upon actual job perfor-mance, and thus, the relationship between dark triad traits and subjective and objective career success is likely to be mediated by the organisational climate with regard to political opportunities and norms (Witt & Spector, 2012). For a more detailed set of hypotheses about interactions between political skills, organisational politics, accountability and organisational factors including transparency, formal policies and culture, see Cohen (2016).

Sex

Men tend to score significantly higher than women on measures of psychopathy in both criminal and noncriminal settings (Miller, Watts, & Jones, 2011), and there is also some evidence that psychopathy manifests differently in women (see Chapter 1). Similarly, in the leadership literature there have been important sex differences reported, including perceptions of effectiveness based on the types of influence tactics used (communal vs agentic; Landay, Harms, & Crede, 2018; Smith et al., 2013), as well as displays of dominance and emotion (Brescoll, 2016). On the interaction between gender, leadership and psychopathy, one study reported that when male leaders displayed dark personality characteristics, they were more likely to be perceived as effective, compared to women who displayed the same characteristics (De Hoogh, Den Hartog, & Nevicka, 2015). In a meta-analytic review, Landay et al. (2018) found that there was a modest negative relationship between psychopathic tendencies and leadership effectiveness for women and a weak positive relationship for men, and similarly, sex differences were found for transformational leadership such that the relationship was strongly negative for females and only moderately negative for men. Finally, for leadership emergence, i.e. the likelihood that an individual has attained a leadership role or is perceived by others in the team as a leader, the relationship with psychopathy was weakly positive for women and stronger for men. While it is noted that the number of studies included in the above analyses was small (e.g. $k = 6$ for transformational leadership), these results do provide support for the contention that higher levels of psychopathic traits are tolerated in men than in women and that there are social and occupational sanctions against women displaying psychopathic traits (Landay et al., 2018). The results of this study were reported for psychopathic traits and not for the dark triad more broadly; therefore, further research is needed on the moderating effects of sex, as well as expanding the outcome variables to include additional work-related criteria such as counterproductive work behaviour.

Conclusions

An overview of research into the relation between DT personality traits and organisational outcomes identifies that each of these contributes in various ways to interpersonal and organisational CWB. It is also acknowledged that empirical literature presents conflicting findings across studies, and this is likely due to several salient concerns. The first of these includes a range of issues relating to the measures that have been used in dark triad research. This has been noted particularly for Machiavellianism, where the shared variance with psychopathy has led some to proposed that existing measures of Machiavellianism are in fact measures of psychopathy (Miller, Vize, Crowe, & Lynam, 2019; Vize, Lynam, Collison, & Miller, 2018). Measurement is also a concern in relation to the other dark triad characteristics. Both narcissism and psychopathy have been found to be multi-dimensional, comprising of facets that have both adaptive and maladaptive aspects. Thus, when studies use total scores to predict CWB, leadership, aggression and other outcomes, it is likely that competing aspects of the measures (reflecting competing aspects of the personality traits themselves) cancel each other out or are weighted disproportionately (Durand, 2017). Secondly, there is a lack of literature investigating the role of contextual factors that may mediate the relationship between the DT and CWB (Blickle et al., 2018; O'Boyle et al., 2012). The variables considered in this chapter are by no means an exhaustive list, and indeed, several of these variables may themselves interact (e.g. gender, political skill and emotional burnout). Thirdly, since the majority of studies have employed a cross-sectional design, it is not possible to know the direction of causality between the personality traits and workplace outcomes (Muris et al., 2017). Fourthly, relying on self-report measures has been noted to be problematic due to common source variance (Blickle et al., 2018). Finally, it is noted that in this chapter, we have focused on the dark triad, whereas a more recently proposed dark tetrad also includes the personality trait of sadism (Međedović & Petrović, 2015; Buckels, Jones & Paulhus, 2013), which in common with the dark triad personality characteristics is understood to have an everyday subclinical component. Recent research has investigated everyday sadism in relation to interpersonal aggression, impulsivity and empathy, but there are no studies as yet investigating its work-related occurrence and behavioural outcomes.

References

Abell, L., Brewer, G., Qualter, P., & Austin, E. (2016). Machiavellianism, emotional manipulation, and friendship functions in women's friendships. *Personality and Individual Differences, 88,* 108–113. https://doi.org/10.1016/j.paid.2015.09.001.

ACFE. (2018). *Report to the nations on occupational fraud and abuse.* Retrieved from www.acfe.com. Association of Certified Fraud Examiners (ACFE).

Ackerman, R., Witt, E., Donnellan, M., Trzesniewski, K., Robins, R., & Kashy, D. (2011). What does the narcissistic personality inventory really measure? *Assessment, 18*(1), 67–87. https://doi.org/10.1177/1073191110382845.

Aghaz, A., Sharifi Atashgah, M. S., & Zoghipour, M. (2014). Narcissism and counterproductive workplace behaviors among Iranian managers and non-managerial employees. *Asian Journal of Business Ethics, 3,* 155–169. https://doi.org/10.1007/s13520-014-0039-2.

Alpers, G., & Eisenbarth, H. (2008). *Psychopathic personality inventory-revised: PPI-R—Manual, deutsche version.* Hogrefe.

American Psychiatric Association. (2013). *Diagnostic and statistical manual of mental disorders* (5th ed.). Arlington, VA: American Psychiatric Publishing.

Amernic, J. H., & Craig, R. J. (2010). Accounting as a facilitator of extreme narcissism. *Journal of Business Ethics, 96,* 79–93. https://doi.org/10.1007/s10551-010-0450-0.

Amir, T. S., & Malik, A. A. (2016). Machiavellianism and counterproductive behaviors at work. *Journal of Education and Social Sciences, 4,* 33–47. https://doi.org/10.5093/jwop2018a10.

Babiak, P., Neumann, C. S., & Hare, R. D. (2010). Corporate psychopathy: Talking the walk. *Behavioral Sciences & the Law, 28,* 174–193. https://doi.org/10.1002/bsl.925.

Baka, Ł. (2018). When do the "dark personalities" become less counterproductive? The moderating role of job control and social support. *International Journal of Occupational Safety and Ergonomics: JOSE, 24*(4), 557–569. https://doi.org/10.1080/10803548.2018.1463670.

Baloch, M. A., Meng, F., Xu, Z., Cepeda-Carrion, I., Danish, & Bari, M. W. (2017). Dark triad, perceptions of organizational politics and counterproductive work behaviors: The moderating effect of political skills. *Frontiers in Psychology, 8,* 1972. https://doi.org/10.3389/fpsyg.2017.01972.

Bandura, A., Barbaranelli, C., Caprara, G. V., & Pastorelli, C. (1996). Mechanisms of moral disengagement in the exercise of moral agency. *Journal of Personality and Social Psychology, 71*(2), 364–374.

Bauer, J. A., & Spector, P. E. (2015). Discrete negative emotions and counterproductive work behavior. *Human Performance, 28,* 307–331. https://doi.org/10.1080/08959285.2015.1021040.

Baughman, H. M., Dearing, S., Giammarco, E., & Vernon, P. A. (2012). Relationships between bullying behaviours and the dark triad: A study with adults. *Personality and Individual Differences, 52,* 571–575. https://doi.org/10.1016/j.paid.2011.11.020.

Beasley, M. S., Carcello, J. V., Hermanson, D. R., & Neal, T. L. (2010). *Fraudulent financial reporting: 1998–2007: An analysis of U.S. public companies.* www.coso.org. The Committee of Sponsoring Organizations of the Treadway Commission (COSO).

Belschak, F. D., Den Hartog, D. N., & Kalshoven, K. (2015). Leading Machiavellians: How to translate Machiavellians' selfishness into pro-organizational behavior. *Journal of Management, 41,* 1934–1956. https://doi.org/10.1177/0149206313484513.

Bennett, R. J., & Robinson, S. L. (2000). Development of a measure of workplace deviance. *Journal of Applied Psychology, 85,* 349–360. https://doi.org/10.1037/21-10.85.3.349.

Benning, S. D., Venables, N. C., & Hall, J. R. (2018). Successful psychopathy. In C. J. Patrick (Ed.), *Handbook of psychopathy* (2nd ed., pp. 585–608). New York: Guilford Press.

Berry, C. M., Carpenter, N. C., & Barratt, C. L. (2012). Do other-reports of counterproductive work behavior provide an incremental contribution over selfreports? A meta-analytic comparison. *Journal of Applied Psychology, 97,* 613–636. https://doi.org/10.1037/a0026739.

Birkás, B., Csathó, Á., Gács, B., & Bereczkei, T. (2015). Nothing ventured nothing gained: Strong associations between reward sensitivity and two measures of Machiavellianism. *Personality and Individual Differences, 74*(C), 112–115. https://doi.org/10.1016/j.paid.2014.09.046.

Blair, C. A., Hoffman, B. J., & Helland, K. R. (2008). Narcissism in organizations: A multisource appraisal reflects different perspectives. *Human Performance, 21,* 254–276. https://doi.org/10.1080/08959280802137705.

Blau, P. M. (1964). *The dynamics of bureaucracy.* Chicago, IL: University of Chicago Press.

Blickle, G., Schütte, N., & Genau, H. (2018). Manager psychopathy, trait activation, and job performance: a multi-source study. *European Journal of Work and Organizational Psychology, 27*(4), 450–461. https://doi.org/10.1080/1359432X.2018.1475354.

Blickle, G., Kramer, J., Schneider, P. B., Meurs, J. A., Ferris, G. R., Mierke, J., ... Momm, T. D. (2011). Role of political skill in job performance prediction beyond general mental ability and personality in cross-sectional and predictive studies. *Journal of Applied Social Psychology, 41*, 488–514.

Boddy, C. (2010). Corporate psychopaths and organizational type. *Journal of Public Affairs, 10*, 300–312. https://doi.org/10.1002/pa.365.

Boddy, C. R. (2011). Corporate psychopaths, bullying and unfair supervision in the workplace. *Journal of Business Ethics, 100*, 367–379. https://doi.org/10.1007/s10551-010-0689-5.

Boddy, C. R. (2014). Corporate psychopaths, conflict, employee affective well-being and counterproductive work behaviour. *Journal of Business Ethics, 121*, 107–121. https://doi.org/10.1007/s10551-013-1688-0.

Boddy, C. R. (2015). Organisational psychopaths: A ten year update. *Management Decisions, 53*, 2407–2432. https://doi.org/10.1108/MD-04-2015-0114.

Boddy, C. R. (2017). Psychopathic leadership a case study of a corporate psychopath CEO. *Journal of Business Ethics, 145*, 141–156. https://doi.org/10.1007/s10551-015-2908-6.

Boddy, C. R., Galvin, P., & Ladyshewsky, R. (2011). Corporate psychopaths. In C. Millar & E. Poole (Eds.), *Ethical leadership* (pp. 17–33). London: Springer.

Boddy, C. R., Ladyshewsky, R. K., & Galvin, P. (2010). The influence of corporate psychopaths on corporate social responsibility and organizational commitment to employees. *Journal of Business Ethics, 97*, 1–19. https://doi.org/10.1007/s10551-010-0492-3.

Boddy, C. R., Miles, D., Sanyal, C., & Hartog, M. (2015). Extreme managers, extreme workplaces: Capitalism, organizations and corporate psychopaths. *Organization, 22*, 530–551. https://doi.org/10.1177/1350508415572508.

Bolton, L. R., Harvey, R. D., Grawitch, M. J., & Barber, L. K. (2012). Counterproductive work behaviours in response to emotional exhaustion: A moderated mediational approach. *Stress and Health, 28*, 222–233. https://doi.org/10.1002/smi.1425.

Bowling, N. A. (2010). Effects of job satisfaction and conscientiousness on extra-role behaviours. *Journal of Business and Psychology, 25*, 119–130.

Bowling, N. A., & Michel, J. S. (2011). Why do you treat me badly? The role of attributions regarding the cause of abuse in subordinates' responses to abusive supervision. *Work & Stress, 25,* 309–320. https://doi.org/10.1080/02678373. 2011.634281.

Braun, S. (2017). Leader narcissism and outcomes in organisations: A review at multiple levels of analysis and implications for future research. *Frontiers in Psychology, 8,* 773. https://doi.org/10.3389/fpsyg.2017.00773.

Breaugh, J. (1998). The development of a new measure of global work autonomy. *Educational and Psychological Measurement, 58*(1), 119–128. https://doi.org/ 10.1177/0013164498058001010.

Brescoll, V. (2016). Leading with their hearts? How gender stereotypes of emotion lead to biased evaluations of female leaders. *The Leadership Quarterly, 27*(3), 415–428. https://doi.org/10.1016/j.leaqua.2016.02.005.

Brewer, G., & Abell, L. (2017). Machiavellianism, relationship satisfaction, and romantic relationship quality. *Europe's Journal of Psychology, 13,* 491–502. https://doi.org/10.5964/ejop.v13i3.1217.

Brewer, G., Abell, L., Glăveanu, V., & Wentink Martin, N. (2017). Machiavellianism, relationship satisfaction, and romantic relationship quality. *Europe's Journal of Psychology, 13*(3), 491–502. https://doi.org/10.5964/ejop.v13i3. 1217.

Brummelman, E., Thomaes, S., & Sedikides, C. (2016). Separating narcissism from self-esteem. *Current Directions in Psychological Science, 25*(1), 8–13. https://doi.org/10.1177/0963721415619737.

Buckels, E., Jones, D., & Paulhus, D. (2013). Behavioral confirmation of everyday sadism. *Psychological Science, 24*(11), 2201–2209. https://doi.org/10. 1177/0956797613490749.

Budean, A., & Pitariu, H. D. (2015). The relationship between trust in manager and the attitude towards change in the context of an international merger. *Psihologia Resurselor Umane, 7*(1), 29–42.

Campbell, W., Bonacci, A., Shelton, J., Exline, J., & Bushman, B. (2004). Psychological entitlement: Interpersonal consequences and validation of a self-report measure. *Journal of Personality Assessment, 83*(1), 29–45. https://doi.org/10. 1207/s15327752jpa8301_04.

Campbell, W., Hoffman, B., Campbell, S., & Marchisio, G. (2011). Narcissism in organizational contexts. *Human Resource Management Review, 21*(4), 268–284. https://doi.org/10.1016/j.hrmr.2010.10.007.

Caponecchia, C., Sun, A. Y. Z., & Wyatt, A. (2012). 'Psychopaths' at work? Implications of lay persons' use of labels and behavioural criteria for psychopathy. *Journal of Business Ethics, 107*, 399–408. https://doi.org/10.1007/s10551-011-1049-9.

Caspi, A., Elder, G. H., & Bem, D. J. (1988). Moving away from the world: Life-course patterns of shy children. *Developmental Psychology, 24*, 824–831. https://doi.org/10.1037//0012-1649.24.6.824.

Chabrak, N., & Daidj, N. (2007). Enron: Widespread myopia. *Critical Perspectives on Accounting, 18*, 539–557. https://doi.org/10.1016/j.cpa.2005.10.004.

Chatterjee, A., & Hambrick, D. (2011). Executive personality, capability cues, and risk taking: How narcissistic CEOs react to their successes and stumbles. *Administrative Science Quarterly, 56*, 202–237. Retrieved from http://www.jstor.org/stable/41410260.

Christie, R., & Geis, F. L. (1970). *Machiavellianism*. New York: Academic Press.

Clarke, J. (2005). *Working with monsters: How to identify and protect yourself from the workplace psychopath*. Sydney: Random House.

CNN Library. (2019, April 25). *Enron fast facts*. CNN. Retrieved from https://edition.cnn.com/2013/07/02/us/enron-fast-facts/index.html.

Cohen, A. (2016). Are they among us? A conceptual framework of the relationship between the dark triad personality and counterproductive work behaviours. *Human Resource Management Review, 16*, 69–85. https://doi.org/10.1016/j.hrmr.2015.07.003.

Cohen, A. (2018). *Counterproductive work behaviors: Understanding the dark side of personalities in organizational life*. New York: Routledge.

Cohen, T., Panter, A., Turan, N., Morse, L., & Kim, Y. (2014). Moral character in the workplace. *Journal of Personality and Social Psychology, 107*(5), 943–963. https://doi.org/10.1037/a0037245.

Colbert, A. E., Mount, M. K., Harter, J. K., Witt, L. A., & Barrick, M. R. (2004). Interactive effects of personality and perceptions of the work situation on workplace deviance. *Journal of Applied Psychology, 89*, 599–609. https://doi.org/10.1037/0021-9010.89.4.599.

Costa, P. T., Jr., & McCrae, R. R. (1992). *Revised NEO Personality Inventory (NEO–PI–R) and NEO Five-Factor Inventory (NEO–FFI) professional manual*. Odessa, FL: Psychological Assessment Resources.

Cropanzano, R., & Mitchell, M. S. (2005). Social exchange theory: An interdisciplinary review. *Journal of Management, 31*, 874–900. https://doi.org/10.1177/0149206305279602.

Crush, P. (2014, May). Every business needs a psychopath. *People Management (CIPD)*.

Cuplan, R., & Trussel, J. (2005). Applying the agency and stakeholder theories to the Enron debacle: An ethical perspective. *Business and Society Review, 110,* 59–76.

Dahling, J. J., Kuyumcu, D., & Librizzi, E. (2012). *Machiavellianism, unethical behavior, and well-being in organizational life.* New York: M.E. Sharpe.

Dahling, J., Whitaker, B., & Levy, P. (2009). The development and validation of a new Machiavellianism scale. *Journal of Management, 35*(2), 219–257. https://doi.org/10.1177/0149206308318618.

Dalal, R. S., Lam, H., Weiss, H. M., Welch, E. R., & Hulin, C. L. (2009). A within-person approach to work behavior and performance: Concurrent and lagged citizenship-counter productivity associations, and dynamic relationships with affect and overall job performance. *Academy of Management Journal, 52*(5), 1051–1066.

Deakin, S., & Konzelmann, S. J. (2004). Learning from Enron. *Corporate Governance, 12,* 134–142.

De Hoogh, A. H., Den Hartog, D. N., & Nevicka, B. (2015). Gender differences in the perceived effectiveness of narcissistic leaders. *Applied Psychology: An International Review, 64,* 473–498. https://doi.org/10.1111/apps.12015.

DeShong, H., Grant, D., & Mullins-Sweatt, S. (2015). Comparing models of counterproductive workplace behaviors: The five-factor model and the dark triad. *Personality and Individual Differences, 74*(C), 55–60. https://doi.org/10.1016/j.paid.2014.10.001.

Detert, J. R., Trevino, L. K., & Sweitzer, V. L. (2008). Moral disengagement in ethical decision making: A study of antecedents and outcomes. *Journal of Applied Psychology, 93*(2), 374–391.

Dorfman, P., Hanges, P. J., & Broadbeck, F. C. (2004). Leadership and cultural variation: The identification of culturally endorsed leadership profiles. In R. J. House, M. Javidan, P. Dorfman, & V. Gupta (Eds.), *Leadership, culture, and organizations: The GLOBE study of 62 societies* (pp. 669–719). Thousand Oaks, CA: Sage.

Dorminey, J., Fleming, A., Kranacher, M., & Riley, R. (2012). The evolution of Fraud Theory. *Issues in Accounting Education, 27*(2), 555–579. https://doi.org/10.2308/iace-50131.

Douglas, S., Martinko, M., & Murphy, K. (2001). Exploring the role of individual differences in the prediction of workplace aggression. *Journal of Applied Psychology, 86*(4), 547–559. https://doi.org/10.1037/0021-9010.86.4.547.

DuBrin, A. (2012). *Narcissism in the workplace: Research, opinion and practice.* Cheltenham: Edward Elgar.

Dunlop, P., & Lee, K. (2004). Workplace deviance, organizational citizenship behavior, and business unit performance: The bad apples do spoil the whole barrel. *Journal of Organizational Behavior, 25*(1), 67–80. https://doi.org/10.1002/job.243.

Durand, G. (2017). The Durand adaptive psychopathic traits questionnaire: Development and validation. *Journal of Personality Assessment,* 1–10. https://doi.org/10.1080/00223891.2017.1372443.

Edens, J., Marcus, D., Lilienfeld, S., Poythress, N., & Watson, D. (2006). Psychopathic, not psychopath: Taxometric evidence for the dimensional structure of psychopathy. *Journal of Abnormal Psychology, 115*(1), 131–144. https://doi.org/10.1037/0021-843X.115.1.131.

Edens, J., Skopp, N., & Cahill, M. (2008). Psychopathic features moderate the relationship between harsh and inconsistent parental discipline and adolescent antisocial behavior. *Journal of Clinical Child & Adolescent Psychology, 37*(2), 472–476. https://doi.org/10.1080/15374410801955938.

Eder, P., & Eisenberger, R. (2008). Perceived organizational support: Reducing the negative influence of coworker withdrawal behavior. *Journal of Management, 34,* 55–68. https://doi.org/10.1177/0149206307309259.

Eisenberger, R., Huntington, R., Hutchison, S., & Sowa, D. (1986). Perceived organizational support. *Journal of Applied Psychology, 71,* 500.

Eschleman, K. J., Bowling, N. A., Michel, J. S., & Burns, G. N. (2014). Perceived intent of supervisor as a moderator of the relationships between abusive supervision and counterproductive work behaviours. *Work & Stress, 28,* 362–375. https://doi.org/10.1080/02678373.2014.961183.

Falkenbach, D. M., Howe, J. R., & Falki, M. (2013). Using self-esteem to disaggregate psychopathy, narcissism, and aggression. *Personality and Individual Differences, 54,* 815–820. https://doi.org/10.1016/j.paid.2012.12.017.

Fehr, B., Samsom, D., & Paulhus, D. L. (1992). The construct of Machiavellianism: Twenty years later. In C. D. Spielberger & J. N. Butcher (Eds.), *Advances in personality assessment* (Vol. 9, pp. 77–116). Hillsdale, NJ: Erlbaum.

Ferris, G. R., Treadway, D. C., Kolodinsky, R. W., Hochwarter, W. A., Kacmar, C. J., Douglas, C., & Frink, D. D. (2005). Development and validation of the political skill inventory. *Journal of Management, 31,* 126–152. https://doi.org/10.1177/0149206304271386.

Fersch, E. L. (2006). *Thinking about psychopaths and psychopathy.* New York: iUniverse.

Fox, S., Kessler, S. R., & Spector, P. E. (2013). It's all about me: The role of narcissism in exacerbating the relationship between stressors and counterproductive work behaviour. *Work & Stress, 27*, 368–382. https://doi.org/10.1080/02678373.2013.849776.

Fox, S., & Spector, P. (1999). A model of work frustration–aggression. *Journal of Organizational Behavior, 20*(6), 915–931. https://doi.org/10.1002/(SICI)1099-1379(199911)20:6<915::AID-JOB918>3.0.CO;2-6.

Fox, S., Spector, P. E., Goh, A., Bruursema, K., & Kessler, S. R. (2012). The deviant citizen: Measuring potential positive relations between counterproductive work behaviour and organizational citizenship behaviour. *Journal of Occupational and Organizational Psychology, 85*, 199–220. https://doi.org/10.1111/j.2044-8325.2011.02032.x.

Fox, S., Spector, P., & Miles, D. (2001). Counterproductive Work Behavior (CWB) in response to job stressors and organizational justice: Some mediator and moderator tests for autonomy and emotions. *Journal of Vocational Behavior, 59*(3), 291–309. https://doi.org/10.1006/jvbe.2001.1803.

Freud, S. (1914/1991). *On narcissism: An introduction.* London: Read Books.

Fritzon, K., & Board, B. J. (2005). Disordered personalities at work. *Psychology, Crime & Law, 11*, 17–32. https://doi.org/10.1080/10683160310001634304.

Fritzon, K., Bailey, C., Croom, S., & Brooks, N. (2017). Problem personalities in the workplace: Development of the corporate personality inventory. In R. B. In P.-A. Granhag, A. Shaboltas, & E. Dozortseva (Eds.), *Psychology and law in Europe: When west meets east* (pp. 139–165). Boca Raton: CRC Press.

Furnham, A., & Crump, J. (2014). A Big Five facet analysis of sub-clinical narcissism: Understanding boldness in terms of well-known personality traits. *Personality and Mental Health, 8*(3), 209–217. https://doi.org/10.1002/pmh.1262.

Furnham, A., Richards, S. C., & Paulhus, D. L. (2013). The dark triad of personality: A 10-year review. *Social and Personality Psychology Compass, 7*, 199–216. https://doi.org/10.1111/spc3.12018.

Gable, M., & Dangello, F. (1994). Locus of control, Machiavellianism, and managerial job performance. *The Journal of Psychology, 128*(5), 599–608. https://doi.org/10.1080/00223980.1994.9914917.

Garcia, D., Adrianson, L., Archer, T., & Rosenberg, P. (2015). The dark side of the affective profiles: Differences and similarities in psychopathy, Machiavellianism, and narcissism. *SAGE Open, 5*(4), 1–14. https://doi.org/10.1177/2158244015615167.

Gee, J., & Button, M. (2018). *The financial cost of fraud 2018 report.* Crowe U.K. LLP. Retrieved May 12, 2019 from https://www.crowe.

com/uk/croweuk/-/media/Crowe/Firms/Europe/uk/CroweUK/PDF-publications/Financial-Cost-of-Fraud-2018.ashx?la=en-GB&hash=F3D9DED968C59B2469729C7FDCDDFF9B481C65BC.

Gerstner, W. C., König, A., Enders, A., & Hambrick, D. C. (2013). CEO narcissism, audience engagement, and organizational adoption of technological discontinuities. *Administrative Science Quarterly, 58,* 257–291. https://doi.org/10.1177/0001839213488773.

Gkorezis, P., Petridou, E., & Krouklidou, T. (2015). The detrimental effect of Machiavellian leadership on employees' emotional exhaustion: Organizational cynicism as a mediator. *Europe's Journal of Psychology, 11,* 619–631. https://doi.org/10.5964/ejop.v11i4.98.

Glenn, A. L., & Sellbom, M. (2015). Theoretical and empirical concerns regarding the dark triad as a construct. *Journal of Personality Disorders, 29,* 360–377. https://doi.org/10.1521/pedi_2014_28_162.

Glover, N., Miller, J., Lynam, D., Crego, C., & Widiger, T. (2012). The five-factor narcissism inventory: A five-factor measure of narcissistic personality traits. *Journal of Personality Assessment, 94*(5), 500–512. https://doi.org/10.1080/00223891.2012.670680.

Goldstein, M. (2011, April). From Hannibal Lector to Bernie Madoff. *Reuters.* Retrieved from https://www.reuters.com/article/us-profiling-whitecollarcrime/special-report-from-hannibal-lecter-to-bernie-madoff-idUSTRE73J2W920110420.

Graham, W. J., & Cooper, W. H. (2013). Taking credit. *Journal of Business Ethics, 115,* 403–425. https://doi.org/10.1007/s10551-012-1406-3.

Greenidge, D., Devonish, D., & Alleyne, P. (2014). The relationship between ability-based emotional intelligence and contextual performance and counterproductive work behaviors: A test of the mediating effects of job satisfaction. *Human Performance, 27,* 225–242. https://doi.org/10.1080/08959285.2014.913591.

Grijalva, E., & Newman, D. A. (2015). Narcissism and counterproductive work behavior (CWB): Meta-analysis and consideration of collectivist culture, big five personality, and narcissism's facet structure. *Applied Psychology, 64,* 93–126. https://doi.org/10.1111/apps.12025.

Hare, R. D. (2003). *Manual for the revised psychopathy checklist* (2nd ed.). Toronto, ON, Canada: Multi-Health Systems.

Hare, R. D., & Neumann, C. S. (2009). Psychopathy: Assessment and forensic implications. *Canadian Journal of Psychiatry* [*Revue Canadienne De Psychiatrie*], *54*(12), 791.

Harrison, A., Summers, J., & Mennecke, B. (2018). The effects of the dark triad on unethical behavior. *Journal of Business Ethics, 153*(1), 53–77. https://doi.org/10.1007/s10551-016-3368-3.

Harms, P. D., & Spain, S. M. (2015). Beyond the bright side: Dark personality at work. *Applied Psychology, 64*(1), 15–24. https://doi.org/10.1111/apps.12042.

Hasanati, N., Winarsunu, T., & Karina, V. D. (2017). The influence of interpersonal conflict on counterproductive work behaviour mediated by job stress. In *Proceedings of 3rd ASEAN Conference on Psychology, Counselling, and Humanities (ACPCH 2017). Advances in Social Science, Education and Humanities Research* (Vol. 133). Atlantis Press.

Heilbrun, A. (1979). Psychopathy and violent crime. *Journal of Consulting and Clinical Psychology, 47*(3), 509–516. https://doi.org/10.1037/0022-006X.47.3.509.

Hershcovis, M., & Barling, J. (2010). Toward a multi-foci approach to workplace aggression: A meta-analytic review of outcomes from different perpetrators. *Journal of Organizational Behavior, 31,* 24–44.

Hershcovis, M. S., Turner, N., Barling, J., Arnold, K. A., Dupré, K. E., Inness, M., … Sivanathan, N. (2007). Predicting workplace aggression: A meta-analysis. *Journal of Applied Psychology, 92*(1), 228–238.

Holland, J. L. (1997). *Making vocational choices: A theory of vocational personalities and work environments* (3rd ed.). Odessa, FL: Psychological Assessment Resources.

Holtzman, N. S., & Donnellan, M. B. (2015). The roots of narcissus: Old and new models of the evolution of narcissism. In V. Zeigler-Hill, L. Welling, & T. Shackelford (Eds.), *Evolutionary perspectives on social psychology* (pp. 479–489). New York, NY: Springer.

Howell, J., & Avolio, B. (2013). Transformational, transactional leadership styles and job performance of academic leaders. In. J. B. Ciulla, M. Uhl-Bien, & P. H. Werhane (Eds.), *Leadership ethics* (pp. 93–108). London: Sage. https://doi.org/10.4135/9781446286357.

Inancsi, T., Lang, A., & Bereczkei, T. (2015). Machiavellianism and adult attachment in general interpersonal relationships and close relationships. *Europe's Journal of Psychology, 11,* 139–154. https://doi.org/10.5964/ejop.v11i1.80.

Ishikawa, S., Raine, A., Lencz, T., Bihrle, S., & Lacasse, L. (2001). Autonomic stress reactivity and executive functions in successful and unsuccessful criminal psychopaths from the community. *Journal of Abnormal Psychology, 110*(3), 423–432. https://doi.org/10.1037/0021-843X.110.3.423.

Jakobwitz, S., & Egan, V. (2006). The dark triad and normal personality traits. *Personality and Individual Differences, 40,* 331–339. https://doi.org/10.1016/j.paid.2005.07.006.

Jennings, M. M. (2006). *The seven signs of ethical collapse.* New York: St. Martin Press.

Johnson, E. N., Kuhn, J. R., Jr., Apostolou, B. A., & Hassell, J. M. (2012). Auditor perceptions of client narcissism as a fraud attitude risk factor. *Auditing: A Journal of Practice & Theory, 32*(1), 203–219.

Jonason, P. K., & Webster, G. D. (2010). The dirty dozen: A concise measure of the dark triad. *Psychological Assessment, 22,* 420–432. https://doi.org/10.1037/a0019265.

Jonason, P. K., Slomski, S., & Partyka, J. (2012). The dark triad at work: How toxic employees get their way. *Personality and Individual Differences, 52,* 449–453. https://doi.org/10.1016/j.paid.2011.11.008.

Jonason, P. K., Wee, S., & Li, N. P. (2015). Competition, autonomy, and prestige: Mechanisms through which the dark triad predict job satisfaction. *Personality and Individual Differences, 72,* 112–116. https://doi.org/10.1016/j.paid.2014.08.026.

Jones, D. (2014). Risk in the face of retribution: Psychopathic individuals persist in financial misbehavior among the Dark Triad. *Personality and Individual Differences, 67,* 109–113. https://doi.org/10.1016/j.paid.2014.01.030.

Jones, D. N., & Paulhus, D. L. (2009). Machiavellianism. In M. R. Leary & R. H. Hoyle (Eds.), *Individual differences in social behavior* (pp. 93–108). New York: Guilford.

Jones, D. N., & Paulhus, D. L. (2010). Different provocations trigger aggression in narcissists and psychopaths. *Social Psychological and Personality Science, 1,* 12–18. https://doi.org/10.1177/1948550609347591.

Jones, D. N., & Paulhus, D. L. (2011). The role of impulsivity in the dark triad of personality. *Personality and Individual Differences, 51,* 679–682. https://doi.org/10.1016/j.paid.2011.04.011.

Jones, D. N., & Paulhus, D. L. (2014). Introducing the short dark triad (SD3) a brief measure of dark personality traits. *Assessment, 21,* 28–41. https://doi.org/10.1177/1073191113514105.

Judge, T. A., Higgins, C. A., Thoresen, C. J., & Barrick, M. R. (1999). The big five personality traits, general mental ability, and career success across the life span. *Personnel Psychology, 52,* 621–652. https://doi.org/10.1111/j.1744-6570.1999.tb00174.x.

Kadlec, D. (2002). Who's accountable? Inside the growing Enron scandal: How evidence was shredded and top executives fished for a bailout as the company imploded. *Inside Politics.* Retrieved from http://edition.cnn.com/ ALLPOLITICS/time/2002/01/21/accountable.html.

Kaiser, R., & Kaplan, R. (2006). The deeper work of executive development: Outgrowing sensitivities. *Academy of Management Learning and Education, 5*(4), 463–483. https://doi.org/10.5465/AMLE.2006.23473207.

Kantan, P., Yyesiltas, M., & Arslan, R. (2015). The moderating role of psychological contract in the effect of dark side of personality on counterproductive work behaviors. *Ataturk University Journal of Economics & Administrative Sciences, 29,* 23–34. https://doi.org/10.13140/RG.2.2.34488.96004.

Katwyk, P., Fox, S., Spector, P., Kelloway, E., & Barling, J. (2000). Using the Job-Related Affective Well-Being Scale (JAWS) to investigate affective responses to work stressors. *Journal of Occupational Health Psychology, 5*(2), 219–230. https://doi.org/10.1037/1076-8998.5.2.219.

Kessler, S. R., Bandelli, A. C., Spector, P. E., Borman, W. C., Nelson, C. E., & Penney, L. M. (2010). Re-examining Machiavelli: A three-dimensional model of Machiavellianism in the workplace. *Journal of Applied Social Psychology, 40,* 1868–1896. https://doi.org/10.1111/j.1559-1816.2010.00643.x.

Kessler, S., Bruursema, K., Rodopman, B., & Spector, P. (2013). Leadership, interpersonal conflict, and counterproductive work behavior: An examination of the stressor-strain process. *Negotiation and Conflict Management Research, 6*(3), 180–190. https://doi.org/10.1111/ncmr.12009.

Khoo, H., & Burch, G. (2008). The "dark side" of leadership personality and transformational leadership: An exploratory study. *Personality and Individual Differences, 44*(1), 86–97. https://doi.org/10.1016/j.paid.2007.07.018.

Kiazad, K., Restubog, S. L. D., Zagenczyk, T. J., Kiewitz, C., & Tang, R. L. (2010). In pursuit of power: The role of authoritarian leadership in the relationship between supervisors' Machiavellianism and subordinates' perceptions of abusive supervisory behavior. *Journal of Research in Personality, 44,* 512–519. https://doi.org/10.1016/j.jrp.2010.06.004.

Kish-Gephart, J. J., Harrison, D. A., & Trevino, L. K. (2010). Bad apples, bad cases, and bad barrels: Meta-analytic evidence about sources of unethical decisions at work. *Journal of Applied Psychology, 95,* 1–31. https://doi.org/10.1037/a0017103.

Klarskov Jeppesen, K., & Leder, C. (2016). Auditors' experience with corporate psychopaths. *Journal of Financial Crime, 23*(4), 870–881.

Klotz, A., He, W., Yam, K., Bolino, M., Wei, W., & Houston, L. (2018). Good actors but bad apples: Deviant consequences of daily impression management at work. *Journal of Applied Psychology, 103*(10), 1145–1154.

Knapp, M. (2009). *Contemporary auditing.* Cincinnati, OH: South-Western.

Kranacher, M.-J., Riley, R., & Wells, J. T. (2011). *Forensic accounting and fraud examination.* Hoboken, NJ: Wiley.

Krizan, Z., & Herlache, A. D. (2018). The narcissism spectrum model: A synthetic view of narcissistic personality. *Personality and Social Psychology Review, 22,* 3–31. https://doi.org/10.1177/1088868316685018.

Landay, K., Harms, P. D., & Crede, M. (2018). Shall we serve the dark lords? A meta-analytic review of psychopathy and leadership. *Journal of Applied Psychology,* 1–14. https://doi.org/10.1037/apl0000357.

Larsen, R. J., & Ketelaar, T. (1991). Personality and susceptibility to positive and negative emotional states. *Journal of Personality and Social Psychology, 61*(1), 132–140.

Lebreton, J., Binning, J., Adorno, A., & Melcher, K. (2004). Importance of personality and job-specific affect for predicting job attitudes and withdrawal behavior. *Organizational Research Methods, 7*(3), 300–325. https://doi.org/10.1177/1094428104266015.

Leung, R. (2005, March 11). *Enron's Ken Lay: I was fooled.* 60 Minutes. Retrieved from https://www.cbsnews.com/news/enrons-ken-lay-i-was-fooled-11-03-2005/.

Lilienfeld, S. O., & Widows, M. R. (2005). *Psychopathic personality inventory—Revised: Professional manual.* Lutz, FL: Psychological Assessment Resources.

Lilienfeld, S. O., Waldman, I. D., Landfield, K., Watts, A. L., Rubenzer, S., & Faschingbauer, T. R. (2012). Fearless dominance and the U.S. presidency: Implications of psychopathic personality traits for successful and unsuccessful political leadership. *Journal of Personality and Social Psychology, 103*(3), 489.

Lingnau, V., Fuchs, F., & Dehne-Niemann, T. E. (2017). The influence of psychopathic traits on the acceptance of white-collar crime: Do corporate psychopaths cook the books and misuse the news? *Journal of Business Economics, 87*(9), 1193–1227.

Linton, D. K., & Power, J. L. (2013). The personality traits of workplace bullies are often shared by their victims: Is there a dark side to victims? *Personality and Individual Differences, 54,* 738–743. https://doi.org/10.1016/j.paid.2012.11.026.

Lynam, D., Gaughan, E., Miller, J., Miller, D., Mullins-Sweatt, S., & Widiger, T. (2011). Assessing the basic traits associated with psychopathy: Development and validation of the elemental psychopathy assessment. *Psychological Assessment, 23*(1), 108–124. https://doi.org/10.1037/a0021146.

Maccoby, M. (2000). Narcissistic leaders: The incredible pros and the inevitable cons. *Harvard Business Review,* pp. 92–101.

Machiavelli, N. (1984). *The prince.* New York: Bantam.

Marcus, D. K., John, S. L., & Edens, J. F. (2004). A taxometric analysis of psychopathic personality. *Journal of Abnormal Psychology, 113*, 626–635. https://doi.org/10.1037/0021-843x.113.4.626.

Marcus, B., Taylor, O., Hastings, S., Sturm, A., & Weigelt, O. (2016). The structure of counterproductive work behavior: A review, a structural meta-analysis, and a primary study. *Journal of Management, 42*(1), 203–233. https://doi.org/10.1177/0149206313503019.

Mathieu, C., Neumann, C. S., Hare, R. D., & Babiak, P. (2014). A dark side of leadership: Corporate psychopathy and its influence on employee well-being and job satisfaction. *Personality and Individual Differences, 59*, 83–88. https://doi.org/10.1016/j.paid.2013.11.010.

McKay, R., Stevens, C., & Fratzl, J. (2010). A 12-step process of white-collar crime. *International Journal of Business Governance and Ethics, 5*(1), 14–32. https://doi.org/10.1504/IJBGE.2010.029552.

McLean, B., & Elkind, P. (2003). *The smartest guys in the room: The amazing rise and scandalous fall of Enron.* New York: Portfolio.

Međedović, J., & Petrović, B. (2015). The Dark Tetrad. *Journal of Individual Differences, 36*(4), 228–236. https://doi.org/10.1027/1614-0001/a000179.

Meurs, J., Fox, S., Kessler, S., & Spector, P. (2013). It's all about me: The role of narcissism in exacerbating the relationship between stressors and counterproductive work behaviour. *Work & Stress, 27*(4), 368–382. https://doi.org/10.1080/02678373.2013.849776.

Michel, J., Newness, K., & Duniewicz, K. (2016). How abusive supervision affects workplace deviance: A moderated-mediation examination of aggressiveness and work-related negative affect. *Journal of Business and Psychology, 31*(1), 1–22. https://doi.org/10.1007/s10869-015-9400-2.

Miller, J. D., & Campbell, W. K. (2010). The case for using research on trait narcissism as a building block for understanding narcissistic personality disorder. *Personality Disorders: Theory, Research, and Treatment, 1*, 180–191. https://doi.org/10.1037/a0018229.

Miller, J. D., Price, J., Gentile, B., Lynam, D. R., & Campbell, W. K. (2012). Grandiose and vulnerable narcissism from the perspective of the interpersonal circumplex. *Personality and Individual Differences, 53*, 507–512. https://doi.org/10.1016/j.paid.2012.04.026.

Miller, J., Vize, C., Crowe, M., & Lynam, D. (2019). A critical appraisal of the Dark-Triad literature and suggestions for moving forward. *Current Directions in Psychological Science, 28*(4), 353–360. https://doi.org/10.1177/0963721419838233.

Miller, J. D., Watts, A., & Jones, S. E. (2011). Does psychopathy manifest divergent relations with components of its nomological network depending on gender? *Personality and Individual Differences, 50,* 564–569. https://doi.org/10.1016/j.paid.2010.11.028.

Miller, J. D., Widiger, T. A., & Campbell, W. K. (2010). Narcissistic personality disorder and the DSM-V. *Journal of Abnormal Psychology, 119,* 640. https://doi.org/10.1037/a0019529.

Morf, C., & Rhodewalt, F. (2001). Unravelling the paradoxes of narcissism: A dynamic self-regulatory processing model. *Psychological Inquiry, 12,* 177–196.

Mount, M., Ilies, R., & Johnson, E. (2006). Relationship of personality traits and counterproductive work behaviors: The mediating effect of job satisfaction. *Personnel Psychology, 59,* 591–622. https://doi.org/10.1111/j.1744-6570.2006.00048.x.

Muris, P., Merckelbach, H., Otgaar, H., & Meijer, E. (2017). The malevolent side of human nature: A meta-analysis and critical review of the literature on the dark triad (narcissism, Machiavellianism, and psychopathy). *Perspectives on Psychological Science, 12,* 183–204. https://doi.org/10.1177/1745691616666070.

Neumann, C. S., Hare, R. D., & Pardini, D. A. (2015). Antisociality and the construct of psychopathy: Data from across the globe. *Journal of Personality, 83,* 678–692. https://doi.org/10.1111/jopy.12127.

O'Boyle, E. H., Forsyth, D. R., Banks, G. C., & McDaniel, M. A. (2012). A meta-analysis of the dark triad and work behavior: A social exchange perspective. *Journal of Applied Psychology, 97,* 557–579. https://doi.org/10.1037/a0025679.

Offermann, L. R., Kennedy, J. K., & Wirtz, P. W. (1994). Implicit leadership theories: Content, structure, and generalizability. *Leadership Quarterly, 5,* 43–58.

Okada, R. (2010). The relationship between vulnerable narcissism and aggression in Japanese undergraduate students. *Personality and Individual Differences, 49*(2), 113–118. https://doi.org/10.1016/j.paid.2010.03.017.

Olver, M., & Wong, S. (2015). Short- and long-term recidivism prediction of the PCL-R and the effects of age: A 24-year follow-up. *Personality Disorders: Theory, Research, and Treatment, 6*(1), 97–105. https://doi.org/10.1037/per0000095.

Özsoy, E. (2018). Dark triad and counterproductive work behaviors: Which of the dark triad traits is more malevolent? *Journal of Business Research Turkey, 10,* 74–756. https://doi.org/10.20491/isarder.2018.546.

Palmer, J., Komarraju, M., Carter, M., & Karau, S. (2017). Angel on one shoulder: Can perceived organizational support moderate the relationship between the Dark Triad traits and counterproductive work behavior? *Personality and Individual Differences, 110,* 31–37. https://doi.org/10.1016/j.paid.2017.01.018.

Patel, P., & Cooper, D. (2014). The harder they fall, the faster they rise: Approach and avoidance focus in narcissistic CEOs. *Strategic Management Journal, 35*(10), 1528–1540. https://doi.org/10.1002/smj.2162.

Patrick, C. J. (Ed.). (2018). *Handbook of psychopathy* (2nd ed.). New York: Guilford Press.

Paulhus, D. L., & Williams, K. M. (2002). The dark triad of personality: Narcissism, Machiavellianism, and psychopathy. *Journal of Research in Personality, 36,* 556–563. https://doi.org/10.1016/S0092-6566(02)00505-6.

Paunonen, S., Lönnqvist, J., Verkasalo, M., Leikas, S., & Nissinen, V. (2006). Narcissism and emergent leadership in military cadets. *The Leadership Quarterly, 17*(5), 475–486. https://doi.org/10.1016/j.leaqua.2006.06.003.

Peeters, M., Cillessen, A. H. N., & Scholte, R. H. J. (2010). Clueless or powerful? Identifying subtypes of bullies in adolescents. *Journal of Youth and Adolescents, 39,* 1041–1052. https://doi.org/10.1007/s10964-009-9478-9.

Penney, L. M., & Spector, P. E. (2002). Narcissism and counterproductive work behavior: Do bigger egos mean bigger problems? *International Journal of Selection and Assessment, 10,* 126–134. https://doi.org/10.1111/1468-2389.00199.

Penney, L. M., & Spector, P. E. (2005). Job stress, incivility, and counterproductive work behavior (CWB): The moderating role of negative affectivity. *Journal of Organizational Behavior, 26*(7), 777–796.

Perri, F. S. (2013). Visionaries or false prophets. *Journal of Contemporary Criminal Justice, 29,* 331–350. https://doi.org/10.1177/1043986213496008.

Perri, F. S., & Brody, R. G. (2011). The Sallie Rohrbach story: Lessons for auditors and fraud examiners. *Journal of Financial Crime, 18*(1), 93–104.

Pilch, I., & Turska, E. (2015). Relationships between machiavellianism, organizational culture, and workplace bullying: Emotional abuse from the target's and the perpetrator's perspective. *Journal of Business Ethics, 128,* 83–93. https://doi.org/10.1007/s10551-014-2081-3.

Porath, C., & Erez, A. (2007). Does rudeness really matter? The effects of rudeness on task performance and helpfulness. *The Academy of Management Journal, 50*(5), 1181–1197. https://doi.org/10.2307/20159919.

PwC. (2018). *Pulling fraud out of the shadows: Global Economic Crime and Fraud Survey 2018.* Retrieved from www.pwc.com/fraudsurvey.

Raine, A., Ishikawa, S., Arce, E., Lencz, T., Knuth, K., Bihrle, S., ... Colletti, P. (2004). Hippocampal structural asymmetry in unsuccessful psychopaths. *Biological Psychiatry, 55*(2), 185–191. https://doi.org/10.1016/S0006-3223(03)00727-3.

Raman, P., Sambasivan, M., & Kumar, N. (2016). Counterproductive work behavior among frontline government employees: Role of personality, emotional intelligence, affectivity, emotional labor, and emotional exhaustion. *Revista de Psicología DelTrabajo Y de Las Organizaciones, 32*(1), 25–37. https://doi.org/10.1016/j.rpto.2015.11.002.

Ramamoorti, S., Morrison, D., & Koletar, J. W. (2009). *Bringing Freud to fraud: Understanding the state-of-mind of the C-level suite/white collar offender through "A-B-C" analysis* (Working paper). Institute for Fraud Prevention.

Raskin, R. N., & Hall, C. S. (1979). A narcissistic personality inventory. *Psychological Reports, 45*(2), 590. https://doi.org/10.2466/pr0.1979.45.2.590.

Raskin, R., & Terry, H. (1988). A principal-components analysis of the narcissistic personality inventory and further evidence of its construct validity. *Journal of Personality and Social Psychology, 54*(5), 890–902. https://doi.org/10.1037/0022-3514.54.5.890.

Rauthmann, J. F., & Will, T. (2011). Proposing a multidimensional Machiavellianism conceptualization. *Social Behavior and Personality, 39*, 391–403. https://doi.org/10.2224/sbp.2011.39.3.391.

Ray, J., & Ray, J. (1982). Some apparent advantages of subclinical psychopathy. *The Journal of Social Psychology, 117*(1), 135–142.

Rehman, U., & Shahnawaz, M. G. (2018). Machiavellianism, job autonomy, and counterproductive work behaviour among Indian managers. *Revistade Psicologiadel Trabajoydelas Organizaciones, 34*, 83–88. https://doi.org/10.5093/jwop2018a10.

Resick, C. J., Whitman, D. S., Weingarden, S. M., & Hiller, N. J. (2009). The bright-side and the dark-side of CEO personality: Examining core self-evaluations, narcissism, transformational leadership, and strategic influence. *Journal of Applied Psychology, 94*, 1365. https://doi.org/10.1037/a0016238.

Rhoades, L., & Eisenberger, R. (2002). Perceived organizational support: A review of the literature. *Journal of Applied Psychology, 87*, 698–714. https://doi.org/10.1037/0021-9010.87.4.698.

Roberts, B. W. (2006). Personality development and organizational behavior. *Research in Organizational Behavior, 27*, 1–40. https://doi.org/10.1016/S0191-3085(06)27001-1.

Roberts, B. W., Caspi, A., & Moffitt, T. E. (2003). Work experiences and personality development in young adulthood. *Journal of Personality and Social Psychology, 84,* 582–593. https://doi.org/10.1037/0022-3514.84.3.582.

Roberts, R., Woodman, T., & Sedikides, C. (2018). Pass me the ball: Narcissism in performance settings. *International Review of Sport and Exercise Psychology, 11,* 190–213. https://doi.org/10.1080/1750984X.2017.1290815.

Robinson, S., & Bennett, R. (1995). A typology of deviant workplace behaviors: A multidimensional scaling study. *The Academy of Management Journal, 38*(2), 555–572. https://doi.org/10.2307/256693.

Roeser, K., McGregor, V. E., Stegmaier, S., Mathew, J., Kubler, A., & Meule, A. (2016). The dark triad of personality and unethical behaviour at different times of the day. *Personality and Individual Differences, 88,* 73–77.

Rose, K., Shuck, B., Twyford, D., & Bergman, M. (2015). Skunked: An integrative review exploring the consequences of the dysfunctional leader and implications for those employees who work for them. *Human Resource Development Review, 14*(1), 64–90. https://doi.org/10.1177/1534484314552437.

Salgado, J. (2002). The Big Five personality dimensions and counterproductive behaviors. *International Journal of Selection and Assessment, 10*(1–2), 117–125. https://doi.org/10.1111/1468-2389.00198.

Sakalaki, M., Kanellaki, S., & Richardson, C. (2009). Is a manipulator's externality paradoxical? The relationship between Machiavellianism, economic opportunism, and economic locus of control. *Journal of Applied Social Psychology, 39,* 2591–2603. https://doi.org/10.1111/j.1559-1816.2009.00539.x.

Samnani, A., Salamon, S., & Singh, P. (2014). Negative affect and counterproductive workplace behavior: The moderating role of moral disengagement and gender. *Journal of Business Ethics, 119*(2), 235–244. https://doi.org/10.1007/s10551-013-1635-0.

Scherer, K., Baysinger, M., Zolynsky, D., & Lebreton, J. (2013). Predicting counterproductive work behaviors with sub-clinical psychopathy: Beyond the five factor model of personality. *Personality and Individual Differences, 55*(3), 300–305. https://doi.org/10.1016/j.paid.2013.03.007.

Schneider, B. (1987). The people make the place. *Personnel Psychology, 40*(3), 437–453.

Schyns, B. (2015). Dark personality in the workplace: Introduction to the special issue. *Applied Psychology, 64*(1), 1–14. https://doi.org/10.1111/apps.12041.

Schyns, B., & Schilling, J. (2013). How bad are the effects of bad leaders? A meta-analysis of destructive leadership and its outcomes. *The Leadership Quarterly, 24,* 138–158. https://doi.org/10.1016/j.leaqua.2012.09.001.

Seifert, K. H., & Bergmann, C. (1983). German adaptation of Super's work values inventory [Deutschsprachige adaptation des work values inventory von Super]. *Zeitschrift Für Arbeits- Und Organisationspsychologie, 27*, 160–172.

Shoss, M. K., Eisenberger, R., Restubog, S. L. D., & Zagenczyk, T. J. (2013). Blaming the organization for abusive supervision: The role of perceived organization support and supervisor's organizational embodiment. *Journal of Applied Psychology, 98*(1), 158–168. https://doi.org/10.1037/a0030687.

Sims, R., & Brinkmann, J. (2003). Enron ethics (Or: Culture matters more than codes). *Journal of Business Ethics, 45*(3), 243–256. https://doi.org/10.1023/A:1024194519384.

Smith, M. (2015). Review of the Americanization of Narcissism by Elizabeth Lunbeck. *Bulletin of the History of Medicine, 89*(4), 825–826. https://doi.org/10.1353/bhm.2015.0119.

Smith, S. F., & Lilienfeld, S. O. (2013). Psychopathy in the workplace: The knowns and unknowns. *Aggression and Violent Behavior, 18*, 204–218. https://doi.org/10.1016/j.avb.2012.11.007.

Smith, A. N., Watkins, M. B., Burke, M. J., Christian, M. S., Smith, C. E., Hall, A., & Simms, S. (2013). Gendered influence: A gender role perspective on the use and effectiveness of influence tactics. *Journal of Management, 39*, 1156–1183. https://doi.org/10.1177/0149206313478183.

Smith, M. B., & Webster, B. D. (2017). A moderated mediation model of Machiavellianism, social undermining, political skill, and supervisor-rated job performance. *Personality and Individual Differences, 104*, 453–459. https://doi.org/10.1016/j.paid.2016.09.010.

Southard, A. C., Noser, A. E., Pollock, N. C., Mercer, S. H., Zeigler-Hill, V. (2015). The interpersonal nature of dark personality features. *Journal of Social and Clinical Psychology, 34*, 555–586. https://doi.org/10.1521/jscp.2015.34.7.555.

Spector, P. (1982). Behavior in organizations as a function of employee's locus of control. *Psychological Bulletin, 91*(3), 482–497. https://doi.org/10.1037/0033-2909.91.3.482.

Spector, P. E. (1988). Development of the work locus of control scale. *Journal of Occupational Psychology, 61*, 335–340.

Spector, P., Bauer, J., & Fox, S. (2010). Measurement artifacts in the assessment of counterproductive work behavior and organizational citizenship behavior: Do we know what we think we know? *Journal of Applied Psychology, 95*(4), 781–790. https://doi.org/10.1037/a0019477.

Spector, P. E., & Fox, S. (2002). An emotion-centered model of voluntary work behavior: Some parallels between counterproductive work behavior and organizational citizenship behavior. *Human Resource Management Review, 12*, 269–292. https://doi.org/10.1016/S1053-4822(02)00049-9.

Spector, P. E., & Fox, S. (2005). The stressor-emotion model of counterproductive work behavior. *Counterproductive work behavior: Investigations of actors and targets* (pp. 151–174). Washington: American Psychological Association.

Spector, P. E., Fox, S., & Domagalski, T. (2005). Emotions, violence and counterproductive work behavior. In E. K. Kelloway, J. Barling, & J. J. Hurrell (Eds.), *Handbook of workplace violence* (pp. 29–46). Thousand Oaks, CA: Sage.

Spector, P. E., Fox, S., Penney, L. M., Bruursema, K., Goh, A., & Kessler, S. (2006). The dimensionality of counterproductivity: Are all counterproductive behaviors created equal? *Journal of Vocational Behavior, 68*, 446–460. https://doi.org/10.1016/j.jvb.2005.10.005.

Spector, P. E., & Jex, S. M. (1998). Development of four self-report measures of job stressors and strain: Interpersonal conflict at work scale, organizational constraints scale, quantitative workload inventory, and physical symptoms inventory. *Journal of Occupational Health Psychology, 3*, 356–367.

Stănescu, D. F., Mohorea, L. (2015, May). The dark triad of personality in organisational life – a correlational study with counterproductive work behaviour and work locus of control. *Proceedings of the Strategica: Local vs Global conference.* Bucharest.

Stevens, G. W., Deuling, J. K., & Armenakis, A. A. (2012). Successful psychopaths: Are they unethical decision-makers and why? *Journal of Business Ethics, 105*, 139–149. https://doi.org/10.1007/s10551-011-0963-1.

Stewart, A. E., & Stewart, E. A. (2006). The preference to excel and its relationship to selected personality variables. *Journal of Individual Psychology, 62*, 270–284. https://doi.org/10.1037/t06561-000.

Stogdill, R. M. (1963). *Manual for the leader behavior description questionnaire, form XII.* Columbus, OH: Bureau of Business Research, Ohio State University.

Stradovnik, K., & Stare, J. (2018). Correlation between Machiavellian leadership and emotional exhaustion of employees. *Leadership & Organization Development Journal, 39*(8), 1037–1050. https://doi.org/10.1108/LODJ-06-2018-0232.

Tang, T. L.-P., Chen, Y.-J., & Sutarso, T. (2008). Bad apples in bad (business) barrels. *Management Decision, 46*(2), 243.

Tett, R. P., & Burnett, D. D. (2003). A personality trait-based interactionist model of job performance. *Journal of Applied Psychology, 88*(3), 500–517. https://doi.org/10.1037/0021-9010.88.3.500.

Tonge, A., Greer, L., & Lawton, A. (2003). The Enron story: You can fool some of the people some of the time [...]. *Business Ethics: a European Review, 12,* 4–22. https://doi.org/10.1111/1467-8608.00301.

Tourish, D., & Vatcha, N. (2005). Charismatic leadership and corporate cultism at Enron: The elimination of dissent, the promotion of conformity and organizational collapse. *Leadership, 1,* 455–480.

Treadway, D. C., Yang, J., Bentley, J. R., Williams, L. V., & Reeves, M. (2017). The impact of follower narcissism and LMX perceptions on feeling envied and job performance. *The International Journal of Human Resource Management,* 1–22. https://doi.org/10.1080/09585192.2017.1288151.

Troy, C., Smith, K. G., & Domino, M. A. (2011). CEO demographics and accounting fraud: Who is more likely to rationalize illegal acts? *Strategic Organization, 9*(4), 259–282. https://doi.org/10.1177/1476127011421534.

Turner, I. N., & Webster, G. D. (2018). Narcissism and dark personality traits. In A. Hermann, A. Brunell, & J. Foster (Eds.), *Handbook of trait narcissism* (pp. 195–203). Switzerland: Springer.

Vergauwe, J., Wille, B., Hofmans, J., & De Fruyt, F. (2017). Development of a five-factor model charisma compound and its relations to career outcomes. *Journal of Vocational Behavior, 99,* 24–39. https://doi.org/10.1016/j.jvb.2016.12.005.

Visser, B. A., & Campbell, S. (2018). Measuring the dark side of personality. In V. Zeigler-hill & K. Schakelford (Eds.), *Sage handbook of personality and individual differences* (pp. 573–591). Thousand Oaks: Sage.

Vize, C., Lynam, D., Collison, K., & Miller, J. (2018). Differences among dark triad components: A meta-analytic investigation. *Personality Disorders, 9*(2), 101–111. https://doi.org/10.1037/per0000222.

Wai, M., & Tiliopoulos, N. (2012). The affective and cognitive empathic nature of the dark triad of personality. *Personality and Individual Differences, 52,* 794–799. https://doi.org/10.1016/j.paid.2012.01.008.

Walters, G., Duncan, S., & Mitchell-Perez, K. (2007). The Latent structure of psychopathy: A taxometric investigation of the psychopathy checklist-revised in a heterogeneous sample of male prison inmates. *Assessment, 14*(3), 270–278. https://doi.org/10.1177/1073191107299594.

Watson, D., Clark, L. A., & Tellegen, A. (1988). Development and validation of brief measures of positive and negative affect: The PANAS scales. *Journal of Personality and Social Psychology, 54*(6), 1063–1070.

Watts, A., Lilienfeld, S., Smith, S., Miller, J., Campbell, W., Waldman, I., ... Faschingbauer, T. (2013). The double-edged sword of grandiose narcissism:

Implications for successful and unsuccessful leadership among U.S. presidents. *Psychological Science, 24*(12), 2379–2389. https://doi.org/10.1177/0956797613491970.

Wells, J. T. (Ed.). (2007). *Fraud casebook: Lessons from the bad side of business.* Hoboken, NJ: Wiley.

Westerlaken, K. M., & Woods, P. R. (2013). The relationship between psychopathy and the full range leadership model. *Personality and Individual Differences, 54,* 41–46. https://doi.org/10.1016/j.paid.2012.08.026.

Whigham, N. (2014, October 23). ASIC white-collar crime data 'tip of the iceberg' in Australia. *News.com.au.* Retrieved from http://www.news.com.au/finance/business/asic-whitecollar-crime-data-tip-of-the-iceberg-in-australia/story-fnda1bsz-1227099462601.

Williams, K., Nathanson, C., & Paulhus, D. (2010). Identifying and profiling scholastic cheaters: Their personality, cognitive ability, and motivation. *Journal of Experimental Psychology: Applied, 16*(3), 293–307. https://doi.org/10.1037/a0020773.

Witt, L. A., & Spector, P. E. (2012). Personality and reactions to organizational politics. In G. R. Ferris & D. C. Treadway (Eds.), *Politics in organizations: Theory and research considerations* (pp. 555–588). New York: Routledge.

Wonneberg, D., & Chapman, D. (2007). *The nature of narcissism within organizational leadership.* ProQuest Dissertations Publishing. Retrieved from http://search.proquest.com/docview/304721301/.

Wu, J., & Lebreton, J. M. (2011). Reconsidering the dispositional basis of counterproductive work behavior: The role of aberrant personality. *Personnel Psychology, 64*(3), 593–626. https://doi.org/10.1111/j.1744-6570.2011.01220.x.

Ying, L., & Cohen, A. (2018). Dark triad personalities and counterproductive work behaviors among physicians in China. *The International Journal of Health Planning and Management, 33,* 1–4. https://doi.org/10.1002/hpm.2577.

Zheng, W., Wu, Y., Chen, X., & Lin, S. (2017). Why do employees have counterproductive work behavior? The role of founder's Machiavellianism and the corporate culture in China. *Management Decision, 55*(3), 563–578. https://doi.org/10.1108/MD-10-2016-0696.

Zhu, D., & Chen, G. (2015). Narcissism, director selection, and risk-taking spending. *Strategic Management Journal, 36*(13), 2075–2098. https://doi.org/10.1002/smj.2322.

Zona, F., Minoja, M., & Coda, V. (2013). Antecedents of corporate scandals: CEOs' personal traits, stakeholders' cohesion, managerial fraud, and imbalanced corporate strategy. *Journal of Business Ethics, 113*(2), 265–283.

Zondag, H., van Halen, C., & Wojtkowiak, J. (2009). Overt and covert narcissism in Poland and the Netherlands. *Psychological Reports, 104*(3), 833–843. https://doi.org/10.2466/PR0.104.3.833-843.

8

The Development of a Measure of Dark Triad Traits in a Corporate Sample

Katarina Fritzon

The Dark Triad

While interest in the manifestation of psychopathy in the workplace remains particularly acute (e.g. a 2nd edition of Babiak and Hare's Snakes in Suits will be published in late 2019), most of the recent research into personality predictors of negative workplace outcomes has included psychopathy alongside Narcissism and Machiavellianism, known as the dark triad (Paulhus & Williams, 2002).

Unlike the literature on psychopathy and narcissism, the empirical research on Machiavellianism has primarily been conducted in the field of social and organisational psychology, due to findings of links between this trait and authoritarianism and other socio-political outcomes (Christie & Geis, 1970; Vize, Lynam, Collison, & Miller, 2018). Much of the research on the dark triad and occupational outcomes has involved the use of instruments that assess the components separately, most commonly

K. Fritzon (✉)
Bond University, Robina, QLD, Australia
e-mail: kfritzon@bond.edu.au

© The Author(s) 2020
K. Fritzon et al., *Corporate Psychopathy*,
https://doi.org/10.1007/978-3-030-27188-6_8

the SRP-III (Paulhus, Neumann, & Hare, 2016), the NPI (Raskin & Hall, 1979) and the Mach-IV (Christie & Geis, 1970). More recently, two measures have been developed that contain all three dark triad constructs: the Dirty Dozen (Jonason & Webster, 2010) and the Short Dark Triad (SD3; Jones & Paulhus, 2014). Both measures are very short, containing 12 and 27 items, respectively, raising concerns about whether there is adequate construct coverage.

Problems with Dark Triad Assessment

A number of recently published papers highlight concerns regarding existing DT measures and indeed concerns about the conceptualisation of the dark triad itself, particularly Machiavellianism (McHoskey, Worzel, & Szyarto, 1998; Persson, Kajonius, & Garcia, 2019; Vize et al., 2018). For example, using multiple inventories to examine the construct of Machiavellianism compared to the FFM, Persson (2019) found that the measures of Machiavellianism were heterogeneous and correlated to various FFM domains.

Although some researchers have argued that large proportions of the variance in the dark triad personality traits themselves are explained by the Big Five factors (e.g. O'Boyle, Forsyth, Banks, & Story, & White, 2015; Muris, Merckelbach, Otgaar, & Meijer, 2017), there have been mixed results in terms of whether assessment of dark triad traits does contribute additional variance to prediction models of negative workplace outcomes beyond FFM measurement. DeShong, Grant, and Mullins-Sweatt (2015) examined which personality constructs (DT and FFM) were the best predictors of counterproductive workplace behaviours. The findings suggested that low agreeableness and low conscientiousness predicted 14% of the variance in interpersonal CWB and 22% of the variance in organisational CWB and that adding dark triad constructs did not contribute any additional variance in the model (De Shong et al., 2015). However, in the study two of the three dark triad measures were derived from the FFM—the Elemental Psychopathy Assessment (EPA; Lynam et al., 2011) and the Five-Factor Narcissism Inventory (FFNI; Glover, Miller, Lynam, Crego, & Widiger, 2012)—and therefore the lack of differentiation between the

FFM and DT may have been due to mono-operation bias. In contrast, O'Boyle et al. (2015) found that the dark triad traits explained a substantial amount of variance in the prediction of negative work behaviour, and to a lesser extent, job performance.

A recent meta-analysis (Vize et al., 2018) has highlighted two important concerns regarding existing DT measures. The analysis examined distinctiveness between the DT constructs by investigating their relationship to the Big Five personality dimensions and various associated outcomes including impulsivity, sensation-seeking, altruism and authoritarianism. The results of the meta-analysis, involving 159 independent samples and 15 criterion constructs, found firstly that the average difference between the effect sizes of psychopathy and Machiavellianism across all outcomes was only .06, whereas the difference between narcissism and psychopathy was .17 and between narcissism and Machiavellianism was .14, leading the authors to conclude that current measures of Machiavellianism may be better viewed as measures of psychopathy (Vize et al., 2018). Secondly, the study also conducted separate meta-analyses to compare different measures for the dark triad. The authors concluded from this set of analyses that the SD3 (see Chapter 4 for further description of this measure) assessment produced better results than the other measures overall. For example, the Psychopathy scale of the Dirty Dozen (Jonason & Webster, 2010) (DD-P) failed to capture variance related to disinhibition and antagonism (Vize et al., 2018). There were problems with all three measurement approaches to Narcissism in that the DD-N scale had a smaller positive relationship to Extraversion, whereas both the SD3-N and the DD-N had smaller negative relationships to Agreeableness compared to the NPI. These patterns of correlations with the Big Five run counter to theoretical conceptualisations of Narcissism where it is generally understood to be a mixture of dominance (high Extraversion) and antagonism (low Agreeableness) (Vize et al., 2018).

Similarly, research using the SRP-SF, which is a 64-item self-report measure derived from Hare's four-factor model of psychopathy, failed to find measurement invariance across two large forensic and community samples, leading to the conclusion that this measure cannot be used in the same way with forensic and non-forensic samples (Debowska et al., 2018). As highlighted previously, psychopathy measures derived from the PCL-R contain variables relating to behavioural deviance and antisociality and are therefore probably not suitable for use in high-functioning, noncriminal samples.

Measuring Psychopathy in Business Populations

As discussed in Chapter 4, there have been a number of recent measures developed to assess psychopathy in a business population; namely the Business-Scan 360 (B-Scan 360; Babiak & Hare, 2012) and the Psychopathy Measure-Management Research Version (PM-MRV; Boddy, Ladyshewsky, & Galvin, 2010). The B-Scan 360 is based on Hare's four-factor model of psychopathy and requires respondents to rate their managers on psychopathy-relevant statements (e.g. "comes across as smooth, polished and charming"). Very little information is known about the psychometric properties of the B-Scan 360 beyond its construct validity in terms of factor structure and its external criterion validity, and discriminant validity is yet to be determined. The PM-MRV (Boddy et al., 2010) is also a third-party report measure requiring respondents to rate their managers on psychopathic traits including glibness and superficial charm. There have been no published attempts to validate this measure using external criteria, and Jones and Hare (2016) have suggested that the PM-MRV being based only on Factor 1 of the PCL-R may not adequately discriminate between psychopathy and Machiavellianism and Narcissism.

Studies into the link between employees at senior management level with dark triad traits and counterproductive work behaviour tendencies appear to be constrained by four recurring limitations. First, the current literature is based on tools deemed inappropriate to assess dark triad personality traits in the corporate environment (Fritzon, Bailey, Croom, & Brooks, 2017; Svetina & Croom, 2019). Second, there is a lack of empirical research employing senior management executives where prototypical dark triad (i.e. subclinical narcissism, subclinical psychopathy and Machiavellianism) individuals are more likely to be found. Third, there is a lack of empirical investigation into moderating variables that may influence the relationship between executives with DT personalities and their tendency to engage in CWB (O'Boyle, Forsyth, Banks, & McDaniel, 2012).

Finally, there is lack of clarity surrounding the differentiation between the dark triad constructs (Miller, Vize, Crowe, & Lynam, 2019; Vize et al., 2018) and their relationship to positive and negative workplace outcomes (DeShong et al., 2015; Landay, Harms, & Credé, 2018).

Development of the Corporate Personality Inventory-Revised (CPI-R)

A series of studies have recently been conducted to support the development and validation of a new measure to aid the detection of dark triad personality traits in individuals occupying mid- to senior level corporate positions. The Corporate Personality Inventory-Revised (CPI-R, Fritzon et al., 2017) is a self-report measure consisting of 58 self-belief statements that require a true or false response. The development of the CPI was based on a rational approach to test construction. Items were generated by an expert panel ($n = 4$) comprising of academics with research and professional experience in business management and forensic psychology. An initial item pool of 145 items was drawn from the research literature describing core personality characteristics of psychopathy as written into statements that would reflect the business environment, and a number of these items ($n = 47$) also reflected potentially positive constructions or manifestations of psychopathic personality traits in a business context (e.g. "I am not afraid to make bold business decisions"; "I am a talented communicator"), some of which also reflected the concepts of fearlessness and social influence as central features of the psychopathic personality (Lilienfeld & Widows, 2005). Finally, some items were drawn from previous research that found an association between high-functioning business executives and other personality disorder constructs, including histrionic and narcissistic personality types (Board & Fritzon, 2005).

Construct Validity

The initial validation sample for the CPI consisted of 261 participants from the supply chain industry, comprising 100 females (mean age = 47 years) and 161 males (mean age = 48.5 years). The sample were primarily senior level employees, with 84.3% reporting that they were managers, senior executives or owners (11.9% were senior buyers, and 3.8% were buyers). Participants completed the original 145-item CPI, the Paulhus Deception Scale and the Psychopathic Personality Inventory-Revised (PPI-R; Lilienfeld & Widows, 2005).

Initial exploratory factor analysis (Fritzon et al., 2017) of the 145-item CPI revealed a number of items with cross-loadings or nil loadings on factors. The final solution consisted of 61 items with a four-factor structure accounting for 23.14% of the variance. One of the factors consisted of 25 impression management items, and the remaining three factors reflected the triarchic model of psychopathy (Patrick, Fowles, & Krueger, 2009). A further EFA (Brooks & Fritzon, 2017) was conducted on a larger sample of $n = 373$, consisting of 63% males and 37% females, with an average age of 45.9 years and on the 120 items (without the impression management items). This confirmed the existence of three content subscales accounting for 23.75% of the variance. The three factors were given the same labels as the previous analysis: Bold (e.g. "I am willing to take risks and embark on difficult course of action", $\alpha = .90$), Interpersonal Dominance (e.g. "People fail to accept when they have made a mistake", $\alpha = .70$) and Ruthless ("It is acceptable to gain from other people's weaknesses/mistakes", $\alpha = .78$). The total CPI-R score is derived from a summation of all items and has a Cronbach's alpha of .84 indicating high internal consistency. The 58-item CPI-R with factor loadings is presented in Table 8.1.

Criterion validity of the CPI has been established using existing dark triad and related measures, including the Paulhus Deception Scale (PDS, Paulhus, 1998), the PPI-R (Lilienfeld & Widows, 2005), the Narcissistic Personality Inventory (Raskin & Hall, 1979), the Mach-IV (Christie & Geis, 1970) and the PID-5 (Krueger, Derringer, Markon, Watson, & Skodol, 2012). The results for these analyses are presented in Table 8.2. As all of these analyses have been carried out in a series of individual studies, the n for each sample will be presented in the first column.

In terms of discriminant and concurrent validity, the CPI-R correlates significantly with the Paulhus Deception Scale ($r = .361$, $p < .001$; Fritzon et al., 2017 and the Psychopathy Personality Inventory-Revised ($r = .231$, $p < .001$). The Boldness subscale of the CPI-R correlates with

Table 8.1 Factor loadings for principle axis factoring with direct oblimin rotation of the CPI-R

	B[a]	ID[b]	R[c]
I am quick-witted	.50		
My knowledge and skills far exceed the average person	.46		
If I wanted to, I could be anything I wanted to be	.45		
I like being where the action is happening	.53		
I thrive off excitement and challenges	.47		
I am able to adapt to any situation or interaction	.49		
Life is full of givers and takers			.45
Once I have made a decision, I do not doubt myself	.55		
I am able to remain calm in the face of danger	.52		
People often react emotionally to small things in the workplace and should instead just move on			.43
Sometimes in life, you need to put yourself first			.41
People make their own decisions and must handle the mistakes			.52
I am able to adapt and change quickly to any task, job or requirement.	.57		
People fail to accept when they have made a mistake			.49
I am often helping colleagues who struggle at keeping up with their work		−.41	
When a colleague makes a mistake, I am quick to help point it out		.44	
I am mentally stronger than others	.50		
I need new and exciting things in my life	.36		
It is not practical to always make appointments on time		.38	
It is enjoyable to test your own limits and learn about the limits of others	.37		
I can usually tell if people are lying	.41		
I am able to persuade people to see what matters	.50		

(continued)

Table 8.1 (continued)

	B[a]	ID[b]	R[c]
It is difficult for people to hear the truth			.50
Waiting patiently for others to complete work requirements that "should have been finished" is arduous at times			.46
It is not uncommon for others to try and show each other up at work			.50
People can treat the workplace like a battlefield at times			.51
I find I have often had to remind colleagues of imminent deadlines			.50
If I am confronted by a hostile colleague, I am able to handle the situation with ease	.41		
It is important for me to be considered as a leader in the workplace	.54		
When it really matters, I can talk most people into anything	.54		
Smiling is an easy way to attract the interest of others			.41
I know what to expect and how to handle people's reactions	.44		
I can handle being the centre of attention	.64		
I am a talented communicator	.54		
I rarely get nervous in the workplace	.51		
I often insist on having things my own way		.36	
I'm always looking for a new challenge	.53		
I find no trouble in speaking out against unjust or unnecessary company policies	.38		
I'm the first to admit when I have made a mistake	.40	−.36	
Challenging someone with authority does not bother me	.47		
A person's first impression of me is always positive	.36		
In some situations, honesty is not necessary		.45	
Success at any cost to others is justifiable		.54	
It is acceptable to gain from other people's weaknesses/mistakes		.54	
I wouldn't feel guilty making an employee cry if they made me look bad		.51	
Lying and deceit are integral to successful business		.56	
I believe I am more important than other people in the workplace		.57	
Feelings of guilt and remorse are a sign of weakness in others		.43	

	B^a	ID^b	R^c
It is acceptable to place extra pressure on colleagues to meet deadlines			.41
When others fail to meet deadlines, this may reflect badly on me.			.49
Having allies helps me achieve my goals			.44
Taking on multiple tasks at once is exciting	.57		
Conflict amongst colleagues is inevitable			.53
It's good to challenge young people in the workplace to test their limits			.36
In the past, I have found that most people are unreliable		.40	
Most relationships in the workplace are superficial and impersonal		.35	
I possess the ability to read people at face value	.41		
When someone in my department has success, I believe my role in that should be acknowledged		.51	
I believe I am an amusing and entertaining conversationalist	.44		
I am able to move on quickly from negative consequences	.50		
Applying pressure to decision-makers is a necessity at times			.51
I would be good in a high stake or pressured situation as I make fast decisions	.67		
Being different and standing out from others has its benefits	.48		
I am willing to take risks and embark on difficult courses of action	.66		
A fast-paced workplace environment excites me	.61		
I admire those who can work the system to get ahead		.48	
All staff members, regardless of authority/status, meaningfully contribute to the company		−.48	
Some people in the workplace will be more valuable and important to me than others			.39

^{a} Bold, ^{b} Interpersonal Dominance, ^{c} Ruthlessness

Table 8.2 Summary of Pearson correlations between CPI-R and related measures

Variable	CPI Boldness	CPI Ruthlessness	CPI Interpersonal Dominance	CPI Total
$N = 261^a$				
PDS total	.43**	−.15*	−.21*	.36**
Self-deceptive	.57**	.01	−.08	
Impression Mgt	.14	−.26*	−.27*	
PPI-R total				.23*
Fearless Dominance	.11	.30**	.47**	
Self-centred impulsivity	.10	.42**	.50**	
Cold-hearted	−.19*	.29**	.32**	
Stress immunity			.32**	
$N = 122^b$				
NPI	.51**	.52**		
Mach tactics		.25*		
Mach views		.27*		
PID **Disinhibition**	.19	.17	.02	.22*
Impulsivity	.16	−.21*	−.07	.15
Irresponsibility	.16	.42**	−.09	
PID **Antagonism**	.48**	.31**	.25*	.30**
Callous	−.06	.44**	.07	.25*
Deceitful	−.01	.25*	.05	.08
Grandiose	.16	.35**	.49**	.35**
Manipulative	.31**	.22*	.10	.17
PID **Neg affect**	−.42**	.00	.15	−.28*
Anxiousness	−.30*	.16	−.34*	−.32*
Emotional lability	.01	−.10	−.24*	−.15
Separation insecurity	.02	.13	−.16	.10
Submissiveness	−.38**	−.19	−.03	−.22
PID **Detached**	−.16	−.01	.20*	.09
Anhedonia	.25*	.08	.26*	.14
Withdrawal	−.27*	−.36**	−.18	
PID **Psychoticism**	.22	−.10	−.15	−.12

$*p < .005, **p < .001$
^{a}Fritzon et al. (2017); ^{b}Rodrigo (2016) and Hughes (2016)

the NPI, and with the self-deceptive enhancement subscale of the PDS, whereas the Ruthlessness subscale correlates moderately with the Tactics and Views subscales of the Mach-IV. The fact that Ruthlessness did not correlate with the Morality subscale implies that high-functioning Ruthless individuals know what is morally "right" and "wrong", and this may be a factor that is protective against engagement in antisocial behaviours. It is also noted that the Morality subscale of the Mach-IV is only comprised of two items. The third subscale of the CPI-R, named Interpersonal Dominance is also negatively correlated with impression management and positively correlated with all subscales of the PPI-R. While the results of these correlational analyses require further replication with larger and more diverse samples, there is some indication from this pattern of results that the subscales of the CPI-R are measuring constructs related to psychopathy as well as other dark triad personality traits and therefore may be a potentially useful measure of derailing personality and behaviours in the workplace.

Significant correlations have also been found between the CPI-R total and sub-facets of the Personality Inventory for the DSM-5 (PID-5) associated with antagonistic maladaptive personality traits (Anderson, Sellbom, Wygant, Salekin, & Krueger, 2014; Strickland, Drislane, Lucy, Krueger, & Patrick, 2013). For example, using the TriPM measure of psychopathy, Strickland et al. (2013) found that the PID-5 scales Disinhibition and Antagonism were the best predictors of the total score of the TriPM. In addition, the Boldness subscale of the TriPM had negative correlations with both Negative Affect and Detachment, whereas TriPM Disinhibition had positive correlations with Negative Affect and Detachment. Comparing these results with the results presented in Table 8.2, we see that the Interpersonal Dominance subscale of the CPI-R is positively correlated with Antagonism and negatively correlated with Negative Affect; in other words, it displays a similar pattern of correlations to the Boldness subscale of the TriPM (Strickland et al., 2013). The Ruthlessness subscale of the CPI-R has the strongest relationships with the facets of the PID-5 that would seem to conceptually align with the Meanness facet of the triarchic model of psychopathy (Patrick et al., 2009), namely callous, deceitful and antagonistic. It is interesting to note the negative correlation between Ruthlessness and Impulsivity, while there is a positive correlation with

Irresponsibility. Impulsivity is noted to be a variable that differentiates psychopathy from Machiavellianism (Vize et al., 2018), with the latter being associated with more planful, deliberate action than the former. Behaving irresponsibly is not the same as behaving impulsively, and so it is noted that individuals high on the Ruthlessness subscale may engage in *planned* irresponsible behaviour, i.e. act without regard for the consequences to others. Finally, the Boldness subscale of the CPI-R had a strong positive correlation with the domain score for PID-5 Antagonism, as well as negative correlations for several of the facet scores of the Negative Affect Domain. Boldness was also negatively correlated with the withdrawn facet of the detached domain, which implies that people who score high on the CPI-R Boldness subscale have a tendency towards self-promotion and forwardness, similar to the previous relationship noted between Boldness and narcissism.

Concurrent validity of the CPI-R has also been examined in relation to workplace outcomes that are of interest, including counterproductive work behaviour (CWB–C; Spector et al., 2006), and the Interpersonal Conflict at Work Scale (ICAWS; Spector & Jex, 1998), career success (Volmer, Koch, & Göritz, 2016), leadership style (Avolio, Gardner, & Walumbwa, 2007; Walsh, 2018) and career satisfaction (Greenhaus, Parasuraman, & Wormley, 1990; Uechtritz, 2018). A set of hypotheses about the relative contributions of the CPI-R personality traits to the aforementioned workplace outcomes were tested using hierarchical multiple regression. Results are presented in the following sections, examining each outcome variable.

Counterproductive Work Behaviour

As discussed in Chapter 7, dark triad traits have been found to be associated with a range of negative workplace outcomes including bullying (Boddy et al., 2010; van Geel, Goemans, Toprak, & Vedder, 2017) interpersonal aggression (Barlett, 2016; Bogart, Benotsch, & Pavlovic, 2004), theft in the workplace (Lyons & Jonason, 2015), abusive supervision (Tepper, 2007) and leadership derailment (Hogan & Hogan, 2001). Counterproductive behaviour in the workplace is the most reliable negative predictor of job performance (Spain, Harms, & LeBreton, 2014), and so it is important to develop valid personality predictors that can potentially be used to identify and screen individuals who may be likely to engage in these behaviours. The results reported in the following section were conducted on a sample of $n = 101$ individuals who were all in a supervisory role (Team Leader or above) primarily in the IT industry (Ray, 2019). Of the sample, 60.4% were male, and the mode age range was 30–39 (24.6%). The study employed the CWB–C (Spector et al., 2006) as an outcome measure. The CWB–C is a 45-item self-report instrument that contains 21 items about behaviours directed at the organisation (CWB–O) and 22 items measuring interpersonal behaviours (e.g. "started or continued a damaging rumour at work"). The subscales of the CPI-R were entered into two multiple regression analyses to predict CWB–O and CWB–I, respectively.

The standard multiple regression analysis revealed that all five predictors significantly explained 30% of the variance in CWB–O ($R^2 = .300$, $F(5, 91) = 7.650$, $p = .000$). Ruthlessness made the strongest unique contribution to CWB–O ($\beta = .319$, $p = .002$), with higher scores on Ruthlessness predicting higher CWB–O scores. Age made the second strongest yet significantly negative contribution to CWB–O ($\beta = -.312$, $p = .001$), with higher age scores predicting lower levels of CWB–O and lower age scores predicting lower levels of CWB–O. Interpersonal Dominance did not make a significant contribution to CWB–O ($p = .255$), nor did Boldness ($p = .057$) or gender ($p = .444$).

The multiple regression analysis indicated that the model explained 36% of the variance in CWB–I ($R^2 = .360$, $F(5, 91) = 10.255$, $p = .000$). Interpersonal Dominance made the strongest unique contribution to CWB–I, such that higher scores on interpersonal dominance significantly predicted higher levels of CWB–I ($\beta = .335$, $p = .001$). Boldness made the second strongest unique contribution to CWB–I ($\beta = -.330$, $p = .000$); however, in the opposite direction anticipated, such that that higher scores on boldness predicted lower CWB–I scores. Ruthlessness also made a significant and unique contribution to CWB–I ($\beta = .303$, $p = .003$), with higher scores on ruthlessness significantly predicting higher scores on CWB–I. Gender did not make a significant contribution to CWB–I ($p = .164$), nor did age ($p = .066$).

Moderation Effects of Interpersonal Conflict in the Workplace

Interpersonal conflict at work was examined as a simple moderator of the relation between the subscales of the CPI-R and the Organisational and Interpersonal subscales of CWB. Interpersonal conflict was measured by the four-item Interpersonal Conflict at Work Scale (ICAWS) developed by Spector and Jex (1998). A significant moderation effect was found only for the Interpersonal Dominance subscale and the Interpersonal CWB. The overall model was significant F (3, 93) = 17.20, $p = .000$, accounting for 36% of overall variance in CWB–I ($R^2 = .360$). Interpersonal Dominance was indicated as a significant predictor of CWB–I ($\beta = .661$, $t(93) = 4.25$, $p = .000$), as was interpersonal conflict at work ($\beta = .780$, t (93) = 4.80 $p = .000$). Further, the interaction between interpersonal dominance and interpersonal conflict at work was significant ($\beta = .188$, t (93) = 2.23, $p = .028$). That is, interpersonal conflict at work was a significant moderator of the psychopathy and CWB–I relationship. This interaction is presented in Fig. 8.1.

When interpersonal conflict at work is low, it has no effect on the relation between interpersonal dominance and CWB–I ($\beta = .287$, $t(93) = 1.17$, $p = .241$). When interpersonal conflict is moderate, it has a significant moderating effect on interpersonal dominance and CWB–I ($\beta = .66$, $t(93) = 4.25$, $p = .000$). When interpersonal conflict at work is high, it also has a significant moderating effect on interpersonal dominance and CWB–I ($\beta = 1.03$, $t(93) = 4.90$, $p = .000$).

Career Success

As indicated above, research on the relationship between dark triad personality traits and workplace outcomes has typically focused on negative aspects even though theories of successful psychopathy have emphasised

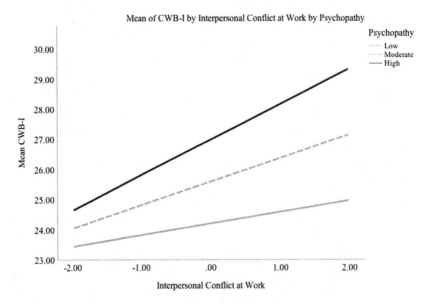

Fig. 8.1 The relationship between interpersonal dominance and CWB-I at low, moderate and high levels of interpersonal conflict

the adaptive traits and protective factors that enable the individual possessing a psychopathic disposition to achieve successful outcomes. Very few studies, for example, have examined the link between dark triad personality traits and career success (Boehm & Lyubomirsky, 2008; Spurk, Keller, & Hirschi, 2016). Aspects of the dark triad personality traits that may indeed be advantageous in workplace settings include interpersonal skills such as superficial charm, a positive attributional style (Snyder, 2010) and stress immunity can increase goal-oriented and problem-solving capacities (O'Boyle et al., 2012), while high self-esteem and belief in one's superiority can give individual with narcissistic traits a potential advantage in terms of seeking early leadership and promotion opportunities (Grijalva & Newman, 2015). Finally, individuals with Machiavellian characteristics can use subtle manipulation alongside resisting impulsiveness to achieve long-term strategic planning goals (Jones & Paulhus, 2011).

The links between the subscales of the CPI-R and career success, defined both objectively (salary and leadership status) and subjectively (via a career satisfaction scale), were addressed in a study employing a sample of $n = 148$ community participants who were all employed at least 20 hours per week. Of the sample, 61% were female, and the modal age (39.6%) was 18–24 years old (Uechtritz, 2018). The study employed the Career Satisfaction Scale (CSS; Greenhaus et al., 1990) which consists of 5 items including "*I am satisfied with the progress I have made toward meeting my overall career goals*", and the Authentic Leadership Questionnaire (ALQ; Avolio et al., 2007). In addition to using the CPI-R, the study also used the Mach-IV scale (Jakobwitz & Egan, 2006) and the NPI (Raskin & Hall, 1979), which was scored into adaptive and maladaptive subscales according to the recommendations of Ackerman et al. (2011).

The overall model for objective career success with all five predictor variables was significant, $F(5, 131) = 3.90$, $p = .002$. In step 1, gender accounted for 8.2% of the variance in objective career success, with males scoring significantly higher ($M = 15.09$, $SD = 5.17$) than females ($M = 12.34$, $SD = 4.34$), $F(1, 135) = 12.03$, $p = .001$. In step 2, Psychopathy, Machiavellianism, healthy narcissism and pathological narcissism accounted for an additional 13% of the variance of objective career success; however, this was not significant, $\Delta F(4, 131) = 1.80$, $p = .133$. Of the personality traits, psychopathy was the only significant predictor of objective career success ($p = .027$), with higher scores on the CPI-R predicting lower objective career success (Uechtritz, 2018).

Subjective Career Success

Table 8.3 also shows the results for the multiple regression model predicting subjective career success, $F(4, 132) = 3.19$, $p = .015$. Out of the four variables, psychopathy and Machiavellianism were the only personality traits that added significantly to the prediction ($p < .05$), with higher scores predicting higher subjective career success (Uechtritz, 2018).

Leadership

The tendency to engage in high levels of impression management, over inflated-claims of competency, devalue the contribution of others and

Table 8.3 Multiple regression analysis predicting work outcomes from CPI-R subscales, Mach-IV and NPI

Work behaviour	CPI-R subscale	β	B (SEB)
CWB–O (n = 97; Ray, 2019)	Boldness	−.17	[−.284, .004]
	Ruthlessness	.31**	[.190, .858]
	I/P Dominance	.11	[−2.13, .791]
CWB–I	Boldness	−.33***	[−.299, −.091]
	Ruthlessness	.30**	[.134, .615]
	I/P Dominance	.33***	[.257, .079]
Objective career success (n = 137; Uechtritz, 2018)	CPI-R	−.24**	−.15 (.07)
	Mach-IV	−.04	−.03 (.05)
	NPI	−.16	−.23 (.18)
Subjective career success	CPI-R	0.26**	0.15 (.06)
	Mach-IV	0.24**	0.13 (.05)
	NPI	0.06	0.11 (.17)

Notes CI = confidence interval. β = standardised coefficient, B = unstandardised coefficient, SE = standard error; *p < .05, **p < .01, ***p < .001

respond negatively to feedback is not conducive to establishing a strong leadership role (Padilla, Hogan, & Kaiser, 2007; Sanecka, 2013). Research is somewhat mixed on the association between dark triad personality traits and leadership outcomes. On the one hand, adaptive traits including low levels of anxiety and stress (Fearlessness), social charm, the ability to discard unnecessary relationships and good problem-solving are putatively associated with good leadership outcomes (Babiak, Neumann, & Hare, 2010; Smith, Lilienfeld, Coffey, & Dabbs, 2013). On the other hand, research has noted that it is important to consider a variety of moderating variables when considering the relationship between dark triad personality traits and leadership (Landay et al. 2018; O'Boyle et al., 2012). For example, while it has been found that individuals with narcissistic traits may obtain positions of authority more quickly than individuals without those traits (Leadership emergence; Lord, De Vader, & Alliger, 1986), once they have reached those positions they are not necessarily effective (Hogan & Kaiser, 2005), because they belittle their subordinates and focus more on their individual needs rather than broader organisational goals (Hogan & Hogan, 2001; Judge, Piccolo, & Kosalka, 2009; O'Boyle et al., 2012;

Watts et al., 2013). O'Boyle et al. (2012) found that being in a position of authority moderated the effect between psychopathic personality traits and counterproductive work behaviour, with those at higher levels in the organisation being better able to control impulsivity and antisocial behaviours. However, O'Boyle et al. (2012) also noted that this finding may have been an artefact of a large number of samples within the meta-analysis comprising positions of authority (e.g. police officers, military and prison guards).

In order to examine the relationships between dark triad personality traits and specific leadership dimensions, a series of multiple regressions were performed predicting the four subscales of the Leadership Style Questionnaire (Avolio et al., 2007) from the CPI-R, the Mach-IV and the NPI (Walsh, 2018). It was found that for relationship transparency (leader presents his/her authentic self to others and reinforces openness with others) and self-aware (understands how he/she makes sense of the world and is aware of strengths and limitations) leadership, there was a small effect for Mach-IV ($\beta = -.28$, $p < .001$ and $\beta = -.26$, $p < .005$, respectively) and CPI-R ($\beta = -.32$, $p < .005$ and $\beta = -.23$, $p < .05$, respectively), while for Moral Perspective (sets a high standard for moral and ethical conduct) there was only an effect for Mach-IV ($\beta = -.44$, $p < .001$). None of the variables predicted balanced processing (leader objectively analyses the relevant data before coming to a decision and solicits views that challenge deeply held position), and Narcissism did not predict any of the Leadership dimensions (Walsh, 2018). The results did not examine individual subscales of the CPI-R, but together they imply that the CPI-R negatively predicts aspects of leadership that are consistent with previous findings for dark triad personality traits. Specifically, the findings for relationship transparency are consistent with the previous suggestion that corporate psychopathy is associated with higher levels of impression management (i.e. presentation of "false self") than non-successful psychopathy, and similarly, narcissism is reliably associated with high levels of impression management and self-deceptive enhancement (on the PDS) in particular. Lack of insight, which is the cornerstone of self-aware Leadership, was once believed to be a central defining characteristic of psychopathy (Cleckley, 1941), although a recent study by Miller, Jones, and Lynam (2011) comparing self- and informant-report psychopathy scores concluded that psychopathic individuals do not appear to lack insight (i.e. report accurately on their own psychopathic characteristics) when there are no direct negative consequences for doing so. Regarding the role of lack of insight into Machiavellianism, Sleep, Miller, Lynam, and Campbell (2018) similarly reported a convergence between self- and informant-report of .36. However, it is important to note that both of these studies involved ratings of *impairment* arising from antagonistic personality traits as assessed by clinical measures (e.g. the Mach-IV and EPA), whereas in the Walsh (2018) study the lack of insight was in relation to its role in Leadership. Therefore, it is possible that an assessment of leadership quality or potential signalled an ego-protection motive to those individuals high in psychopathy and Machiavellianism to engage in the impression management distortion that they are so famously known for (Jaiswal & Bhal, 2014; Kwon & Seo, 2017). This suggestion is supported by the findings of a study conducted by Blickle, Schütte and Genau (2018) who noted that the correlations that they obtained between psychopathy and leadership style, which was through a combination of self-report, subordinate ratings and superior ratings, were much smaller than those obtained by Mathieu and Babiak (2015), which were obtained via other ratings only. For Mathieu and Babiak (2015), the correlations between psychopathy and the consideration leadership style ranged from $r \leq -.34$ and $r \geq -.52$, whereas in the later study they ranged from $r \leq -.09$ to $r \geq -.32$ (Blickle et al., 2018, p. 22). Thus, the contribution of self-rated psychopathy appeared to ameliorate the negative correlations between psychopathy and leadership overall, which has important implications for studies where only self-reported ratings of psychopathy are used.

Finally, the finding that the Mach-IV negatively predicted the Moral Perspective subscale of Leadership is not surprising given that questionable morality is a defining feature of the Machiavellian personality. Future research will examine these leadership dynamics in relation to the subscales of the CPI-R, particularly Ruthlessness which correlated with the Mach-IV. Also, future research using the CPI-R will attempt to replicate the findings by Landay et al. (2018), who identified a curvilinear relationship between psychopathy and leadership effectiveness (as rated by subordinates and peers), such that moderate scores for psychopathy were associated with higher ratings of effectiveness than either very low or very high ratings.

Third-Party Version of the CPI

Researchers have raised several concerns about the validity of self-report measures in assessing psychopathy and other dark triad personality characteristics (Sellbom, Lilienfeld, Fowler, & McCrary, 2018). The issues of dishonesty and lack of insight have already been discussed previously in this chapter, with mixed findings depending perhaps on the motive for self- or other-directed distortion (Miller et al., 2011; Sleep et al., 2018). A further issue that is particularly salient for psychopathy and dark triad measures generally is that "it may be inherently problematic to ask individuals who have never experienced an emotion… to report on its absence" (Sellbom et al. 2018, p. 214). A final issue also raised previously is that of mono-source bias (Blickle et al., 2018). In an attempt to overcome these limitations, the Corporate Personality Inventory also contains a third-party report version, which asks respondents to bring to mind a senior colleague *with whom they have had a difficult relationship or interaction*. This instruction was added so as to maximise the likelihood that respondents would focus their attention on a senior colleague/supervisor who might possess the personality traits that the measure was designed to capture. The CPI-3R consists of 57 items that are derived from the self-report version, but exclude items that could not easily be known or observed by a third party. For example, the self-report item *I believe I am an amusing and entertaining conversationalist* is translated to *My manager believes he/she is an amusing and entertaining conversationalist*. On the other hand, the self-report item *Life is full of givers and takers* is not included in the third-party report version.

For the third-party rater version, exploratory factor analysis also yielded a three-factor structure accounting for 58.23% of the variance (Wiseman, 2014). Factor labels were selected to reflect the items that loaded onto each factor with subscale alphas of .91 for adaptive façade, .92 for Ruthlessness and .89 for Impulsive egocentricity. The subscales were highly inter-correlated with adaptive façade correlating with Ruthlessness at $r =$

.73, $p < .001$, and Impulsive Egocentricity at $r = .53$, $p < .001$; while the correlation between Ruthlessness and Impulsive Egocentricity was $r = .91$, $p < .001$. Results of the EFA for $n = 385$ cases are presented in Table 8.4.

Adaptive façade reflects positive, charming and personable traits. These characteristics may be presented initially by individuals high in psychopathy to appear as ideal workplace candidates (Boddy, 2010) and thus reflect the concept of *superficial charm* as measured by the PCL-R. While the variables that comprise the adaptive façade subscale may at face value seem entirely positive, it is important to note the inter-correlations amongst the subscales highlighting that these adaptive qualities exist alongside the more malevolent behaviours reflected in the other two subscales. Ruthlessness measures a lack of concern for the personal consequences of actions, motivation to get ahead and manipulation of others. This also reflects the prototypical description of the "corporate psychopath" (Boddy, 2006). Finally, impulsive egocentricity was defined by variables reflecting a grandiose sense of self-worth and recklessness. These traits have been described by other researchers as being revealed through the actions and attitudes of corporate psychopaths over time (Skeem, Polaschek, Patrick, & Lilienfeld, 2011). Cronbach's alphas for the factors indicated that there may be some item redundancy, particularly for the adaptive façade and ruthlessness factors, with $n = 23$ and $n = 28$ items, respectively.

The three factors of the CPI-3R are also conceptually consistent with the triarchic model (Patrick et al., 2009), with Boldness being represented by the adaptive façade in terms of an individual's ability to remain calm, recover quickly from stressful events and persuade others. The triarchic element of Meanness is represented by Ruthlessness in the CPI-3R in terms of defiance of authority, exploitation of others and destructiveness (Patrick et al., 2009). Finally, the Disinhibition element of the triarchic model is similar to Impulsive Egocentricity in the CPI-3R in terms of impulsiveness, lack of planfulness and failure to meet obligations.

Criterion validity for the CPI-3R has been examined using the NEO-PI-R, the Psychopathy Workplace Behaviours (Boddy, 2011) and the Comprehensive Assessment of Psychopathic Personality (CAPP; Cooke, Hart, Logan & Michie, 2012). These are presented in Table 8.5.

Table 8.4 Factor loadings for principle axis factoring with direct oblimin rotation of the CPI-3R

	AF[a]	IE[b]	R[c]
My manager believes they are an amusing and entertaining conversationalist	.45	**.54**	.22
My manager is quick-witted	**.70**	.21	.29
My manager believes that their knowledge and skills far exceed the average person	.30	**.68**	.32
My manager likes being where the action is happening	.49	**.52**	.37
My manager lives life in the fast lane	.18	.23	**.48**
My manager is able to adapt to any situation or interaction	**.75**	.11	.28
My manager is not perplexed or embarrassed when found to be wrong	**.62**	.37	−.12
My manager is adept at noticing weakness in others	.39	.34	**.56**
My manager is able to move on quickly from negative consequences	**.75**	.34	−.21
My manager is able to remain calm in the face of danger	**.83**	.02	.20
My manager easily gets caught up in others problems	.16	.32	**.32**
My manager believes that applying pressure to decision-makers is a necessity at times	.44	**.59**	.30
My manager is able to adapt and change quickly to any task, job or requirement	**.80**	.05	.37
My manager is often helping colleagues who struggle to keep up with their work	**.65**	−.09	.11
When a colleague makes a mistake, my manager does not forget	.12	**.71**	.33
My manager is mentally stronger than others	**.70**	.08	.39
My manager is good at noticing aspects on which to compliment another person	**.68**	−.19	.33
My manager would be good in a high stake or pressured situation as they make fast decisions	**.67**	−.03	.42
My manager always make appointments on time	.45	−.16	**.61**
My manager finds it difficult to talk others into seeing my side or point of view	**.65**	.40	−.25
My manager seems to be able to tell if people are lying	**.69**	.20	.14
My manager is very nervous about taking a risk for a big payoff	**.67**	.36	.05

	AF[a]	IE[b]	R[c]
My manager is able to persuade people to see what matters	.74	.22	.24
My manager makes bold business decisions that come at a personal cost to others	.15	**.82**	−.05
My manager does not wait patiently for others to complete work requirements that "should have been finished"	.26	**.78**	.10
My manager shows up others at work	.12	**.79**	.09
My manager treats the workplace like a battlefield at times	−.03	**.82**	.21
If my manager is confronted by a hostile colleague, they are able to handle the situation with ease	**.79**	.17	.20
It is important for my manager to be considered as a leader in the workplace	.50	**.65**	.30
Sometimes I find my manager is nervous without knowing why	**.74**	.34	−.03
My manager likes to be the centre of attention	.09	**.67**	.32
My manager is a talented communicator	**.80**	.13	.16
My manager rarely gets nervous in the workplace	**.75**	.22	.16
My manager is willing to take risks and embark on difficult courses of action	**.71**	.20	.29
My manager often insists on having things their own way	.21	**.79**	.35
My manager speaks out against unnecessary company policies	.35	.04	.51
My manager challenges others in authority	.37	**.48**	.22
My manager believes that they are is entertaining and theatrical	.27	**.57**	.20
My manager shows admiration for those who can work the system to get ahead	.32	.24	**.48**
My manager is tested by anyone who challenges their work/position	.13	**.68**	.25
My manager is not afraid to publicly point out others' mistakes	.26	**.79**	.20
I would describe their mentality as being "for the moment"	.13	**.75**	−.13
My manager gains from other people's weaknesses/mistakes	−.00	**.75**	.14
My manager feels guilty after reprimanding an employee or colleague	.32	**.68**	.15
It wouldn't bother my manager making an employee cry if they challenged their decisions on a matter of importance	.03	**.74**	.11
My manager is a valuable asset to any workplace	**.82**	.03	.27

(continued)

Table 8.4 (continued)

	AF[a]	IE[b]	R[c]
My manager gives people a chance to rectify mistakes	-.18	.70	-.10
My manager places extra pressure on colleagues to meet deadlines	.35	.72	.16
My manager is careful to select an inner circle of supporters at work	.40	.55	.29
My manager always sticks to company rules and procedures	.12	.59	-.10
My manager likes to challenge young people in the workplace to test their limits	.52	.58	.10
My manager employs humiliation and intimidation in the workplace	-.17	.75	.14
My manager believes that authority and status within the company is the most important thing	-.14	.17	.79
My manager possesses the ability to read people	.70	.21	.17
My manager likes to create his own "culture" at work	.31	.46	.53
When someone in the department has success, my manager insists that their role in that be acknowledged	.12	.73	-.07
My manager is the person for colleagues to confide in	.72	-.12	.09
Work defines who my manager is	.29	.46	.49

[a]Adaptive façade, [b]Impulsive Egocentricity, [c]Ruthlessness

Table 8.5 Summary of Pearson correlations between CPI-3R and related measures

Variable	Adaptive façade	Ruthless	Impulsive egocentricity	CPI-3R Total
NEO-PI-R[a]				
Neuroticism	-.70**	.44**	.21*	-.01
Anxiety	-.59**	.21*	.15	-.39**
Angry Hostility	-.37**	.66**	.25**	.39**
Depression	-.55**	-.01	.04	-.33**
Self-consciousness	-.54**	.16	-.03	-.37**
Impulsiveness	-.46**	.40**	.31**	.12
Vulnerability	-.68**	.41**	.21*	-.03
Extraversion	.56**	-.26**	.41**	.24**
Warmth	.52**	-.61**	.13	-.15
Gregariousness	.31**	-.20*	.37**	.13
Assertiveness	.48**	.30**	.33**	.63**
Activity	.27**	.22**	.38**	.45**
Excitement-seeking	.23**	-.01	.51**	.29**
Positive emotions	.50**	-.50**	.16	-.06
Openness	.42**	-.45**	.20*	-.06
Fantasy	-.07	-.04	.33**	.00
Aesthetics	.16	-.40**	.18*	-.18*
Feelings	.12	-.05	.43**	.15
Actions	.46**	-.41**	.05	-.05
Ideas	.48**	-.32**	.02	.05
Values	.49**	-.50**	-.16	-.16

(continued)

Table 8.5 (continued)

Variable	Adaptive façade	Ruthless	Impulsive egocentricity	CPI-3R Total
Agreeableness	.42**	-.82**	-.32**	-.50**
Trust	.42**	-.64**	-.16	-.30**
Straightforwardness	.22**	-.62**	-.36**	-.47**
Altruism	.43**	-.76**	-.15	-.40**
Compliance	.27**	-.71**	-.33**	-.51**
Modesty	.28**	-.71**	-.48**	-.53**
Tender-mindedness	.47**	-.60**	-.12	-.23**
Conscientiousness	.66**	-.32**	-.20*	.11
Competence	.69**	-.44**	-.15	.04
Order	.24**	.09	-.06	.21*
Dutifulness	.58**	-.49**	-.27**	-.09
Achievement striving	.50**	.07	.24**	.44**
Self-discipline	.50**	.07	-.17*	.21
Deliberation	.49**	-.56**	-.45**	-.27**
Psychopathy workplace behaviours[b]	-.54**	.75**	.24*	.30**
CAPP[c]	-.55**	.60**	-.03	.07

[a]$N = 174$, [b]Psychopathy workplace behaviours were comprised of items from Boddy (2011, pp. 15–18), [3]$n = 93$ (Anderson, 2018)

*$p < .005$, **$p < .001$

Individuals obtaining high scores on the CPI-3R were rated as low on Agreeableness on the NEO-PI-R. The total score of the CPI-3R also correlated negatively with most of the facets of the Neuroticism subscale (except for angry hostility) and positively with Extraversion at both the domain and facet level. Gender differences were also noted, in that female participants with high ratings on the CPI-3R had higher ratings on Openness and Conscientiousness, than male participants. Some interesting patterns were observed for the subscales of the CPI-R. The adaptive façade actually had positive correlations with all domains of the NEO, except for Neuroticism, whereas Ruthlessness had the strongest negative correlations for Agreeableness, as well as low Openness and low Extraversion (particularly positive emotions). Finally, Ruthlessness had a strong negative correlation with Conscientiousness. Impulsive Egocentricity had a positive association with Extraversion (particularly excitement seeking) and with the fantasy and feelings facets of Openness.

Although each of the dark triad constructs has been found to relate somewhat differently to specific FFM domains (Furnham, Richards, Rangel, & Jones, 2014), all three have significant negative associations to Agreeableness. Narcissism tends to have higher correlations with Extraversion than the other dark triad traits, while Machiavellianism and Psychopathy have low Conscientiousness. Finally, Neuroticism is generally (though not always) lower for Narcissism than for the other two DT personality traits (Furnham et al., 2014). Employing meta-analysis to study the combined statistical effects of the FFM on the DT personality traits, O'Boyle et al. (2015) examined the degree of overlap between the DT and the Big Five, at both the global traits and facet domain levels. The meta-analysis identified 310 independent samples that had employed FFM measures (90% the NEO-PI, Costa & McCrae, 1992) and explicit DT measures including expert ratings. The samples were all non-clinical samples. Findings revealed that Machiavellianism was significantly negatively associated with Agreeableness and Conscientiousness and positively correlated with Neuroticism. Narcissism was significantly positively associated with Extraversion, Openness and Conscientiousness and significantly negatively associated with Agreeableness and Neuroticism. Psychopathy was significantly negatively associated with Agreeableness and Conscientiousness and slightly positively associated with Extraversion, Neuroticism and

Openness. Collectively, the FFM traits explained approximately a third of the variance in Machiavellianism, 88% of the variance in psychopathy and 42% of the variance in narcissism.

The pattern of correlations between the CPI-3R and the CAPP revealed that only the Ruthlessness subscale of the CPI-3R correlated significantly with the CAPP, and that the total CPI-3R score did not correlate significantly with the CAPP (Anderson, 2018). There are several possible interpretations of this pattern of results when taken together with the results obtained for the NEO-third-party rating. Firstly, as was the case for the self-report version of the CPI-R, some of the subscales of the third-party version may represent constructs other than psychopathy. The Ruthlessness subscale correlates significantly with the CAPP; thus, this may be the closest conceptually to psychopathy, with the other subscales representing alternative dark triad personality domains. This interpretation is also partially supported by noting correlations between the Ruthlessness subscale and the NEO facets that have been identified in previous literature to align with psychopathy. Namely, Ruthlessness correlates negatively with Agreeableness and Extraversion, while the correlations between the NEO and Impulsive Egocentricity are closely aligned with those for Narcissism (high E, low A).

An alternative explanation for the overall lack of correlation between the CPI-3R total score and the CAPP total score is also suggested, which is that the CAPP does not contain items relating to the putative positive characteristics that may accompany high-functioning psychopathy, particularly in individuals who have achieved positions of success in business. The adaptive façade subscale of the CPI-3R identifies individuals who possess the ability to read people, adapt to situations, but also notice and exploit weaknesses in others. These may be the positive characteristics that act as moderators, differentiating high-functioning and low-functioning psychopathy. The need for measures of successful psychopathy to include positive adaptive characteristics has been highlighted by Durand (2017) who has created a scale comprising amongst other things, Leadership, Logical Thinking, Composure, Fearlessness and Focus. As many of these characteristics are also captured in the adaptive façade subscale of the CPI-3R, future research should validate the CPI-3R with this and other measures of psychopathy that incorporate positive traits.

Overall Discussion

The finding that the PDS correlated positively with the CPI-R ($r = .361$, $p < .001$) while negatively with the PPI-R ($r = -.275$, $p < .001$) is interesting in light of research by Verschuere et al. (2014) finding an inverse relationship between psychopathy and impression management based on the assumption that psychopaths have a disregard for social convention. This suggestion appears to hold for a general measure of psychopathy (the PPI-R), whereas the corporate-specific measure (the CPI-R) had a positive correlation with impression management, suggesting that impression management may be a central part of the defining criteria for corporate psychopathy and differentiates the successful psychopath from the non-successful variant. This finding also supports the moderated expression theory of corporate psychopathy (Hall & Benning, 2006) in that the ability to successfully create and maintain a positive impression acts as a protective factor that buffers against the negative aspects of psychopathy and allows individuals to succeed in a business environment, at least up to a point (Landay et al., 2018).

At the subscale level, the pattern of correlations for the three subscales of the CPI-R suggest that it may be measuring dark triad traits more broadly, rather than just psychopathy. The correlations between the Boldness subscale of the CPI-R, with the NPI and self-deceptive enhancement of the PDS suggests that the Boldness subscale is close to a measure of narcissism, although its negative correlation with the Negative Affect facet of the PID-5, as well as Manipulativeness indicates a broader correspondence with elements of the interpersonal and affective domains of psychopathy. Indeed research on the construct of Boldness within psychopathy has highlighted its considerable overlap with Narcissism (Miller, Sleep, Crowe, & Lynam, 2019) particularly the grandiose elements of Narcissism. Similarly, very high correlations have been observed between Boldness and self-esteem, which also appears to be reflected in the adaptive façade subscale of the CPI-3R (the third-party report version). This subscale correlated positively with many of the facets that have been found to be associated with high self-esteem, emotionally stable, extraverted and conscientious, somewhat agreeable and open to experience (Robins, Tracey, Trzesniewski, Potter, &

Gosling, 2001). While this suggests a correspondence between the Boldness subscale of the CPI-R and the adaptive façade subscale of the CPI-3R, at the item level there is less than a 50% overlap, and at this point, correlations between the two measures have not been tested as this would require overcoming the ethical hurdle of being able to link participant data with data collected by an informant co-worker of the participant. The procedure employed by Blickle et al. (2018) offers a promising solution, that is to request that participant provide email addresses of superior and subordinate colleagues, who are then invited to complete questionnaires using a randomly generated code.

The worry is that the findings presented in this chapter for the CPI-R and CPI-3R are equivalent to a Dodo-Bird verdict; there is a lack of clear differentiation amongst the subscales as to whether they are assessing subcomponents of psychopathy, or dark triad personality traits more broadly. Dark triad researchers have been categorised as "splitters" or "lumpers" (Furnham et al., 2014), and it is unclear as yet which of those prosaic descriptors best applies to the research presented in this chapter. Given the average effect size for the relationship between the three dark triad constructs is very high ($r = .58$ for M and P; $r = .38$ for N and P; and $r = .34$ for N and M; Muris et al., 2017), and that recent research by Jones and Figueredo (2013) identified that the combination of callousness and manipulation accounted for the entirety of the overlap between the dark triad traits, the question remains as to whether there is value in continuing to partial these constructs (Persson, 2019), i.e. what is Machiavellianism measuring when Narcissism and Psychopathy are removed (Sleep, Lynam, Hyatt, & Miller, 2017). The question of whether the subscales of the CPI-R are measuring dark triad traits more broadly or conceptual domains of psychopathy specifically requires further investigation, using additional measures beyond the NPI and Mach-IV. For example, a recently created inventory of Machiavellianism which was derived from expert ratings on FFM facets (Collison, Vize, Miller, & Lynam, 2018) was found to differentiate more clearly from the other elements of the dark triad. Future research should test the convergent validity of the CPI-R against this measure, as well as the Elemental Psychopathy Assessment (Lynam et al. 2011), and the Five-Factor Narcissism Inventory (Glover et al., 2012) to test the robustness of the CPI-R's ability to discriminate amongst the three elements of the dark triad.

The construct of psychopathy generally attracts negative connotations related to the pathologic nature of the disorder. The findings from the above body of research, however, confirms what other researchers have posited; namely that there are some positive and adaptive qualities possessed by individuals with dark triad traits that can be potentially advantageous in a corporate setting (Babiak et al., 2010). These adaptive qualities include being creative, decisive, confident, strategic and skilful communicators who often possess strong personal presentation skills (Babiak et al., 2010). Thus, it is important, as researchers, that we consider a well-rounded approach in how we research and report on these individuals particularly in the context of developing effective management strategies.

References

Ackerman, R. A., Witt, E. A., Donnellan, M. B., Trzesniewski, K. H., Robins, R. W., & Kashy, D. A. (2011). What does the Narcissistic Personality Inventory really measure? *Assessment, 18,* 67–87. https://doi.org/10.1177/1073191110382845.

Anderson, K. (2018). *Gender differences in five factor model representations of corporate psychopathy as measured using the Corporate Personality Inventory—3rd Party Report.* Thesis submitted in partial fulfilment of the Masters of Psychology (Forensic), Bond University.

Anderson, J. L., Sellbom, M., Wygant, D., Salekin, R. T., & Krueger, R. F. (2014). Examining the associations between DSM-5 section III antisocial personality disorder traits and psychopathy in community and university samples. *Journal of Personality Disorders, 28*(5), 675–697.

Avolio, B. J., Gardner, W. L., & Walumbwa, F. O. (2007). *Authentic leadership questionnaire.* Mindgarden.

Babiak, P., & Hare, R. D. (2012). *The B-Scan 360 manual.* Manuscript in preparation.

Babiak, P., Neumann, C. S., & Hare, R. D. (2010). Corporate psychopathy: Talking the walk. *Behavioral Sciences & the Law, 28,* 174–193. https://doi.org/10.1002/bsl.925.

Barlett, C. (2016). Exploring the correlations between emerging adulthood, dark triad traits, and aggressive behavior. *Personality and Individual Differences, 101*, 293–298. https://doi.org/10.1016/j.paid.2016.05.061.

Blickle, G., Schütte, N., & Genau, H. (2018). Manager psychopathy, trait activation, and job performance: A multi-source study. *European Journal of Work and Organizational Psychology, 27*(4), 450–461. https://doi.org/10.1080/1359432X.2018.1475354.

Board, B., & Fritzon, K. (2005). Disordered personalities at work. *Psychology, Crime & Law, 11*(1), 17–32. https://doi.org/10.1080/10683160310001634304.

Boddy, C. R. (2006). The dark side of management decisions: Organisational psychopaths. *Management Decision, 44*(9/10), 1461–1475.

Boddy, C. (2010). Corporate psychopaths and organizational type. *Journal of Public Affairs, 10*(4), 300–312. https://doi.org/10.1002/pa.365.

Boddy, C. (2011). Corporate psychopaths, bullying and unfair supervision in the workplace. *Journal of Business Ethics, 100*(3), 367–379. https://doi.org/10.1007/s10551-010-0689-5.

Boddy, C. R., Ladyshewsky, R. K., & Galvin, P. (2010). The influence of corporate psychopaths on corporate social responsibility and organizational commitment to employees. *Journal of Business Ethics, 97*, 1–19. https://doi.org/10.1007/s10551-010-0492-3.

Boehm, J. K., & Lyubomirsky, S. (2008). Does happiness promote career success? *Journal of Career Assessment, 16*, 101–116.

Bogart, L., Benotsch, E., & Pavlovic, J. (2004). Feeling superior but threatened: The relation of narcissism to social comparison. *Basic and Applied Social Psychology, 26*(1), 35–44. https://doi.org/10.1207/s15324834basp2601_4.

Brooks, N., & Fritzon, K. (2017). *Manual for the corporate personality inventory-revised.* Manuscript in preparation.

Christie, R., & Geis, F. L. (1970). *Studies in machiavellianism.* London: Academic Press.

Cleckley, H. (1941). *The mask of sanity: An attempt to reinterpret the so-called psychopathic personality.* Oxford, England: Mosby.

Collison, K. L., Vize, C. E., Miller, J. D., & Lynam, D. R. (2018). Development and preliminary validation of a five factor model measure of Machiavellianism. *Psychological Assessment, 30*(10), 1401–1407. https://doi.org/10.1037/pas0000637.

Cooke, D., Hart, S., Logan, C., & Michie, C. (2012). Explicating the construct of psychopathy: Development and validation of a conceptual model, the Comprehensive Assessment of Psychopathic Personality (CAPP). *International Journal of Forensic Mental Health, 11*(4), 242–252. https://doi.org/10.1080/14999013.2012.746759.

Costa, P. T., Jr., & McCrae, R. R. (1992). *Professional manual: Revised NEO Personality Inventory (NEO PI-R) and NEO Fivefactor Inventory (NEO-FFI)*. Odessa: Psychological Assessment Resources.

Debowska, A., Boduszek, D., Dhingra, K., Sherretts, N., Willmott, D., & Delisi, M. (2018). Can we use hare's psychopathy model within forensic and non-forensic populations? An empirical investigation. *Deviant Behavior, 39*(2), 224–242. https://doi.org/10.1080/01639625.2016.1266887.

DeShong, H., Grant, D., & Mullins-Sweatt, S. (2015). Comparing models of counterproductive workplace behaviors: The five-factor model and the dark triad. *Personality and Individual Differences, 74*(C), 55–60. https://doi.org/10.1016/j.paid.2014.10.001.

Durand, G. (2017). The durand adaptive psychopathic traits questionnaire: Development and validation. *Journal of Personality Assessment*, 1–10. Advance online publication. https://doi.org/10.1080/00223891.2017.1372443.

Fritzon, K., Bailey, C., Croom, S., & Brooks, N. (2017). Problem personalities in the workplace: Development of the corporate personality inventory. In P. A. Granhag, A. Shabolatas, & E. Dozortseva (Eds.), *Psychology and law in Europe: When west meets east* (pp.139–165). Boco Raton: CRC Press.

Furnham, A., Richards, S., Rangel, L., & Jones, D. N. (2014). Measuring malevolence: Quantitative issues surrounding the Dark triad of personality. *Personality and Individual Differences, 67*, 114–121. https://doi.org/10.1016/j.paid.2014.02.001.

Glover, N., Miller, J., Lynam, D., Crego, C., & Widiger, T. (2012). The five-factor narcissism inventory: A five-factor measure of narcissistic personality traits. *Journal of Personality Assessment, 94*(5), 500–512. https://doi.org/10.1080/00223891.2012.670680.

Greenhaus, J. H., Parasuraman, S., & Wormley, W. M. (1990). Effects of race on organizational experiences, job performance evaluations, and career outcomes. *Academy of Management Journal, 33*, 64–86. https://doi.org/10.2307/256352.

Grijalva, E., & Newman, D. A. (2015). Narcissism and counterproductive work behavior (CWB): Meta-analysis and consideration of collectivist culture, big five personality, and narcissism's facet structure. *Applied Psychology, 64*, 93–126. https://doi.org/10.1111/apps.12025.

Hall, J., & Benning, S. (2006). The "successful" psychopath: Adaptive and sub-clinical manifestations of psychopathy in the general population. In C. J.

Patrick (Ed.), *Handbook of psychopathy* (pp. 459–478). New York, NY: Guilford Press.

Hogan, R., & Hogan, J. (2001). Assessing leadership: A view from the dark side. *International Journal of Selection and Assessment, 9*(1–2), 40–51. https://doi.org/10.1111/1468-2389.00162.

Hogan, R., & Kaiser, R. (2005). What we know about leadership. *Review of General Psychology, 9*(2), 169–180. https://doi.org/10.1037/1089-2680.9.2.169.

Hughes, M. (2016). *Corporate psychopathy: An empirical investigation and dimensional trait-based conceptualization.* Thesis submitted in partial fulfillment of the requirements for the Graduate Diploma of Psychological Science, Bond University.

Jaiswal, P., & Bhal, K. (2014). Behavioural flexibility: The use of upward impression management tactics by subordinates for good performance rating from leader and impact of organizational & leader's machiavellianism. *Global Journal of Flexible Systems Management, 15*(4), 313–326. https://doi.org/10.1007/s40171-014-0077-6.

Jakobwitz, S., & Egan, V. (2006). The dark triad and normal personality traits. *Personality and Individual Differences, 40,* 331–339. https://doi.org/10.1016/j.paid.2005.07.006.

Jonason, P. K., & Webster, G. D. (2010). The dirty dozen: A concise measure of the dark triad. *Psychological Assessment, 22,* 420–432.

Jones, D. N., & Figueredo, A. J. (2013). The core of darkness: Uncovering the heart of the Dark Triad. *European Journal of Personality, 27,* 521–531. https://doi.org/10.1002/per.1893.

Jones, D., & Hare, R. (2016). The mismeasure of psychopathy: A commentary on boddy's PM-MRV. *Journal of Business Ethics, 138*(3), 579–588. https://doi.org/10.1007/s10551-015-2584-6.

Jones, D. N., & Paulhus, D. L. (2011). The role of impulsivity in the dark triad of personality. *Personality and Individual Differences, 51,* 679–682. https://doi.org/10.1016/j.paid.2011.04.011.

Jones, D. N., & Paulhus, D. L. (2014). Introducing the short dark triad (SD3) a brief measure of dark personality traits. *Assessment, 21,* 28–41. https://doi.org/10.1177/1073191113514105.

Judge, T., Piccolo, R., & Kosalka, T. (2009). The bright and dark sides of leader traits: A review and theoretical extension of the leader trait paradigm. *The Leadership Quarterly, 20*(6), 855–875. https://doi.org/10.1016/j.leaqua.2009.09.004.

Krueger, R. F., Derringer, J., Markon, K. E., Watson, D., & Skodol, A. E. (2012). Initial construction of a maladaptive personality trait model and inventory for DSM–5. *Psychological Medicine, 42,* 1879–1890. https://doi.org/10.1017/S0033291711002674.

Kwon, I., & Seo, M. (2017). The impact of machiavellianism on the impression management: The mediating effect of organizational politics. *Korea International Trade Research Institute, 13*(4), 523–537. https://doi.org/10.16980/jitc.13.4.201708.523.

Landay, K., Harms, P. D., & Crede, M. (2018). Shall we serve the dark lords? A meta-analytic review of psychopathy and leadership. *Journal of Applied Psychology.* http://dx.doi.org/10.1037/apl0000357.

Lilienfeld, S. O., & Widows, M. R. (2005). *Psychopathic personality inventory-revised: Professional manual.* Lutz, FL: Psychological Assessment Resources.

Lord, R., De Vader, C., & Alliger, G. (1986). A meta-analysis of the relation between personality traits and leadership perceptions: An application of validity generalization procedures. *Journal of Applied Psychology, 71*(3), 402–410. https://doi.org/10.1037/0021-9010.71.3.402.

Lynam, D. R., Gaughan, E. T., Miller, J. D., Miller, D. J., Mullins-Sweatt, S., & Widiger, T. A. (2011). Assessing the basic traits associated with psychopathy: Development and validation of the Elemental Psychopathy Assessment. *Psychological Assessment, 23*(1), 108–124. http://dx.doi.org/10.1037/a0021146.

Lyons, M., & Jonason, P. (2015). Dark triad, tramps, and thieves. *Journal of Individual Differences, 36*(4), 215–220. https://doi.org/10.1027/1614-0001/a000177.

Mathieu, C., & Babiak, P. (2015). Tell me who you are, I'll tell you how you lead: Beyond the full-range leadership model, the role of corporate psychopathy on employee attitudes. *Personality and Individual Differences, 87,* 8–12. https://doi.org/10.1016/j.paid.2015.07.016.

McHoskey, J. W., Worzel, W., & Szyarto, C. (1998) Machiavellianism and psychopathy. *Journal of Personality and Social Psychology, 74,* 192–210. http://dx.doi.org/10.1037/0022-3514.74.1.192.

Miller, J. D., Jones, S. E., & Lynam, D. R. (2011). Psychopathic traits from the perspective of self and informant reports: Is there evidence for a lack of insight? *Journal of Abnormal Psychology.* https://doi.org/10.1037/a0022477.

Miller, J. D., Sleep, C. E., Crowe, M. L., & Lynam, D. R. (2019). *Psychopathic boldness: Narcissism, self-esteem, or something in between?* https://doi.org/10.31234/osf.io/5mfyr.

Miller, J., Vize, C., Crowe, M., & Lynam, D. (2019). A critical appraisal of the dark-triad literature and suggestions for moving forward. *Current*

Directions in Psychological Science, 28(4), 353–360. https://doi.org/10.1177/0963721419838233.

Muris, P., Merckelbach, H., Otgaar, H., & Meijer, E. (2017). The malevolent side of human nature: A meta-analysis and critical review of the literature on the dark triad (narcissism, Machiavellianism, and psychopathy). *Perspectives on Psychological Science, 12,* 183–204. https://doi.org/10.1177/1745691616666070.

O'Boyle, E. H., Forsyth, D. R., Banks, G. C., Story, P. A., & White, C. D. (2015). A meta-analytic test of redundancy and relative importance of the dark triad and the five-factor model of personality. *Journal of Personality, 83,* 644–664. https://doi.org/10.1111/jopy.12126.

O'Boyle, E. H., Forsyth, D. R., Banks, G. C., & McDaniel, M. A. (2012). A meta-analysis of the dark triad and work behavior: A social exchange perspective. *Journal of Applied Psychology, 97*(3), 557–579. https://doi.org/10.1037/a0025679.

Padilla, A., Hogan, R., & Kaiser, R. B. (2007). The toxic triangle: Destructive leaders, susceptible followers, and conducive environments. *The Leadership Quarterly, 18,* 176–194. http://doi.org/10.1016/j.leaqua.2007.03.001.

Patrick, C., Fowles, D., & Krueger, R. (2009). Triarchic conceptualization of psychopathy: Developmental origins of disinhibition, boldness, and meanness. *Development and Psychopathology, 21*(3), 913–938. https://doi.org/10.1017/S0954579409000492.

Paulhus, D. L. (1998). *Paulhus deception scales: Manual of the balanced inventory of desirable responding (BIDR-7).* Toronto, Canada: Multi-Health Systems.

Paulhus, D. L., Neumann, C. S., & Hare, R. D. (2016). *Manual for the hare self-report psychopathy scale.* Toronto, Ontario, Canada: Multi-Health Systems.

Paulhus, D., & Williams, K. (2002). The dark triad of personality: Narcissism, machiavellianism, and psychopathy. *Journal of Research in Personality, 36*(6), 556–563. https://doi.org/10.1016/S0092-6566(02)00505-6.

Persson, B. N. (2019). Searching for Machiavelli but finding psychopathy and narcissism. *Personality Disorders: Theory, Research and Treatment, 10*(3), 235–245. http://dx.doi.org/10.1037/per0000323.

Persson, B., Kajonius, P., & Garcia, D. (2019). Revisiting the structure of the short dark triad. *Assessment, 26*(1), 3–16. https://doi.org/10.1177/1073191117701192.

Ray, S. (2019). *Unmasking a darker side to management: Dark triad personality traits as predictors of counterproductive work behaviour.* Thesis submitted in partial fulfilment of Masters of Psychology (Clinical), Bond University.

Robins, R., Tracy, J., Trzesniewski, K., Potter, J., & Gosling, S. (2001). Personality correlates of self-esteem. *Journal of Research in Personality, 35,* 463–482. https://doi.org/10.1006/jrpe.2001.2324.

Rodrigo, S. (2016). *Corporate psychopathy: An empirical investigation and dimensional trait-based conceptualization.* Thesis submitted in partial fulfillment of the requirements for the Graduate Diploma of Psychological Science, Bond University.

Raskin, R. N., & Hall, C. S. (1979). A narcissistic personality inventory. *Psychological Reports, 45,* 590.

Sanecka, E. (2013). The effects of supervisor's subclinical psychopathy on subordinates organizational commitment, job satisfaction and satisfaction with supervisor. *The Journal of Education, Culture, and Society, 2,* 172–191.

Sellbom, M., Lilienfeld, S. O., Fowler, K. A., & McCrary, K. L. (2018). The self-report assessment of psychopathy: Challenges, pitfalls, and promises. In C. J. Patrick (Ed.), *Handbook of psychopathy* (pp. 211–258). New York: Guilford Press.

Skeem, J., Polaschek, D., Patrick, C., & Lilienfeld, S. (2011). Psychopathic personality: Bridging the gap between scientific evidence and public policy. *Psychological Science in the Public Interest, 12*(3), 95–162. https://doi.org/10.1177/1529100611426706.

Sleep, C., Lynam, D., Hyatt, C., & Miller, J. (2017). Perils of partialing redux: The case of the dark triad. *Journal of Abnormal Psychology, 126*(7), 939–950. https://doi.org/10.1037/abn0000278.

Sleep, C., Miller, J., Lynam, D., & Campbell, W. K. (2018, August 22). *Insight regarding the presence of antagonism-related traits and their subsequent impairment in relation to psychopathy, narcissism, and Machiavellianism.* https://doi.org/10.31234/osf.io/vrcng.

Smith, S., Lilienfeld, S., Coffey, K., & Dabbs, J. (2013). Are psychopaths and heroes twigs off the same branch? Evidence from college, community, and presidential samples. *Journal of Research in Personality, 47*(5), 634–646. https://doi.org/10.1016/j.jrp.2013.05.006.

Snyder, S. (2010). *Adaptive traits associated with psychopathy in a "successful", non-criminal population.* Retrieved from https://psychology.yale.edu/sites/default/files/snyder_senior_essay.pdf.

Spain, S. M., Harms, P., & LeBreton, J. M. (2014). The dark side of personality at work. *Journal of Organizational Behavior, 35,* 41–60.

Spector, P. E., Fox, S., Penney, L. M., Bruursema, K., Goh, A., & Kessler, S. (2006). The dimensionality of counterproductivity: Are all counterproductive behaviors created equal? *Journal of Vocational Behavior, 68,* 446–460. https://doi.org/10.1016/j.jvb.2005.10.005.

Spector, P. E., & Jex, S. M. (1998). Development of four self-report measures of job stressors and strain: Interpersonal conflict at work scale, organizational constraints scale, quantitative workload inventory, and physical symptoms inventory. *Journal of Occupational Health Psychology, 3,* 356–367.

Spurk, D., Keller, A. C., & Hirschi, A. (2016). Do bad guys get ahead or fall behind? Relationships of the dark triad of personality with objective and subjective career success. *Social Psychological and Personality Science, 7,* 113–121. https://doi.org/10.1177/1948550615609735.

Strickland, C., Drislane, L., Lucy, M., Krueger, R., & Patrick, C. (2013). Characterizing psychopathy using DSM-5 personality traits. *Assessment, 20*(3), 327–338. https://doi.org/10.1177/1073191113486691.

Svetina, M., & Croom, S. (2019). *Psychometric properties of the psychopathic personality inventory: Application to high functioning business population.* Unpublished manuscript.

Tepper, B. J. (2007). Abusive supervision in work organizations: Review synthesis, and research agenda. *Journal of Management, 33,* 261–289.

Uechtritz, N. (2018). *The dark triad: Personality characteristics in the workplace.* Thesis submitted in partial fulfillment of the requirements for the Graduate Diploma of Psychological Science, Bond University.

van Geel, M., Goemans, A., Toprak, F., & Vedder, P. (2017). Which personality traits are related to traditional bullying and cyberbullying? A study with the big five, dark triad and sadism. *Personality and Individual Differences, 106,* 231–235. https://doi.org/10.1016/j.paid.2016.10.063.

Verschuere, B., Uzieblo, K., De Schryver, M., Douma, H., Onraedt, T., & Crombez, G. (2014). The inverse relation between psychopathy and faking good: Not response bias, but true variance in psychopathic personality. *The Journal of Forensic Psychiatry & Psychology, 25*(6), 705–713. https://doi.org/10.1080/14789949.2014.952767.

Vize, C. E., Lynam, D. R., Collison, K. L., & Miller, J. D. (2018). Differences among dark triad components: A meta-analytic investigation. *Personality Disorders: Theory, Research, and Treatment, 9*(2), 101–111. https://doi.org/10.1037/per0000222.

Volmer, J., Koch, I., & Göritz, A. (2016). The bright and dark sides of leaders' dark triad traits: Effects on subordinates' career success and well-being. *Personality and Individual Differences, 101,* 413–418. https://doi.org/10.1016/j.paid.2016.06.046.

Walsh, C. (2018). *The dark triad in the realm of career success and leadership authenticity.* Thesis submitted in partial fulfilment of the requirements for the Graduate Diploma of Psychological Science, Bond University.

Watts, A., Lilienfeld, S., Smith, S., Miller, J., Campbell, W., Waldman, I., ... Faschingbauer, T. (2013). The double-edged sword of grandiose narcissism: Implications for successful and unsuccessful leadership among U.S. presidents. *Psychological Science, 24*(12), 2379–2389. https://doi.org/10.1177/0956797613491970.

Wiseman, E. (2014). *The Corporate Psychopathy Inventory: A potential screening tool in the workplace.* Thesis submitted in partial fulfillment of the requirements for the Graduate Diploma of Psychological Science, Bond University.

9

The Tangled Web: Psychopathic Personality, Vulnerability and Victim Selection

Nathan Brooks

The Mask of Psychopathy

The construct of psychopathy is associated with manipulation, feigning of emotions and the appearance of a veneer of stability, normality and friendliness (Hickey, 2010). The ability to defraud, con, cheat and manipulate people without the slightest concern about their victim or the repercussions of their actions is a central characteristic of psychopathy (Hare, 1999, 2003). As Hare states, "a good looking, fast talking psychopath and a victim who has 'weak spots' is a devastating combination" (p. 145). The ability to rapidly determine the personality styles, emotional states and intentions of others requires skilled interpersonal perception. Despite much speculation about the interpersonal skills of psychopaths, there is a limited understanding of the exploitative strategies used by psychopathic individuals in selecting and targeting victims (Black, Woodworth, & Porter, 2014). Preliminary research investigating these phenomena has

N. Brooks (✉)
Central Queensland University, Townsville, QLD, Australia
e-mail: nathan@nathanbrooks.com.au

© The Author(s) 2020
K. Fritzon et al., *Corporate Psychopathy*,
https://doi.org/10.1007/978-3-030-27188-6_9

suggested that higher levels of psychopathy are associated with a greater likelihood of detecting vulnerabilities in others (Brooks, Fritzon, Watt, in press; Wheeler, Book, & Costello, 2009; Wilson, Demetrioff, & Porter, 2008). It has been postulated that psychopathic people are adept at identifying these vulnerabilities, callously taking advantage of weakness, fulfilling their need for power, dominance and gratification (Hare, 1999). In the famous novel, *The Silence of the Lambs*, by Thomas Harris (1989), a fascinating description is provided of the first encounter between Dr. Hannibal Lecter, "a pure sociopath" (p. 13), and young FBI agent Clarice Starling. In the interaction, Starling seeks to garner the help of Lecter; however, he seizes the opportunity, viewing the conversation as a game, quick to establish an advantage over Starling by identifying her weakness—the fear of being "common". The relationship between psychopathic personality and assessing and exploiting vulnerability in others has significant implications for understanding the interpersonal processes associated with manipulation and deceit, the strategies of victim selection and the vulnerabilities that may predispose individuals to being targeted.

Jonason, Lyons, Baughman, and Vernon (2014) investigated the propensity of individuals with psychopathy to lie, deceive and cheat in a large sample of participants ($n = 447$). Psychopathy was assessed using the Self-Report Psychopathy Scale-III (SRP-III; Paulhus, Hemphill, & Hare, in press), while narcissism (Narcissistic Personality Inventory; Raskin & Terry, 1988) and Machiavellianism (Mach-IV Scale; Christie & Geis, 1970) were also assessed. To examine deception, the authors utilised a series of questions that addressed participant deception tendencies over the past seven days. These included: how many lies the participant had told, the number of different people lied to, the number of self-gain lies told, lies told to avoid hurting someone and lies told for convenience. The Deceptive Mating Tactics Scale (Tooke & Camire, 1991) was used in the study to examine participant's intersexual and intrasexual deception. Results of the study found a positive correlation between both Psychopathy and Machiavellianism in regard to the number of lies told, but not narcissism. Psychopathy was related to telling lies pertaining to dominance, sincerity and sexual intentions. Individuals with higher levels of psychopathy were more likely to lie for no reason and have a greater perceived ability to lie (Jonason et al., 2014). Notably, psychopathy was found to have a significant positive relationship with a greater perceived ability to lie for both genders; however, this relationship was stronger for females. The research provided an understanding of the relationship between psychopathy and deception, including the similarities between males and females with higher levels of psychopathy that engage in deception.

Baughman, Jonason, Lyons, and Vernon (2014) investigated the relationship between psychopathy, gender and lying, in Canadian undergraduate students ($n = 462$). Psychopathy was assessed using the Short Dark Triad (SD3; Jones & Paulhus, 2014) self-report measure, which assesses for traits of psychopathy, narcissism and Machiavellianism. The propensity of participants to lie was evaluated through a series of questions that were rated on a seven-point Likert scale and included: how often the individual lies, how often they believed their lies were detected, their emotional state after lying, the cognitive effort required to lie and who they perceived as believing their lies. Using a regression analysis, results of the study found that psychopathy was associated with greater positive emotions when lying, while Machiavellianism was related to planning ahead and constructing a lie. The authors conducted a hierarchical regression to examine whether the dark triad traits mediated gender differences in lying. Gender differences in participants emotional state when lying were partially mediated by the dark triad traits; however, the direct effect was reduced with the addition of the indirect effects of psychopathy, Machiavellianism and narcissism. At the final step of the model, psychopathy, narcissism and Machiavellianism were not found to add significant unique variance, suggesting that these traits partially mediated the relationship but alone did not significantly predict gender differences in lying. The research by Baughman et al. (2014) provided support for the relationship between psychopathy and deception; however, due to sampling only students, the research has limited applicability to understanding psychopathy in other domains, including custodial and professional contexts.

Research has supported the relationship between psychopathy, lying and deception (Baughman et al., 2014; Hare, 1999; Jonason et al., 2014). While deception and lying are key characteristics of psychopathy, manipulation is another trait associated with the personality construct (Hare, 2003). Manipulation is the deliberate act of attempting to create a favourable outcome through the calculated use of actions and words

(Hare, 1999; Simon, 2010). Manipulation often requires an awareness of another's values or weaknesses and typically involves the exploitation of these. Many of the skills used in manipulation require the ability to understand another's emotional state. The ability to regulate emotions and present in a manner that shows an understanding of another's perspective is often referred to as social and emotional intelligence (Goleman, 1995). Emotional intelligence refers to the abilities and skills needed to manage both the intrapersonal (awareness of own feelings and states) and interpersonal (ability to interact and understand another) components of emotional and social interactions (Goleman, 1995). However, although emotional intelligence is considered an important attribute for interpersonal interactions (Baron-Cohen, 2011), some researchers have suggested that a "darker side" of social and emotional intelligence exits. A darker emotional intelligence is characterised by exploitative personality constructs (psychopathy, Machiavellianism and narcissism) using social and emotional skills for self-gratifying advances and pursuits (Grieve & Panebianco, 2013; Nagler, Reiter, Furtner, & Rauthmann, 2014; Simon, 2010).

The relationship between the dark triad personalities (psychopathy, narcissism and Machiavellianism) and social and emotional intelligence was examined in a large sample of 594 community participants (438 females and 138 males). The study used self-report measures to examine the personality constructs and social and emotional intelligence and emotional manipulation (Nagler et al., 2014). Results of the study found that narcissism had a significant positive relationship with socio-emotional expressivity and control and a negative relationship with social and emotional sensitivity (subscales of the Social Skills Inventory; Riggio & Carney, 2003). Psychopathy was found to have no relationship with socio-emotional expressivity, but a significant positive relationship with socio-emotional control and significant negative relationship with socio-emotional sensitivity. Machiavellianism had a positive relationship with emotional control and a negative relationship with the other subscales of the SSI. All three of the dark triad personality types were found to have a significant relationship with emotional manipulation. Moderation analyses revealed that narcissism significantly moderated the relationship between emotional control and emotional manipulation, suggesting that higher levels of narcissism were associated with greater levels of emotional control and emotional manipulation (Nagler et al., 2014). Psychopathy was also found to significantly moderate the relationship between emotional control and emotional manipulation. A moderated relationship was found between emotional sensitivity and emotional manipulation, with psychopathy moderating this relationship. The results of the study provide evidence that psychopathy and narcissism were related to the use of social and emotional intelligence for emotional manipulation (Nagler et al., 2014). The authors of the study identified that psychopathy was associated with emotional manipulation and emotional control; however, the authors did not investigate whether this relationship was influenced by gender and if males and females employed different forms of emotional manipulation.

Grieve and Panebianco (2013) investigated emotional manipulation and social and emotional intelligence in males and females. In a study of 243 participants from an Australian university, higher levels of social information processing skills, emotional intelligence, indirect aggression and self-serving cognitive distortions were found to be significant predictors of emotional manipulation by males (Grieve & Panebianco, 2013). Interestingly, although the authors examined psychopathy, this was not found to be a predictor of emotional manipulation by males. For females, a younger age, indirect aggression, traits of primary psychopathy, higher levels of emotional intelligence and lower levels of social awareness were found to significantly predict emotional manipulation. The authors concluded that although there were overlapping predictors of emotional manipulation (indirect aggression and emotional intelligence) between the two genders, emotional manipulation differed as a function of gender, with primary psychopathy (interpersonal traits of psychopathy, rather than behavioural) a greater predictive factor of emotional manipulation by females rather than males. The findings by Grieve and Panebianco (2013) provide support for primary psychopathy being more dominant and calculated in comparison with secondary psychopathy. The research provides important findings for understanding the relationship between the types of psychopathy, gender and emotional processing skills in a non-incarcerated sample. However, as the research was conducted on a student sample, further analysis of the relationship between these constructs in the community is required.

Mechanisms in the Psychopath's Armoury

People with psychopathic personality traits appear to have the ability to understand another's emotions and behaviour, allowing them to manipulate and deceive others for self-gain. The manipulation associated with psychopathy, while ruthless and callous, appears to involve a level of social and emotional understanding that suggests that individuals with psychopathy possess the ability to understand the psychological motivations and desires of others (Babiak & Hare, 2006). Lyons, Healy and Bruno (2013) investigated the social information processing skills related to psychopathy. The authors used 26 real-life video clips of emotional lies (13 truthful and 13 lies) to examine participants ($n = 150$) abilities to correctly detect lying. Psychopathy was assessed based on the Self Report Psychopathy Scale-III (SRP-III; Paulhus et al., in press). The researchers found that males with higher levels of primary psychopathy had a greater ability to successfully detect lying, in comparison with females. Although females in the sample had a greater ability to distinguish between lairs and non-liars, females high on psychopathy and secondary psychopathy had poorer accuracy at detecting lies (Lyons et al., 2013). The authors concluded that the ability to detect deception and lying behaviour may differ between gender and forms of psychopathy. The finding that males higher on primary psychopathy were better at detecting deception supports literature that describes primary psychopathy as more successful and socially skilled than secondary psychopathy (Cleckley, 1976; Lyons et al., 2013; Newman, MacCoon, Vaughn, & Sadeh, 2005). The authors concluded that primary psychopathy may be a male adaption of psychopathy (Jonason, Li, Webster, & Schmitt, 2009; Lyons et al., 2013); however, due to the lack of research investigating psychopathy in females (Hare, 2003), particularly in relation to the primary and secondary types, a greater body of research is required to support this conclusion.

The ability of psychopathic offenders to manipulate has been highlighted in research based on offenders and criminal justice outcomes. The ability to manipulate and deceive people within the criminal justice system provides evidence that psychopaths are successful at creating confusion and achieving outcomes in complex and high-stakes situations. Research has found the psychopathic offenders are successful at obtaining parole and gaining early release from custody, challenging sentencing verdicts and denying responsibility for their behaviour (Häkkänen-Nyholm & Hare, 2009; Hare, 2003; Porter, ten Brinke, & Wilson, 2009). The findings from research by Häkkänen-Nyholm and Hare (2009) and Porter et al. (2009) indicate that psychopathic individuals manage their image and adjust this to the criminal justice system for their own personal benefit. Despite empirical findings suggesting manipulation of the justice system, this process is poorly understood and in need of greater appreciation and research (Häkkänen-Nyholm & Hare, 2009). The research by Porter et al. (2009) and Häkkänen-Nyholm and Hare (2009) has important implications for understanding the ability of individuals with psychopathic traits to successfully present a positive image and manipulate others across numerous settings. The findings highlight the capacity of psychopathic people to manipulate and deceive others, explaining why some psychopathic individuals reach positions of corporate status, likely due to their charming and manipulate tendencies (Babiak & Hare, 2006; Boddy, 2011; Dutton, 2012; Hare, 1999).

The extent to which people with psychopathic traits are capable of detecting cues from body language and inferring vulnerability is an area of research that is limited. Several studies have documented the inference that can be established from observing body language, particularly walking gait. For example, based on observations of walking gait, Montepare, Goldstein, and Clausen (1987) found that subjects were able to identify emotional states of walkers, while another study found that sexologists could determine history of vaginal orgasm based on observing females walking gait (Nicholas, Brody, de Sutter, & de Carufel, 2008). In an early study on walking gait conducted by Grayson and Stein (1981), the authors found that physical attributes could differentiate victims from non-victims. Most notably, those more vulnerable to victimisation were prone to have less synchronous movements in comparison with those less vulnerable to victimisation. This was evidenced by longer or shorter stride length, non-lateral weight shifts, gestured rather than postural body movements and a tendency to lift feet higher while walking. The association between walking gait (abnormal pattern of walking strides, typically shorter or longer strides) and vulnerability to victimisation has been supported by research suggesting that walking gait can act as an indicator of potential victimisation and vulnerability (Murzynski & Degelman, 1996; Sakaguchi & Hasegawa, 2006).

Wheeler et al. (2009) investigated whether higher levels of psychopathic traits were associated with accurate victim selection, specifically determining a person most vulnerable to victimisation. The authors contended that due to people with psychopathic characteristics readily victimising others, psychopathic individuals should possess the skills to perceive cues of vulnerability, such as basic emotional states in others (Wheeler et al., 2009). The authors employed a methodology that videotaped participants walking down a hallway, then asked the participant through a demographic questionnaire whether they had previously been victimised and on how many occasions. Victimisation was defined as being equal to or greater than bullying behaviour (Wheeler et al., 2009). A total of 12 video clips (eight females and four males) were used for participants to determine vulnerability, and of these, four women and two men identified past victimisation. Psychopathy was assessed by the SPR-III (Paulhus et al., in press). The study required 47 male students to rate targets in the video clips based on their vulnerability to victimisation. Results of the study found a significant correlation between subjects body language and previous victimisation, suggesting that targets who reported past victimisation had noticeable difference in their walking gait. A significant positive relationship was found between total psychopathy scores and accuracy at identifying victims. Notably, a significant positive relationship was observed between Factor 1 of the SRP-III and accurate identification of victims; however, a non-significant relationship between Factor 2 of the SRP-III and victim identification was found.

Similar findings were reported by Book, Quinsey, and Langford (2007) in a community and correctional sample. The authors investigated the relationship between psychopathic personality traits and perceived vulnerability in a community ($n = 60$) and correctional sample ($n = 59$). The authors utilised the Levenson Self Report Psychopathy Scale (LSRP;

Levenson, Kiehl, & Fitzpatrick, 1995) to examine psychopathic personality traits in both the community and correctional setting, while the PCL-R was used solely to evaluate inmates for psychopathy. The study examined the ability of participants to read emotional facial expressions, judge vulnerability based on videotapes of interpersonal interactions and determine the assertiveness levels of those in the videotaped interaction. The correctional sample was found to have higher total and primary psychopathy scores on the LSRP in comparison with the community sample, but no difference was found for secondary psychopathy traits. Correlational analysis revealed that psychopathy was not found to be associated with any deficits in recognition of facial expressions of emotion, suggesting that psychopathy was associated with greater accuracy at identifying emotions and emotional intensity. The results also demonstrated that total scores on the LSRP as well as primary and secondary scores for the measure were found to have a significant positive relationship with accuracy to rate assertiveness in other people. Although the PCL-R total scores were not found to be significant, Factor 1 of the PCL-R was found to have a significant positive relationship with accuracy in rating assertiveness. The authors concluded that psychopathy may in fact lead to more accurate judgements of emotional intensity and vulnerability, suggesting that people with psychopathic traits have the ability to perceive and understand the emotional states of others, yet lack the feeling and response that is associated with empathy towards others (Blair, Jones, Clark, & Smith, 1997; Book et al., 2007).

Alternative findings regarding psychopathy and vulnerability were reported by Black et al. (2014). Utilising a sample of undergraduate students ($n = 101$), the authors had participants complete a series of self-report measures (i.e. SRP-III) and view, listen, listen and view, and read clips of a stimuli target considered to be extremely assertive or extremely under-assertive based on scores from the Rathus Assertiveness Scale (Rathus, 1973). In total, 15 clips were developed of different stimuli targets describing themselves. Each participant viewed two clips with video and audio, two audio clips, two video clips and read the details of two clips, overall exposed to 8 clips. Results of the study revealed that regardless of assertiveness levels, participants with higher levels of psychopathy perceived targets as being disagreeable, neurotic, depressed and anxious. Overall, higher scorers on psychopathy, narcissism and Machi-avellianism perceived targets as having low self-esteem, suffering from negative mood states and being less agreeable. The findings suggested that psychopathy and the other dark personalities perceived everyone as being prone to vulnerability, characterised by weakness and emotionality (Black et al., 2014). The tendency to perceive everyone as vulnerable to victim-isation and having an emotional weak point is a unique perspective on psychopathic victim selection and exploitation. However, as the study was comprised of undergraduate students who completed a short self-report measure of psychopathy, it is not clear whether any participants displayed clinical levels of psychopathy, reducing the generalisation of the findings.

In contrast, the research by Wheeler et al. (2009) and Book et al. (2007) suggested that people with psychopathic traits had greater ability to detect vulnerability and submissiveness in others. The ability to detect vulnera-bility may explain why psychopathy is common in custodial settings, due to individuals with psychopathic traits seeking to exploit this vulnerability (Hare, 1999, 2003). This tendency to exploit vulnerability and opportu-nity may also clarify why some individuals with psychopathy are able to work in the professional setting and are termed successful (Babiak, Neu-mann, & Hare, 2010; Dutton, 2012; Hare, 1999). However, despite find-ings suggesting that individuals with psychopathic personality are capable of detecting and exploiting vulnerability, some researchers disagree over the ability of people with psychopathy to process and understand emotions (Black et al., 2014; Johns & Quay, 1962). Hastings, Tagney, and Stuewig (2008) found that psychopathic traits were negatively related to affect recognition, with a poor ability to recognise expressions of sadness. Long and Titone (2007) also observed similar results, finding that participants with higher level of psychopathy were less efficient at processing negative emotional states (e.g. fear and sadness) in comparison with other emo-tions. Conversely, Glass and Newman (2006) and Book et al. (2007) both found results suggesting that people with psychopathic traits were able to recognise facial expressions of emotion without having deficits in this area. In another study, participants with high levels of psychopathic traits were found to have a partial deficit in responding to distress cues (Blair et al., 1997). The authors observed reduced arousal responses to distress cues, yet did not find a deficit in perceiving the distress cues. Blair and colleagues concluded that these results were due to a deficient emotional response to distress (lower physiological reaction) in psychopathic individuals, rather than a deficiency in the perception of distress (Blair et al., 1997). This finding is consistent with the research by Fecteau, Pascual-Leone, and Théoret (2008) who suggested that psychopathy may be positively associated with sensory aspects of the empathy construct (ability to observe and understand the affective/emotional state of an individual), although negatively related to emotional, state or trait empathy (Fecteau et al., 2008).

Further explanations for the discrepancies in findings across the research may be explained by the methodologies employed by the researcher/s when examining the relationship between psychopathic traits and ability to recognise emotion. Differentiating psychopathy based on Factor 1 and Factor 2 traits may account for varied findings across studies. Book et al. (2007) found that Factor 1 traits were positively related to the accurate identification of emotional intensity judgements. Similarly, in another study, total psychopathy scores on the PCL-R were found to be negativity related to the accurate identification of facial expressions of emotions, but Factor 1 scores were positively related to accuracy in identifying facial emotions (Habel, Kühn, Salloum, Devos, & Schneider, 2002). This suggests that individuals with psychopathic characteristics may in fact have intact emotional recognition capabilities; however, this may vary as a function of the clustering of psychopathic traits and/or the specific type or subtype of psychopathy. It also remains possible that other developmental factors consistent with the moderated expression pathway of psychopathy (see Hall & Benning, 2006) may account for research and individual differences, with variable such as education, history of trauma, and social integration and achievement, likely to influence social and emotional understanding and ability.

Case Examples of Psychopathic Victimisation

The style and type of victimisation perpetrated by psychopathic individuals can be considerably varied, targeting victims for specific reasons and outcomes, or simply due to a greater desire for dominance and control.

The following section provides an overview of four separate cases of psychopathic victimisation, with unique motivations, exploitation strategies, observational skills and outcomes. The cases include two examples of criminal psychopathy and two related to noncriminal psychopathy (psychopathic individuals residing in the community).

John Jackson

John (name altered) had a long history of incarceration and had established himself within the prison hierarchy, a person who could resolve issues if they arose, receiving respect from most inmates and also many prison officers. His position amongst the other inmates led Chris, a recently transferred prisoner, to seek out his assistance due to being fearful for his life. Chris had been getting threatened, intimidated and physically assaulted by a few prisoners who appeared to have strong anger and hostility towards him. He was struggling to cope; feeling a sense of despair and out of desperation approached John to ask for his help in dealing with the issue. John listened to Chris's concerns and considered his request, agreeing to assist Chris with one condition. The condition was that if he resolved the problem for Chris, then as a favour, Chris would allow him to engage in sexual acts with him. It would be one-off deal and John would be able to have sexual gratification, something that he was rarely able to engage in while incarcerated. Chris was confronted by the deal, presenting him with a dilemma, continue to suffer the victimisation by the other inmates and risk his life, or suffer a brief period of discomfort and engage in sex with John. Reluctantly, he agreed to John's condition. John delivered on his promise to Chris, speaking with the inmates that had been standing over and intimidating him, leading to this behaviour ceasing and Chris being able to feel safe in the custodial environment. Chris met John's term and engaged in the sexual acts that John had requested.

After he had completed his agreement with John, Chris believed that everything was resolved and that his time in custody would continue incident free. Unfortunately for Chris, this was not the case, and as time went on, he heard whispers and was told information by other fellow prisoners that greatly distressed him. The pieces of the puzzle began to fall in place for Chris, painting an alarming and horrifying picture. It was revealed that John had masterfully orchestrated the whole situation, targeting Chris and exploiting him for sex. John had requested that some of his fellow prisoners harass Chris, intimidate him and make him fearful. While this occurred, John welcomed Chris in casual interactions, remaining open and conveying his approachability. Chris took the bait and John successfully manipulated Chris into agreeing to engage in sexual acts with him. The case of John Jackson highlights the complexity of psychopathic exploitation. From a distance patterns or warning signs may be observable, yet when a victim is resource deprived, emotional, and unable to identify alternative solutions, the likelihood of vulnerability and victimisation significantly increases.

Reggie Jones

Numerous psychologists and psychiatrists had assessed Reggie (name changed) as psychopathic. He was exceptionally interpersonally skilled, a talented communicator—despite limited education, manipulative, charming, fearless and ruthless. His offending was considerably deviant and exploitative, raping several women through a combination of opportunistic encounters and targeted offences where he waited inside residences for victims to return home. His offending behaviour and personality disposition were best viewed under the guise of a sexual psychopath (Porter et al., 2001).

The severity and nature of Reggie's offending resulted in him spending the majority of his living life in custody, incarcerated for in-excess of 40 years. Despite being small in stature, although physically fit, Reggie's exploits did not cease when he was incarcerated. He was continuously subject to allegations while in custody, regularly accused of victimising other prisoners through sexual assaults, while dividing custodial officers, and establishing his position in the prison hierarchy. His tendency to prey on younger and vulnerable prisoners resulted in Reggie spending extended periods in isolation, at one stage ordered to a 10-year period in maximum security, isolated to a single cell and deprived of contact with other inmates.

Reggie was sexually deviant and his behaviour was driven by power, control and a desire for sexual gratification. He was astute in identifying weaknesses and vulnerabilities in others, claiming that "*emotions make people weak*", able to identify weakness in people based on the "*things they say*". Reggie believed that women in particular were weak and easy victims, advising that a "*scorned*" woman was a vulnerable person, suffering from the loss of a relationship, burdened by self-doubt and emotion, and seeking comfort. Despite having spent several decades in custody, he believed that violence was a last resort and that it was not hard to intimidate someone, as simple as walking over to someone, getting close and "*laughing at them*". According to Reggie, victimisation was not complicated, and it was about planting the idea and allowing the rest to follow. He stated, "*you laugh at someone, it gets them thinking, makes them wonder, makes them worried.*" Even though Reggie had spent the majority of his life in custody, his insights into victimisation highlight how subtle behaviour can be more powerful than overt actions in victimising someone.

Sam Vaknin

Sam Vaknin was the subject of the 2009 documentary *I, Psychopath*, produced by film director Ian Walker. The documentary chronicles Vaknin's claims that he is in fact a psychopath. Vaknin, the author of the book, *Malignant Self Love: Narcissism Revisited*, undertakes a series of assessments investigating his personality. During the course of the documentary, several issues arise, including, the validity of Vaknin's proclaimed Ph.D. and the bullying which he perpetrates towards the film director behind the scenes when the camera is turned off.

According to the film, Vaknin was born to migrant parents and had a modest upbringing. He was a gifted child, of considerable intellect, believed to have an IQ of 185. The documentary reported that he commenced university at 11 years of age and was taken on by one of Israel's richest businessmen, and at 21 years old, he was travelling around the world in a private jet for business. He then went on to find success as a "dot.com" entrepreneur before being charged and sentenced to imprisonment in 1995 for securities fraud.

During the course of the film, Vaknin is assessed by psychologist Dr. Belinda Board and Professor Niels Birbaumer. Dr. Board completes a consultation with Vaknin and assesses him on the Million Clinical Multiaxial Inventory (MCMI), determining that his profile is more reflective of a psychiatric patient, rather than indicating psychopathy or narcissism. Vaknin is not deterred by Dr. Board's results, instead seeking further opinion and assessment. He is next examined by Professor Birbaumer, who completes a series of assessments with Vaknin to examine his personality features and response to emotional stimuli. The findings reveal that Vaknin displays neuropsychological deficits in response to testing, and through a clinical interview, Professor Birbaumer determines that Vaknin has a total score of 18 on the Psychopathy Checklist Revised: Screening Version (PCL-R:SV); meeting the threshold to be considered as having a psychopathic personality.

Arguably one the most startling aspects of the documentary are the explanations that Vaknin regularly offers on psychopathy. For example, when discussing his perceptions of psychopaths, Vaknin states the following:

> The vast majority of psychopaths, like an iceberg are under the water and like an iceberg they are inert, they do nothing, they are just there. They torment their spouse by being unempathic, but they don't beat her or kill her. They bully co-workers, but they don't burn the office. They are not dramatic, they are pernicious. Most psychopaths are subtle, they are more like poison than a knife, they are more like slow working poison than cyanide.

Vaknin's opinion provides one explanation (possibly from a psychopathic perspective) as to why many psychopathic individuals may be able to reside in the community, functioning as noncriminal psychopaths. This appears consistent with many expert views on noncriminal psychopathy, contending that psychopathic people in the community operate on the moral fringes, rather than perpetrating violent and overt acts of crime (Babiak & Hare, 2006; Boddy, 2011; Fritzon, Bailey, Croom, & Brooks, 2016; Hall & Benning, 2006; Hare, 1999). Considerably more troubling is Vaknin's detailed account of the physiological impact that bullying has on victims, providing this explanation to filmmaker Ian Walker during the midst of conflict between the pair. Vaknin states:

> Your body was flooded instantly by adrenalin and its relatives like nore-pinephrine. Now when these hormones evade the blood stream, your brain reacts, it shuts down certain centres and activates others, this is called a stress reaction or a stress syndrome. Then when the abuse recedes, the adrenalin levels begin to drop. As they drop the entire system goes into mayhem. The heart that received the adrenalin shock and pounded about 30% faster has to readjust. Blood pressure drops precipitously, and you move from hypertension to hypotension. Many systems in the body go haywire within a session of bullying and especially after the session is over. So what bullies usually do is they start and stop, start and stop, that achieves the maximum physiological arousal and the maximum stress syndrome – and this is the great secret of bullying, never over do it, small doses, the victim will do the rest.

Dave

The case of Dave is documented by Dr. Paul Babiak (1995) in the paper titled *When Psychopaths go to work: A Case Study of an Industrial Psychopath*. Babiak provides a detailed overview and analysis of Dave, a newly employed individual within an organisation who has created considerable conflict and divided many co-workers. The initial description of Dave at the time of employment was:

> Dave was in his mid-thirties, a good looking well spoken professional, married for the third time with four children. He had a degree from a large university and had been hired into a newly created position during a hiring surge. Dave interviewed well, impressing his prospective boss as well as the department director with his creative mind, high energy level, and technical expertise. Routine reference checks seemed positive as did a security check. (pp. 177–178)

Having started out positively, Dave was quick to create problems in the organisation, critical of his co-workers, demanding staff were fired, engaging in verbal tirades towards colleagues, leaving during the middle of meeting, plagiarising work material and failing to meet deadlines. After three months, his supervisor Frank called a meeting with Dave, outlining his concerns, particularly his inability to get along with co-workers, unwillingness to complete work and inappropriate emotionality. Dave was surprised by Frank's comments, denying that there was a problem and suggesting that some aggression was necessary to achieve outcomes. Frank continued to monitor Dave's performance and despite many co-workers being troubled by Dave, others found him humorous, entertaining, flirtatious, creative and bright. Dave formed unusual friendships within the business, finding allies in different levels and positions; these included a middle-aged staff assistant, a secretary, a number of executives and a young female security guard. However, Frank's concern about Dave came to a culmination when he discovered evidence of misconduct that he believed violated the companies policies and had to be actioned. The account of this is as follows:

> Frank discovered that Dave had been using company time and materials to start his own business. After collecting enough physical evidence to undertake disciplinary action, Frank went to his own boss [the director] for support, only to find out that Dave had been complaining to him about Frank since he joined the company. After hearing the other side of a lot of stories, the director realised that Dave was distorting the truth to make Frank look bad and gain sympathy for himself. Convinced that Dave was a liar and possible thief, the executive went to the president and vice president only to discover that Dave was well regarded by them and considered a high potential employee. They told him to leave Dave alone! Within a couple of weeks a reorganisation took place; Frank ended up in a new function and Dave was promoted. (pp. 180–181)

Upon becoming involved in the matter, Babiak (1995) assessed Dave on the PCL-R:SV, scoring him 19 (above cut-off threshold), while his score on the PCL-R was 29.4, suggesting Dave had a psychopathic personality. In Babiak's review of the case, he determined that Dave's ability to climb the corporate ladder and successfully achieve an advantage over his co-workers was due to a series of factors: (1) establishing a network of useful and powerful relationships; (2) avoiding situations and meetings where maintaining multiple façades was difficult; (3) creating conflicts which led to distraction and prevented co-workers from sharing information about him; (4) abandoning co-workers who were no longer useful once he had established a level of power; and (5) neutralising critics and detractors by raising doubts regarding their competence and loyalty. Babiak also believed that inadequate management, unstable cultural factors and the changing nature of the organisation further served to provide cover for Dave's psychopathic behaviour.

Understanding Psychopathic Manipulation and Victimisation in the Workplace

Organisations are diverse and layered systems, encompassing people of different socio-economic backgrounds, educational standards and inter-personal skills. As noted by Babiak (1995), corporations can be chaotic, comprised of unstable cultural factors, rapidly changing and balancing an elusive dynamic between individual and corporate needs. Organisa-tions and businesses commonly exercise significant power, influence and control over others both within and at a broader societal level (Shank, 2018). This combination of power and chaos is perfect scenario for psy-chopathic individuals who are able to adapt to a system comprising of both significant vulnerability and limitless opportunity. Although there are several dimensions to psychopathic personality, there appears to be two central elements to psychopathic manipulation and victimisation in the workplace, the first being a *crafted persona* conveying competence and charisma, and the second concerns astute *observational and interpersonal skills*.

Crafted Persona

The act of self-presentation and impression management plays a piv-otal role in the management of one's immediate environment (Goff-man, 1959, 1967; Paulhus, 1998). Babiak and Hare (2006) proposed that the psychopathic individual is adept at managing the three faces of their personality. The authors suggested that a personality comprises of three pathways/components, with these pathways/components influencing both personality expression and others interpretation of the personality or individual. The first component of the personality is characterised as the internal or *private* personality. The private personality consists of our own thoughts, attitudes, perceptions, values, drives and emotions, commonly referred to as "me" (Babiak & Hare, 2006). The second pathway for personality is the *persona*; which related to what we want others to see and associate with us. The persona is an edited version of our private self, with some individuals more conscious of how they may appear and able to make considered attempts to convey a specific impression or appearance (Babiak & Hare, 2006; Goffman, 1959, 1967). The persona reveals selective details and traits about a person, commonly a controlled or deliberate attempt (whether conscious, unconscious or socially influenced) to influence how others judge or see us. The third component of the personality is the *attributed personality* or *reputation*, an element of personality that is externally determined and subject to limited control or influence (Babiak & Hare, 2006). The attributed personality comes from others perceptions of our personality, interpreted based on what we say and do and coupled with others views and biases that may influence this interpretation.

The three faces of personality are of particular importance when considering psychopathy. The private personality of the psychopath is something that can only be postulated, likely characterised by a grandiose self-centeredness and a desire for self-gain and gratification. However, the persona of psychopathic individuals, like a "chameleon" is often crafted or adapted to their environment, portraying the traits and features that are perceived as being socially expected of that situation or interaction. As Mathieu (2016) states, *"the difference between psychopathy in the business world and general psychopathy is the suit"*, explaining that the behaviour is the same except *"it comes in a more expensive and well-spoken package"* (p. 3). Psychopathic individuals are astute learners; for example, in the case of John Jackson as aforementioned, John had undertaken extensive psychological treatment with no behavioural change, although improved social understanding, informing, *"treatment taught me how to push their buttons, get what I want"*. By understanding that faults and weakness exist in individuals and systems, psychopathic people are flexible in the engagement style, may often alter appearance, profess to having knowledge or skills relevant to the setting, and convey a veneer of credibility and competence. According to Cleckley (1941), "*his rational power enables him to mimic directly the complex play of the human living*" (p. 383). Through a crafted image, selective language, instrumental lies and modelling sincerity, psychopathic individuals attempt to portray the "perfect" persona.

When considering psychopathy in corporate settings, it would not be amiss to suggest that the ideal CEO profile is of "*an extraverted charismatic individual who shows no sign of emotion under stressful circumstances, who is goal-oriented, aggressive with the competition, and able to sell anything to anyone and who will be able to take drastic actions when needed. Coupled with nice clothes, the charming smile, the expensive watch and the promise of bringing more money or wealth to the company*" (Mathieu, 2016, p. 3). Unfortunately, this type of profile or perception of a successful CEO shares many similarities to the characteristics of psychopathic personality, with differences only distinguished by an astute observer. At the surface level, differentiating a psychopathic person from a suitable CEO would be challenging, requiring sound assessment and meticulous interview processes and encompassing integrity testing and moral reasoning tasks. Failure to do so would mean that assessments and judgements of character and competence would be based on impressions and preferences, likely resulting in problematic outcomes (Babiak & Hare, 2006).

One of the central issues of relying on first impressions to determine competence, trustworthiness and character is that people's evaluations of others are inherently flawed and error-prone (Baker, Porter, ten Brinke, & Udala, 2015). For example, research has shown that facial symmetry, attractiveness, larger eyes, higher eyebrows, rounder faces and "babyfacedness" are associated with greater signalising and perceptions of trustworthiness (Baker et al., 2015; Bar, Neta, & Linz, 2006; Bull & Rumsey, 1988; Bull & Vine, 2003; Todorov, 2008; Todorov, Baron, & Oosterhof, 2008). Several studies have found that parole boards, psychologists, mental health practitioners and legal professionals detected lies at less than or at chance levels (Ekman & O'Sullivan, 1991; Shaw, Porter, & ten Brinke, 2013; Vrij & Mann, 2001), while more emotionally intelligent individuals were worse at detecting deception (Barker, ten Brinke, & Porter, 2012). In another study, a mock-jury rendered a guilty verdict for an untrustworthy-looking defendant compared to a trustworthy-looking one based on fewer pieces of evidence (Porter, ten Brinke, & Gustaw, 2010), highlighting the implications of faulty judgements and decision-making related to assessing a person's character.

Intuitive judgements on a person's character are problematic, and generally, humans are unable to determine the correct information upon which to base their conclusions. Studies suggest that within approximately 100 milliseconds of meeting someone, established first impressions are formed, and once formed, these first impressions become solidified (Babiak & Hare, 2006; Baker et al., 2015; Bar et al., 2006; Porter & ten Brinke, 2009; Willis & Todorov, 2006). The observer focuses on any subsequent information that supports this initial impression, filtering out and selectively ignoring details that contradict this early impression. Therefore, only preferential information that is supportive of this first impression is considered (Babiak & Hare, 2006), suggesting that people we like at first meeting become more likeable, and those we do not like remain that way (Babiak & Hare, 2006). This filter system works to the advantage of those with psychopathy, who present as confident, socially poised, charming and charismatic regularly at first meeting (Hall & Benning, 2006; Hare, 1999). The problem with a filtering system that dictates the formation of/and determines a person's character is that if the persona of that person is misjudged at the time of the first impression then problems can arise (Babiak & Hare, 2006). Porter and ten Brinke (2009) coined the term, *Dangerous Decision Theory* (DDT), to account for instantaneous impressions of character, determined by details such as facial appearance. These impressions result in broad assumptions about a person based on irrelevant information, leading a person to make conclusions related to trustworthiness, personality and character and credibility. The authors believed that in high-stakes cases or situations (i.e., jurors determining guilt), incorrect and irrelevant details were commonly used to make judgements and decisions, often resulting in "tunnel vision", reflective of a selective focus on detail, noticing only preferential information and ignoring the rest.

DDT highlights the flaws in human perception and character judgement. These flaws have considerable implications for understanding psychopathic manipulation and victimisation. In essence, humans place value on traits such as confidence, charm, humour, fearlessness and material goods (e.g. trendy clothing and expensive accessories), features that are easily influenced and vulnerable to exploitation. Psychopathic individuals are skilled at wearing the right mask, being the wolf in sheep's clothing or walking the walk (Babiak et al., 2010; Cleckley, 1941; Hare, 2003). However, as capable as a psychopathic person may be in crafting a persona, in time cracks in character will emerge and the private inner personality and intentions will leak through. Nonetheless, the greatest challenge to identifying what is beneath the crack in the mask is in overcoming established and solidified character judgements, which even in the face of contradictory information remains firm and are rarely easily altered.

Observational and Interpersonal Skills

Devoid of a desire to find acceptance and belonging amongst co-workers, psychopathic individuals are quick to meet as many people within an organisation as they can, gathering as much information and understanding as to the value of each person they encounter. By determining the value, role, and utility of each individual, the psychopathic person is able to identify whom to allocate their time and attention to. Value is commonly identified based on a person's position in the organisational hierarchy (position power), access to information (knowledge power), control over resources (resource power) and technical abilities (expert power) (Babiak & Hare, 2006). Through observation and interaction, psychopathic individuals identify the core players within an organisation, analyse the interaction and communication between co-workers and through interpersonal interactions determine the personality styles (strengths, weakness, assertiveness and submissiveness) of potentially useful colleagues. According to Babiak and Hare (2006) during the early stages of employment, the psychopathic individual sets about planning their success, establishing the pawns, partisans, patrons, patsies and police. By categorising co-workers into useful, irrelevant, and prohibiting, the psychopathic person is able to identify weak points within the organisation, obstacles to overcome, potential allies and suitable victims.

An important first step is to identify the "pawns" within a business, those that can be easily manipulated and also provide needed resources and information such as money, contacts, influence and expertise (Babiak & Hare, 2006). Pawns become primary targets, with the psychopathic person seeking to convey their honesty and integrity, developing a friendship and expressing their loyalty towards individuals that fit this role (Babiak, 1996). A pawn serves as a momentary person of value for a psychopathic individual, often assisting in the pursuit of establishing a relationship with a "patron", an influential person within the organisation, commonly an executive or person of seniority. Forming a relationship with a patron is of considerable importance, with the aim of being taken "under their wing" and "mentored" (Babiak, 1996; Babiak & Hare, 2006). Once this patronage is established, an alliance is formed, and with the patron on their side, the psychopathic individual is protected and their games and manipulation become difficult to overcome. Ultimately for pawns and patrons, the outcomes of supporting the psychopathic individual are adverse, often most costly for the patron, who is a high-power and high-status individual (Babiak, 1996). Commonly patrons become the "patsies", the "fall person" who is blamed for mistakes, poor practices or particular indiscretions. Superseding the patron is the whole purpose of the game, with pawns assisting the psychopathic individual in this quest (Babiak, 1996; Babiak & Hare, 2006).

Balancing the interaction between pawns and patrons requires psychopathic individuals to carefully manage relationships with "partisans" and "police" in the organisation. Partisans are considered to be co-workers who are often oblivious, disengaged, dealing with their own personal issues or with limited goals and ambitions. These low utility people rarely present as a barrier or obstacle for the psychopathic person, instead the psychopath avoids contact or interaction with partisans as they serve little purpose (Babiak & Hare, 2006). By far the greatest obstacle to the psychopath is the organisational police and the detractors, those responsible for maintaining order and control, or people who have a grievance with the psychopathic person. These individuals may see through the psychopathic manipulation or attempt to place rules and regulations around the psychopaths conduct. The police keep oversight of business matters and deal with any complaints or behaviour issues, commonly holding positions related to human resources, auditing or quality control (Babiak, 1996; Babiak & Hare, 2006). Psychopathic individuals will strive at all costs to avoid coming to the attention of police, while often creating chaos for detractors such as creating doubts about their competence or loyalty to the business. It is not uncommon for psychopaths to make efforts to manipulate those in policing positions within an organisation, such as in the case of Dave who targeted a young female employee working in security. Even establishing relationships with secretaries that work for people in policing positions can serve as a further method of gaining information and remaining a step ahead of any sanctions.

Conclusion

The corporate setting, like the criminal justice systems, has several systems in place to protect against deceit and exploitation; however, despite these barriers, psychopathic individuals are able to successfully navigate challenges and achieve personal pursuits (Babiak, 1995; Häkkänen-Nyholm & Hare, 2009; Porter et al., 2009). Research has demonstrated that psychopathic personality is associated with several outcomes in relation to manipulation and deception, including: a greater propensity to tell lies related to dominance, conveying sincerity and masking sexual intentions (Jonason et al., 2014); the experience of positive emotions, or a "duping delight" when lying (Baughman et al., 2014); the use of social and emotional skills for self-gain and gratification, reflective of a "darker side" to emotional intelligence (Grieve & Panebianco, 2013; Nagler et al., 2014); the ability to identify submissiveness, assertiveness and proneness to victimisation (Book et al., 2007; Wheeler et al., 2009); and a demonstrated pattern of gaining early release from custody and having the severity of offences reduced in legal proceedings (Häkkänen-Nyholm & Hare, 2009; Porter et al., 2009). The research suggests that manipulation and deceit are prominent traits associated with psychopathic personality, with psychopaths often successfully duping others, creating chaos and confusion, and triumphing at a cost to others. The case of John Jackson highlighted the complexity of psychopathic victimisation, while author and subject of the film *I, Psychopath*—Sam Vaknin—provided a concerning account of the knowledge that some psychopaths have regarding human emotions and vulnerabilities.

Unlike the criminal justice system where assessment and oversight is common practice, corporate environments can be vast and varied. The issue of psychopathy in the workplace and preventing disruption and victimisation is ultimately related to the structures, process and systems within an organisation. The research on psychopathy in the business sector suggests that one of the major shortcomings relates to the recruitment process of employees, with many misconceptions about what constitutes success and a suitable candidate (Babiak, 1995; Babiak & Hare, 2006; Boddy 2011; Mathieu & Babiak, 2016). As highlighted by Mathieu (2016, p. 1), "*we judge how successful people are by external cues: how they dress, how confident they are, how 'driven' they seem to be*", having a poor awareness of character and the operational attributes of success (such as long-term prosperity rather than immediate results). Psychopathic individuals are capable of adjusting their presentation to match the environment or conditions, a problematic issue for recruiters, who place value on confidence, charm, charisma, fearlessness and vision, traits characteristic of psychopathy. Furthermore, the research by Porter and ten Brinke (2009) emphasises the downfalls of human judgement of character, described by DDT, indicating that decisions are based on the inaccurate information, characterised by biases and "tunnel vision".

In high-stake contexts (i.e. interviewing for a job), the recruiters and the candidate each try to read one another, with recruiters making observations based on appearance, response style, response content and general demeanour and candidates carefully attempting to portray a positive impression and convey their suitability for the job (Baker et al., 2015). This method of recruitment, although well intentioned, highlights many of the aforementioned issues associated with determining likeability, suitability and trustworthiness based on initial impressions. There is also a lack of consideration for deceit and manipulation in this process, failing to anticipate individuals who have astute observation skills, willing to present a façade of competence and openly lie. For psychopathic individuals, the recruitment process often provides insight into the inner workings and systems of a company, with an absence of assessment, referee checks or follow-up interviews, suggestive of lax processes and organisational over-sight, a company vulnerable for exploitation. Once hired, psychopathic individuals then commence the process of identifying victims, devising strategies for victimisation and finding "weak points" within the business (Babiak & Hare, 2006). Preventing or managing victimisation by psychopaths has significant challenges if psychopathic personality traits are not accurately identified at the screening or beginning stages. Whether in business or in custody, it is only a matter of time until problems arise, and the complexity and the extent of these issues result in chaos and disruption.

References

Babiak, P. (1995). When psychopaths go to work: A case study of an industrial psychopath. *Applied Psychology: An International Review, 44,* 171–188.

Babiak, P. (1996). Psychopathic manipulation in organizations: Pawns, patrons, and patsies. *Issues in Criminological and Legal Psychology, 24,* 12–17.

Babiak, P., & Hare, R. D. (2006). *Snakes in suits: When psychopaths go to work.* New York: HarperCollins.

Babiak, P., Neumann, C. S., & Hare, R. D. (2010). Corporate psychopathy: Talking the walk. *Behavioural Sciences and the Law, 28,* 174–193. https://doi.org/10.1002/bsl.925.

Baker, A., Porter, S., ten Brinke, L., & Udala, M. (2015). Risky business: Incorporating informed deception detection strategies in violence risk assessment. *Archives of Forensic Psychology, 1,* 55–77.

Baker, A., ten Brinke, L., & Porter, S. (2012). Will get fooled again: Emotionally intelligent people are easily duped by high-stakes deceivers. *Legal and Criminological Psychology, 18,* 300–313. https://doi.org/10.1111/j.2044.8333.2012.02054.x.

Bar, M., Neta, M., & Linz, H. (2006). Very first impressions. *Emotions, 6,* 269–278. https://doi.org/10.1037/1528-3542.6.6.269.

Baron-Cohen, S. (2011). *The science of evil.* New York: Basic Books.

Baughman, H., Jonason, P. K., Lyons, M., & Vernon, P. A. (2014). Liar liar pants on fire: Cheater strategies linked to the dark triad. *Personality and Individual Differences, 71,* 35–38. https://doi.org/10.1016/j.paid.2014.07.019.

Black, P. J., Woodworth, M., & Porter, S. (2014). The big bad wolf? The relation between the dark triad and the interpersonal assessment of vulnerability.

Personality and Individual Differences, 67, 52–56. https://doi.org/10.1016/j.
paid.2013.10.026.

Blair, R. J. R., Jones, L., Clark, F., & Smith, M. (1997). The psychopathic
individual: A lack of responsiveness to distress cues? *Psychophysiology, 34,* 192–
198. https://doi.org/10.1111/j.1469-8986.1997.tb02131.x.

Boddy, C. R. (2011). *Corporate psychopaths: Organisational destroyers.* London:
Palgrave Macmillan.

Book, A. S., Quinsey, V. L., & Langford, D. (2007). Psychopathy and the perception of affect and vulnerability. *Criminal Justice and Behavior, 34,* 531–544.
https://doi.org/10.1177/0093854806293554.

Brooks, N., Fritzon, K., & Watt, B. (in press). "You can tell a victim by the
tilt of her head as she walks": Psychopathic personality and social-emotional
processing (Paper submitted). *Psychiatry, Psychology & Law.*

Bull, R., & Rumsey, N. (1988). *The social psychology of facial appearance.* New
York: Springer.

Bull, R., & Vine, M. (2003). *Attractive people tell the truth: Can you believe it?*
Poster presented at the Annual Conference of the European Association of
Psychology and Law, Edinburg.

Christie, R., & Geis, F. L. (1970). *Studies in Machiavellianism.* New York: Academic Press.

Cleckley, H. M. (1941). *The mask of sanity: An attempt to reinterpret the so-called
psychopathic personality.* London: The C. V. Mosby Company.

Cleckley, H. M. (1976). *The mask of sanity* (5th ed.). St Louis: Mosby.

Dutton, K. (2012). *The wisdom of psychopaths: What saints, spies, and serial killers
can teach us about success.* New York: Scientific American.

Ekman, P., & O'Sullivan, M. (1991). Who can catch a lair? *American Psychologist,
46,* 913–920. https://doi.org/10.1037/0003-066x.46.9.913.

Fecteau, S., Pascual-Leone, A., & Théoret, H. (2008). Psychopathy and the
mirror neuron system: Preliminary findings from a non-psychiatric sample.
Psychiatry Research, 160, 137–144. https://doi.org/10.1016/j.psychres.2007.
08.022.

Fritzon, K., Bailey, C., Croom, S., & Brooks, N. (2016). Problematic personalities
in the workplace: Development of the corporate personality inventory. In P.
Granhag, R. Bull, A. Shaboltas, & E. Dozortseva (Eds.), *Psychology and law
in Europe: When west meets east.* Boca Raton: CRC Press.

Glass, S. J., & Newman, J. P. (2006). Recognition of facial affect in psychopathic
offenders. *Journal of Abnormal Psychology, 115,* 815–820. https://doi.org/10.
1037/0021-843X.115.4.815.

Goffman, E. (1959). *The presentation of self in everyday life*. New York: Anchor Books.

Goffman, E. (1967). *Interaction rituals: Essays on face-to-face behaviour*. New York: Pantheon Books.

Goleman, D. (1995). *Emotional intelligence*. London: Bloomsbury.

Grayson, B., & Stein, M. I. (1981). Attracting assault: Victims' nonverbal cues. *Journal of Communication, 31*, 68–75. https://doi.org/10.1111/j.1460-2466. 1981.tb01206.x.

Grieve, R., & Panebianco, L. (2013). Assessing the role of aggression, empathy, and self-serving cognitive distortions in trait emotional manipulation. *Australian Journal of Psychology, 65*, 79–88. https://doi.org/10.1111/j/1743-9536.2012.00059.x.

Habel, U., Kühn, E., Salloum, J. B., Devos, H., & Schneider, F. (2002). Emotional processing in psychopathic personality. *Aggressive Behaviour, 28*, 394–400. https://doi.org/10.1002/ab.80015.

Häkkänen-Nyholm, H., & Hare, R. D. (2009). Psychopathy, homicide, and the courts: Working the system. *Criminal Justice and Behavior, 36*, 761–777. https://doi.org/10.1177/0093854809336946.

Hall, J. R., & Benning, S. D. (2006). The "successful" psychopath: Adaptive and subclinical manifestations of psychopathy in the general population. In C. J. Patrick (Ed.), *Handbook of psychopathy* (pp. 459–478). New York: Guilford Press.

Hare, R. D. (1999). *Without conscience: The disturbing world of psychopaths among us*. New York: Guilford Press.

Hare, R. D. (2003). *The Hare psychopathy checklist—Revised* (2nd ed.). Toronto: Multi-Health Systems.

Harris, T. (1989). *The silence of the lambs*. London: Arrow Books.

Hastings, M. E., Tangney, J. P., & Stuewig, J. (2008). Psychopathy and identification of facial expressions of emotions. *Personality and Individual Differences, 44*, 1474–1483. https://doi.org/10.1016/j.paid.2008.01.004.

Hickey, E. W. (2010). *Serial murderers and their victims* (5th ed.). Belmont, CA: Wadsworth Cengage Learning.

Johns, J. H., & Quay, H. C. (1962). The effect of social reward on verbal conditioning in psychopathic and neurotic military offenders. *Journal of Consulting Psychology, 26*, 217–220.

Jonason, P. K., Li, N. P., Webster, G. D., & Schmitt, D. P. (2009). The dark triad: Facilitating a short-term mating strategy for men. *European Journal of Personality, 23*, 5–18.

Jonason, P. K., Lyons, M., Baughman, H. M., & Vernon, P. A. (2014). What a tangled web we weave: The dark triad traits and deception. *Personality and Individual Differences, 70,* 117–119. https://doi.org/10.1016/j.paid.2014.06.038.

Jones, D. N., & Paulhus, D. L. (2014). Introducing the Short Dark Triad (SD3): A brief measure of the dark triad personality traits. *Assessment, 21,* 28–41.

Levenson, M. R., Kiehl, K. A., & Fitzpatrick, C. M. (1995). Assessing psychopathic attributes in a non institutionalized population. *Journal of Personality and Social Psychology, 68,* 151–158. https://doi.org/10.1037/0022-3514.68.1.151.

Long, S. L., & Titone, D. A. (2007). Psychopathy and verbal emotional processing in non-incarcerated males. *Cognition and Emotion, 21,* 119–145. https://doi.org/10.1080/02699930600551766.

Lyons, M., Healy, N., & Bruno, D. (2013). It takes one to know one: Relationship between lie detection and psychopathy. *Personality and Individual Differences, 55,* 676–679. https://doi.org/10.1016/j.paid.2013.05.018.

Mathieu, C. (2016). The devil lurks in the suit. *Aftermath: Surviving Psychopathy Newsletter, October,* 1–8.

Mathieu, C., & Babiak, P. (2016). Validating the B-scan self: A self-report measure of psychopathy in the workplace. *International Journal of Selection and Assessment, 24,* 272–284. https://doi.org/10.1111/ijsa.12146.

Montepare, J. M., Goldstein, S. B., & Clausen, A. (1987). The identification of emotions from gait information. *Journal of Nonverbal Behavior, 11,* 33–43.

Murzynski, J., & Degelman, D. (1996). Body language of women and judgements of vulnerability to sexual assault. *Journal of Applied Social Psychology, 26,* 1617–1626. https://doi.org/10.1111/j.1559-1816.1996.tb00088.x.

Nagler, U. K. J., Reiter, K. J., Furtner, M. R., & Rauthmann, J. F. (2014). Is there a "dark intelligence"? Emotional intelligence is used by dark personalities to emotionally manipulate others. *Personality and Individual Differences.* Retrieved from http://dx.doi.org/10.1016/j.paid.2014.01.025.

Newman, J. P., MacCoon, D. G., Vaughn, L. J., & Sadeh, N. (2005). Validating a distinction between primary and secondary psychopathy with measures of Gray's BIS and BAS constructs. *Journal of Abnormal Psychology, 114,* 319–323. https://doi.org/10.1037/0021-843X.114.2.319.

Nicholas, A., Brody, S., de Sutter, P., & de Carufel, F. (2008). A woman's history of vaginal orgasm is discernible from her walk. *The Journal of Sexual Medicine, 5,* 2119–2124. https://doi.org/10.1111/j.1743-6109.2008.00942.x.

Paulhus, D. L. (1998). *Paulhus Deception Scales (PDS): The balanced inventory of desirable responding-7.* New York: Multi-Health Systems.

Paulhus, D. L., Hemphill, J. F., & Hare, R. D. (in press). Manual for the *Self-report psychopathy scale*. Toronto: Multi-Health Systems.

Porter, S., Fairweather, D., Drugge, J., Hervé., Birt, A., & Boer, D. P. (2001). Profiles of psychopathy in incarcerated sexual offenders. *Criminal Justice and Behavior, 27*, 216–233. Retrieved from https://www.researchgate.net/publication/247744685_Profiles_of_Psychopathy_in_Incarcerated_Sexual_Offenders.

Porter, S., & ten Brinke, L. (2009). Dangerous decisions: A theoretical framework for understanding how judges assess credibility in the courtroom. *Legal and Criminological Psychology, 14*, 119–134. https://doi.org/10.1348/135532508X281520.

Porter, S., ten Brinke, L., & Gustaw, C. (2010). Dangerous decisions: The impact of first impressions of trustworthiness on the evaluation of legal evidence and defendant culpability. *Psychology, Crime & Law, 16*, 477–491. https://doi.org/10.1080/10683160902926141.

Porter, S., ten Brinke, L., & Wilson, K. (2009). Crime profiles and conditional release performance of psychopathic and non-psychopathic sexual offenders. *Legal and Criminological Psychology, 14*, 109–118. https://doi.org/10.1348/135532508X284310.

Raskin, R. N., & Terry, H. (1988). A principle components analysis of the Narcissistic Personality Inventory and further evidence of its construct validity. *Journal of Personality and Social Psychology, 54*, 890–902.

Rathus, S. (1973). A 30-item schedule for assessing assertive behaviour. *Behavior Therapy, 4*, 398–406.

Riggio, R. E., & Carney, D. C. (2003). *Manual for the social skills inventory* (2nd ed.). Menlo Park, CA: Mind Garden.

Sakaguchi, K., & Hasegawa, T. (2006). Person perception through gait information and target choice for sexual advances: Comparison of likely targets in experiments and real life. *Journal of Nonverbal Behavior, 30*, 63–85. https://doi.org/10.1007/s10919-006-0006-2.

Shank, C. A. (2018). Deconstructing the corporate psychopath: An examination of deceptive behavior. *Review of Behavioral Finance, 10*, 163–182. https://doi.org/10.1180/RBF-03-2017-0028.

Shaw, J., Porter, S., & ten Brinke, L. (2013). Catching liars: Training mental health and legal professionals to detect high-stakes lies. *The Journal of Forensic Psychiatry & Psychology, 24*, 145–159. https://doi.org/10.1080/14789949.2012.752025.

Simon, G. K., Jr. (2010). *Character disturbance: The phenomenon of our age*. Marion, MI: Parkhurst Brothers.

Todorov, A. (2008). Evaluating faces of trustworthiness: An extension of systems for recognition of emotions signaling approach/avoidance behaviours. *Annals of the New York Academy of Sciences, 1124,* 208–224. https://doi.org/10.1196/annals.1440.012.

Todorov, A., Baron, S. G., & Oosterhof, N. N. (2008). Evaluating face trustworthiness: A model based approach. *Social Cognitive and Affective Neuroscience, 3,* 119–127. https://doi.org/10.1093/scan/nsn009.

Tooke, W., & Camire, L. (1991). Patterns of deception in intersexual and intrasexual mating strategies. *Ethology and Sociobiology, 12,* 345–364.

Vrij, A., & Mann, S. (2001). Who killed my relative? Police officers ability to detect real-life high-stakes lies. *Psychology, Crime, & Law, 7,* 119–132. https://doi.org/10.1080/10683160108401791.

Walker, I. (Director). (1994). *I, psychopath* [Documentary picture].

Wheeler, S., Book, A., & Costello, K. (2009). Psychopathic traits and perceptions of victim vulnerability. *Criminal Justice and Behaviour, 36,* 635–648. https://doi.org/10.1177.0093854809333958.

Willis, J., & Todorov, A. (2006). First impressions: Making up your mind after a 100-Ms exposure to a face. *Psychological Science, 17,* 592–598. https://doi.org/10.1111/j.1467-9280.2006.01750.x.

Wilson, K., Demetrioff, S., & Porter, S. (2008). A pawn by any other name? Social information processing as a function of psychopathic traits. *Journal of Research in Personality, 42,* 1651–1656. https://doi.org/10.1016/j.jrp.2008.07.006.

10

Corporate Psychopathy: Entering the Paradox and Emerging Unscathed

Nathan Brooks, Katarina Fritzon and Simon Croom

Peeling Back the Psychopathy Paradox

Over recent years, particular disagreement amongst researchers has centred on the role that potentially positive characteristics such as immunity from stress and anxiety, a fearless ability to make bold decisions unimpaired by concerns about the distress of others (Ketelaar & Tung Au, 2003), and the ability to make a positive first impression have in the defining characteristics of psychopathy. For some, this debate has centred around the apparently oxymoronic concept that a condition that is considered pathological

N. Brooks (✉)
Central Queensland University, Townsville, QLD, Australia
e-mail: nathan@nathanbrooks.com.au

K. Fritzon
Bond University, Robina, QLD, Australia
e-mail: kfrtizon@bond.edu.au

S. Croom
University of San Diego, San Diego, CA, USA
e-mail: scroom@sandiego.edu

© The Author(s) 2020
K. Fritzon et al., *Corporate Psychopathy*,
https://doi.org/10.1007/978-3-030-27188-6_10

can ever involve non-impairment in social or occupational functioning, as encapsulated in the DSM-5 definitions of personality disorder (American Psychiatric Association, 2013). However, as Benning, Venables, and Hall (2018) discussed in their important chapter on successful psychopathy, there are several notable examples in human history of individuals who have achieved extraordinary success, despite having neurological or psychological impairments. These include Temple Grandin (Grandin, 2012), Kay Redfield Jamison (1993), and Elyn Saks (2007) and John Nash (Nazar, 1998). Indeed, the neuroscientist James Fallon (2014) portrays himself as an example of a successful psychopath, believing that positive experiences in childhood ameliorated any negative effects brought about by the presence of neurological and genetic markers for psychopathy.

There has been a significant increase in research investigating the core constructs associated with psychopathy in noncriminal and non-clinical samples. This research is important as it attempts to uncover the potentially protective factors that mitigate against the tendency for individuals with psychopathic personality traits to engage in chronic, serious and prolonged antisocial behaviour (Lilienfeld, 1994). The focus of this book has been to describe this body of research, as well as to add to knowledge particularly in relation to how psychopathic and other difficult personality traits may manifest both positively and negatively in the workplace. The position that we have adopted throughout is premised on the assumption that the core affective and interpersonal personality deficits associated with psychopathy *can* but do not *necessarily* give rise to certain behavioural outcomes. In essence, there are numerous individual differences that may moderate or mediate the relationships between psychopathic personality traits and the violation of social norms (Benning et al., 2018).

An overview of theory and empirical findings relating to psychopathy in general was the focus of Chapter 1, which reviewed literature on both criminal and noncriminal samples. Chapter 2 described subtypes and typologies and provided an overview of research on clinical samples and characteristics associated with psychopathy. The challenges of operationalising varied presentations of psychopathic personality were discussed, with the Clinical Classification Criteria of Psychopathy (CCCP) proposed to determine clinical differences in psychopathic individuals. In Chapter 3, psychopathic personality was examined across contexts, with research and assessment findings in relation to criminal and noncriminal psychopathy explored. Chapter 4 provided an overview of the various ways that psychopathy can be measured, beginning with the PCL-R, and including self-report questionnaires that have been derived from the PCL-R as well as instruments that are based on alternative models of psychopathy, such as the triarchic model and the five-factor model. Chapter 5 focused particularly on the PPI-R, which is one of the most comprehensive of the self-report measures, as well as having been the first such measure that was created, thus generating a large body of research. Within the broader context of organisational psychology, many assessment measures have been developed that attempt to predict individuals' work-related performance, both positive and negative. Chapter 6, therefore, describes these measures and the research that supports their ability to predict negative outcomes in particular.

In Chapter 7, the impact of psychopathic traits and behaviours in the workplace specifically examined the relationship between dark triad traits of psychopathy, narcissism and Machiavellianism and counterproductive work behaviour (CWB). The consequences from the interactions between personality and workplace behaviour manifest in serious ways, from harassment, bullying, aggression and occupational stress through to fraud. Given the massive effects from CWB, Chapter 8 provided a detailed examination of the development of a measure of dark triad traits—the Corporate Personality Inventory-Revised (CPI-R). Much of the chapter explored the development and validity of the CPI-R and discussed the benefits of assessment. In Chapter 9, not only was the issue of CWB expanded, significant insights were provided into the specific strategies often used by psychopathic individuals in their assessment of their organisational and social environment, particularly how predatory motives cause the psychopath to envisage a "tangled web" of patrons, partisans, pawns, police and patsies. In many ways, this chapter served a dual role providing both explanation and warning about the victimisation strategies in diverse contexts.

In the search for theoretical explanations accounting for the tendency for individuals with dark traid personality traits to engage in counterproductive work behaviours, two leading perspectives have emerged. The first is social exchange theory, which is based on the evolutionary function of personality, that is to solve socially based problems resulting from humans living together in groups (Buss, 1991). Some researchers have speculated that psychopathic personality traits evolved as an adaptive strategy alongside more prosocial characteristics including agreeableness and conscientiousness. Specifically, it is suggested that in an environment in which the majority of people adopt a strategy of cooperation, a small number of individuals may be able to maintain an exploitative, socially parasitic strategy (Glenn, Kurzban, & Raine, 2011). Social exchange theory when applied to the work context posits that the average person's work-related outcomes are based on the principle that employees work in exchange for direct and indirect rewards including pay, fringe benefits, status and admiration. Dark triad personality traits however involve attempts to extract resources for the individual from the collective, and this strategy may only be successful to the extent that colleagues are unaware of the subterfuge (O'Boyle, Forsyth, Banks, & McDaniel, 2012). Thus, if an individual relies on interpersonal manipulation but lacks social effectiveness then workplace relationships will be weakened due to inequity in the exchange process (Witt & Ferris, 2003). Findings supporting the social exchange perspective include that Machiavellians are more likely to engage in interpersonal forms of CWB (Kish-Gephart, Harrison, & Trevin~o, 2010) and have poor job performance (Molm, 2010), Narcissists can gain early promotion (Hogan & Kaiser, 2005) but are ineffective in positions of authority (Campbell, Hoffman, Campbell, & Marchisio, 2011), and Psychopaths have poor job performance ratings but engage in less CWB if they are in positions of authority (O'Boyle et al., 2012).

Another theoretical perspective that appears promising in the context of explaining links between dark triad personality traits and CWB is trait activation theory (Holland, 1997; Tett, Simonet, Walser, & Brown, 2013). Building on the previous findings showing only weak relationships between psychopathy and CWB and job performance (O'Boyle et al., 2012), this theory emphasises the importance of contextual factors in activating the predatory orientation of dark triad personalities. As yet, this theory has only been tested in relation to psychopathy (Blickle, Schutte, & Genau, 2018), where it was found that specific job characteristics including ascendancy and income rise prospects (associated with Enterprising work environments, Holland, 1997) were significant in moderating the relationships between psychopathy and inconsiderate leadership behaviour (Kaiser, LeBrenton, & Hogan, 2015) as assessed by subordinates. At the subscale level, this effect was particularly strong for the meanness score of the PPI-R (Blickle et al., 2018), highlighting the importance of further examination of trait level relationships between particular sub-components of the dark triad and their behavioural expression in a work context.

Trait activation theory and social exchange theory are both consistent with the moderated expression model applied to successful psychopathy (Lilienfeld, Watts, & Smith, 2015), and additionally, the above findings have important implications for the development of taxonomies of specific interactions between psychopathy, victim selection and organisational influence.

Paul Babiak (1995) presented perhaps the first conceptual framework outlining the process by which individuals with psychopathic personalities identify targets at various levels of the organisation, from executive level to junior staff with informal power, who are manipulated in order to influence the attitudes and behaviour of others. This process is outlined in more detail in Chapter 9.

Similar to Babiak's proposed process, Wexler (2008) also draws attention to the stages through which successful psychopaths gain increasing amounts of power within organisations, overcoming opposition by manipulating those with authority into not only protecting the psychopath, but effectively creating a "scam environment" (Wexler, 2008, p. 230) involving corrupt corporate governance and systemic corporate psychopathy giving rise to the flurry of corporate scandals that have occurred in recent years (Markham, 2006; Thomas, 2006). Finally, an expanded process model is provided by McKay, Stevens and Fratel (2010) who describe how individuals within an organisation are attracted to and support each other, colluding to allow white-collar crime to occur and go undetected; they describe these actors in terms of leaders and followers, similar to Babiak's conceptualisation of the psychopath and his "patsies". However, McKay et al. (2010) also describe how organisations can create environments that foster performance anxiety and a culture of winners and losers through policies such as "rank-and-yank" (p. 6) whereby the bottom 10% of performers are retrenched from the organisation. Other practices that foster dependence on management included moving junior employees to different departments to "encourage creativity" (p. 7), but this meant that inexperienced employees become dependent on those in senior positions for guidance. These approaches discourage those employees who become aware of illegal activity on the part of management, from reporting it. Once illegal actions have been noticed, McKay et al. (2010) go on to describe the process by which other staff become reluctant participants, overlooking observed irregularities or attempting to take action but being dissuaded from doing so either because they defer to the leader's authority, collude with the need for power, accept false assurances that things will be corrected or imagine their own guilt in not having reported sooner.

While Babiak and Wexler focus primarily on psychopathy, and McKay et al. mention both psychopathic and narcissistic traits, a more recent paper by Fennimore (2017) also emphasises the abilities of those with Machiavellian personalities to use power and influence in self-serving ways (Bagozzi et al., 2013). Unlike the subclinical psychopathic personality style, which may be associated with impulsive strategies that diminish long-term financial benefits or result in damaged reputation (Jones & Paulhus, 2010), the calculated long-term strategising of Machiavellians can be harder to detect (Jones, 2014). It is suggested that the Machiavellian personality is associated with "cautious misbehaviour" (Fennimore, 2017, p. 1634), and they do not engage in needless risks. Furthermore, those with Machiavellian personalities are more likely to terminate financial misbehaviour when caught, or when rewards are not perceived as sufficient (Fehr, Samson, & Paulhus, 1992), unlike psychopaths who are undeterred by punishment or anticipation of punishment (Lykken, 1957). Fennimore suggests that both personality types have the potential to act as "false agents" (p. 1635) in contractual relationships, resulting in potential defection (Gordon & Platek, 2009), non-reciprocation of goodwill (Gervais, Kline, Ludmer, George, & Manson, 2013), and persuasion to persist with a bad deal when presented with a plan for future success (Fennimore, 2017). Furthermore, the contractor who is preoccupied with his/her own choices may not notice agent misbehaviour. Cognitive dissonance may result in persistence with commitment to a decision, despite increasing evidence that it was a bad one (Arkes & Blumer, 1985; Staw, 1981). The ability of subclinical psychopaths to create a positive first impression, and the irascible findings from social psychology research that "first impressions last" (Gunaydin, Selcuk, & Zayas, 2017) and continue to effect personal judgments even in the presence of contradictory evidence about the individual (Rydell, Mcconnell, Mackie, & Strain, 2006), contributes to this process of creating a false sense of trust between the principal and the agent in an economic transaction (Fennimore, 2017).

Finally, Fennimore also draws attention to the difficulties associated with detecting and monitoring opportunistic or dishonest behaviours in particular organisational contexts, for example, public sector or hybrid organisations given complex multi-layered authority structures. She recommends a series of strategies including better screening prior to contract negotiation, and during the life of the term of contract, as well as interventions to improve the self-monitoring of those who may be affected by "false agents" to guard against processes such as acceptance of minor trust violations, the "halo effect" (first impressions last) and making decisions based on intuition and emotion rather than factual evidence.

Fixing the Problem

The cost to an organisation from hiring an unsuitable or problematic individual can be enormous, encompassing loss of salary, cultural disruption, poor team morale, ruptured stakeholder relationships, opportunity loss, potential litigation and damaged reputation. The implications of poor hiring and recruitment are considerable and in the past decade, particularly since the Global Financial Crisis, there has been extensive commentary and recommendations in relation to revised recruitment, policy and management practices to mitigate the consequences of problematic employees (Babiak & Hare, 2006; Babiak, Neumann, & Hare, 2010; Boddy, 2011, 2015; Furnham, 2008; Perri, 2013). Many of those tasked with recruitment and employee management have a generally limited understanding of problematic or dark triad traits and attributes, instead making recruitment decisions based on first impressions and self-reported work and skill history. It is unsurprising that organisations have been prone to vulnerability and exploitation due to weak points within the business, commonly failing at the beginning stages. To assist in addressing many of the shortfalls in recruitment and employee management, the following three aspects will be examined, these include the interview, assessment and screening, and management and policy processes.

The Interview

The interview is often the cornerstone of employee recruitment and arguably the most high-stakes component. If done correctly the interview process can identify an appropriate candidate and streamline the recruitment time, however, if poorly defined, with limited direction and incorrect attribute weightings, significant costs to the organisation can occur. Unstructured interviews are of limited value and conclusions drawn from these have very low validity, yet, structured and planned interviews commonly yield valuable information (Cook, 1998). Organisations around the world rely on the employment interview as a tool for selecting the best applicant (Posthuma, Morgeson, & Campion, 2002), but deception during the interview may invalidate the interview process by biasing the decision in favour of an unqualified or unsuitable candidate (Young & Kacmar, 1998). Research suggests that interviewers are often unable to detect deception during the employment interview (Posthuma et al., 2002) and that faking can lead to interview success (Levashina & Campion, 2007). Furthermore, individuals who are high on dark triad personality traits are more likely to employ deception in job interviews (Hogue, Levashina, & Hang, 2013). There may be a need to employ innovative interviewing techniques to improve the quality of information that candidates provide and to provide interviewers with more contextual and interpersonal information about the candidate to potentially increase the ability to detect deception.

Two such methods that have been developed in the forensic context include the *Cognitive Interview* (CI; Fisher & Geiselman, 1992) and the PEACE model (Home Office, 1992). Collectively these have led to significant improvements in the quantity and quality of information that is gained from witnesses and suspects involved in crime, respectively. The CI is based on the psychological processes of perception, memory, social dynamics and communication and has been found to increase subject recall by approximately 30–50% (Fisher & Geiselman, 1992), improving memory recollection and communication skills in demanding situations (Furnham & Taylor, 2011). Although the CI has primarily been used for memory retrieval in witnesses or victims, the technique requires the interviewer to develop effective methods of engaging with subjects to elicit information.

At a similar time in the UK, the PEACE framework was proposed as a method to implement a consistent and structured approach to police interviewing that could be systematically applied across policing. The model uses conversation management and cognitive interviewing techniques and has utility across a variety of contexts. In the first step, planning and preparation (P) the interviewer is prepared by accessing a range of information about the interviewee. Unlike standard job interview methods, this would potentially involve seeking referee reports prior to interviewing candidates, in order to plan for scenario-based questioning that builds on knowledge gained about past occupational strengths and weaknesses. Engagement and explanation (E) involves building rapport and potentially interacting with the candidate in an unstructured way, which may provide an opportunity to assess the interviewee's interpersonal skills and behaviours when they are "off-guard". In the account (A) phase, the job interview would proceed through the substantive questioning phase, and again it is suggested that through having prior knowledge of the interviewee it may be possible to probe an account of specific events such that inconsistencies emerge. Finally, closure (C) and evaluation (E) would involve summarising key details provided during the interview and following this the interviewer reflects on the interaction and particularly focuses on any unusual or concerning interpersonal events.

According to Shepherd (1986, 2007), in addition to the PEACE steps, interviewers should be able to display six key skills. These skills are observation and memory, listening and assertion, active listening and information processing, appropriate questioning which leads to elicitation and probing, initiation and regulation through control and social reinforcement processes, and confronting feelings through reflection and summarising (Furnham & Taylor, 2011). Shepherd (2007) contends that the PEACE framework provides an overarching process to guide interviews; however, this forms only the basis for a competent interview. For an interviewer to be skilled and capable, the following characteristics are required:

1. The ability to detect and identify changes in non-verbal behaviour, suggestive of evasion or deception.
2. The ability to observe change in emotional states, intent, disposition or attitude.
3. The capacity to form a overall picture of the interview as a whole.
4. The skills to determine indicators of ambiguity, vagueness or contradiction.

The interviewer needs to be able to monitor for acute changes during an interview, above and beyond simply listening to the interviewee's responses and determining their fit to the selection criteria. Research has demonstrated that in the absence of these skills, interviewers are subject to basing decisions on the incorrect information, such as attractiveness, dress, conversational style and interpersonal features (Babiak & Hare, 2006). Porter and ten Brinke (2009) described this tendency to make judgements about a person based on incorrect information as *Dangerous Decision Theory (DDT)*, where people believe that attributes or features (insignificant) are representatives of a person as whole. DDT has been highlighted in mock-jury decision-making, with jurors making decisions about a defendant's guilt based on whether they appeared to be trustworthy or untrustworthy (Porter, ten Brinke, & Gustaw, 2010). Intuitive judgements about a person's character are problematic and generally flawed, with research suggesting that first impressions, once formed, become solidified, with preferential information observed and contradictory indicators ignored (Babiak & Hare, 2006; Baker, Porter, ten Brinke, & Udala, 2015).

Psychopathic individuals are astute learners and quick to identify weakness or vulnerabilities in others, adjusting their engagement style accordingly. Although some research has failed to find a relationship between psychopathy and the ability to perceive emotions and vulnerability in others (see Hastings, Tagney, & Stuewig, 2008; Long & Titone, 2007), several studies have found notable associations. For example, higher levels of psychopathy were found to be associated with greater accuracy of identifying emotions and emotional intensity (Book, Quinsey, & Langford, 2007), determining history of victimisation based on walking gait (Wheeler, Book, & Costello, 2009) and ability to recall and recognise sad, unsuccessful females (Wilson, Demetrioff, & Porter, 2008). Psychopathy has also been associated with a greater judgement and accuracy of sad micro-expressions of emotion, characterised by brief involuntary emotional leakage of an emotion at a rate of 1/25th of second (Demetrioff, Porter, & Baker, 2017). Although slightly inconsistent with the aforementioned research, Black, Woodworth and Porter (2015) failed to find that higher levels of psychopathy were associated with the ability to differentiate assertiveness and submissiveness. Instead, Black et al. (2015) found that those who scored highly on psychopathy and the other dark personality traits perceived all subjects in the study as being vulnerable and characterised by weakness and emotionality.

Without an appropriate understanding of interviewer bias, DDT, and areas of susceptibility for manipulation and deceit, interviewers are likely to make poor judgements and risk being exploited. The four competencies specified by Shepherd (2007), which suggest that interviewers are not only well practised in structured interviewing (e.g. PEACE framework), but skilled in non-verbal behaviour, objectivity, verbal and non-verbal inconsistencies, deception and identifying emotional states. In some police settings, officers have specific roles of expertise, some investigative, while others focused on interrogation and interviewing. In the corporate setting, like in policing, there is a need for specialised interviewers, skilled in the interview modalities, assessment practices and many of the other discussed areas of competence. In situations of high-stakes recruitment, in addition to relevant organisational staff, specialised and trained recruiters should direct interviewing and employee selection. High-stakes positions in the corporate domains may include large salaries, positions of power, financial capacities, leadership roles, significant stakeholder interactions and considerable internal control. It is perhaps not always reasonable to expect HR personnel, managers or other internal professionals to have the skills and expertise to conduct a structured interview, detecting for deception, identifying behavioural and emotional inconsistencies, developing a formulation of character traits, and able to incorporate assessment tools within the interview processes.

At a minimum, without utilising specialised experts trained in interviewing practices, companies should implement formalised and structured processes for conducting an interview. The PEACE model provides an appropriate framework to guide employee interviews; however, Furnham and Taylor (2011, p. 84) have specifically adapted this model to business interviewing. The authors detail nine steps, rather than the five of the PEACE model, suggesting the following focused areas for interviews:

1. *Preparation*—Review files, employee information, selection criteria, interview objectives and set up the room appropriately.
2. *Welcome*—Establish rapport with the interviewee, greet and spend a few minutes conversing. This is often overlooked, particularly in formal and structure interview settings, as this can assist candidates with sufficient skills yet are anxious, whilst also supporting engagement.
3. *Explanation*—Outline the interview process, what will occur, aims, requirements, supporting the interviewee to control and direct the process of responses.
4. *Initiate free report*—Allow the interviewee to have control and freedom in speaking, implementing active listening, open questioning, time for pauses and without interruption. This provides the opportunity for sufficient narrative and also to examine verbal and non-verbal indicators.
5. *Fill the gaps*—Once a open report or account has been given, review notes and gaps in information, also reminding the interviewee that it is okay to say "I don't know", rather than guessing for a response.
6. *Further retrieval*—Review accounts where necessary and request the interviewee to examine information from a different perspective, with specific questions related to that task, such as "how do you feel your colleague felt when that occurred?" Non-verbal and verbal indicators should again be monitored during this stage.
7. *Summarise*—Regular summary should occur throughout the interview or at certain steps; however, a final summary of the interview should be completed at the end.
8. *Closure*—Thank the interviewee and provide details in relation to any additional questions, methods of contact and next steps.

9. *Evaluate*—Analyse the interview, writing up a summary, which reviews strengths, gaps that remain and possible areas of deception or inconsistency. Determine any follow-up action required.

Assessment and Screening

The interview of potential employees should be supported by assessment strategies and tools to support decision-making. Assessment of personality, while at times contested, is generally accepted where suitable and valid instruments are used. Appropriate assessment of potential employee's provides a robust and reliable method of understanding behaviours in the workplace (Furnham, 2008). Some concerns have been raised regarding the legality of some assessments, considered to be intrusive and questioning a candidate's personal life therefore violating Fair Work or Discrimination Acts. In this respect, assessment by tools such as the MMPI are considered inappropriate as it is likely that Courts would deem this to be a pre-employment medical examination (Mathieu & Babiak, 2016). However, the use of instruments examining behaviour, nonclinical personality features, character, integrity, moral reasoning and applied problem-solving is considered suitable for organisational recruitment practices. These areas remain separate from any form of medical investigation and are not considered to require or involve information related to a candidate's personal life, instead specific to the job, attributes, skills and organisational need.

As discussed in Chapter 6, typically the approach in deploying personality measures in occupational selection is to clarify the traits that are likely to be linked to desirable workplace or role outcomes (e.g. conscientiousness or assertiveness) and to seek candidates who demonstrate higher levels of these traits. In other words, the approach is to focus on positive attributes, on the assumption that lower scores on these dimensions will result in less desirable behaviours. This also includes examining the relationship between personality features, honesty and integrity, using this information to formulate an understanding of a candidate's character. Incorporating this combined attribute and performance knowledge from the assessment processes assists in establishing a candidate's character, a central component of the recruitment process, determining preliminary organisational fit and suitability for further progression through the recruitment process.

Integrity Testing. Despite many organisations seeking an employee with sound integrity and moral reasoning, rarely does recruitment examine, let alone assess for these qualities (Furnham & Taylor, 2011). It estimated that up one-third of employees have stolen from their employer (Fine, 2013), while 5% of the annual revenue of US businesses is lost to white-collar crime (O'Brien, 2017). Financial loss is just one component of CWBs, with other impacts including damaged reputation, loss of staff and sabotage. In considering the diverse range of CWBs and traits associated with these, integrity becomes an essential character feature that indicates moral and ethical tendencies. Integrity implies that an individual is incorruptible, unimpeachable and consistent in their words and actions (Furnham & Taylor, 2011; Palanski & Yammarino, 2007).

Integrity assessments are designed to examine consistency in behaviour, moral and ethical reasoning, values, and dependability and response to adversity. Integrity measures also predict the likelihood of an individual engaging in CWBs at work. Example questions may include "*under what circumstances, in your view, is it appropriate to lie?*" and "*your next-door neighbour offers to hook you up with free cable television. Do you take the offer?*" (Furnham & Taylor, 2011, p. 187). Commonly based on either overt (likelihood of engaging in problematic behaviour such as lying or theft) or covert methods (personality-based features including conscientiousness and trustworthiness) of assessment, integrity tests measure a range of constructs including attitudes, beliefs and behaviours. An overt question may include "*How easy is it to get away with stealing?*", while a covert question may be "*How often do you make your bed?*" (Furnham & Taylor, 2011). There are several integrity assessments, including but not limited to, the Giotto (Rust, 1999), IP200 (Integrity International, 2019) and Moral Disengagement Measure (Moore, Detert, Trevino, Baker, & Mayer, 2012). Although each of these measures has strengths and weakness that need to be considered when conducting an evaluation, the overarching aim of using these assessment tools is to further elicit and evaluate a candidate's ethical and moral positions, along with general attitudes.

One of the main criticisms of integrity assessments has related to the accuracy of measurement in determining integrity, with concerns as to the problem of fake-ability and subjects being able to respond in a desirable manner (Brown & Colthern, 2002). As Furnham notes (2008, p. 314), it is possible for people to "beat the test" and appear "virtuous" when indeed they are not. An alternative option to integrity testing, or an additional component of assessment, is a veiled purpose test, designed to examine harmful or deviant behaviour (see Bennet & Robinson, 2000). Veiled purpose measures the degree of frequency of problematic or harmful behaviour displayed by a person. Despite some concerns, integrity testing is valuable, with no assessment full-proof. Integrity measures serve as one tool to assist in evaluating a candidate's character and when combined with other assessments and thorough collateral checking can be a primary feature of employee screening and assessment.

Honesty. There are a range of methods to examine honesty, including integrity testing, indicators of deception or inconsistency during the interview, and collateral checking. Honesty can be examined through integrity testing or in stand-alone measures, where scenarios are provided and a candidate is required to give a forced answer (i.e. yes or no). A further avenue to gather information in relation to honesty is on the validity scales of psychometric instruments, with evaluations on these scales (such as positive impression management) likely to suggest a tendency to respond in a somewhat distorted manner that conveys a favourable impression (Paulhus, 1998).

A specific way to investigate honesty is through response latency. This can be measured through assessment items being administered by computer under a controlled setting (i.e. at the organisation rather than at home), recording the length of time that it takes a candidate to respond to a question. The underlying position of response latency testing is that it takes longer to lie than it does to respond sincerely. In a study where participants were instructed to either respond accurately or falsely to questions, it was possible to correctly differentiate approximately 80% of responses, categorising these as either being honest or faked (Holden & Hibbs, 1995). If suitable assessment instruments are used that can be administered through computer format, then response latency is an additional component of assessment that can be incorporated into examining the honesty and validity of candidate responding (Furnham & Taylor, 2011).

Two primary components of recruitment that are overlooked and provide valuable information in relation to character and honesty are the curriculum vitae (CV) and referee checks. As Furnham and Taylor (2011) note, a central question with a CV is the veridicality of the document, including what details are omitted or exaggerated. Many services are now available to screen CVs and conduct background checks through online platforms in a quick and convenient matter, cross-checking education and work histories through available data. It is recommended that during the interview stage, that a brief discussion of a CV occurs, reviewing the main points and eliciting the candidate's responses in relation to these.

Conducting referee checks is another important step; similar to the significance of reviewing CVs. Boddy (2011, 2015) suggests that this should be a triangulation process, whereby a referee report is obtained from a prior manager or supervision, colleague and subordinate. By gaining feedback on a candidate across multiple levels of an organisation, this provides a complete picture of candidate and their ability to work with others, follow directions, complete tasks and conform to expectations. In addition to referee checks, it is now an emerging practice for vetting to include social media reviews or Internet searches on candidates, providing biographical and retrospective information on the person (Furnham & Taylor, 2011). This can offer insight into interests, relationships, treatment of others, prior criminal history and indicate signs of future possible problems. This form of background check, whether considered moral and appropriate, can offer an indication in relation to a candidate's honesty, with any contradictory information warranting further review and discussion.

Personality. Personality characteristics can have significant implications on the workplace, with personality dimensions observed to be moderate predictors of task performance, job efficiency and contextual performance (Hough, 1992; Salgado, 2003). When appropriate personality measures are used to screen employees, the information derived from the assessment process can "add significant incremental validity" to selection processes, "over and above cognitive ability testing" (Arnold et al., 2005; Furnham, 2008, p. 39). A primary aim of assessment instruments should be to determine how personality traits influence the likelihood of organisation citizenship behaviour (OCB, positive workplace behaviour) and counterproductive workplace behaviour (CWB, problematic or harmful behaviour). The three primary assessment instruments of personality discussed throughout the chapters, which are specifically designed for the workplace, include the Hogan Development Survey (HDS; Hogan & Hogan, 2009), the Business Scan (Mathieu, Hare, Jones, Babiak, & Neumann, 2013) and the Corporate Personality Inventory (Fritzon, Bailey, Croom, & Brooks, 2016).

The HDS is arguably the first and most well-known occupational assessment of personality, developed to examine "common dysfunctional dispositions" or "dark side" traits that can result in "problematic behaviours" in corporate settings (Hogan & Hogan, 2009, p. 1). The HDS is based on the authors' research regarding dark personalities and leadership, with the scales of the instrument considered to be subclinical measures of personality disorders (Mathieu & Babiak, 2016). The measure focuses on the pervasive features of behaviour, rather than predicting CWBs, with the personality features incorporated in the tool derived from the DSM-IV. The HDS has been widely researched, with support found for the personality traits of the measure in predicting negative workplace outcomes (Kaiser et al., 2015; Khoo & Burch, 2008). Some critics of the tool have cited high variability between personality traits and workplace outcomes, a narrow focus on positive attributes and a broad view of personality that fails to adequately capture psychopathy (Furnham, Trickey, & Hyde, 2012; Mathieu & Babiak, 2016).

The B-Scan is based on Hare's four-factor model of psychopathy and comprises of a self-report measure (B-Scan Self; Mathieu & Babiak, 2016) along with a third party measure (B-Scan 360; Mathieu et al., 2013). The B-Scan tools are designed to examine psychopathic personality traits within the workforce and preliminary research has found promising support for the instruments. While the self-report and third party version require further validation and analysis with external workplace criterion, the measures are likely to be available in the near future as assessment instruments of psychopathy in the corporate setting.

The CPI consists of a self-report measure (CPI-R; Fritzon et al., 2016) and also a third party rating version (CPI-3R; Fritzon, Croom, & Brooks,

2013). Unlike the B-Scan, the CPI does not solely measure psychopathy, instead designed to examine dark personality features as applicable to the workplace, this include both problematic behaviours along with possible adaptive features. The CPI assesses behaviours, attitudes and decisions within a work context, and validation research has confirmed its ability to predict both positive (leadership, career success) and negative (CWB, bullying claims) outcomes (see Chapter 8 for further discussion).

Of the three assessment instruments discussed, the HDS has had the most wide-ranging use and application in organisational settings. The instrument has been demonstrated to have operational utility, with personality features demonstrated to predict workplace outcomes, although some minor criticism of the measure has been noted. The CPI shares many similarities with the HDS, however, is more specifically focused on dark personality traits, including psychopathy and has varied assessment methods. The B-Scan is a measure designed exclusively for psychopathy and based on emerging research appears as a potential tool for investigating psychopathic personality in the workplace. A positive feature of the CPI and B-Scan is the third party rater versions, which allow for ongoing assessment beyond recruitment, including in probationary stages or at later time points. The three instruments are considered to all have strengths along with some areas for further development, refinement and empirical analysis. Despite this, the application of these assessment tools in examining dark personalities in the workplace is important to enhancing recruitment practices and preventing individuals with problematic personality traits from reaching high-stakes corporate positions where the costs of harm are high.

Bringing It All Together

Companies have a duty to protect assets, workers and stakeholder interests. There must be reasonable efforts made to adhere to these duties and reduce the risk of harm occurring in any one of these areas. The screening and assessment stage of recruitment is a valuable and data-rich process, whereby essential features relating to a candidate's behaviour, attitudes and decision-making can be garnered. As previously discussed, solely relying on the judgements inferred from an interview places the recruitment process at risk, increasing the likelihood of a poor hire and recruitment mistakes being made. The components of integrity testing, honesty, applied problem-solving skills (specific job-based scenarios) and personality testing provide a formulation of a candidate's character. Character is a crucial feature of a successful leader and employee, often associated with long-term prosperity, rather than short-term change and gain (Mathieu, 2016). It is common practice that recruitment decisions are based on candidate's skill and work history, with character a secondary consideration in progressive recruitment practices. This practice of placing value on skill and past employment is costly for many organisations and the current processes of assessing candidate suitability are backwards, placing weighting on incorrect features. It is proposed that a tiered system to recruitment be implemented, with the first tier focused on examining character and the suitability of this to organisational need. The second step or tier, once character is deemed an appropriate fit, should consider skills, attributes and relevant experience to complete the role. By restructuring the weighting placed on core characteristics of candidate recruitment, it is expected that organisations will be able to employ more suitable candidates, modelling positive character and integrity, coupled with sufficient skill and expertise.

Management and Procedures

While the recruitment process is exceptionally important for identifying the correct candidate, the processes that a company have in place to manage new employees and issues of behavioural concern are equally as valuable. The internal management procedures within an organisation can support or hinder a business, providing sufficient security, power and flexibility, or alternatively exposing the company to exploitation through weakness and gaps in the system. Some of the major areas relevant to management of concerns and issues include the induction, probation period, ongoing assessment, performance reviews, behavioural management processes, record keeping, staff competency, and internal training and development. Studies have also shown that there are important organisational factors that mediate the relationship between personality factors and negative outcomes, including organisational support, burnout and emotional exhaustion or depletion (Raman, Sambasivan, & Kumar, 2016). Therefore, there are a multitude of reasons and motivations for employees to engage in CWB, and organisations need to have suitable support structures and management process to protect the overall company, wellbeing of staff and manage behavioural concerns. Some the reasons for CWB or sabotage may include financial problems, greed, entitlement, anger, revenge, envy, excitement seeking and power (Furnham & Taylor, 2011). For psychopathic individuals or those with dark personality traits, many of the aforementioned motivations can drive behaviour in the workplace; however, a common overarching motivator is the desire for dominance, promoting self-gain regardless of the costs that it may have to others (Boddy, 2011, 2015; Hare, 1999; Perri, 2013). In many incidents of CWBs, a motivation can be identified, yet in the case of psychopathy this is not always clear, instead sometimes psychopathic individuals act this way because it would be foolish not to (Hare, 1999). To protect organisations and staff from the range of implication that can arise from psychopathy and dark personalities within the workplace, a number of key areas relevant to organisational management and procedures will be examined.

The Induction

The induction serves as the first opportunity to establish expectations, outline acceptable and desirable behaviour, detail processes of communication, educate on privacy and security matters and review specific role features (Furnham & Taylor, 2011). Completing a thorough induction over a number of days is important for several reasons: (1) it provides a clear and specified overview of the role requirements and organisational processes; (2) the organisation completes their responsibility to provide the appropriate information to the employee about the company and therefore is protected against any later complaints relating to misinforming or failing to inform of organisational processes; (3) it provides the new employee with the opportunity to ask questions, learn about expectations, shadow current staff and commence the role with adequate organisational understanding; (4) processes of communication, direct reports and hierarchical structures can be established outlining the information sharing steps along with boundaries and limits; and (5) important information about the culture and values of the organisation can be imparted including group norms around collegial behaviour and decision-making processes, making clear distinctions between ethical and unethical behaviours (Cohen, 2016; Kaptein, 2011). The induction should be a written document that is accompanied by periods of observation, discussion and practice. If done appropriately, the induction will provide organisations with a reference point to challenge behaviour that is inconsistent with role requirements, defies hierarchical structures or fails to adhere to specific information sharing processes.

Probation

The probation period of employment should be closely aligned to the induction, supporting the induction process and providing the individual and organisation with the opportunity to monitor adherence to the role and the company expectations. Probationary periods are common practice in many businesses, typically viewed as a "cooling off" period in a contract allowing either party to terminate the contract due to a failure to meet the standards specified in the contractual agreement. The length of a probation period may vary and can be either mutually agreed upon or stipulated by the employer. Employee probation usually relates to the first three months of employment, however, may range up twelve months in some cases. The use of probation clauses in employment contracts is particularly important with respect to psychopathy and dark personalities, as these individuals have the capacity to present a favourable impression and image in the short-term, however, over time this veneer fades and underlying intentions emerge (Babiak & Hare, 2006; Furnham & Taylor, 2011; Mathieu, 2016).

Many organisations consider that the behaviour exhibited by an employee within the first three months of commencing employment will be indicative of future conduct, yet, CWBs often emerge beyond this time frame. Most employees are motivated to convey a positive impression, integrate with others and demonstrate competency within the first few months of employment. It is only after these initial intentions are achieved that problematic behaviours may arise (Babiak & Hare, 2006; Clarke, 2005). To mitigate the risk of CWB and making a poor hiring decision, organisations should look to extend probationary periods for new employees (Clarke, 2005). This may involve reviewing existing policies in relation to probationary processes for all new hires or alternatively incorporating an adjusted probationary period into a contract in situations where pre-employment assessment identifies areas of caution or concern. Another under-utilised component of the probation period is performance reviews, with many probation periods rolling into permanent contracts without any evaluation of the subject's performance or integration within the business. By extending probation periods, organisations have further time to elevate and assess the employee, gaining valuable information on the subject's performance, ability to work with colleagues and willingness to follow direction and strategic aims.

Assessment

One of the common misconceptions about the use of assessment instruments within organisations is that they only apply to initial employee screening. As previously discussed, assessment and evaluation can be valuable during the probationary period for new employees, along with periodic reviews, conduct issues and when investigating complaints. There are a range of instruments designed to evaluate performance beyond the scope this chapter, however, in situations where concerns are evident with behaviour, or inconsistencies are identified in performance reviews, then a case may warrant more specific investigation. The B-Scan 360 (Mathieu et al., 2013) and CPI-3R (Fritzon et al., 2013) are both third party instruments, allowing for a subject to be evaluated by another person. The measures are designed to conduct an objective analysis of an employee who has been identified as exhibiting concerning behaviour.

In the case of the CPI-3R, an evaluator trained in the instrument is able to assess the subject, determining the extent to which their behaviour is reflective of underlying dark personality traits, along with providing recommendations in relation to management or the need for further assessment. The advantage of tools such as the B-Scan 360 and CPI-3R is that they allow for behavioural investigation above and beyond, mediation or management plans, with the instruments able to assess the role of personality and how this impacts workplace conduct and outcomes (Fritzon et al., 2016; Mathieu, 2016; Mathieu et al., 2013). This may include identifying the protective factors of the individual, which serve to reduce the likelihood of engaging in CWB, or determining whether dark personality traits are influencing a person's behaviour in the workplace. For example, in the event that a candidate was identified as having elevations on the CPI-R during recruitment, yet the hiring still proceeded, an extended probationary period (twelve months) with a sixth-month and twelve-month evaluation that encompassed the CPI-3R along with other performance criteria, would allow for sufficient oversight, analysis and duty of care by an organisation.

Ultimately, the role of assessment following recruitment is diverse, serving to assist in employee monitoring or staff investigation. Having a reliable measure that provides an objective analysis of an employee's personality and behaviour within the workplace is important to guide any decision-making or performance management strategies, as without this analysis it can difficult to determine factors relevant an issue and the appropriate methods of resolving or mitigating the problem (Clarke, 2005; Furnham & Taylor, 2011).

Management Processes

Organisations have a difficult task of balancing their duty to support staff when complaints arise, while also allowing the subject of the complaint or problem to have the opportunity to be treated fairly and be managed in a manner that respects their rights (Clarke, 2005). Companies require codes of conduct, specified values, strategic direction and aims, security practices (prevention, protection, detection and deterrence), training standards, levels of transparency and exit policies (Furnham & Taylor, 2011). All these processes and policies need to be clear and established, without these, it is difficult to identify, manage and resolve conduct issues within the workplace. Gaps in any of these internal processes can also leave organisations exposed, with limited options to intervene in cases of CWB. Psychopathic individuals can wreak havoc in a workplace and this can lead to bullying complaints, staff absenteeism, ruptured stakeholder relationships and financial loss (Babiak & Hare, 2006; Boddy, 2011; Hogan & Hogan, 2009; Perri, 2013). It is common practice for human resource departments within a business to deal with complaints and determine a course of action to resolve the issue. However, even if HR sections have proactive complaints processes and assessment practices in place, managing psychopathic or destructive behaviour can be extremely challenging and demanding (Clarke, 2005; Furnham & Taylor, 2011). Subsequently, to sufficiently manage psychopathic behaviour within a business there are several areas that companies need to address, this includes training of staff, reporting of complaints, suitably assessing complaints, developing performance management regimes and having appropriate exit policies.

In training staff, companies should detail the code of conduct within the business, what constitutes a complaint or behavioural issue, how a complaint can be made, what documentation is required and how the complaint investigation process will occur. In essence, this should stipulate what is acceptable and unacceptable behaviour in the workplace and how employees can proceed to report problematic behaviour if it is identified. There are two components to identifying behavioural issues, the first being, keeping detailed accounts through documentation, specifically—what occurred, when, whom it involved and any outcomes that resulted from the issue. Secondly, if concerns with behaviour are observed, staff should never label this behaviour and instead keep record or note of the problem (Babiak & Hare, 2006; Clarke, 2005). If the behaviour is identified over several occasions, then formal notification should be made to suitable parties within the business. Training is intended to provide staff with the knowledge, capability and organisational understanding to action behavioural concerns if they arise. Through this, staff should know who to report a concern too, and if this fails, the next step to seek action. Organisations can support staff in reporting complaints by providing clear criteria outlining what constitutes unacceptable behaviour and facilitate this reporting through either online processes to document concerns or through templates to record behavioural problems.

There are a variety of methods to assessing complaints, including requesting further information, conducting preliminary monitoring, rating the severity of the complaint or conduct, or commencing formal evaluation. As previously discussed, the use of performance rating information and third party assessment tools can serve as a valuable method to determining the extent of the concerning presentation. The result of assessing the complaint is to ultimately determine what course of action is required and if management or intervention is needed. In the case that conduct issues are determined, a performance or behavioural management plan may be implemented, specifying expected conduct and working with the subject to develop strategies to address the areas of concern. This requires considerable information and monitoring for management strategies to be successful, such as weekly review meetings, unscheduled drop-ins on the subject and performance reviews (Clarke, 2005). This can also entail feedback from peers, subordinates, and supervisors to assist in determining the effectiveness of the management plan. One of the proposed methods to managing psychopathic individuals has been to target the person's desire for self-gain, focusing on rewards and incentives as behavioural motivators (Clarke, 2005). Similar to a "star chart" for behaviour with a child, psychopathic individuals can be placed on a performance management plan where they are given specific goals, removed from having regular interaction with colleagues, and financially rewarded based on adherence to the plan and achievement of set goals/performance markers (Clarke, 2005). Although not deterred by punishment, research has consistently found that psychopathic individuals are instrumentally motivated, driven by rewards and self-gratification, suggesting that if an organisation is able to appropriately incentivise behaviour and convey to the psychopathic person their importance to the organisation, this may serve as one method to managing psychopathic personality in the workplace. However, it is not clear whether such a strategy would have long-term viability, with all systems characterised by a level of fragility, along with psychopaths being prone to boredom, needing excitement and stimulation (Babiak & Hare, 2006; Mathieu, 2016).

Exit policies are also an area for focus, needing to be built into contracts and allowing for dismissal from employment if behaviour is considered to violate the organisations code of conduct and attempts at remediation have been unsuccessful. The central principle is that behaviour needs to be incorporated into contracts and if it can be demonstrated that a subject's conduct repeatedly impacts those within the business or places the organisation at risk, then the company must have contractual grounds for exiting the employee. This may involve detailing that attempts at remediation will be made; however, if unsuccessful, then dismissal may occur. This also sets expectations from the start of employment and models to other staff as to the boundaries and limits of conduct (Furnham & Taylor, 2011).

Lastly, as discussed previously, financial institutions may also require higher-level structural policies to be in place to prevent the sort of culturally embedded unethical and illegal practices that were seen in the cases discussed by McKay et al. (2010). Here, we see situations where malpractice was occurring at leadership level, and this is much more challenging than managing an instance of an individual employee who is engaging in interpersonal CWB, such as bullying and intimidation. In these cases, it would seem that there is a need for a level of monitoring and reporting to exist outside of the organisation itself, such as a banking ombudsman, e.g. the Australian Financial Complaints Authority.

Re-visioning organisational culture is a longer-term process requiring a strategic plan including levels of accountability and individual employee plans, an oversight of a board or directors and external stakeholders. A new leadership team may require education and training to re-establish ethical standards (McKay et al., 2010). Changing organisational culture to shift behaviour in the direction of communal rather than individual goals has been suggested as an effective strategy for managing narcissistic leaders (Sedikides & Campbell, 2017), but as yet there have been no known examples of interventions that have demonstrated successful outcomes in relation to ameliorating the negative impact of dark triad personalities at the higher levels of organisations.

The Individual Response

The aforementioned sections have discussed many of the organisational processes that can be implemented to prevent or mitigate psychopathic personality or other dark personality features within the workplace. However, for individuals who are being victimised by a manager or colleague, it can be a troubling and distressing issue to overcome. If companies have sufficient internal processes in place to report these concerns, then this is often the most suitable path to pursue to address the problem. Yet, if someone is being victimised by their CEO, the person tasked with leading the business and managing complaints, this can present quite a dilemma. Having a psychopathic boss can have a debilitating impact on an employee and lead to numerous professional and personal problems (Babiak & Hare, 2006). The following strategies have been identified as approaches that an individual can employ if being victimised by a colleague or manager:

1. *Document everything*—The role of documentation is one of the most important processes for dealing with issues within the workplace (Babiak & Hare, 2006; Furnham & Taylor, 2011). This provides an "evidence trail", documenting a history of directions, requests and patterns of engagement. Documentation serves to protect the individual and can also provide specific examples or incidents of conduct issues. For example, if provided with verbal direction to complete a task, an employee may detail this in an email, seeking clarification on a particular point before moving forward with task. An employee may also make their own notes by creating an email and sending this to themselves, detailing an issue that had arisen in the day, what it related to, who was involved and any outcomes. Overtime, if consistent documentation occurs, an employee develops a record of behaviour and engagement, something that can be taken to a board of directors or external regulators.

2. *Understand organisational processes*—As simple as this may sound, some employees do not know the organisational process for dealing with

internal problems or complaints (Babiak & Hare, 2006). Many companies will have HR departments that are tasked with developing systems for resolving problems and have process and policies stipulating codes of conduct and avenues to report complaints.

3. *Adopt communication tactics*—Implementing some basic communication tactics can change the interaction between an employee and a problematic leader. Firstly, wait for the leader to speak, do not initiate conversation or offer ideas unless requested. This reduces the extent of the interaction and also the likelihood of the leader finding faults in what is said. Secondly, do not respond when emotional, allow time to pass and instead respond later in an email which documents the issue and avoids further face-to-face interaction. Thirdly, when interacting with a problematic leader, keep statements concise, specific to the issues, based on facts and data, without offering opinion (Roter, 2019). A fourth communication tactic is to be assertive and set boundaries, again best approached through email or written correspondence. This may include delaying responding, setting limits or guidelines as to what can be achieved or undertaken or referring back to organisational policies if something is inconsistent. Lastly, where possible, communicate with a difficult leader in the presence of colleagues. This may serve to reduce the likelihood or severity of victimisation and provides a witness to any targeted behaviour.

4. *Avoid labelling*—It is never useful to label a person's behaviour, particularly using names such as "psychopath" (Babiak & Hare, 2006). The use of such labels undermines the employee who does not have the appropriate qualifications to make such statements. By labelling a colleague, an employee places themselves at risk of being accused of bullying or making defamatory comments.

5. *Seek support*—Anyone experiencing victimisation in the workplace often feels isolated and alone. It is important that a person feeling victimised confides in a trusted co-worker, friends or seeks profession support through counselling (Babiak & Hare, 2006). The impact of victimisation is commonly worse when a person fails to share their current difficulties, internalising these and coping through problematic means.

6. *Monitor internalisation*—As discussed in Chapter 9, victimisation is successful when a person begins to experience self-doubt and becomes critical of their self. This may involve rumination, anxiousness about going to work, an inability to concentrate on tasks, repeated sickness and a gradual deterioration in coping. It is essential to be aware of these warning signs and seek support if any of these indicators emerge.

7. *Prioritise self-care*—Protecting wellbeing through consistent self-care practices can reduce the impact of victimisation (Clarke, 2005). In many situations where a person is victimised, self-care reduces, with routines and structures forgotten, and passive or dysfunctional coping adopted.

8. *Review values*—It is important for an individual to reflect on their reasons for working with an organisation reviewing their goals and evaluating whether the current circumstances are consistent with their beliefs and meeting their expectations (Roter, 2019). When there is a discrepancy between values and current circumstances, internal conflict often arises. Ultimately, if a person's values are not being met and conflict is experienced, the most likely resolution is to leave the employment, as the only outcome that can be controlled is the individual's choices and not the behaviour of others (Glasser, 1998).

9. *Explore whistleblowing options*—The option to report wrongdoing by an individual is a strategy that is heavily influenced by the culture of the organisation, relationships with one's immediate supervisor and policies surrounding whistleblowing (Mesmer-Magnus & Viswesvaran, 2005). Clearly, challenges can also arise for whistleblowers from the potential psychopathic individual, given the "tangled web" of relationships and influence they will have spun. Ideally, confidentiality for whistleblowers should be a cornerstone of organisational policies, but the risks have been significant when such safeguards are not enacted (Delk, 2013).

Conclusions

In this chapter, we have provided an outline of some suggestions aimed at managing or changing the outcomes associated with dark personalities in the workplace. We have also acknowledged the role of the organisational culture, and effective policies and processes to manage complaints and to report suspected illegal or anomalous practices. Overall while there is evidence that dark triad personality traits can have both negative and, in some cases, positive outcomes, the positive outcomes are usually only for the individuals themselves and not for those who interact with them in the workplace. Therefore, the paradox would appear to depend on the perspective, whether of the psychopathic individual or a person in their sphere of influence. Effective management and prevention strategies remain paramount in minimising harm to self and others.

At the core of dark personalities is a tendency towards manipulation, callous behaviour, and self-centeredness, resulting in a generally antagonistic style of social behaviour (Jones & Figueredo, 2013; Moshagen, Hilbig, & Zettler, 2018). As aforementioned, due to the implications of these personality types on the workplace, it is important to complete thorough interviews, conduct screening assessments and have sound management policies and procedures in place to respond to conduct issues. However, although the focus on this book has been on psychopathy and the dark triad, one of the fundamental areas of for further research and development is in determining personality traits that are adaptive and positive for the workplace. This includes whether there is a point at which dark personality features shift from functional to dysfunctional, or alternatively, if other corresponding traits may moderate the expression of dark personality features. Interestingly, only recently new research has emerged on a "light triad", considered to be opposing personality traits to those related to the dark triad. The light triad comprises of humanism (valuing the worth of others), faith in humanity (believing in goodness) and Kantianism ("treating people as ends unto themselves") (Kaufman, Yaden, Hyde, & Tsukayama, 2019, p. 1). Compared to the dark triad, the light triad is found to be associated with greater life satisfaction, a beneficence towards others and growth oriented-outcomes. In contrast, the dark triad is related to selfishness, adverse social outcomes, exploitation and aggressiveness (Kaufman et al., 2019). Subsequently, future research would benefit from examining whether a "optimal zone" of personality exits, balanced between both the light and dark ends of the personality spectrum. The presence of light triad features may also serve to protect against or reduce the likelihood of dark personality characteristics, an area that both researchers and organisations may explore in relation to recruitment and organisational assessment.

Finally, throughout the book we have focused on the personality constructs of psychopathy, Machiavellianism and narcissism; recent research has proposed the addition of sadism as a fourth aspect of personality that has demonstrated empirical overlap with both psychopathy (Buckels, Jones, & Paulhus, 2013; Međedović & Petrović, 2015; Paulhus & Jones, 2015) and narcissism (Paulhus & Dutton, 2016). A self-report measure of sadism has been developed (Comprehensive Assessment of Sadistic Tendencies; Buckels & Paulhus, 2014) and preliminary findings indicate that this measure predicts a variety of aggressive and antisocial behaviours, including partner and animal abuse (Paulhus, Jones, Klonsky, & Dutton, 2011). While the behavioural associations for sadism has warranted its inclusion within a *Dark Tetrad* (Buckels et al., 2013), more recent research found considerable overlap between psychopathy, Machiavellianism and sadism, raising concerns about the construct validity of the tetrad (Ritchie, Blais, & Forth, 2019) and echoing the already identified concerns around measurement of these dark personality traits. There is no research as yet investigating workplace outcomes, and so it remains a focus for future research to investigate whether everyday sadism has predictive validity over and above the other dark triad personality traits, or whether it is indeed the case that "psychopathy runs the show" (Muris, Merckelbach, Otgaar, & Meijer, 2017, p. 194).

References

American Psychiatric Association. (2013). *Diagnostic and statistical manual of mental disorders* (5th ed.). Arlington, VA: Author.

Arkes, H., & Blumer, C. (1985). The psychology of sunk cost. *Organizational Behavior and Human Decision Processes, 35*(1), 124–140. https://doi.org/10.1016/0749-5978(85)90049-4.

Arnold, J., Silvester, J., Patterson, F., Robertson, I., Cooper, C., & Burnes, B. (2005). *Work psychology: Understanding human behaviour in the workplace.* Harrow, UK: Prentice Hall.

Babiak, P. (1995). Psychopathic manipulation in organisations: Pawns, patrons, and patsies. *Issues in Criminological and Legal Psychology, 24,* 12–17.

Babiak, P., & Hare, R. D. (2006). *Snakes in suits: When psychopaths go to work.* New York: HarperCollins.

Babiak, P., Neumann, C. S., & Hare, R. D. (2010). Corporate psychopathy: Talking the walk. *Behavioural Science and the Law, 28,* 174–193.

Bagozzi, R., Verbeke, W., Dietvorst, R., Belschak, F., van Den Berg, W., & Rietdijk, W. (2013). Theory of mind and empathic explanations of Machiavellianism: A neuroscience perspective. *Journal of Management, 39*(7), 1760–1798. https://doi.org/10.1177/0149206312471393.

Baker, A., Porter, S., ten Brinke, L., & Udala, M. (2015). Risky business: Incorporating informed deception detection strategies in violence risk assessment. *Archives of Forensic Psychology, 1,* 55–77.

Bennet, R., & Robinson, S. (2000). Development of a measure of workplace deviance. *Journal of Applied Psychology, 85,* 349–360.

Benning, S. D., Venables, N. C., & Hall, J. R. (2018). Successful psychopathy. In C. J. Patrick (Ed.), *Handbook of psychopathy* (2nd ed., pp 585–608). New York, NY: Guilford Press.

Black, P. J., Woodworth, M., & Porter, S. (2015). The big bad wolf? The relation between the dark triad and the interpersonal assessment of vulnerability. *Personality and Individual Differences, 67,* 52–56. https://doi.org/10.1016/j.paid.2013.10.026.

Blickle, G., Schütte, N., & Genau, H. (2018). Manager psychopathy, trait activation, and job performance: A multi-source study. *European Journal of Work and Organizational Psychology, 27*(4), 450–461. https://doi.org/10.1080/1359432X.2018.1475354.

Boddy, C. R. (2011). *Corporate psychopaths: Organisational destroyers.* London: Palgrave Macmillan.

Boddy, C. R. (2015). Organisational psychopaths: A ten year update. *Management Decisions, 53,* 2407–2432. https://doi.org/10.1108/MD-04-2015-0114.

Book, A. S., Quinsey, V. L., & Langford, D. (2007). Psychopathy and the perception of affect and vulnerability. *Criminal Justice and Behavior, 34,* 531–544. https://doi.org/10.1177/0093854806293554.

Brown, R., & Colthern, C. (2002). Individual difference in faking integrity tests. *Psychological Reports, 91,* 691–702.

Buckels, E., Jones, D., & Paulhus, D. (2013). Behavioral confirmation of everyday sadism. *Psychological Science, 24*(11), 2201–2209. https://doi.org/10.1177/0956797613490749.

Buckels, E. E., & Paulus, D. L. (2014). *Comprehensive assessment of sadistic tendencies.* Unpublished instrument. Vancouver, Canada: University of British Columbia.

Buss, D. M. (1991). Evolutionary personality psychology. *Annual Review of Psychology, 42*(1), 459–491.

Campbell, W. K., Hoffman, B. J., Campbell, S. M., & Marchisio, G. (2011). Narcissism in organizational contexts. *Human Resource Management Review, 21,* 268–284.

Clarke, J. (2005). *Working with monsters: How to identify and protect yourself from the workplace psychopath.* Sydney, NSW: Random House Australia.

Cohen, T. R. (2016). The morality factor. *Scientific American Mind, 28*(1), 32–38.

Cook, M. (1998). *Personnel selection.* Chichester: Wiley.

Delk, K. L. (2013). Whistleblowing—Is it really worth the consequences? *Workplace Health & Safety, 61*(2), 61–64.

Demetrioff, S., Porter, S., & Baker, A. (2017). I know how you feel: the influence of psychopathic traits on the ability to identify micro-expressions. *Psychology, Crime & Law, 23,* 274–290. https://doi.org/10.1080/1068316X.2016.1247159.

Fallon, J. (2014). *The psychopath inside: A neuroscientist's personal journey into the dark side of the brain*: New York: Current.

Fehr, B., Samson, D., & Paulhus, D. R. (1992). The construct of Machiavellianism: Twenty years later. In C. D. Spielberger & J. N. Butcher (Eds.), *Advances in personality assessment* (pp. 77–116). Hillsdale, NJ: Erblaum.

Fennimore, A. (2017). Natural born opportunists. *Management Decision, 55*(8), 1629–1644. https://doi.org/10.1108/md-11-2016-0786.

Fine, S. (2013). A look at cross-cultural integrity testing in three banks. *Personnel Review, 42*(3), 266–280.

Fisher, R., & Geiselman, R. (1992). *Memory enhancing techniques for investigative interviewing: The cognitive interview.* Springfield, IL: Charles C. Thomas.

Fritzon, K., Bailey, C., Croom, S., & Brooks, N. (2016). Problematic personalities in the workplace: Development of the Corporate Personality Inventory. In P. Granhag, R. Bull, A. Shaboltas, & E. Dozortseva (Eds.), *Psychology and law in Europe: When west meets east.* Boca Raton: CRC Press.

Fritzon, K., Croom, S., & Brooks, N. (2013). *The corporate personality inventory – Third party report.* Unpublished.

Furnham, A. (2008). *Personality and intelligence at work: Exploring and explaining individual differences at work.* Hove and New York: Psychology Press.

Furnham, A., & Taylor, J. (2011). *Bad apples: Identify, prevent and manage negative behaviour at work.* New York: Palgrave Macmillan.

Furnham, A., Trickey, G., & Hyde, G. (2012). Bright aspects to dark side traits: Dark side traits associated with work success. *Personality and Individual Differences, 52,* 908–913.

Gervais, M., Kline, M., Ludmer, M., George, R., & Manson, J. (2013). The strategy of psychopathy: Primary psychopathic traits predict defection on low-value relationships. *Proceedings of the Royal Society B: Biological Sciences, 280*(1757), 20122773. https://doi.org/10.1098/rspb.2012.2773.

Glasser, W. (1998). *Choice theory: A new psychology of personal freedom.* New York: Harper Collins.

Glenn, A., Kurzban, R., & Raine, A. (2011). Evolutionary theory and psychopathy. *Aggression and Violent Behavior.* https://doi.org/10.1016/j.avb.2011.03.009.

Gordon, D., & Platek, S. (2009). Trustworthy? The brain knows. Implicit neural responses to faces that vary in dark triad personality characteristics and trustworthiness. *Journal of Social, Evolutionary, and Cultural Psychology, 3*(3), 182–200. https://doi.org/10.1037/h0099323.

Grandin, T. (2012). *Different…not less: Inspiring stories of achievement and successful employment from individuals with autism, Asperger's, and ADHD.* Arlington, TX: Future Horizons.

Gunaydin, G., Selcuk, E., & Zayas, V. (2017). Impressions based on a portrait predict, 1-month later, impressions following a live interaction. *Social Psychological and Personality Science, 8*(1), 36–44. https://doi.org/10.1177/1948550616662123.

Hare, R. D. (1999). *Without conscience: The disturbing world of psychopaths among us.* New York: Guilford Press.

Hastings, M. E., Tangney, J. P., & Stuewig, J. (2008). Psychopathy and identification of facial expressions of emotions. *Personality and Individual Differences, 44,* 1474–1483. https://doi.org/10.1016/j.paid.2008.01.004.

Hogan, R., & Hogan, J. (2009). *Hogan development survey manual.* Tulsa, OK: Hogan Press.

Hogan, R., & Kaiser, R. B. (2005). What we know about leadership. *Review of General Psychology, 9,* 169–180. https://doi.org/10.1037/1089-2680.9.2.169.

Hogue, M., Levashina, J., & Hang, H. (2013). Will I fake it? The interplay of gender, Machiavellianism, and self-monitoring on strategies for honesty in job interviews. *Journal of Business Ethics.* https://doi.org/10.1007/s10551-012-1525-x.

Holden, R., & Hibbs, N. (1995). Incremental validity of response latencies for detecting fakes on a personality test. *Journal of Research in Personality, 29,* 362–372.

Holland, J. L. (1997). *Making vocational choices: A theory of vocational personalities and work environments* (3rd ed.). Odessa, FL: Psychological Assessment Resources.

Hough, L. M. (1992). The "big five" personality variables—Construct confusion: Description versus prediction. *Human Performance, 5*(1–2), 139–155.

Integrity International. (2019). Available at https://www.integtests.com. Accessed 12 December 2018.

Jamison, K. R. (1993). *Touched with fire: Manic-depressive illness and the artistic temperament.* New York: Simon & Schuster.

Jones, D. (2014). Risk in the face of retribution: Psychopathic individuals persist in financial misbehavior among the dark triad. *Personality and Individual Differences, 67,* 109–113. https://doi.org/10.1016/j.paid.2014.01.030.

Jones, D. N., & Figueredo, A. J. (2013). The core of darkness: uncovering the heart of the dark triad. *European Journal of Personality, 27,* 521–531. https://doi.org/10.1002/per.1893.

Jones, D., & Paulhus, D. (2010). Different provocations trigger aggression in narcissists and psychopaths. *Social Psychological and Personality Science, 1*(1), 12–18. https://doi.org/10.1177/1948550609347591.

Kaiser, R. B., Le Breton, J. M., & Hogan, J. (2015). The dark side of personality and extreme leader behaviour. *Applied Psychology: An International Review, 64*(1), 55–92.

Kaptein, M. (2011). Understanding unethical behavior by unraveling ethical culture. *Human Relations, 64*(6), 843–869.

Kaufman, S. B., Yaden, D. B., Hyde, E., & Tsukayama, E. (2019). The light triad vs. dark triad of personality: Contrasting two very different profiles of human nature. *Frontiers in Psychology, 10,* 1–26. https://doi.org/10.3389/fpsyg.2019.00467.

Ketelaar, T., & Tung Au, W. (2003). The effects of feelings of guilt on the behaviour of uncooperative individuals in repeated social bargaining games: An affect-as-information interpretation of the role of emotion in social interaction. *Cognition and Emotion, 17*(3), 429–453. https://doi.org/10.1080/02699930143000662.

Khoo, H. S., & Burch, G. S. J. (2008). The 'dark side' of leadership personality and transformational leadership: An exploratory study. *Personality and Individual Differences, 44*(1), 86–89.

Kish-Gephart, J., Harrison, D. A., & Trevin˜o, L. K. (2010). Bad apples, bad cases, and bad barrels: Meta-analytic evidence about sources of unethical decisions at work. *Journal of Applied Psychology, 95*, 1–31. https://doi.org/10.1037/a0017103.

Levashina, J., & Campion, M. A. (2007). Measuring faking in the employment interview: Development and validation of an interview faking behavior scale. *Journal of Applied Psychology, 92*, 1638–1656. https://doi.org/10.1037/0021-9010.92.6.1638.

Lilienfeld, S. O. (1994). Conceptual problems in the assessment of psychopathy. *Clinical Psychology Review, 14*(1), 17–38.

Lilienfeld, S. O., Watts, A. L., & Smith, S. F. (2015). Successful psychopathy: A scientific status report. *Current Directions in Psychological Science, 24*, 298–303.

Long, S. L., & Titone, D. A. (2007). Psychopathy and verbal emotional processing in non-incarcerated males. *Cognition and Emotion, 21*, 119–145. https://doi.org/10.1080/02699930600551766.

Lykken, D. (1957). *The antisocial personalities*. Mahwah, NJ: Erlbaum.

Markham, J. (2006). *A financial history of modern US corporate scandals: From Enron to reform*. Armonk, NY: M. E. Sharpe.

Mathieu, C. (2016, October). The devil lurks in the suit. *Newsletter*, pp. 1–8. Aftermath: Surviving Psychopathy.

Mathieu, C., & Babiak, P. (2016). Validating the B-scan self: A self-report measure of psychopathy in the workplace. *International Journal of Selection and Assessment, 24*, 272–284. https://doi.org/10.1111/ijsa.12146.

Mathieu, C., Hare, R. D., Jones, D. N. Babiak, P., & Neumann, C. S. (2013). The factor structure of the B-scan 360: A measure of corporate psychopathy. *Psychological Assessment, 25*, 288–293.

McKay, R., Stevens, C., & Fratzl, J. (2010). A 12-step process of white-collar crime. *International Journal of Business Governance and Ethics, 5*(1), 14–32. https://doi.org/10.1504/IJBGE.2010.029552.

Međedović, J., & Petrović, B. (2015). The dark tetrad. *Journal of Individual Differences, 36*(4), 228–236.

Mesmer-Magnus, J. R., & Viswesvaran, C. (2005). Whistleblowing in organizations: An examination of correlates of whistleblowing intentions, actions, and retaliation. *Journal of Business Ethics, 62*(3), 277–297.

Molm, L. D. (2010). The structure of reciprocity. *Social Psychology Quarterly, 73*(2), 119–131.

Moore, C., Detert, J. R., Trevino, L. K., Baker, V. L., & Mayer, D. M. (2012). Why employees do bad things: Moral disengagement and unethical organizational behavior. *Personnel Psychology, 65,* 1–48.

Moshagen, M., Hilbig, B., & Zettler, I. (2018). The dark core of personality. *Psychological Review, 125,* 656–688. https://doi.org/10.1037/rev0000111.

Muris, P., Merckelbach, H., Otgaar, H., & Meijer, E. (2017). The malevolent side of human nature. *Perspectives on Psychological Science, 12*(2), 183–204.

Nazar, S. (1998). *A beautiful mind.* New York: Touchstone.

O'Boyle, E., Forsyth, D., Banks, G., Mcdaniel, M., & Kozlowski, S. (2012). A meta-analysis of the dark triad and work behavior: A social exchange perspective. *Journal of Applied Psychology, 97*(3), 557–579. https://doi.org/10.1037/a0025679.

O'Brien, Connie. (2017). Can pre-employment tests identify white collar criminals and reduce fraud risk in your organization? *Journal of Forensic and Investigative Accounting, 9*(1), 621–636.

Office, Home. (1992). *Memorandum of good practice on video recorded interviews with child witnesses for criminal proceedings.* London: Her Majesty's Stationary Office.

Palanski, M., & Yammarino, F. (2007). Integrity and leadership: A multi-level conceptual framework. *Leadership Quarterly, 20,* 405–420.

Paulhus, D. L. (1998). *Paulhus deception scales (PDS): The balanced inventory of desirable responding-7.* New York: Multi-Health Systems.

Paulhus, D. L., & Dutton, D. G. (2016). Everyday sadism. In V. Zeigler-Hill & D. K. Marcus (Eds.), *The dark side of personality: Science and practice in social, personality and clinical psychology* (pp. 109–120). Washington, DC: American Psychological Association.

Paulhus, D. L., & Jones, D. N. (2015). Measures of dark personalities. In G. J. Boyle, D. H. Saklofske, & G. Matthews (Eds.), *Measures of personality and social psychological constructs* (pp. 562–594). San Diego, CA: Elsevier Academic Press.

Paulhus, D. L., Jones, D. N., Klonsky, E. D., & Dutton, D. G. (2011). *Sadistic personality and its everyday correlates.* Unpublished manuscript. University of British Columbia.

Perri, F. S. (2013). Visionaries or false prophets. *Journal of Contemporary Criminal Justice, 29,* 331–350. https://doi.org/10.1177/1043986213496008.

Porter, S., & ten Brinke, L. (2009). Dangerous decisions: A theoretical framework for understanding how judges assess credibility in the courtroom. *Legal and Criminological Psychology, 14,* 119–134. https://doi.org/10.1348/135532508X281520.

Porter, S., ten Brinke, L., & Gustaw, C. (2010). Dangerous decisions: The impact of first impressions of trustworthiness on the evaluation of legal evidence and defendant culpability. *Psychology, Crime & Law, 16,* 477–491. https://doi.org/10.1080/10683160902926141.

Posthuma, R. A., Morgeson, F. P., & Campion, M. A. (2002). Beyond employment interview validity: A comprehensive narrative review of recent research and trends over time. *Personnel Psychology, 55,* 1–81. https://doi.org/10.1111/j.1744-6570.2002.tb00103.x.

Raman, P., Sambasivan, M., & Kumar, N. (2016). Counterproductive work behavior among frontline government employees: Role of personality, emotional intelligence, affectivity, emotional labor, and emotional exhaustion. *Journal of Work and Organizational Psychology, 32,* 25–37. https://doi.org/10.1016/j.rpto.2015.11.002.

Ritchie, M., Blais, J., & Forth, A. (2019). "Evil" intentions: Examining the relationship between the dark tetrad and victim selection based on nonverbal gait cues. *Personality and Individual Differences, 138,* 126–132. https://doi.org/10.1016/j.paid.2018.09.013.

Roter, A. (2019). *The dark side of the workplace: Managing incivility.* New York: Routledge.

Rust, J. (1999). The validity of the Giotto integrity test. *Personality and Individual Differences, 27*(4), 755–768.

Rydell, R., Mcconnell, A., Mackie, D., & Strain, L. (2006). Of two minds: Forming and changing valence-inconsistent implicit and explicit attitudes. *Psychological Science, 17*(11), 954–958. https://doi.org/10.1111/j.1467-9280.2006.01811.x.

Saks, E. R. (2007). *The center cannot hold: My journey through madness.* New York: Hyperion.

Salgado, J. F. (2003). Predicting job performance using FFM and non-FFM personality measures. *Journal of Occupational and Organizational Psychology, 76,* 323–346.

Sedikides, C., & Campbell, W. K. (2017). Narcissistic force meets systemic resistance: The energy clash model. *Perspectives on Psychological Science, 12*(3), 400–421.

Shepherd, E. (1986). Conversational core of policing. *Policing, 2,* 294–303.

Shepherd, E. (2007). *Investigative interviewing: The conversation management approach.* Oxford: Oxford University Press.

Staw, B. (1981). The escalation of commitment to a course of action. *Academy of Management Review, 6*(4), 577–587. https://doi.org/10.5465/amr.1981.4285694.

Tett, R. P., Simonet, D. V., Walser, B., & Brown, C. (2013). Trait activation theory: Applications, developments, and implications for person-workplace fit. In N. D. Christiansen & R. P. Tett (Eds.), *Handbook of personality at work* (pp. 71–100). New York: Routledge.

Thomas, A. (2006). *Corporate scandals: Reverberations and long-term meaning.* New York, NY: Nova Science.

Wexler, M. (2008). Conjectures on systemic psychopathy: Reframing the contemporary corporation. *Society and Business Review, 3*(3), 224–238. https://doi.org/10.1108/17465680810907305.

Wheeler, S., Book, A., & Costello, K. (2009). Psychopathic traits and perceptions of victim vulnerability. *Criminal Justice and Behaviour, 36,* 635–648. https://doi.org/10.1177/0093854809333958.

Wilson, K., Demetrioff, S., & Porter, S. (2008). A pawn by any other name? Social information processing as a function of psychopathic traits. *Journal of Research in Personality, 42,* 1651–1656. https://doi.org/10.1016/j.jrp.2008.07.006.

Witt, L. A., & Ferris, G. R. (2003). Social skill as moderator of the conscientiousness-performance relationship: Convergent results across four studies. *Journal of Applied Psychology, 88,* 809–821. https://doi.org/10.1037/0021-9010.88.5.809.

Young, A. M., & Kacmar, M. K. (1998). ABCs of the interview: The role of affective, behavioral, and cognitive responses by the applicants in the employment interview. *International Journal of Selection and Assessment, 6,* 211–221. https://doi.org/10.1111/1468-2389.00092.

Index

© The Editor(s) (if applicable) and The Author(s), under exclusive license
to Springer Nature Switzerland AG, part of Springer Nature 2020
K. Fritzon et al., *Corporate Psychopathy*,
https://doi.org/10.1007/978-3-030-27188-6

CPSIA information can be obtained
at www.ICGtesting.com
Printed in the USA
LVHW021039090423
743871LV00002B/101